OBJECTIVE	PAGE
Creating User Services *(continued)*	
Instantiate and invoke a COM component: Create a Visual Basic client application that uses a COM component; Create a Visual Basic application that handles events from a COM component.	329, 343
Create call-back procedures to enable asynchronous processing between COM components and Visual Basic client applications.	343
Implement online user assistance in a distributed application: Set appropriate properties to enable user assistance. Help properties include **HelpFile**, **HelpContextID**, and **WhatsThisHelp**; Create HTML Help for an application; Implement messages from a server component to a user interface.	468, 479, 485
Implement error handling for the user interface in distributed applications: Identify and trap run-time errors; Handle inline errors; Determine how to send error information from a COM component to a client computer.	495, 505, 507
Use an active document to present information within a Web browser.	448
Creating and Managing COM Components	
Create a COM component that implements business rules or logic. Components include DLLs, ActiveX controls, and active documents.	165
Create ActiveX controls: Create an ActiveX control that exposes properties; Use control events to save and load persistent properties; Test and debug an ActiveX control; Create and enable property pages for an ActiveX control; Enable the data-binding capabilities of an ActiveX control; Create an ActiveX control that is a data source.	203, 206, 212, 220, 225, 228
Create an active document: Use code within an active document to interact with a container application; Navigate to other active documents.	448
Design and create components that will be used with MTS.	374
Debug Visual Basic code that uses objects from a COM component.	539
Choose the appropriate threading model for a COM component.	167
Create a package by using the MTS Explorer: Use the Package and Deployment Wizard to create a package; Import existing packages; Assign names to packages; Assign security to packages.	365, 368, 386, 581
Add components to an MTS package: Set transactional properties of components; Set security properties of components.	379
Use role-based security to limit use of an MTS package to specific users; Create roles; Assign roles to components or component interfaces; Add users to roles.	368, 381
Compile a project with class modules into a COM component: Implement an object model within a COM component; Set properties to control the instancing of a class within a COM component.	165, 171
Use Visual Component Manager to manage components.	186
Register and unregister a COM component.	185
Creating Data Services	
Access and manipulate a data source by using ADO and the **ADO Data** control.	100
Access and manipulate data by using the Execute Direct model.	125
Access and manipulate data by using the Prepare/Execute model.	125

(list continued on inside back cover)

MCSD: Visual Basic 6
Distributed Applications
Study Guide

MCSD: Visual Basic® 6 Distributed Applications Study Guide

Michael Lee
with Clark Christensen, PhD

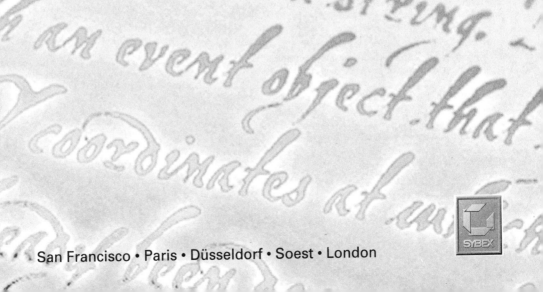

San Francisco • Paris • Düsseldorf • Soest • London

Associate Publisher: Gary Masters
Contracts and Licensing Manager: Kristine O'Callaghan
Acquisitions & Developmental Editor: Brenda Frink
Editor: Sally Engelfried
Project Editor: Ed Copony
Technical Editor: Ed Larkin
Book Designer: Bill Gibson
Graphic Illustrator: Tony Jonick
Electronic Publishing Specialist: Bill Gibson
Production Coordinator: Julie Sakaue
Indexer: Ted Laux
Companion CD: Ginger Warner
Cover Designer: Design Site
Cover Illustrator/Photographer: Design Site

Screen reproductions produced with Collage Complete.
Collage Complete is a trademark of Inner Media Inc.

Library of Congress Card Number: 98-83173
ISBN: 0-7821-2433-X

Manufactured in the United States of America

10 9 8 7 6 5 4 3 2 1

November 1, 1997

Dear SYBEX Customer:

Microsoft is pleased to inform you that SYBEX is a participant in the Microsoft® Independent Courseware Vendor (ICV) program. Microsoft ICVs design, develop, and market self-paced courseware, books, and other products that support Microsoft software and the Microsoft Certified Professional (MCP) program.

To be accepted into the Microsoft ICV program, an ICV must meet set criteria. In addition, Microsoft reviews and approves each ICV training product before permission is granted to use the Microsoft Certified Professional Approved Study Guide logo on that product. This logo assures the consumer that the product has passed the following Microsoft standards:

- The course contains accurate product information.
- The course includes labs and activities during which the student can apply knowledge and skills learned from the course.
- The course teaches skills that help prepare the student to take corresponding MCP exams.

Microsoft ICVs continually develop and release new MCP Approved Study Guides. To prepare for a particular Microsoft certification exam, a student may choose one or more single, self-paced training courses or a series of training courses.

You will be pleased with the quality and effectiveness of the MCP Approved Study Guides available from SYBEX.

Sincerely,

Holly Heath
ICV Account Manager
Microsoft Training & Certification

MICROSOFT INDEPENDENT COURSEWARE VENDOR PROGRAM

To all of the teachers and trainers who have granted to us their knowledge and wisdom over the years. Thank you for the inspiration.

Acknowledgments

This project, like all worthwhile pursuits, has been a team effort. To all of those involved, I wish to express my sincere gratitude. The Sybex team is the very best in the business. In my many projects with Sybex, I have had such positive experiences, and every new project is a delight. Special thanks to Peter Kuhns, Brenda Frink, Ed Copony, and Neil Edde for giving me the opportunities to grow personally and professionally with this and other projects.

Our editor for this project, Sally Engelfried, has been a pleasure to work with. Thanks to the entire editorial team including Ed Larkin, the technical editor, and the artists and proofreaders. I appreciate your dedication to perfection. Thanks for the time that you have spent on this project. Thanks also to Clark Christensen, who worked with me on this book. You came through when it counted, and I appreciate your hard work and devotion to excellence.

Special thanks to my wife Raelynn for her sacrifices. Whenever I tackle a new book project, it always comes at her expense. This book is no exception. Thanks for reminding me that there is more to life than work. Your support makes it all possible. This year, I'll be home for Christmas.

I owe much to those who have influenced me as teachers and mentors. My parents and colleagues are always there with encouragement and support. Bob Taylor from Productivity Point International has been a mentor and role model for me from the very beginning of my professional IT career. Jon Hansen, my friend and comrade, has been my greatest supporter over the years. Thanks to both of you for the encouragement and guidance.

Finally, thanks to you, the reader, for your interest in this volume. I appreciate the trust that you have placed in us to help guide you through to your certification goals. Without you, none of this is possible.

—Michael Lee

My thanks to those who have given me hope and chances to grow. To my parents for planting my feet firmly on the ground and teaching me the love of learning. Also to my older brother, Richard, for exemplifying the passion for science and technology. I have had many teachers and mentors over the years, and I am grateful to all of you.

The folks at Sybex have been great to work with: competent, professional, and sociable. It doesn't get much better than that.

I would like to give particular thanks to my wife, for sacrificing so that I could be a part of this project. For roughly half my life she has been supporting me, encouraging me, and traveling the journey of life with me. Without her I am nothing.

Finally, I owe a huge debt of thanks to Mike Lee, an old and dear friend, who has supported my transition into a formal IT career in more ways than I can count. More explicitly, I'm grateful that Mike gave me the chance to be a part of this project. I trust and respect Mike tremendously, both personally and professionally.

Whatever the reasons for your reading this book, I hope this volume meets your needs.

—Clark Christensen

Contents at a Glance

Table of Contents

Table of Exercises

Introduction

Microsoft is a company for and about developers. Even though developer tools represent a small portion of Microsoft's total revenues, Microsoft has a firm strategic commitment to the developer market. Every year, Microsoft sponsors events such as the Professional Developer's Conference (PDC) and Developer Days for the purpose of getting Microsoft technology in the hands of developers. In addition, Microsoft participates in countless third-party events targeted at the developer audience. Microsoft also makes available every development tool, operating system, and BackOffice product in the Microsoft Developer Network and competitively prices them. In other words, their developer support is enormous.

This support is emphasized in the Microsoft Certified Solution Developer (MCSD) certification. This certification, the first of its kind in the industry, gives developers the opportunity to showcase their skills and familiarity with Microsoft platforms and development tools. The industry response has been significant. MCSD certification provides a way for developers to prove their skills and adds credibility to their job applications and promotions.

For database developers and administrators, Microsoft's support has never been stronger. With the announcement of the Microsoft Certified Database Administrator (MCDBA) certification, Microsoft has committed to supporting all aspects of the database professional's role. The certification exam supports both the MCSD and MCDBA certifications.

About This Book

Writing this book was an exercise in trade-offs. With a subject as large as this, we had to make some sacrifices and judgment calls about the important content for this book. First of all, this is not a book for beginners. Although Chapter 6 does cover some basic form development concepts, you will not find introductory discussions in this book about the Visual Basic language and syntax. This knowledge is assumed. This book also assumes that you have some experience with relational database design. Some experience with Microsoft SQL Server is helpful, but not required.

Although we have tried to be as comprehensive as possible, writing a book that covers every aspect of distributed application development is almost impossible. Since this is a study guide, we focus on certification. Every effort has been made to cover the exam objectives in plenty of detail; in addition, we provide a little extra information that will make you a more productive developer but we don't burden you with unnecessary detail.

To do all of the exercises in this book, you will need to install a significant amount of software. The installation requirements include:

- Microsoft Windows NT Server 4 Service Pack 4 or later
- Microsoft Windows NT 4 Option Pack including:
  - Microsoft Transaction Server 2
  - Microsoft Internet Information Server 4
- Microsoft Internet Explorer 4 Service Pack 1 or later
- Microsoft Visual Basic 6
- Microsoft Office 97 Professional
- Microsoft SQL Server 7

Your Key to Passing Exam 70-175

This book provides you with the key to passing Exam 70-175, Designing and Implementing Distributed Applications with Microsoft Visual Basic 6.0. Inside, you'll find information and practice questions relevant to this exam, all designed to make sure that when you take the exam, you are ready.

To help you prepare for certification exams, Microsoft provides a list of exam objectives for each test. This book is structured according to the objectives for Exam 70-175, which is designed to measure your understanding of Windows architecture and development.

Is This Book for You?

If you are interested in preparing for the Designing and Implementing Distributed Applications with Microsoft Visual Basic 6.0 exam, this book is for you. If you are trying to complement your general understanding of Microsoft development tools and procedures, this book is also for you. For both of these purposes, this book covers a wide array of topics in substantial detail without overburdening you with unnecessary information.

Understanding Microsoft Certification

Microsoft offers several levels of certification for anyone who has or is pursuing a career as a network professional working with Microsoft products:

- Microsoft Certified Professional (MCP)
- Microsoft Certified Professional + Internet
- Microsoft Certified Solution Developer (MCSD)
- Microsoft Certified Systems Engineer (MCSE)
- Microsoft Certified Systems Engineer + Internet
- Microsoft Certified Database Administrator (MCDBA)
- Microsoft Certified Trainer (MCT)

(Internet certification qualifies professionals to enhance, deploy, and manage intranet and Internet solutions.)

Microsoft Certified Professional (MCP)

This certification is for individuals with expertise in one specific area. MCP certification is often a stepping stone to MCSE certification and allows you some benefits of Microsoft certification after just one exam.

You can become an MCP by passing one core exam, meaning any Microsoft exam except Networking Essentials.

Microsoft Certified Solution Developer (MCSD)

The MCSD certification identifies developers with experience working with Microsoft operating systems, development tools, and technologies. To achieve the MCSD certification, you must pass four exams:

- Analyzing Requirements and Defining Solution Architectures
- A desktop application development exam selected from the following:
  - Designing and Implementing Desktop Applications with Visual Basic 6.0
  - Designing and Implementing Desktop Applications with Microsoft Visual C++ 6.0
- A distributed application development exam selected from the following:
  - Designing and Implementing Distributed Applications with Microsoft Visual Basic 6.0

- Designing and Implementing Distributed Applications with Microsoft Visual C++ 6.0

- One elective exam. Some of the electives include:

  - Implementing a Database Design on Microsoft SQL Server 6.5

  - Designing and Implementing Databases with Microsoft SQL Server 7.0

  - Designing and Implementing Data Warehouses with Microsoft SQL Server 7.0

  - Developing Applications with Microsoft Visual C++ Using the Microsoft Foundation Class Library

  - Designing and Implementing Web Sites with Microsoft Front-Page 98

  - Designing and Implementing Commerce Solutions with Microsoft Site Server 3.0, Commerce Edition

  - Designing and Implementing Web Solutions with Microsoft Visual InterDev 6.0

 Desktop and distributed application development exams for Microsoft Visual J++ 6 and Microsoft Visual FoxPro 6 are in development and will be available in 1999.

Microsoft Certified Systems Engineer (MCSE)

The MCSE certification requires commitment from network professionals. You need to complete all of the steps required for certification. Passing the exams shows that you meet the high standards that Microsoft has set for MSCEs.

To become an MCSE, you must pass a series of six exams:

- Networking Essentials (waived for Novell CNEs)

- Implementing and Supporting Microsoft Windows NT Workstation 4.0 (or Windows 95)

- Implementing and Supporting Microsoft Windows NT Server 4.0

- Implementing and Supporting Microsoft Windows NT Server 4.0 in the Enterprise

- Two elective exams. Some of the electives include:

  - Internetworking with Microsoft TCP/IP on Microsoft Windows NT 4.0

  - Implementing and Supporting Microsoft Internet Information Server 4.0

  - Implementing and Supporting Microsoft Exchange Server 5.5

  - Implementing and Supporting Microsoft SNA Server 4.0

  - Implementing and Supporting Microsoft Systems Management Server 1.2

  - Implementing a Database Design on Microsoft SQL Server 6.5

  - System Administration for Microsoft SQL Server 6.5

Microsoft Certified Database Administrator (MCDBA)

The MCDBA certification is the premier certification for database support and development professionals. This certification requires four core exams in the subjects of Microsoft SQL Server 7 and Windows NT platform support. The core exams include:

- Implementing and Supporting Microsoft Windows NT 4.0

- Implementing and Supporting Microsoft Windows NT 4.0 in the Enterprise

- System Administration of Microsoft SQL Server 7.0

- Designing and Implementing a Database with Microsoft SQL Server 7.0

In addition, you must pass one elective exam. Some of the more popular include:

- Designing and Implementing Distributed Applications with Microsoft Visual Basic 6.0

- Designing and Implementing Distributed Applications with Microsoft Visual C++ 6.0

- Designing and Implementing Data Warehouses with Microsoft SQL Server 7.0

- Implementing and Supporting Microsoft Internet Information Server 4.0

- Internetworking with Microsoft TCP/IP on Microsoft Windows NT 4.0

Microsoft Certified Trainer (MCT)

As an MCT, you can deliver Microsoft certified courseware through official Microsoft channels. The number of exams you are required to pass depends on the number of courses you want to deliver. Certification is granted on a course-by-course basis.

In addition to passing exams for the courses that you want to deliver, you must also attend a trainer skills course that is approved by Microsoft and demonstrate that you have prepared adequately for each new class. This can be done either by attending the class or completing a self-study checklist and sending it to Microsoft.

For the most up-to-date certification information, visit Microsoft's Web site at www.microsoft.com/train_cert.

Preparing for the MCSD Exams

To prepare for the MCSD certification exams, you should try to work with the products as much as possible. In addition, a variety of resources from which you can learn about the products and exams are available:

- You can take instructor-led courses.

- You can participate in online training as an alternative to instructor-led courses. This is a useful option for people who cannot find any courses in their area or who do not have the time to attend classes.

- If you prefer to use a book to help you prepare for the MCSD tests, you can choose from a wide variety of publications. These include study guides, such as the Network Press *MCSD Study Guide* series, which cover the core MCSD exams and key electives.

For more MCSD information, point your browser to the Sybex Web site, where you'll find information about the MCP program, job links, and descriptions of other quality titles in the Network Press line of MCSD-related books. Go to http://www.sybex.com, and click on the MCSD logo.

Scheduling and Taking an Exam

Once you think you are ready to take an exam, call Prometric Testing Centers at (800) 755-EXAM (755-3926). They'll tell you where to find the closest testing center. Before you call, however, get out your credit card—each exam costs $100.00. (If you've used this book to prepare yourself thoroughly, chances are you'll only have to shell out that $100.00 once!)

You can schedule the exam for a time that is convenient for you. The exams are downloaded from Prometric to the testing center, and you show up at your scheduled time and take the exam on a computer.

Once you complete the exam, you will know right away whether you have passed or not. At the end of the exam, you will receive a score report that will list the six areas that you were tested on and how you performed. If you pass the exam, you don't need to do anything else—Prometric uploads the test results to Microsoft. If you don't pass, it's another $100.00 to schedule the exam again, but at least you will know from the score report where you did poorly, so you can study that particular information more carefully.

Test-Taking Hints

If you know what to expect, your chances of passing the exam will be much greater. The following sections cover some tips that can help you achieve success. For greater detail on these and other test-taking strategies, see Appendix B.

Get There Early and Be Prepared   This is your last chance to review. Bring your book and review any areas about which you feel unsure. If you need a quick drink of water or a visit to the restroom, take care of it before the exam. Once your exam starts, it cannot be paused for these needs.

When you arrive for your exam, you will be asked to present two forms of ID. You will also be asked to sign a piece of paper verifying that you understand the testing rules and that you will not disclose the content of the exam to others.

Before you start the exam, you will have an opportunity to take a practice exam. It is not related to the topic of your exam and is simply offered so that you will have a feel for the exam-taking process.

What You Can and Can't Take in with You   First, be aware that Prometric Testing Centers take the test-taking process and the test validation very seriously. These are closed-book exams. The only thing you can take in is scratch paper provided by the testing center. Use this paper as much as possible to diagram the questions. Many times, diagramming questions will help make the answer clear. You will have to give this paper back to the test administrator at the end of the exam.

Many testing centers are very strict about what you can take into the testing room. Some centers will not even allow you to bring in items like a zipped purse. If you feel tempted to take in any outside material, be aware that many testing centers use monitoring devices such as video and audio equipment (so don't swear, even if you are alone in the room!)

Test Approach   As you take the test, if you know the answer to a question, fill it in and move on. If you're not sure of the answer, mark your best guess, then mark the question.

At the end of the exam, you can review the questions. Depending on the amount of time remaining, you can view all of the questions again, or you can view only the questions about which you were unsure. Double-check your answers, just in case you misread any of the questions on the first pass. (Sometimes half of the battle is in trying to figure out exactly what the question is asking you.) You may find that a related question that you had no problem answering will provide a clue for a troublesome question.

Be sure to answer all questions. Unanswered questions are scored as incorrect and will count against you. There is no penalty for guessing. Also, make sure you keep an eye on the remaining time so that you can pace yourself accordingly.

If you do not pass the exam, write down everything that you can remember while the exam is still fresh on your mind. This will help you prepare for your next try. Although the next exam will not be exactly the same, the questions will be similar, and you want to avoid making the same mistakes.

After You Become Certified

Once you become an MCSD, Microsoft kicks in some goodies, including:

- A one-year subscription to the Microsoft Beta Evaluation program, which is a great way to get your hands on new software and be the first kid on the block to play with new and upcoming software.

- Access to a secured area of the Microsoft Web site that provides technical support and product information. This certification benefit is also available for MCP certification.

- Permission to use the Microsoft Certified Professional logos (each certification has its own logo), which look great on letterhead and business cards.

- An MCSD certificate (you will get a certificate for each level of certification you reach), suitable for framing or sending copies to Mom.

- A one-year subscription to *Microsoft Certified Professional Magazine*, which provides information on professional and career development.

How to Use This Book

All of the exercises in the book assume that products have been installed according to the defaults. No consideration is given for additional customizations that you have made on the installation.

As you work through this book, you may want to follow these general procedures:

1. Review the exam objectives as you work through each chapter. (You may want to check the Microsoft Train_Cert Web site at http://www .microsoft.com/train_cert to make sure the objectives haven't changed.)

2. Study each chapter carefully, making sure you fully understand the information.

3. Complete all hands-on exercises in each chapter, referring to the appropriate text so that you understand every step you take.

4. Answer the practice questions at the end of the chapter. (You will find the answers to these questions in Appendix A.)

5. Note which questions you did not understand, and study those sections of the book again.

To learn all of the material covered in this book, you will need to study regularly and with discipline. Try to set aside the same time every day to study, and select a comfortable and quiet place in which to do it. Good luck!

What's on the CD?

The companion CD contains shareware, freeware, and demo programs, as well as articles and URLs of interest to MCSD students.

About the Authors

Michael Lee

Michael Lee is an MCT, MCSD, and MCSE with over five years of experience developing client/server and Web-based applications with Microsoft tools. He is the owner of SabrePoint Software, a Microsoft Certified Solution Provider located in North Salt Lake, Utah. He has also authored and contributed to many other articles and books including *MCSE: SQL Server 6.5 Administration Study Guide* and *MCSD: Windows Architecture II*, both published by Sybex.

Clark Christensen

Clark Christensen, PhD., MCSD, MCT, is a Microsoft Development Trainer for Keane, Inc., in Salt Lake City, Utah. He has been building database-enabled solutions since 1992, primarily for research and clinical counseling functions.

How to Contact the Authors and Sybex

You can e-mail Mike or Clark at the following addresses:

Michael Lee: mlee@sabrepoint.org

Clark Christensen: clarkmct@earthlink.net

Sybex's e-mail and Web site are as follows:

Technical Support: support@sybex.com

Web site: www.sybex.com

To find information on this book, click on catalog, then type **2433** in the search field and press enter.

CHAPTER

1

Designing a
Distributed Solution

Every business has different data needs; some businesses even have applications distributed on different network architectures. In the world of custom application development, this poses interesting challenges. Because no two businesses' needs are exactly alike, no two application architectures are exactly alike.

General Application Architecture

It is impossible to begin any discussion of application architecture without starting at the most fundamental level. This section will cover the general differences between file server applications and applications built for the client/server model. Choosing between these general architectures is by no means a trivial decision. It carries with it some substantial performance implications, some of which may never be overcome if you make the wrong choice.

Let's take a closer look at both of these architectural approaches. In this section, we will address the basic structure and the pros and cons of each of these architectural approaches.

File Server Architecture

Even though *client/server* is the buzzword heard around town these days, traditional file server architectures still have their place in the world. The file-based database, sometimes called a *flat-file database*, is as old as computing, and ISAM data structures and data extraction methods are as old as the oldest mainframes. If they have been around for that long, there must be a reason.

ISAM (Indexed Sequential Access Method) is a method of working with data in a large data file that assigns a key value to every record and then creates multiple indexes that arrange these keys in various indexed orders. Invoking an index allows a record to be located faster than reading the entire table in a single sequential order.

File-based databases are very efficient for extracting information from large data files. Each workstation on the network has access to a central file server where the data is stored. The data file can also reside on the workstation with the client application. The PC network version of this architecture is illustrated in Figure 1.1.

F I G U R E 1.1

The file server database

Workstation   Server

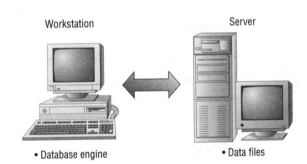

• Database engine   • Data files

As shown in the figure, multiple workstations will access the same file server where the data is stored. The file server is centrally located so that it can be reached easily and efficiently by all workstations. In addition to the data, other files may be needed on the server to manage any multi-user considerations. Ensuring compliance with multi-user policy may be the responsibility of the workstation. As functionality increases on the server, it may even become a client/server system. The user's application (including the interactive portion of the application *and* the database engine) resides on the workstation. The fact that the database engine resides on the workstation implies that ISAM database engines are essentially single-user engines. Although multi-user considerations can be a factor of the engine design or application design, the engines themselves are substantially biased toward single-user data processing.

Another fact inherent in file server design is that the file server stores only data and support files. It is not an application server and as such does not host any server-side processes. This means that the file server is a passive participant in the application process, requiring the engine residing on each individual workstation to do all of the processing in the application.

To illustrate this last point, consider the following scenario. Suppose you have a data file hosted on a file server. This data file contains 10,000 records. A user submits a request from the workstation application to extract 10 records from this data file. How many records does the file server send back to the workstation to fulfill this request?

If you answered 10,000, you are right. The file server hosts no program to process the data. The entire file requested must be sent back to the client application and processed at the workstation where the database engine resides. A few sophisticated ISAM data engines, such as Microsoft's Joint Engine Technology (JET), use a process of client-side page caching to make this process more efficient; however, even in these cases, the workstation-resident engine is still responsible for the entire process.

NOTE   Many file-based database systems are starting to look more and more like *relational* databases. For example, both Microsoft Access and Microsoft FoxPro can implement normalized data structures. Even so, they remain ISAM data systems and are not true relational databases. Judge them by the rules of file server databases.

Now that you know the network performance implications and the additional client overhead of the file server approach, you might wonder where that implementation is reasonable. Let's look at Microsoft Access as an example.

Microsoft Access stores all of its objects in Microsoft Database files (*.mdb). This includes interface objects such as forms and reports; processing objects such as macros, queries, and code modules; and data objects, namely tables. These can all be implemented into a single local database providing outstanding stand-alone support. In this case, there is no file server. Everything is hosted on the local PC.

If a stand-alone application is not possible, then the data objects (tables) can be stored on a central file server. Multiple users can access this file by pointing their client applications to this central server. To support multiple users, a file with an extension of *.ldb will be stored in the same directory as the data file source. This locking database will track which 2K pages of data are currently in use by other applications to prevent them from being accessed by other applications. Figure 1.2 illustrates this architecture.

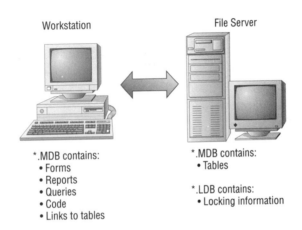

FIGURE 1.2

Microsoft Access application architecture

Workstation

*.MDB contains:
• Forms
• Reports
• Queries
• Code
• Links to tables

File Server

*.MDB contains:
• Tables

*.LDB contains:
• Locking information

Exercise 1.1 will give you the opportunity to implement a prototype of this architecture. Notice especially how locking support is managed.

EXERCISE 1.1

Implementing Microsoft Access File Server Architecture

1. Be sure Microsoft Access 97 is not running. To investigate the current data structure, open the Windows Explorer and navigate to \Program Files\Microsoft Office\Office\Samples. In this location, you should see the Northwind.mdb file. Minimize the Windows Explorer.

2. Start Microsoft Access 97. When prompted to open or create a database file, select the option button labeled Blank Database and click OK.

EXERCISE 1.1 (CONTINUED)

3. You must now save the database. Accept the default name (db1.mdb) and place the database wherever you want. Save it by clicking the Create button. A blank database window should open.

4. To link this database to tables stored in the Northwind database, select File ➤ Get External Data ➤ Link Tables from the menu. Navigate to the location of the Northwind database given in Step 1. Select Northwind.mdb and click Link.

5. From the list of tables, select Customers and Products and click OK. Your database window should now look like the one illustrated here. The black arrow icon beside each table name represents a linked object.

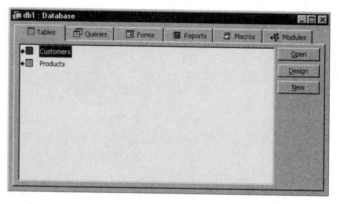

6. Double-click the Customers table in the database window to open it. You should now see the list of Northwind customers.

7. Maximize the Windows Explorer, which should still be open to the Samples folder. Notice that a new file has been created in the folder called Northwind.ldb.

8. Switch back to Microsoft Access. Close the Customers table and close Microsoft Access. Switch back to the Windows Explorer. The Northwind.ldb file should now be gone.

9. Close the Windows Explorer.

File server database architecture is sometimes referred to as *single-tier architecture* because all of the processing takes place at one point in the architecture, the client workstation. Based on this discussion, single-tier database applications are the most appropriate for either stand-alone or small workgroup applications. With a limited number of users, all in close proximity to the file server, this architecture can be extremely efficient and cost effective. It removes the need for a large server to handle central processing and puts the task on the local workstation. If the hardware in the workgroup is sufficient to handle the processing needs, this model works very well.

However, implementing this architecture for large applications supporting many users can often be a costly mistake. Migrating from Microsoft Access data files to Microsoft SQL Server or client/server database back-ends is a significant trend today. As a company matures and grows, the file-based application that once worked very well may no longer be able to support the application.

Client/Server Architecture

The driving concept in client/server architecture is flexibility. Client/server architecture is often referred to as *multiple-tier* architecture because the execution of tasks is divided between applications and components in the architecture. A *tier* in client/server technology is a layer of software that accepts requests and offers services to an application. For example, the client application represents the user services layer of the application. This is a tier of the application. As a system architect, you have discretion to allocate tasks and processing to different tiers in the model. You can use a traditional two-tier model or increase application independence by moving to a multiple-tier model. Within these models, you still have full control over the technology used to implement the solution and your chosen level of systems abstraction.

Figure 1.3 illustrates a basic client/server scenario. Although this theme has many variations, you will notice some common threads running throughout all client/server implementations.

Figure 1.3 illustrates some distinguishing characteristics of client/server design. You will notice immediately that the database engine has been moved from the client to the server. The server in this scenario is no longer a file server simply providing file services to the network. It is an application server hosting a process such as Microsoft SQL Server or Oracle.

F I G U R E   1.3

Client/server
architecture

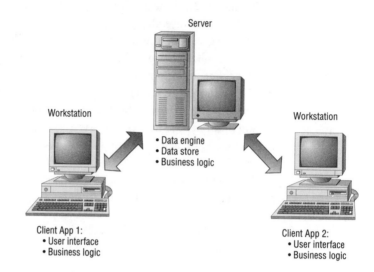

This transition is significant because it means that the client workstation is no longer responsible for all of the work involved in implementing the application. Tasks can be distributed between client and server, allowing each to participate in the process. In fact, you could say that the definition of client/server architecture is the intelligent distribution of tasks across tiers in the architecture.

Because the database engine now resides on the server, the behavior of the previous scenario changes. Remember that the data table held 10,000 records. Now assume that a Microsoft SQL Server is hosting this data table. When the client application submits a request for 10 records, only 10 rows will be returned across the network to the client because a process on the server can satisfy the request.

Because the server is an active participant in the process of data reduction and modification, a client/server database is not limited to small workgroup applications the way file server applications are limited. However, because client/server systems usually have much larger numbers of users, an increased load might be put on the network, so managing network resources becomes paramount in a client/server design.

In most cases, the primary role of the database server when returning results should be *data reduction* (minimizing the amount of data going across the network). This may leave many other activities, such as sorting and further data processing, to the client.

The Services Design Model

Microsoft ✓ *Exam* *Objective* — **Given a conceptual design, apply the principles of modular design to derive the components and services of the logical design.**

When designing client/server solutions, you must make many choices concerning which pieces of the application will reside on which tiers of the architecture. The Services design model can aid significantly in this process. This model divides application tasks into different services, which in turn can be applied to different tiers in the architecture.

The Services design model defines three services:

- User services

- Business services

- Data services

Most client/server models implement user and data services at roughly the same points in the architecture; however, the business services layer is unique in its ability to morph to various tiers, providing different advantages and creating different challenges. Figure 1.4 illustrates the Services model and its possible mappings to physical architecture.

NOTE

User, business, and data services do not directly relate to the three "tiers" (presentation, business, and data) of the three-tier application environment. Even a single-tier application will contain user, business, and data services. These services all simply reside on the same machine and, usually, in the same application.

FIGURE 1.4

Client/server
application services

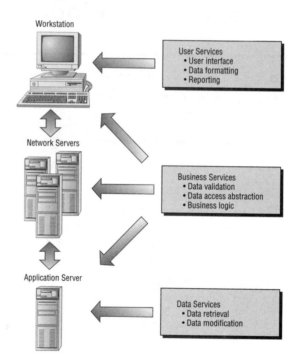

User Services

User services deal with the interaction between the user and the application, as well as the preparation of data for user requirements. The following types of tasks usually fall into the category of user services:

- Receiving data input from users

- Packaging user input for further validation or server processing

- Data formatting

- Reporting

- Managing user preferences

User services define any and all client-side activities, no matter what the goals of those activities may be. For example, a single SQL Server database might actually be the data source for a number of different client applications. Some of these will perform standard business functions (such as inputting or extracting information) while others may perform administrative duties (such as adding new users to the application or handling security concerns). All of these activities respond directly to the request of a user.

Developmental concerns for user services deal primarily with user interface design and user requirements. Applications should be as intuitive as possible to their users. Users should have flexible approaches to working with data and application features.

Other user services include data formatting functions not utilized at the data services level. For example, if you want to have a result set sorted in a particular order, you can choose where that is to be done. Sorting can be done at the server or it can be done at the client. Because the server's primary role in data extraction is actually data reduction, operations (such as sorting) that have no reductive effect are frequently better implemented as part of the client application as a user service.

The implementation of client-side transactions is also a user services issue. Client transactions are used for logically organizing tasks and buffering data on the client so larger batches of data can be passed back to the server.

Data Services

Data services interact with the actual data source. The functionality of the data services layer is implemented at the database engine level, forcing data services to reside on the application server in the client/server scenario. Four functional areas are in the data services layer:

- Retrieving data and building result sets

- Inserting data

- Updating data

- Deleting data

The actual request for data interaction can come to the server in a variety of ways. It can come directly from the client application through the database server's proprietary Application Programming Interface (API), through the Open Database Connectivity Application Programming Interface (ODBC API), or even from a business component through OLE DB, Microsoft's Component Object Model (COM) specification for database access. How the request gets to the server is irrelevant. Once there, it is handled in exactly the same way, through the database engine running on the server.

Not all of the functionality implemented by the database server actually qualifies as a data service. For example, the sorting of data might better qualify as a data formatting user service. The fact that the database server is able to implement a particular functionality does not mean that this is the best place in the architecture to do that implementation.

Transactions also play very important roles in data services implementation. True relational databases support *atomic edits*. This means that any group of changes made to a database can be marked as a transaction which will be guaranteed to commit in its entirety or roll back to a consistent state before the edits took place. In other words, when a transaction is issued to the server, either all of the transaction commits or none of it will commit. This is an atomic transaction. The database provides a transaction log that records all changes even before they physically occur to the data. This log can be used to roll back the transactions or roll forward in a server crash, if needed.

Business Services

Business services often make up the largest portion of the coding in a client/ server application. The physical process of the client talking to the server takes place at the business services layer. However, this layer also has many other tasks. Business services may include any of the following:

- Business rule and logic implementation
- Data validation
- Data access logic

- System administration logic

- Transaction support

Unlike user and data services that are usually implemented as a monolithic client or server application residing entirely on one machine, the business services can be located in the client application, the server application, both, or even neither. The following discussion classifies each of these approaches.

Smart Client

The smart client approach stores business rules and logic in the client application. All data access logic is also found at the client. This approach utilizes all resources at the client level and frees precious resources at the server for data services, as shown in Figure 1.5.

FIGURE 1.5

The smart client

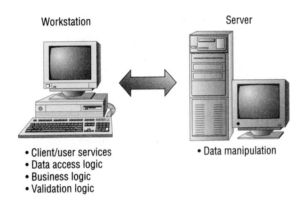

The primary disadvantage of this approach is update deployment. Updating the business or data access logic would require redeploying the entire client application, or at least the supporting DLLs (Dynamic Link Libraries) on every client machine. As the developer, you must also be concerned with the hardware level available on each of the clients. In this approach, it is critical that the hardware level be sufficient to handle the load that is being placed on it.

Smart Server

The smart server approach consolidates all of the business and validation logic onto a central server. In your server-side application, you would include all the necessary code to ensure that business rules were being followed. The advantage is obvious. By consolidating the logic in one location in the server application, you avoid the update/redeployment problem that you saw in the smart client model. Instead of updating the logic on every client, you need only update the logic once in the server. If the logic ever changes, you only need to make the change in the server application. Figure 1.6 illustrates this approach.

F I G U R E 1.6

The smart server

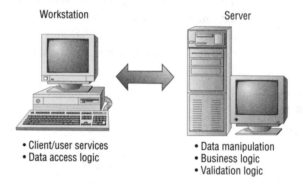

Workstation   Server

- Client/user services   • Data manipulation
- Data access logic   • Business logic
                                • Validation logic

The primary disadvantage of this approach is that it places an enormous strain on the server. By shifting the logic to the server, you are forcing the server to perform all of those functions for every connected client. Whether or not this will have a performance impact on your application depends on how many users connect and the services provided by the server, but the effect can be significant.

The Mixed Solution

Dividing the business and validation logic between the client and the server is possible. Dividing them allows each piece of the architecture to focus on its core strengths. This approach is illustrated in Figure 1.7.

Once again, there are disadvantages to this approach. Although you are making the most of the resources provided by every machine in the architecture, you still have the update/deployment problem found in the smart client approach. In addition, your logic is distributed throughout your application

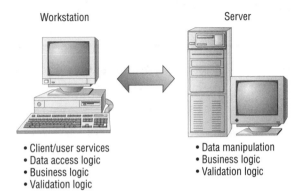

FIGURE 1.7

The mixed solution

Workstation

Server

- Client/user services
- Data access logic
- Business logic
- Validation logic

- Data manipulation
- Business logic
- Validation logic

at many levels, making it very difficult to maintain without excellent documentation. Even with documentation, you will most likely have to alter both client and server structures to upgrade the application.

Architectural Options

The architectural examples discussed so far are all examples of traditional two-tier design, so-called because two components participate in the process. This may be a very effective design under certain conditions. For example, if your application is not volatile (i.e., it will not need significant updates in the future) and you have workstations that can handle more sophisticated applications, a two-tier smart client may be exactly what you need.

On the other hand, you may have a very powerful server machine. Even if the logic occasionally needs to be updated, as long as the user base does not overwhelm the capacity of the server, you have another two-tier option, the smart server. Both of these options are entirely viable.

However, the conditions favoring the two-tier approach may not be valid. Remember that the business logic may be located in a combination of the client and server applications, but it may also be independent of both the client and the server. In this case, create components that are separate from both the client and the server and distribute them throughout the network. These components can define all business services. This approach is called three-tier, n-tier, or multiple-tier client/server architecture.

Multiple-Tier Architecture

When implementing a multiple-tier solution, all business services are placed inside small components that provide services to both the client application and the server application. These components, created in a language such as Microsoft Visual Basic or Microsoft Visual C++, are implemented as COM (Component Object Model) objects. They may be accessed from the client application using the Distributed Component Object Model (DCOM).

Figure 1.8 illustrates a basic multiple-tier architecture and shows that these components can be distributed, running on multiple servers in the network. These components can also be placed on the application server if necessary. This approach is very modular, each component object providing different services to the application. One component may focus on the implementation of business logic, while another might implement data access logic.

FIGURE 1.8

Multiple-tier client/
server architecture

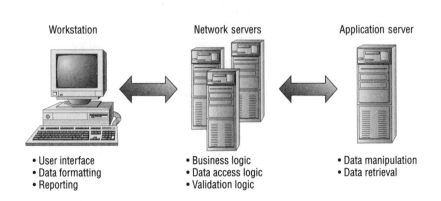

Workstation	Network servers	Application server
• User interface	• Business logic	• Data manipulation
• Data formatting	• Data access logic	• Data retrieval
• Reporting	• Validation logic	

Abstracting Data Access Logic

One of the most useful elements of multiple-tier development is the ability to conceal from both the client and server applications any implementation detail about how database connectivity is being made. As you already know, databases can be accessed many different ways. You can use the proprietary API of the database server, OLE DB, ODBC (Open Database Connectivity), or you can use one of many object models designed for simplifying the process of accessing database resources. To make matters more complex, new approaches are being developed all the time, thereby exposing your application to an obsolescence risk if the method of data access you are using is no longer supported by its vendor.

Using component objects, you can place the actual implementation logic in the component and simply provide consistent public interfaces to the client and the server that access these components. This will enable you to entirely conceal the method of data access from the rest of the application.

Assume for a moment that you are writing a client application in Visual Basic that will be accessing a Microsoft SQL Server database. The following options allow you to access the SQL Server data:

- Visual Basic will allow you to use the JET engine to access data from SQL Server through ODBC.

- If you are using Visual Basic 5 Enterprise Edition or later, you also have the option of using the Remote Data Objects (RDO 2 or later).

- You can use the ActiveX Data Objects (ADO 2 or later) to access the data through the new OLE DB standard.

- You can write to ODBC directly using DLL calls from within Visual Basic.

Assume that in this scenario, you decide to use RDO to access your SQL Server database. Traditional two-tier design would require you to write the RDO data access code in the client application, which would then connect to the SQL Server database directly. This approach poses a problem, however, if Microsoft stops supporting RDO. You may want to upgrade your application to a new RDO version or even go to another data access model entirely, such as ADO. Using the two-tier approach, the client application would have to be redesigned and redeployed.

The alternative is to place the RDO code in a component object. This COM object would support properties and methods that would be visible to the client application through OLE automation. You could create methods such as "ConnectDB" or "InsertEmployee" that would be exposed through this COM object. Inside the component where the method is defined, the RDO code will be used to perform the task. Figure 1.9 illustrates a scenario where this approach might be used.

F I G U R E   1.9

Data access in a
component object

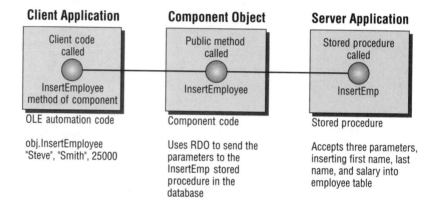

If the component object in this example supports a method called "Insert-Employee," this method would accept values for all required fields as required parameters and values for all optional fields as optional parameters. Additional parameters may be specified for special types of inserts of other definable behavior. This method would be a public interface of the component.

This component would be called from the client application using OLE automation. In a Visual Basic application, you would first create an object variable that referenced the component. Then you would call the Insert-Employee method through the object variable and pass all necessary parameters. The component, using RDO code, would accept these parameters and call the *InsertEmp* stored procedure on the server passing the parameters received from the client application.

The SQL Server would make the actual data modifications to the employee table through the stored procedure. The insert can be created as a transaction in a stored procedure on the server, guaranteeing that the record is inserted in its entirety or not at all.

Now assume that Microsoft has just announced that they will no longer support RDO. You need to readdress the issue of data access methodology. Fortunately, no matter which approach to data access you choose, neither the client nor server applications need to be touched. As long as you do not alter the public interfaces and parameters that the component exposes, you can make the necessary data access changes by redesigning the component and then deploying the component in the network.

When using this approach to abstracting data access logic, it is very important for you to consider the future of your application before designing your component. As you change data access methods, you may need to provide additional parameters that your existing method does not require. Chapter 4 will further explore the design issues surrounding business objects in the business tier.

In Exercise 1.2, you will use Visual Basic 6 to implement a simple component. As you work through this exercise, consider how you could apply these techniques to the concepts of data access and business logic abstraction. You will create a component that interacts with Win32 API to return the directory location where Windows is installed.

EXERCISE 1.2

Creating and Calling a Simple Component

1. Start Visual Basic 6. By default this should be accessible through Start ➢ Programs ➢ Microsoft Visual Studio 6.0 ➢ Microsoft Visual Basic 6.0. When prompted for a type of project, select ActiveX DLL. Click OK.

2. You should see a code window called Class1. In the Properties window, change the name of the module from Class1 to Directory by typing the new name in the properties window. Leave the instancing property as 5-Multiuse.

3. Open the API Text Viewer utility. This should be available by default from Start ➢ Programs ➢ Microsoft Visual Studio 6.0 ➢ Microsoft Visual Studio 6.0 Tools ➢ API Text Viewer. From the API Viewer menu, select File ➢ Load Text File. Select the Win32api.txt file and click Open.

4. Under Available Items, find the entry for GetWindowsDirectory. The entries are in alphabetical order. Choose Private Scope for the declaration. Select the GetWindowsDirectory entry and click Add from the command buttons on the right side of the window. This will place the declaration in the bottom box.

EXERCISE 1.2 (CONTINUED)

5. Click the Copy button in the viewer window. This will copy the entry to your Clipboard. Close the viewer utility.

6. Back in Visual Basic, paste the declaration into the general declarations section of the Directory class module. The declaration should now read like the following (note that your entry will all be on one line):

```
Private Declare Function GetWindowsDirectory Lib
"kernel32" Alias "GetWindowsDirectoryA" (ByVal lpBuffer As
String, ByVal nSize As Long) As Long
```

7. To add a method of the class, from the Visual Basic menu, select Tools ➤ Add Procedure. Fill in the dialog as shown in the following graphic.

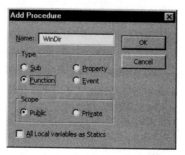

8. Click OK. You will be taken to the procedure template for the Public Function WinDir. Between the Function and End Function statements, enter the following code:

```
Dim strBuffer As String, lngLength As Long
strBuffer = String$(255, 0)
lngLength = GetWindowsDirectory(strBuffer, Len(strBuffer))
strBuffer = Left$(strBuffer, lngLength)
WinDir = strBuffer
```

9. Name the project by selecting Project ➤ Project1 Properties from the Visual Basic menu. In the Project Name box, enter **TestProj**. Click OK. Save the project in a location of your choice. Accept the default file names.

10. To test the component, add a new project to the project group by selecting File ➤ Add Project from the Visual Basic menu. When prompted for a project type, select Standard Exe and click Open. You should now see two projects in the project window.

11. Point to the icon for Project1 in the project group window and click the right mouse button. Select Set As Start Up from the pop-up menu. This will bold Project1, and your project window should now look like the following figure.

12. Select Project1 in the project window. Make a reference to TestProj by selecting Project ➤ References from the menu. Click in the check box next to the TestProj entry and click OK.

13. In the Visual Basic toolbox, locate the command button control. Double-click this control in the toolbox to add an instance of the control to your form.

14. Double-click the command button in the form to expose the click event procedure of the command button. In this procedure, type the following code:

```
Dim obj As TestProj.Directory
Set obj = New TestProj.Directory
MsgBox obj.WinDir
```

15. Save the project group in the location of your choice, accepting all of the defaults. Run the application and click on the Command1 button. A message box will indicate the location where Windows is installed.

16. Close Visual Basic.

Multiple-Tier Design and Performance

One advantage to implementing multiple-tier design is that the modifiable components can be reused as libraries in a variety of applications. Another advantage is that deployment and updating are much simpler because the components only need to be implemented in one location (or just a few locations) on the network.

Notwithstanding these advantages, component architecture comes at a price, and that price is often performance. When you evaluate the structure of a multiple-tier architecture, this is perfectly reasonable. In the two-tier model, the entire application exists as two processes, one running on the client and the other running on the server. Multiple-tier architecture changes this structure significantly. Elements of the application run in at least three processes, maybe even more, depending on the way the components were designed.

Problems with Three-Tier Architectures

One problem with three-tier architecture is simply a matter of network traffic. Now, instead of a single communication between client and server, you have communication between client and component, server and component, and perhaps even component and component. This will obviously increase network traffic and reduce network response time. Figure 1.10 illustrates how dramatic this effect can be.

FIGURE 1.10

Network traffic in a two-tier and n-tier client/server

2-Tier C/S

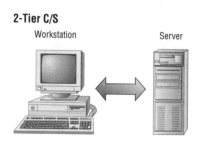
Workstation   Server

N-Tier C/S

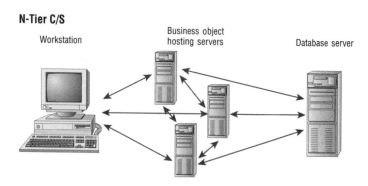
Workstation   Business object hosting servers   Database server

This is not the only problem, however. Remember that all clients will be working with the same components. When every client was interacting with the server directly, this did not usually pose much of a threat. After all, large database servers such as Microsoft SQL Server and Oracle are designed to be *scalable* (able to handle greater traffic or volume). Unfortunately, the components are not usually scalable to the same degree that the database servers are. This means that if you plan to implement this design on a network with a very large number of users, the components will almost certainly create a bottleneck in the application. Although it is possible to build objects that scale, this requires a significant amount of additional code, as scalable components can be quite complex to build.

Another problem is that while we are able to define true atomic transactions at the data services level, we may need to have the same functionality at the business services level. Suppose you have a group of components that are designed to be used together. When any one component is used, it must be enlisted in a transaction with other components. Each component sends its own independent data modification requests to the server, so these transactions cannot be enforced at the data services layer.

These problems can certainly be overcome (as you will see in the next section); however, they add an element of additional complexity to our multiple-tier designs. When selecting an appropriate multiple-tier design, you must think about where in the network your objects will be implemented, the development system that will be used to create the components, and other issues which may impact overall client/server application performance.

Microsoft Transaction Server

Multiple-tier client/server design is much too good of an idea to scrap because of a few problems, especially if those problems can be overcome. In the previous discussion, two primary complications in the multiple-tier scenario were identified: the inability of objects to effectively scale and the inability of objects to enlist other objects in atomic transactions.

Microsoft Transaction Server (MTS) was created to address these problems. First, MTS can be used to manage all multi-user considerations for a component architecture. In other words, you do not need to write sophisticated threading and multi-user support in your components. MTS will provide that support for the components.

Second, MTS extends transaction support from the data services layer into the business services layer. This allows you to write components that focus on a core business function, and MTS can enlist various components into transactions, providing true and reliable transaction support. Let's look at each of these two main functions individually.

Scalability

To provide scalability to a component, MTS provides all of the necessary services to manage multiple users, scaling resources, and other issues central to scalability. Before MTS, to create an object that would truly scale, the developer had to incorporate all of this functionality inside the component. With MTS, the developer need only write a single-user object, which will be managed in a multi-user environment by MTS.

Scalability became an issue during the development of distributed processing architectures such as multiple-tier client/server. Because these systems could theoretically handle more users, it was imperative that all elements of the application be created to scale. This was easy for some elements. The database server, for example, has scalability as one of its central features. Products such as Oracle and Microsoft SQL Server can scale to unbelievable levels. It was the component, not the database server that was the weak link in this chain.

Although the popularity of client/server architectures introduced the problem of scalable component architectures, the Internet brought it to a whole new level. You can conceivably get by in a small to moderate client/server environment with objects that do not really scale, but scalability issues can no longer be brushed aside if the application is exposed to the Internet.

Microsoft created MTS with the Internet in mind. Because of scalability problems, traditional n-tier client/server applications would never survive if Internet traffic were allowed access to the applications' business objects. MTS provides the internal plumbing necessary to allow business objects to scale to the enterprise and beyond.

A serious transition has been occurring in many businesses over the last year or two. This transition involves the seemingly infinite volume of access coming from the Internet. Taking an existing client/server application and putting it on the Internet so that remote employees, customers, suppliers, and in some cases, the general public can access the information in a database is problematic. Managing security and ensuring scalability to Internet application levels is also problematic.

Figure 1.11 illustrates the path of this transition. Note that the internal client/server applications and the Internet application share some common elements, such as a data store and even components.

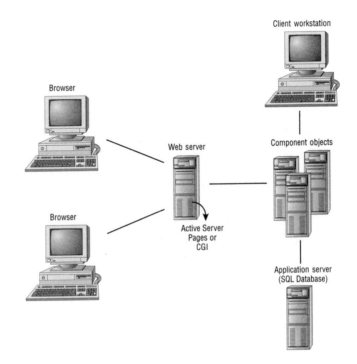

In this scenario, the component objects are required to handle Internet traffic as well as internal client/server traffic, creating a true scalability nightmare. The components are accessed from the Web server through an Internet Service API (ISAPI) application such as an Active Server Page or possibly a Common Gateway Interface (CGI) application. The client to the component is actually the application running on the Web server, not the Web browser. Assuming that we use Active Service Pages, ASP are responsible for collecting data from the data source and creating an HTML (Hypertext Markup Language) response that is sent back to the browser. Every time a browser makes a request for data in the database, an ISAPI routine will execute. Because data can be extracted from the database only by going through the component objects, this becomes a real scalability issue.

Now suppose you install Microsoft Transaction Server on the same machine that hosts the components. By allowing the components to be managed by MTS, scalability is automatically provided, even if the objects are written as single-user components, and the focus of scalability shifts. The component no longer creates the bottleneck. Now the bottleneck is created by the Windows NT Operating System or the SQL Server database. Windows NT clustering solves some of this problem, but the future lies in the next wave of products.

Transaction Support

In addition to supporting scalability, MTS supports transactions across objects at the business-logic layer. This support allows you to focus the properties and methods of components on nondecomposable units of work because these objects can be combined into transactions later when the components need to work together.

To illustrate this functionality, suppose that you are responsible for developing the accounts database application for a bank. Your application must support the functionality to deposit funds into an account as well as to withdraw funds from an account. You determine that the best way to do this is to use a multiple-tier solution so that you can update business and data access logic more easily if it is needed later.

To support this functionality at the middle tier, you create one component called Deposit and another called Withdrawal. These components are used to encapsulate all the business and data access logic needed to deposit or withdraw funds from an account.

The bank manager decides that the tellers must be able to transfer money from one account to another. This poses an interesting dilemma for you because there are a few ways you can accomplish this task. One option is to create a stored procedure on the server that will perform the transfer as a single transaction and call that stored procedure from a component. This option would achieve the desired result, but it would require an additional stored procedure on the server that would need to be managed.

Another option is to create a component that calls the Deposit and Withdrawal components to perform the transfer. This is a fairly thin solution because the new component does not need to do much other than call the other components. It's true that not having to make additional modifications to the server applications is an advantage, but the problem with this is that the two called components would actually be individual transactions. This could cause a problem with data integrity.

The second solution is preferable except for the transaction problem. Fortunately, MTS can solve that problem. The three components (Deposit, Withdrawal, and Transfer) can be included in a Transaction Server *package*, which allows the three objects to work together under the context of a single transaction when necessary but still allows them to work independently if required. The resulting model is illustrated in Figure 1.12.

F I G U R E   1.12

Component trans-
action support
through MTS

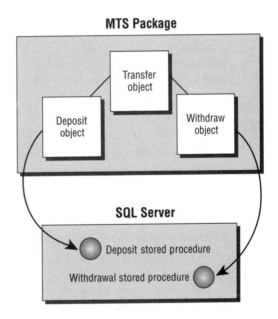

To provide this type of transaction support, the components' code must be slightly modified. All of the components will recognize a special object called a *Context object*. This Context object will control the context of the transaction. By informing the Context object about the success or failure in completing the work in the components, the Context object can track the progress of the entire transaction.

Suppose that as a transfer is in progress, the Withdrawal component identifies three funds that are insufficient to perform the withdrawal. The

Withdrawal object would inform the Context object that the transaction cannot continue. When the Context object reports to MTS that the transaction failed in at least one if its components, the entire transaction is forced to roll back.

As you can see from this brief discussion, MTS has a definite place in client/server architecture. MTS also supports mainframe connectivity that allows mainframe architectures to participate in distributed transactions without requiring any modifications to the mainframe application.

MTS can take your client/server application to the next level, providing multi-user support, distributed transaction support, and even support for legacy applications running on an SNA architecture. The technology is readily available and ships with a number of different packages, including Visual Studio 97 Enterprise Edition and the Windows NT 4 option pack. When combined with other technologies, such as Microsoft Cluster Server and Microsoft Message Queue Server, MTS will provide outstanding support for your scalability needs.

Security

Another advantage of implementing MTS is security. MTS defines a security model called *package security*. This approach allows the developer to assign user identity to packages, thus allowing the packages to act as a virtual user. In some respects, the package can be thought of as a logical grouping of users, just like a network group. The package identity is given rights to perform any required activities on the underlying data sources. Then each network user or group is given access to the components in the package as needed.

The advantage to this approach is tremendous. Instead of managing security at many tiers throughout the application, MTS manages the security at the package level. This unburdens the administrator significantly, as database security is only managed by granting access to the packages. The packages then act as a user filter to allow only qualified users into the database.

Data Source Availability with Microsoft Message Queue

Another of the problems often faced in multiple-tier development is the availability of the data source. What if, for some reason, the business object cannot contact the data source? Does this prevent a transaction from committing? The Microsoft Message Queue (MSMQ) helps to resolve this problem.

Suppose that your client application interacts with a database that is available only across a slow link or unreliable network connection. The database is not always available, yet your client application must continue to write modifications to the data source without error. This may seem like an impossible task; however, MSMQ makes this possible.

With MSMQ installed, the target database may be unavailable and the data modifications can still commit. Consider the MSMQ to be a store-and-forward database. Messages are placed in the queue and, when the database is available, the modifications are written to the data source.

The MSMQ can also search for a data source that can accept and commit the modification. Now suppose that you have a client application that places orders for products with vendors. Using MSMQ, if the client application or business object contacts the first vendor and is unable to commit, then another vendor can be contacted. This can continue until a vendor is found that can satisfy the request. All the while, the transactions are stored in the message queue and the client can continue without waiting for the transaction to commit. Even though the transaction is sent from the client asynchronously, the message queue maintains the integrity of the transaction.

Optimization of Database Roles

Not all databases are created equal. The functions that databases are designed to fulfill can be quite different from each other. While some databases are designed to provide information for reporting, others are intended for handling data entry or modification for archival purposes. Still others are a combination of both of these roles. Whichever role a database plays in the business process, the way that you design and maintain that database can have a significant impact on the performance of the database, either positive or negative.

In this section, we will discuss the various roles that a database can play in the business process. We will then look at different design approaches that we can use to maximize the efficiency of each of these roles.

Decision-Support Systems

A decision-support system (DSS) is a database used primarily for reporting purposes. Although there may be some data entry and data modification, the main goal of the DSS is to provide information through queries for various management reports intended to aid the business decision-making process.

Although DSS does not necessarily imply a completely static or read-only database, it will definitely be much less volatile than other databases. This lack of volatility enables us to incorporate two elements into the database design that might otherwise raise concern: denormalizations and indexes.

- *Denormalization* is the deliberate breaking of the normal forms for the purpose of enhancing performance. While this approach may very well increase performance, there is a cost to be paid in maintenance of existing data and input of new data. A DSS will tend to be much less costly in terms of denormalization support because the data is less likely to change.

- *Indexes* are a two-edged sword. It is impossible to assemble a good database without them, yet too many can also negatively impact performance. It is possible to have too much of a good thing!

Indexes make the process of locating data faster. When data is requested, a query optimizer that is part of the DBMS will analyze the query to identify the potential indexes that could be used to satisfy the query, and the best possible index will be chosen. How this index is chosen is an issue that is very specific to the DBMS and is a factor that makes some DBMS products superior to others. Microsoft SQL Server 7 uses a cost-based optimizer that estimates the amount of page input/output and other resources that would be required to resolve the query and then selects the index that results in the lowest estimated resource usage score.

Generally speaking, the more indexes that exist, the better selection the query optimizer will have when indexes are selected; this should, therefore, result in better performance. Also, if the number of indexes is not a concern, the developer can create indexes targeted to specific queries. This allows the developer to improve system performance on a query-by-query basis.

The problem with this perspective is that indexes also come at a cost. There are two main costs associated with indexes. First, storage space is always a concern. It is not uncommon in products like Microsoft SQL Server to see indexes that are 25 percent of the table or more in size. If you have disk space to burn, you may want to create indexes, but for most of us, disk space is always at a premium. However, if you are managing a DSS and you want the advantages that the extra indexes can provide, you might work these extra disk requirements into your storage space estimates from the very beginning.

 As the cost of hard disk storage continues to decline, conservation of disk space is becoming less of a concern.

The other cost associated with indexes is the high maintenance costs required whenever data is inserted or updated. An index stores the location of every indexed value in its structure. If data is regularly inserted or updated, the indexes must also be updated. If you have a large number of indexes, this can result in a substantial negative effect on update and insert performance.

Since DSS environments have much less data volatility, you may be free to use more indexes. The lack of data volatility essentially exempts your database from the maintenance costs usually associated with extensive indexing.

Online Transaction Processing Systems

The online transaction processing (OLTP) database is not primarily concerned with reporting, but rather with data maintenance. This type of database is constantly receiving transactions that need to be processed and data that needs to be updated on a regular basis. This differs from the DSS in that the DSS might be receiving a heavy load of data requests that are not transactions. Transactions are responsible for data modifications, insertions, or deletions.

How will the architecture of the database differ for an OLTP database? The two constructs that were realistic for DSS databases, namely denormalizations and high index levels, would be totally inappropriate for an OLTP database. This will have an impact on the design of that database.

It is quite important that an OLTP database be extremely well normalized. Although you may have some specific nonvolatile areas in the database where denormalization might be appropriate, the general rule is that normalized is preferred in most cases.

Indexes will also be affected. The high level of indexes that you would see in a DSS database is simply too costly for an OLTP database. It is very important to keep the number of indexes reasonable; you must also make sure that you are getting the most mileage out of the indexes that you do choose to use.

WARNING Although it might be tempting, do not remove all indexes from an OLTP database. While the maintenance cost for indexes in an OLTP environment is very high, some indexes are needed to effectively locate the records that need to be modified. Look at the WHERE clauses in your SQL statements to identify those few fields that might benefit the most from indexes.

The Balancing Act

I'm sure that, as you have been reading this section defining DSS and OLTP database processes, you have been thinking about your databases and how they would be classified. If your databases are like most, there is no easy way to categorize them. After all, most production databases are involved in activities that could be classified as both DSS and OLTP in nature. How do you balance these various tasks?

The question is a good one and is the very issue that has plagued database developers and administrators since the invention of the index. Where do you draw the line and how do you effectively create an architecture that will support both types of database systems? There is no easy answer, but there are some things that you can do: namely divide, conquer, and kill.

Divide

Perhaps the database can be easily divided into logical partitions that perform specific functions. For example, if you have a customer order database, this encompasses multiple functionalities. Assume for the sake of illustration that the customer-tracking portion of this database is used primarily for reporting. You generate reports based on customer information, but the customer information itself is not very volatile. You may treat this customer portion as a DSS.

Although the customer portion of the database is extremely static, the orders portion of the database is extremely volatile. Data is inserted and updated with great frequency. This portion of the database can be treated as an OLTP system.

While there will be some minimal crossover between the two sides of the database, you can essentially practice standard optimization techniques by treating the different parts of the database as if they were different databases entirely.

Another approach to dividing databases is to create two full databases. One database can be used for handling the transaction traffic and can be optimized accordingly. This data can then be periodically replicated to the second database, which can be used for reporting purposes and optimized as a DSS.

Conquer

You may not be able to divide the database as neatly as discussed in the previous section, but you may still be able to select certain tasks that will have priority over other tasks in the database and optimize for those tasks. Every query has a priority. It may be a high-priority report that is delivered to the president's desk every Monday or perhaps a low-priority update that does not require real-time reflection in the database.

For those tasks that you determine are higher priorities, you will optimize. The other tasks of lower priorities will be subject to the tasks higher on the food chain. Although the division will not be as surgical as in the previous example, it will still enable you to set some relative priorities and optimize your system based on those priorities.

Kill

Sometimes there is no choice but to pick a victim. A database simply cannot be all things to all people and, if no other choice is reasonable, you may have to favor one optimization over the other. Of course, this should also be done based on priorities, ensuring that the lower priority optimizations will be victim.

Although this approach may sound like giving up in a way—and it certainly is a last resort—remember that your ultimate goal is to provide the best possible performance to as many users as possible. While some users will disagree with your choice of optimizations, if you have done your job correctly, these will be the vocal minority.

Installing and Configuring Visual Studio 6 Components

The installation process for Visual Studio 6 has changed from the installer for Visual Studio 97. Getting comfortable with this installation process and proper configuration is sure to make your job of creating distributed applications an easier one. In this section, we will address the installation process for Visual Basic 6 and the Visual SourceSafe source-code control utility.

Since this book covers subjects concerning distributed application development, this installation discussion assumes that you are installing from the Visual Studio 6 Enterprise edition. All of the screenshots in this section assume an installation on Windows NT 4 with Service Pack 3 installed.

Installing and Configuring Visual Basic 6

Microsoft ✓ *Exam Objective*

Install and configure Visual Basic for developing distributed applications.

The installation process for Visual Basic 6 starts with the first CD in the Visual Studio 6 suite. All of the development products except for Visual J++ install from this first CD. The rest of the discs in the set provide other supporting utilities as well as a Visual Studio version of Microsoft BackOffice and the NT 4 Option Pack.

One of the most critical installation steps in preparing for distributed application development is installing the correct version of Visual Basic. The Enterprise version was created with distributed applications in mind. If you plan to create distributed applications, you should install the Enterprise version.

If you haven't installed Visual Basic 6 yet, you might want to follow along as this section illustrates the process. This will not be structured as a formal exercise.

The first Visual Studio CD should autoplay when inserted into your CD-ROM drive. If it does not autoplay, run the setup by double-clicking the Setup.exe icon. The first screen that you will see is the introductory screen. This screen, pictured in Figure 1.13, gives you the opportunity to view the readme file which provides an overview of the installation notes on all of the products in the Visual Studio 6 suite. You will advance to more screens by clicking the Next button.

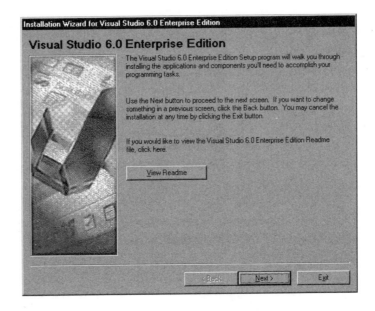

Before you can continue, you must accept all of the terms of the license agreement. Be sure to read the license agreement carefully. After accepting it, you are legally bound to the terms of the agreement.

The next installation dialog screen asks you for information about the licensing of this installation. You must provide a CD key, which you will find on the packaging of your Visual Studio CD set. You must also provide the name and organization of the license holder. Figure 1.14 illustrates this screen.

If you do not have the most recent version of Microsoft Internet Explorer 4 installed, the Visual Studio installer will now raise a dialog asking you to install this product. You must have IE version 4 or later so that Visual Studio 6's help utilities and console screens will install and operate properly. If you do have to install IE 4 at this time, the Visual Studio installer will take you to the appropriate screen to continue when the IE installation process is complete.

WARNING   Windows NT 4 Service Pack 3 or higher must be installed in order for IE 4.*x* to install properly. When installing IE 4.*x*, bear in mind that the screenshots in this book assume that the active desktop features have *not* been installed.

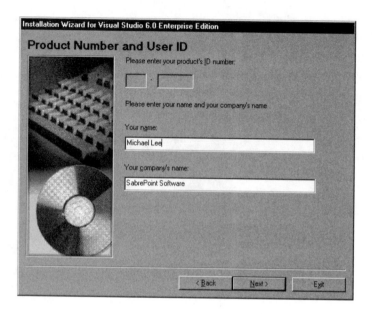

The next screen queries as to what should be installed. You have three choices: Custom, Products, or Server Applications. Choose Custom if you wish to install both Products and Server Applications. Since you are concerned only with the installation of Visual Basic 6 in this step, you will choose Products.

The next screen asks for a location for the Visual Studio 6 common files. These are files that are used by all of the Visual Studio products, such as graphics and other binaries and executables. The default location is C:\Program Files\Microsoft Visual Studio\Common. There should be no need to change this location.

The next screen, illustrated in Figure 1.15, lists the Visual Studio products that can be installed. Select Visual Basic 6.0 as shown. The other tools can be installed on the same computer if desired; however, they are not needed at this time. Click the Next button to begin the Visual Basic 6.0 installer.

Advance through the information screens until you are presented with a list of components to install. The Visual Studio elements that are selected for you are the ones that are the most common for use with Visual Basic 6. To provide the best support for distributed applications development, you will want to make a few changes to this list.

F I G U R E 1.15

Selecting the
appropriate Visual
Studio product

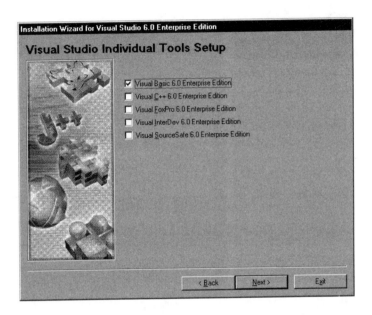

First, remove the check next to Visual SourceSafe 6.0. Although this is an extremely helpful tool for distributed applications development, we will install this tool later in this chapter.

Next, click Data Access and click the Change Option button. The resulting list addresses all of the Data Access technologies that ship with Visual Studio 6. The default selections should look like Figure 1.16. By default, Visual Basic will install with all available OLE DB providers, but only ODBC drivers for SQL Server, Oracle, Jet, and FoxPro. No Jet ISAM drivers are installed by default. If you wish to install any of these components, click the appropriate category and click the Change Option button to select the tool desired. As a shortcut, simply click Select All. Click the OK button to return to the main screen.

Using a similar process, advance to the Enterprise Tools installer and add the Visual Studio Analyzer to the list of components. This useful tool can aid you in locating bottlenecks in a distributed application. In the main screen, also select the checkbox for Graphics. This installs the icons, bitmaps, and other graphics that you may use when developing the presentation tier of your distributed application. When finished selecting items, click Continue.

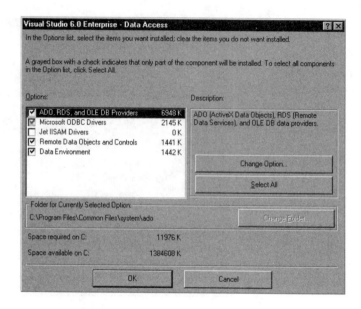

Visual Basic 6 will now install on your computer. After the file copy is completed, setup will update your computer's Registry. You will then be prompted to restart your computer to complete the installation. After restarting, you will be prompted to install Microsoft Developer Network (MSDN). MSDN is now the source for all of the Visual Studio documentation. If you don't have a subscription to MSDN, you can install the version that ships with Visual Studio.

It is highly recommended that you install MSDN on your development computer. It provides a wealth of information that can be invaluable as you develop applications with Visual Studio.

The next installation screen allows you to install InstallShield for Visual C++. If you wish to install this tool, click on the name of the tool in the list box and click the Install button. When finished, click the Next button.

The next screen allows you to install other components such as the Visual SourceSafe Server and other Microsoft BackOffice products as needed. We will skip these installations at this time.

The last screen gives you the opportunity to register online with Microsoft. Click the Finish button; your Visual Basic installation is now complete.

Installing SQL Debugging

Another of the helpful enterprise utilities that ships with Visual Studio is SQL debugging. This tool allows you to debug client/server applications completely by allowing breaks in SQL stored procedures. This brings desktop ease to distributed application development. This tool must be installed on the computer that hosts the SQL Server. Exercise 1.3 walks you through the process of installing SQL debugging.

Before you can install SQL debugging, SQL Server must be installed on your Windows NT Server. For details on installing SQL Server 7, consult Appendix C, SQL Server 7 Primer.

Although you can install any of the tools using the Visual Studio installer, if you wish to install a single tool, you can go directly to the appropriate folder in the CD set. This is often easier than wading through the installer.

EXERCISE 1.3

Installing SQL Debugging

1. Insert *Visual Studio Enterprise* disc 2 into the CD-ROM drive. Navigate into the sqdbg_ss folder and launch Setup.exe.

2. Continue through the screens until you reach the dialog that sets the installation folder. The default folder is C:\Program Files\ Microsoft Visual Studio\Common\Tools\SQL Debugging. There should be no need to change this location. Click the large setup button at the top of the dialog.

3. After the files copy to the computer, you will be informed that the setup is complete.

Installing and Using Microsoft Visual SourceSafe

Microsoft ✓ *Exam* *Objective*	**Establish the environment for source-code version control.**

One of the most common problems associated with team application development is the control of source code. When more than one individual is responsible for the development of an application object, it is not uncommon for conflicts to occur. Visual SourceSafe can solve this problem by providing a central database and repository for all of your source code.

Visual SourceSafe can also track the history of your source code. This gives you the ability to revert to a former version of your application if needed. This feature is useful even when you are working as a single developer, because it provides one more layer of protection against work loss.

Visual SourceSafe requires the installation of both client and server components. Exercise 1.4 takes you through the process of installing the Visual SourceSafe server components.

EXERCISE 1.4

Installing Visual SourceSafe Server

1. Insert Visual Studio disc 1. Run Setup.exe in the root folder of the CD. From the Installation Wizard dialog, select Server Applications and Tools. Click Next.

2. In the Server Setups dialog, click Visual SourceSafe Server from the Server Components list. Click the Install button. When prompted, insert disc 2 into the CD-ROM drive and click OK.

3. Click Continue from the initial information screen and click OK from the product information screen. In the Installation dialog, accept the default installation location by clicking the large button picturing the server.

4. If prompted to use the new SourceSafe Server database format, select Yes. This format is not compatible with Visual Basic 5 projects, but it can offer superior performance for Visual Basic 6 projects.

5. The server files will now copy to your computer. When prompted, restart you computer. You will eventually return to the Server Components installer. Click Finish to complete the installation.

Exercise 1.5 illustrates the installation of the Visual SourceSafe client components.

EXERCISE 1.5

Installing and Implementing the Visual SourceSafe Client

1. Insert Visual Studio disc 1. Run Setup.exe in the root folder of the CD. From the Installation Wizard dialog, select Workstation Tools and Components and click Next.

2. Since you have run the Products installation previously, you will be prompted as to whether you wish to Add/Remove, Reinstall, or Remove All of a previous install. Click Add/Remove.

3. Click the checkbox for Microsoft Visual SourceSafe. Do not deselect any elements from the list (this would uninstall those elements). Click Continue.

4. When prompted to upgrade your database, click Yes. After the file copy, you will be informed that the installation is complete. Click the OK button.

5. To test the Visual SourceSafe installation, start a new project in Visual Basic. From the Start menu click Start ➢ Programs ➢ Microsoft Visual Studio 6 ➢ Microsoft Visual Basic 6. When prompted for a project type, click Standard Exe and click OK.

6. Immediately save the project. From the Visual Basic menu, click File ➤ Save Project. Save the form and the project file to a location of your choice. When prompted to add the project to SourceSafe, click Yes.

7. For the username, type **Admin**. Leave the password blank. Leave the database set to common. Click OK.

8. In the project text box type **NewProj**. Click OK. When asked to confirm the SourceSafe project creation, click Yes. Add all files to the project and click OK.

9. In the Visual Basic Project window, you should see that the icons have changed and now show locks next to the forms and project icons. This means that the files are under source code control. Close Visual Basic.

10. View the new project using the Visual SourceSafe Client utility. From the Start menu click Start ➤ Programs ➤ Microsoft Visual Studio 6 ➤ Microsoft Visual SourceSafe ➤ Microsoft Visual SourceSafe 6. Login as Admin with a blank password. Leave the database as Common. You should now see the project as displayed in the following graphic.

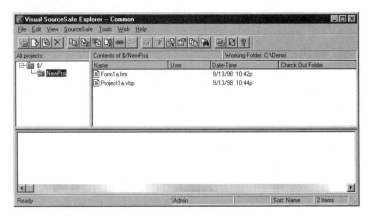

11. Leave the Visual SourceSafe Client running and Start Visual Basic 6. Open the project that you just saved. You will be prompted for a login. Again, enter **Admin** with a blank password.

12. In the Visual Basic Project window, click on the icon for form1 with your right mouse button. This will open the pop-up menu. At the bottom of the menu, select Check Out. This will check the file out of the SourceSafe database so that changes can be saved and tracked.

13. Switch to the Visual SourceSafe Client. Refresh the window by pressing the F5 key on your keyboard. You should now see that the form file is checked out.

14. Switch back to Visual Basic. Right-click on the form file icon in the Project Window once more, exposing the pop-up menu. Click Undo Check Out, rather than Check In. This will cancel the Check Out operation, and a historical iteration will not be saved in the database.

15. Exit Visual Basic. In the SourceSafe Client, press the F5 key again to refresh. Notice that the file is no longer checked out. Exit the Visual SourceSafe Client.

Review Questions

1. The Microsoft JET database engine is structured to be a very robust multi-user engine scaling to thousands of users.

   A. True

   B. False

2. In a typical client/server implementation, the database engine will reside on a:

   A. Windows NT primary domain controller

   B. Central database application server

   C. Client workstation

   D. Business component object

3. When dealing with data extraction, the database server application's primary role is:

   A. Data reduction

   B. Data formatting

   C. Reporting

   D. Sorting

4. Which service defines data modification and data extraction?

   A. User

   B. Business

   C. Data

   D. Application

5. Which service defines formatting and reporting activities?

   A. User

   B. Business

   C. Data

   D. Application

6. Which service defines validation and data access logic?

   A. User

   B. Business

   C. Data

   D. Application

7. You have decided to implement a two-tier client/server architecture, but you are concerned with the maintainability of business logic. Which architecture should you implement?

   A. Smart client

   B. Smart server

C. Smart component

D. Mixed

8. You have decided that you will implement a two-tier client/server architecture, but you are concerned about the strain that may be placed on the server. The client workstations have excess processing capacity. Which architecture should you implement?

   A. Smart client

   B. Smart server

   C. Smart component

   D. Mixed

9. Business objects will most often be created as which type of object?

   A. True DLL

   B. Java applet

   C. Active Server Page

   D. COM object

10. Which of the following Microsoft tools provides for data availability by preventing a transaction from failing if the data source is unavailable?

    A. Microsoft SQL Server

    B. Microsoft Message Queue

    C. Microsoft Transaction Server

    D. Microsoft Windows NT Server Enterprise

11. Which of the following is not part of the ACID test by which transactions are measured?

    A. Anonymity

    B. Consistency

    C. Isolation

    D. Durability

12. The ability to provide support for user bases ranging from very small to very large without suffering performance degradation is called:

 A. Responsiveness

 B. Threading

 C. User pooling

 D. Scalability

13. Which of the following is not a benefit of using Microsoft Visual SourceSafe?

 A. Each object can have different levels of permissions for every user created through the Visual SourceSafe Administrative Utility.

 B. SourceSafe provides for a historical repository of source code modifications.

 C. SourceSafe guarantees that a read/write copy of the source code will be available whenever it is requested by a user.

 D. SourceSafe protects source code from simultaneous revisions by multiple users.

14. Which of the following database application classifications would be considered appropriate for a database designed to accept numerous real-time data modifications?

 A. Data warehouse

 B. Online Transaction Processing System (OLTP)

 C. Online Analytical Processing System (OLAP)

 D. Decision Support System (DSS)

15. Which of the following is NOT considered a true relational database management system? (select two)

 A. Microsoft SQL Server

 B. Oracle

 C. Microsoft Access

 D. Microsoft FoxPro

CHAPTER

2

Designing and Implementing the Data Tier

In this chapter, we will look at the data tools supported by Visual Basic. We will begin by discussing how to structure your data, including proper normalization techniques. We will then create SQL Server tables using Visual Basic tools. With our data defined, we will then look at different ways to query and update information using the SQL language. Finally, we will look at the role of transactions at the data tier, examining different approaches to enforcing transactions at the data and other tiers.

Although the most glamorous part of any distributed application is the presentation tier or user interface, the data tier is also of significant importance. Even the most exciting and compelling user interface is wasted without a reliable and persistent data store. In the past, creating the data tier meant using a separate environment such as SQL Server for all of the data work, including creating tables, queries, stored procedures, etc. Although it is still very helpful to understand how to work with products like SQL Server, Visual Basic now gives us the ability to define much of our data tier without switching to an alternate tool.

Designing the Data Tier

Design of the data tier is critical. Without a well-planned design, the entire application is prone to inefficiencies and instabilities. What you do at the yellow pad and pencil stage often has much more to do with the performance of an application than anything that you will have the power to do after the application has been built.

In this section, we will first look at the design issues involved in creating a data tier, primarily the development of a normalized structure for the database. We will then walk through the process of creating database objects in Microsoft SQL Server 7 using Visual Basic and OLE DB.

The Rules of Normalization

Normalization is the process of removing all redundancy from your data storage. When the database design is fully normalized, there is no repetition of data across tables with the exception of the keys used to join the tables together. The advantages of data normalization can be enormous in terms of space and cost savings, as well as the increased efficiency with which data can be updated and maintained.

In this section, you will look at the rules of normalization, otherwise known as the *normal forms*. The normal forms define exactly what information can be placed in each table and how this information relates to the fields defined as Primary Keys. Entire books have been written on the subject of normalization; however, this section will simply hit the highlights and illustrate the first three normal forms, which are the most critical in preserving the integrity of your data.

Table 2.1 shows a few of the terms that are used in talking about normalization. Before we discuss the rules of normalization, let's review these terms. As an example, imagine that you have written a check to a vendor for a product that you will resell to a customer. Think of your check register as a table. It has records (or rows) that represent each check written. It also has fields (or columns) that define the individual attributes of each check. This type of modeling is often called *Entity Relationship Analysis* (ERA).

T A B L E 2.1:   Terms Used to Discuss Normalization

Term	What It Means	Example	How It's Created
Entity	A topic or subject that you will describe	A customer, an order, or a check	Entities are represented in databases by creating tables.
Field	An attribute of an entity	If the entity is a check, its attributes include check number, date, amount, payee, etc.	Because entities are represented in databases as tables, attributes are the fields of the table.
Record	An instance of an entity	Every check you write is an instance of the entity. When these checks are entered into a check register, each line of the register represents an individual check or an instance of the check entity.	Adding rows to a table creates records of the table. Each record (or row) acts as a unique instance of that entity defined by the table.

The First Normal Form

The first normal form dictates that tables should contain no repeating groups of data. Every instance of an entity referenced in a table will be unique and all of the fields in the table contain data that is *nondecomposable*. Nondecomposable data is data that cannot be broken down into smaller pieces. This means two things. First, a single column must have only one piece of data. Second, a row cannot have any repeated values.

Every record in the table must be unique. This means that every time you enter information about an instance of an entity, that instance will not be repeated again in the table. The easiest way to identify a record as being unique is to declare a Primary Key on the table. In fact, that is just what the first normal form requires you to do.

Primary Keys must comply with a number of different conditions:

- Any data entered into a Primary Key field anywhere in that table must be unique to that table.

- No duplications can occur in the primary field.

- The Primary Key must not allow null entries.

- There must be a Primary Key entry for every record.

- It is preferable that the Primary Key be a small numeric value for efficiency; however, it is critical that the Primary Key be relevant to the data, even if relevancy requires the numeric value to be large.

Data entered in the table must also be *nondecomposable*. This means that data can't be broken down into smaller meaningful parts. Consider, for example, a field in the table called *name* in which we enter the first name, middle initial (if any), and last name of every customer. Such a field is a violation of the first normal form because it can be broken down into smaller pieces.

If you create a field called *name*, you can still sort by either first name or last name by parsing the name value for every single record and pulling out only the information with which you want to work. Then you can write a custom procedure to sort, search, or otherwise manipulate the data you have extracted. However, this is a high overhead solution.

For efficiency, data in a table should be broken down into the smallest possible pieces for which you will search or modify. Each piece should be a single field so that is can be searched, sorted, or modified as an individual unit.

If you break the field down into pieces, you don't have to go through as much effort to re-create the field in its entirety. Fortunately for us, most database management systems assume that you will be working with nondecomposable data as a general rule and have included in their languages and development systems easy mechanisms that can reassemble data. Even the ANSI standard SQL language contains the tools needed to reassemble data that has been broken apart because of the first normal form.

The nondecomposable data rule applies to records as well as individual fields. Sometimes it is better to break a single record into multiple records to avoid decomposable data at the record level. For example, assume that in your order table you have a field for *order number*, *order date*, *customer number*, and then a series of fields called *product1*, *product2*, *product3*, and so forth that represent all of the individual products requested in a single order. This structure is actually a violation of the first normal form because the record itself is decomposable. Figure 2.1 shows an example of this structure. Note that the product table is aliased three times to support each of the three relationships.

Aliasing is a very useful technique that allows us to refer to a single object in different ways at the same point in time. For example, if you go to the tailor to get a suit altered, the tailor will have you stand in front of a three-way mirror. This way the tailor can look at the suit from three different perspectives at the same time. There is only one suit, but it is being presented in three different ways at the same time. Object aliasing is the virtual version of a three-way mirror.

F I G U R E   2.1

The structure shown here violates the first normal form.

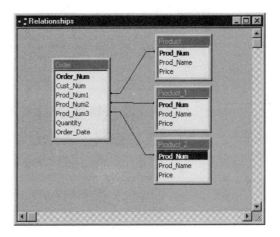

This situation can be rectified in a couple of different ways. One way is to change the Primary Key on the order table to a composite key of two fields, which include the order number and an invoice line number. The composite key will then represent a single line item in the invoice. Although this solves the initial problem, it still violates the ERA model because now we are treating an order and a line item within an order as individual entities. Figure 2.2 illustrates this approach.

FIGURE 2.2

A composite key solution to the problem shown in Figure 2.1

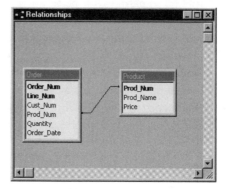

The most appropriate solution to this problem would be to create a *many-to-many relationship* between the order table and the product table. A many-to-many relationship means that you have a one-to-many relationship in both directions. A row in one table relates to many rows in a second table, and the reverse is also true.

Creating this type of relationship requires another table to be created to hold the detail between the order table and the product table. In the example in Figure 2.3, it is called the Invoice_Line table and represents a single line item on an invoice. Note that the Primary Key on this table is a composite of the invoice number and the product number, a combination that will never be repeated.

FIGURE 2.3

A many-to-many solution

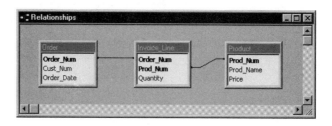

The Second Normal Form

The second normal form states that every field in a table should relate to the Primary Key field in its entirety. This is primarily an issue when tables have composite Primary Keys consisting of multiple fields. If a composite key is present, then every field in that table must relate to all fields comprising that key, not just to one or some of the fields.

In our previous example, we created a table called Invoice_Line that held a many-to-many relationship between the order table and the product table. The entity being described by this table is a single line item on an invoice. Referring back to Figure 2.1, notice that the *price* field is being stored in the product table and not the Invoice_Line table. If the Invoice_Line table defines a single line item in an invoice, why isn't the *price* field held in this table?

The answer relates to the second normal form. If the *price* field were included in the Invoice_Line table, it would be a violation of the second normal form because the price of a product is really an attribute of the product itself, not of the entire order. If the *price* field were included in the Invoice_Line table, that field would relate only to one of the fields in the composite key, namely the *prod_num* field. This is a textbook violation of the second normal form rule.

The Third Normal Form

The third normal form states that any nonkey field in a table must relate to the Primary Key of the table and not to any other field. The Primary Key in this case may be either composite or single. This form forces all data found in a table to relate exclusively to the entity that the table describes.

Using our previous business model example, let's assume that customers will only order a single product from the firm. This restriction eliminates the need for a many-to-many relationship and an Invoice_Line table. In this scenario, all of the information needed to track an order is found in the order table.

In Figure 2.4, there is a violation of the third normal form. Note that the *price* field is included in the order table. As discussed previously, the price relates to the product, not the order. If you needed to record specific customer discounts, they could be included by providing an appropriate *discount* field in the customer table and relating it to the order. Although the *prod_num* field is found in the table, it acts as a foreign key field relating to the product table, not as a *Primary Key* field. Because every field in the table must relate to a key (meaning Primary Key) field and not to any other field, this violates the third normal form.

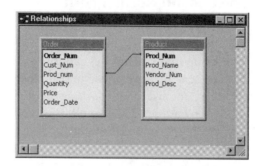

Advantages and Disadvantages of Normalization

Normalized data structures can have significant advantages over denormalized structures as they relate to data entry and data maintenance, yet these same structures can suffer from some prohibitive performance problems.

On the positive side of the normalization picture is the complete removal of data redundancy, thereby optimizing storage space on the data source. With redundancy virtually eliminated, you can use the space to store more data instead of restoring old data.

The maintenance tasks also get much easier when you have a truly normalized design. Because there is no data redundancy, you will never have to change a value in more than one place. If your data is extremely volatile, this is an advantage that usually outweighs all possible disadvantages.

The primary weakness of normalization lies in its very strength, that is, the subdividing of information into single-entity tables. This separation of information requires multiple tables to be joined together to get all of the information that you need, and these joins can be quite costly.

Joins are usually resolved using a process called *nested iteration*. Nested iteration arranges the joined tables sequentially so that when a qualifying record is found in an outside table, an inside table is scanned to find all matching records. For example, assume that you are joining two tables together. Further assume that there will be a total of 25 qualifying records that will be extracted from the outside table. This means that for every qualifying record in the outside table, you must scan the inside table once to find all matching and qualifying records. If there are a total of 25 qualifying records in the outside table, there will be a total of 26 accesses to the set of tables, 1 on the outside and 25 on the inside.

Although indexes and join orders can make this process much more efficient, it is still a time-consuming and I/O-intensive process. If joining two tables together is this troublesome, imagine what happens when you start joining three and four tables together. More tables simply multiply this effort, making it nearly impossible to join large numbers of tables together with any reasonable performance.

Denormalization

Even if you have taken the time to build a normalized database your old college professor would be proud of, it still may not be perfect. The performance problems caused by a normalized design might be far too substantial for you to accept. If this is the case, it is time to start considering various approaches to denormalization.

Denormalization is the process of deliberately breaking the rules of normalization in the hope that you will gain some performance benefits in needed areas. There is no magic ticket to denormalization. It is a process of cost-benefit analysis, testing and retesting, and constant reevaluation.

Of course, every denormalization will carry with it its costs to maintain. These must be considered before a denormalized design is chosen, and you should only consider those designs where the cost of maintaining the denormalization is outweighed by the benefits.

It is very important that you start with a normalized design and use it as your benchmark for testing purposes before you consider a denormalized database design. One of the worst mistakes you can make is to assume that a particular design will be either good or bad without testing it first.

Duplicate Attributes

There are numerous approaches to denormalization. One approach is to provide redundant attributes in tables. In the previous examples, you determined that placing the *price* field in the order table violated the third normal form. If you follow the rules exactly, you will need to do a join from the order table to the product table to access pricing information for the ordered products.

This may be a time-consuming join statement if you are constantly running reports to calculate the total cost of goods sold. You may consider placing the *price* field in the order table as well as in the product table. Although this violates the rules, the benefits are obvious. You no longer have to perform a join statement to access price information for ordered products.

The maintenance cost involved in this approach includes updating the duplicate attributes when the original attributes are updated. Although this can be handled very easily by using an update trigger on the original table, it may significantly slow the update process if the attributes are modified on a regular basis. It is best if duplicate attributes are nonvolatile.

Duplicate Keys

As discussed earlier, every table that you add to the join list multiplies the number of scans required exponentially. The fewer scans required, the less I/O will be needed to satisfy the data request. Providing redundant keys may be one way to reduce the number of joins.

Take a look at another join scenario. Figure 2.5 illustrates an employee table that is related to a customer table. Customers have one employee assigned to them. The customer table is then related to an order table that shows the orders made by that customer. To generate a report about the orders sold by an employee, a join must be made between all three tables.

The costs associated with this approach mirror those incurred with the duplicate-attribute approach. Whenever a key value changes, the value must be updated in all tables. Once again, this approach is best when used with nonvolatile values.

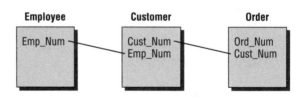

F I G U R E 2.5

A normalized three-table join

Although it will require breaking some rules, you can reduce the total number of joins required to execute this query. Including the *emp_num* field in the order table will provide a direct relationship between employees and orders. Identifying the orders placed by every employee's customers will be more efficient because you won't need to go through the customer table if customer information is not needed.

Table Partitioning

The ERA model and rules of normalization both specify that only one table per entity should exist inside a database. This is a perfectly reasonable requirement; however, this means that tables often become quite large and may contain a significant amount of data that is not frequently used. If the data can be broken into multiple tables, a query has much less data to wade through to find what is actually desired. The tables can be broken apart in two ways, either by row or by column.

If you regularly work with every record in the table but tend to use only a few fields of the table, you may consider partitioning the table by column. Using this strategy, you will create two tables, each with different structures. Although they will both contain the Primary Key value for each record, the other fields will be placed in the tables based solely on their frequency of access. One table will have the fields that are accessed on a regular basis, and the other table will contain less frequently accessed fields. Because each of these tables contains the Primary Key, they can be easily related to reconstruct the entire table, if needed.

Perhaps you have very large tables full of both current and historical information. When these types of tables are present in a database, the current information usually is accessed quite frequently and the historical data is accessed much less often. This situation may lend itself to breaking down a table by row.

To accomplish this, create two identical tables, each with every field being tracked. Place the current information in one table and the historical information in the other table. Periodically move data from the current table to the historical table as the data ages. Once again, using a union statement to reconstruct the original table can easily reassemble this data.

Most sophisticated database management systems allow the developer to create views that contain union operators, further reducing the cost of row-based partitioning of information. Union operators allow two or more distinct result sets to be combined into a single result set.

As you can clearly see, normalized designs are not perfect. Although a normalized design is certainly the best place to start, you may find some unacceptable performance problems as you begin to test your database. If this is the case, you may want to evaluate denormalization as a method of optimizing your database.

As with any optimization tactic, denormalization does not come without its costs. The fields that are the best candidates for denormalization will always be nonvolatile fields, and the fewer times a denormalized field must be updated, the less costly the approach.

The key to effective denormalization is trial and error. Starting with a normalized design, you can test your modifications for efficiency and performance. If the modifications result in benefits that you determine outweigh the costs, then the strategy was probably a good choice. If not, try something else and test again.

Creating and Managing Database Objects

Visual Basic 6 includes many new tools for working with your data. Among these is the Data View window. This window gives you the ability to connect to any data source and browse data structures dynamically at runtime. The Data View window supports two approaches to viewing data and data structures, Data Environment connections and Data Links. We will turn our attention to Data Environment connections.

The Data Environment is a collection of data connections, each of which contains a set of parameters required to access a specific data source. The parameters may include information such as a data source name, a server name, and other logon information. Connections are stored in a project and are activated when the user performs an action that requires access to the database.

For example, a connection for a Microsoft SQL Server database consists of the name of the database, the location of the server on which it resides, network information used to access that server, and a user ID and password. Figure 2.6 illustrates the Data View window browsing the pubs database hosted on a Microsoft SQL Server.

Exploring Databases

Using the Data View window and the DataEnvironment object, we can view existing database structures at design time. If you have ever shuffled paper back and forth between your data schema documentation and your application development environment, you know what a benefit this design-time viewing capability can be.

Creating the Data Environment Connection

The first step in the process is to add a Data Environment and create a data connection. Exercise 2.1 will take you through this process in preparation for the exercises to follow. Do not skip this step, or the remainder of the exercises in this chapter will not function correctly.

Although Microsoft SQL Server 6.5 Developer Edition ships with Visual Studio 6, this book targets SQL Server 7. Two SQL Server configurations are used throughout the book. One is a SQL 7 installation on NT Server 4 called Server 1. The other is the Desktop installation of SQL Server 7 on a Windows 98 Notebook computer called Mobile1. If you are unfamiliar with SQL Server 7, you can refer to Appendix C, *SQL Server 7 Primer*.

EXERCISE 2.1

Creating a Data Environment Connection

1. Start Visual Basic from the Windows start menu. Click Start ➤ Programs ➤ Microsoft Visual Studio 6.0 ➤ Microsoft Visual Basic 6.0. From the New Project window, select Standard EXE and click the Open button.

2. Select View ➤ Data View window from the Visual Basic menu. You will see two folders, Data Links and Data Environment Connections.

3. Select Project ➤ Add Data Environment from the Visual Basic menu. This item might also appear under Project ➤ More ActiveX Designers ➤ Data Environment. This will open a Data Environment window ready for configuration. Point to the Connection1 object in this window and click the right mouse button. Select Properties from the pop-up menu. You are now ready to configure your data connection.

4. From the provider list, select Microsoft OLE DB provider for SQL Server. Click the Next button.

5. In step 1 of the dialog, provide the server name where your SQL Server is installed. In this example, the name of the server is Server1.

6. Step 2 of the dialog provides the server with authentication. For these exercises, we will use a specific user name and password. In the User name text box, type **sa**. Leave the Password text box empty.

7. Step 3 of the dialog points the data connection to a specific database. Open the combo box and select the pubs database from the list. The connection configuration is now complete. The completed dialog should look like the one below. Click OK to close the dialog.

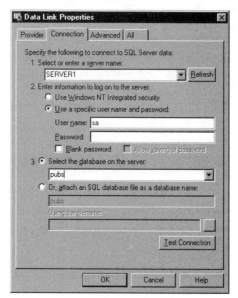

8. Click the Test Connection command button to test the connection. In the Data Environment window, point to Connection1 and right-click. Select Rename from the pop-up menu. Type **pubs** and hit the Enter key.

9. Close the Data Environment window by clicking the Close box in the upper-right corner of the window. The data connection should be showing in the Data View window.

10. Click the plus sign next to the data connection to drill down into the connection. Continue this process to view the structure of the pubs database. When finished, close the Data View window. Do not exit the project.

Creating a Database Diagram

Now that the data connection has been created, you are ready to start exploring, creating, and modifying the structure of your data source. One of the most useful features of the data connection is the database diagram. Those of you that have worked with Microsoft Visual InterDev 1 will immediately find this familiar. The database diagram illustrates the structure of tables and the relationships between tables in a data source, thus simplifying the process of creating queries, especially those that depend on joins between multiple tables. Figure 2.7 illustrates a database diagram showing the relationships among the tables that track author and title information in the pubs database.

F I G U R E   2.7

A typical database diagram

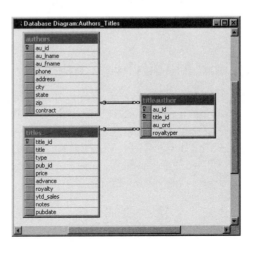

Exercise 2.2 takes you through the process of creating a database diagram. This diagram is identical to the one pictured in Figure 2.7 that illustrates the relationships between the authors and titles tables.

EXERCISE 2.2

Creating a Database Diagram

1. This exercise is a continuation of the project from Exercise 2.1. Select View ➤ Data View window from the Visual Basic menu. Drill down into the pubs database connection and point to the Database Diagrams folder. Click the right mouse button and select New Diagram from the pop-up menu.

2. The blank window that appears must be arranged on the screen so that you can see both the Data View window and the Database Diagram window.

3. In the Data View window, drill down into the Tables folder so that the table names are exposed. Drag the icons for the authors, titles, and titleauthor tables from the Data View window to the blank Database Diagram window. Arrange the table representations in the desired fashion.

4. Close the database diagram. When prompted, save the diagram. Type the name Authors_Titles in the Save As dialog box. Click OK. Note that Authors_Titles now appears in the Database Diagrams folder of the Data View window.

5. Save the project and form files in a folder of your choice. Name the project file `datatier.vbp`. Do not close the project.

Viewing and Modifying Tables

Most of the time we think of a table as a collection of data relating to a specific topic or subject. In reality, a table can also be viewed as a template for storing that data. In simple terms, we can look at a table in either a data view or a design view. Visual Basic 6 puts these different views at our fingertips. Through the data connection, we can view and modify both the structure and data of any table.

Figure 2.8 illustrates the data view of the authors table in the pubs database. This view can be obtained simply by double-clicking the table name in the Data View window. The data view is both read and write, so you can make all data modifications directly to the data grid.

F I G U R E   2.8

The authors table in
data view

au_id	au_lname	au_fname	phone	address	city
172-32-1176	White	Johnson	408 496-7223	10932 Bigge Rd.	Menlo Park
213-46-8915	Green	Marjorie	415 986-7020	309 63rd St. #411	Oakland
238-95-7766	Carson	Cheryl	415 548-7723	589 Darwin Ln.	Berkeley
267-41-2394	O'Leary	Michael	408 286-2428	22 Cleveland Av. #	San Jose
274-80-9391	Straight	Dean	415 834-2919	5420 College Av.	Oakland
341-22-1782	Smith	Meander	913 843-0462	10 Mississippi Dr.	Lawrence
409-56-7008	Bennet	Abraham	415 658-9932	6223 Bateman St.	Berkeley
427-17-2319	Dull	Ann	415 836-7128	3410 Blonde St.	Palo Alto
472-27-2349	Gringlesby	Burt	707 938-6445	PO Box 792	Covelo
486-29-1786	Locksley	Charlene	415 585-4620	18 Broadway Av.	San Francisco
527-72-3246	Greene	Morningstar	615 297-2723	22 Graybar House I	Nashville
648-92-1872	Blotchet-Halls	Reginald	503 745-6402	55 Hillsdale Bl.	Corvallis
672-71-3249	Yokomoto	Akiko	415 935-4228	3 Silver Ct.	Walnut Creek
712-45-1867	del Castillo	Innes	615 996-8275	2286 Cram Pl. #86	Ann Arbor
722-51-5454	DeFrance	Michel	219 547-9982	3 Balding Pl.	Gary
724-08-9931	Stringer	Dirk	415 843-2991	5420 Telegraph Av	Oakland
724-80-9391	MacFeather	Stearns	415 354-7128	44 Upland Hts.	Oakland
756-30-7391	Karsen	Livia	415 534-9219	5720 McAuley St.	Oakland
807-91-6654	Panteley	Sylvia	301 946-8853	1956 Arlington Pl.	Rockville
846-92-7186	Hunter	Sheryl	415 836-7128	3410 Blonde St.	Palo Alto
893-72-1158	McBadden	Heather	707 448-4982	301 Putnam	Vacaville
899-46-2035	Ringer	Anne	801 826-0752	67 Seventh Av.	Salt Lake City
998-72-3567	Ringer	Albert	801 826-0752	67 Seventh Av.	Salt Lake City

Figure 2.9 illustrates the design view of the authors table. To obtain this view of the table, point to the table name in the Data View window and select Design from the pop-up menu. Like the data view, the design view is both read and write. After making all table modifications and closing the table, you will be asked whether you wish to save your changes to the table. Other affected tables might also be saved as prompted.

F I G U R E   2.9

The authors table in
design view

Column Name	Datatype	Length	Precision	Scale	Allow Nulls	Default Value	Identity	Identity Seed	Identity Increment
au_id	id (varchar)	11	0	0					
au_lname	varchar	40	0	0					
au_fname	varchar	20	0	0					
phone	char	12	0	0		('UNKNOWN')			
address	varchar	40	0	0	✓				
city	varchar	20	0	0	✓				
state	char	2	0	0	✓				
zip	char	5	0	0	✓				
contract	bit	1	0	0					

Creating a SQL Server Table

Creating a SQL Server table with Visual Basic is as easy as modifying a table. Simply navigate to design view for a new table and add the desired columns. Exercise 2.3 takes you through the process of creating a new SQL Server table in Visual Basic.

Although Visual Basic allows you to create tables and other database objects in a SQL Server database, it does not have the ability to create the database itself. Before you can create database objects, you must first create the database.

EXERCISE 2.3

Creating a SQL Server Table

1. Activate the Data View window by selecting View ➢ Data View window from the Visual Basic menu. Drill down into the pubs database connection and point to the Tables folder. Click the right mouse button and select New Table from the pop-up menu.

2. Name the table by typing **NewTable** in the Choose Name dialog. Click the OK button.

3. Fill in the data view grid as illustrated in the following graphic. This will create three columns called *FirstName*, *LastName*, and *Salary* respectively.

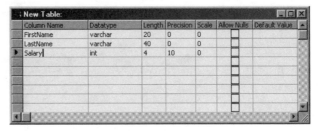

4. Close the table design window. When prompted to save, click Yes. You should now see NewTable in the tables list.

5. Double-click NewTable in the tables folder to enter data view for the table. Enter a few rows of data and close the data view. Save the data tier project.

Although it is customary to refer to data storage in nonrelational database environments (such as Microsoft Access or FoxPro) as fields and records, the accepted terminology in relational data structures is rows and columns.

Retrieving and Modifying Data with SQL Statements

The next logical step in the process of creating the data tier is building stored procedures that can be called from a data client or a data access component created in Visual Basic. Before we can accomplish this, however, we must first become familiar with the structure of the SQL statements that operate on the data. SQL (Structured Query Language) has two major divisions, Data Definition Language (DDL) and Data Manipulation Language (DML). We use DDL to create objects such as databases, tables, stored procedures, etc. DML controls data selection and modification.

In this section, we will focus on the use of DML, specifically ANSI SQL, which defines the standard SQL syntax that provides the foundation for all other dialects of SQL. A database developer can use the same general syntax when writing SQL statements to create stored procedures in SQL Server or manipulate data through the ActiveX Data Objects (ADO) from a Visual Basic client.

Retrieving Data with SQL

Microsoft Exam Objective | **Write SQL statements that retrieve and modify data.**

To retrieve data from a database, we use a SELECT statement. This extremely flexible statement allows the developer to extract the exact data required in precisely the format needed. The basic syntax of the SELECT statement looks like this:

```
SELECT select_list
[FROM table1_name [JOIN STATEMENT table2_name …]]
[WHERE conditions]
[GROUP BY columns]
[HAVING conditions]
[ORDER BY columns]
```

This syntax provides support for queries ranging from the very simple to the very complex. Although there are many variations on this syntax, the structure above is almost universally supported.

When writing SQL statements, the convention is to place the clause commands such as SELECT and FROM in upper case. Database objects are traditionally all lower case. This convention makes it very easy to differentiate the commands from the objects. It is also conventional that all commands begin a new line of text in the statement. This section follows these conventions for clarity; however, when writing a SQL statement in a Visual Basic module, the new line convention cannot be honored without breaking the string and inserting a line continuation character.

Simple SELECT Statements

The most basic SQL statement is SELECT. The asterisk (*) is a special wild-card symbol that requests all columns in the tables mentioned in the FROM clause. For example:

```
SELECT *
FROM authors
```

This query would return every column and every row in the entire authors table. Although this approach is very likely to return the required information, it is extremely inefficient. One way to improve the efficiency of the

SELECT statement is to restrict the columns returned to the user. For example, if the only information that is required for this query is the first name and last name of each author, instead of using the asterisk, the query could be rewritten like this:

```
SELECT au_fname, au_lname
FROM authors
```

Since the first name and last name columns of the authors table are actually called *au_fname* and *au_lname*, this query would offer the required results. If desired, these columns can be renamed in the result set under a different name than the one stored in the table. For example, suppose that you wanted to reference the columns in the result set as *firstname* and *lastname* instead of *au_fname* and *au_lname* respectively. The following query would do the trick.

```
SELECT au_fname firstname, au_lname lastname
FROM authors
```

You could even combine the two columns to make a whole new column that didn't exist in the original table. This process is called concatenation. The following query concatenates the *au_fname* column and the *au_lname* column to create a new column called *name*.

```
SELECT au_fname + ' ' + au_lname name
FROM authors
```

You can use the same basic technique to manipulate numeric data. This process of deriving data based on calculations allows the use of the standard arithmetic operators (+, -, *, /, %). The following example illustrates this with the sales table, creating a derived column called *newquant* which is the quantity value plus 10 percent.

```
SELECT ord_num, (qty * 1.1) newquant
FROM sales
```

Exercise 2.4 takes you through the process of executing a simple SELECT statement using Microsoft SQL Server 7. This will give you the opportunity to see the results of these queries very quickly and easily.

EXERCISE 2.4

Executing a Simple SELECT Statement with SQL Server 7

1. From the Windows Start menu, select Start ➤ Programs ➤ Microsoft SQL Server 7.0 ➤ Query Analyzer. In the SQL Server combo box, enter the name of your SQL Server. The example shows a server name of Server1. Use SQL Server authentication and enter a Login Name of **sa**. Leave the password blank. Click OK.

2. Open the Database list box at the top of the Query Analyzer window. Select pubs from the list. In the blank window, type the following code.

   ```
   SELECT au_fname + ' ' + au_lname name
   FROM authors
   ```

3. Select Query ➤ Execute Query from the menu. You should now see the results of the query in the bottom pane of the window.

4. Experiment with additional queries of your own, typing the query in the top pane and then executing the code. When you are finished, close the Query Analyzer and do not save changes to the current query.

Using Data Restrictions

The approaches previously described work very well when you want all of the rows in a table returned, but what if you want to be a little more restrictive? For example, rather than getting all of the authors in the authors table, suppose that you only wanted to see the authors in the list whose last name is Smith? Using SQL, we accomplish this with a WHERE clause. The code for this example would appear as follows.

```
SELECT *
FROM authors
WHERE au_lname = 'Smith'
```

This query would return every column for those rows that match the given criteria. Although this example returns every column, you could rewrite the query to extract only the columns desired and concatenate or calculate them in any way.

WARNING One of the installation options with SQL Server is the sort order. The default sort order is dictionary order, case insensitive. If you choose to install SQL Server with a case sensitive sort order, results of comparisons may vary from the examples in this book.

When using restrictive statements, you can employ a number of different operators. These operators allow you to perform numerous searches, such as comparisons between values, ranges, approximate searches, and others.

Using Comparison Operators   Table 2.2 lists the valid comparison operators.

TABLE 2.2	Operator	Meaning
The Valid Comparison Operators	=	Equal to
	>	Greater than
	>=	Greater than or equal to
	<	Less than
	<=	Less than or equal to
	<>	Not equal to

These comparison operators can be used to restrict both string and numeric data. However, be sure to use a single quote to identify all string information.

Using Ranges   Ranges can be handled in two different ways, using either multiple comparison operators or the BETWEEN operator. For example, the following two statements would execute identically.

```
SELECT *
FROM sales
```

```
WHERE qty >= 10
AND qty <= 50

SELECT *
FROM sales
WHERE qty BETWEEN 10 AND 50
```

As you can see from the previous example, the BETWEEN operator assumes that the values used in the BETWEEN clause are included in the result set.

Using Lists   Sometimes you may want to select from a table based on possible matches from a list of items. For these cases, you again have two choices. You can either use a series of OR operators, or you can precede the list with the IN operator. For example, the following two statements would execute identically.

```
SELECT *
FROM authors
WHERE au_lname = 'Smith'
     OR au_lname = 'Jones'

SELECT *
FROM authors
WHERE au_lname IN ('Smith', 'Jones')
```

Although the two approaches give you the same result, using the IN operator creates a query that is much easier to read and maintain later. The IN operator also provides a much easier way of managing nested SELECT statements, also known as subqueries. A subquery can be used anywhere that an expression is expected, but it can also present a list of values to be evaluated by the IN operator. The example below illustrates the use of a subquery. This query returns a set of records that list all of the authors that have a mailing address in the same city as one of the stores in the pubs database.

```
SELECT *
FROM authors
WHERE city IN (SELECT city FROM stores)
```

The inner query (the one inside the parentheses) returns a list of cities, which is then used to restrict the list of authors that is returned by the outer query.

Approximate Searches   Sometimes you may not have complete information when doing a search, or perhaps you wish to select broader ranges of information by providing approximate search criteria. For these cases, SQL provides a set of wildcards and a special operator called LIKE. Table 2.3 lists the SQL wildcard characters and their uses.

T A B L E 2.3 Transact SQL Wild- card Characters	**Character**	**Use**
	%	Replaces any string of zero or more characters
	_ (underscore)	Replaces any single character
	[]	Defines a group of characters, any one of which replaces a single character in that position
	[^]	Defines a group of characters, all of which are excluded from representing a single character in that position

For example, if you were searching the authors table for a last name that began with the letter S, you might write a query like the following.

```
SELECT *
FROM authors
WHERE au_lname LIKE 'S%'
```

However, if you were looking for a three-letter name that had the letter A as the middle character, the query would be written very differently.

```
SELECT *
FROM authors
WHERE au_lname LIKE '_a_'
```

You could also use the wildcards to exclude specific characters. Assume that you wanted to find all the authors whose last names began with the letter M, but did not have the letter C as the second character. The query would look like this.

```
SELECT *
FROM authors
WHERE au_lname LIKE 'M[^c]%'
```

As you experiment with the wildcards, you will find that they are flexible enough to satisfy any data search need.

Searching Using Nulls   The value of null is something very difficult to pin down. Then again, that is the very idea! Null does not mean zero or empty; it simply means that it is unknown or undefined.

As an example, I was at the grocery store with my family recently. We were standing at the checkout counter and, as the clerk passed each item over the scanner, the cost of each item appeared on a display for us to see. A minute or so into this routine, a product was waved over the scanner that resulted in a rather nasty beeping. The clerk tried again and again but was informed by the computer that there was no price for that product in the database.

"I suppose that means that it's free," I joked. As a database developer, I should have known better. After all, it was a perfect opportunity to give everyone in the checkout line a lesson on the meaning of the concept of null. Just because there was no price for the item in the database didn't mean that the store management was going to let me waltz out of the store without paying for the item. Sure enough, before long, the price was determined and the money to pay for it was extracted from my pocket.

Sometimes in database development, the absence of meaningful data can be as useful as the actual data itself. Suppose that you are working with a company database that tracks order dates and ship dates in an orders table. If you query the table and extract the rows where the ship date is null, you have learned something very important about those orders: They are the orders that have not shipped yet. When they do ship, the data will be entered into the database and the ship date will no longer be null. The following example shows the proper use of null in a SQL query.

```
SELECT *
FROM titleauthor
WHERE royaltyper IS NULL
```

Although many data engines will allow it, you should never use the equal comparison operator when testing for null. In some data engines it may fail; however, at the very least, it violates the entire concept of null, since nothing can equal an undefined value.

As in Exercise 2.4, try using the SQL 7 Query Analyzer to enter some of the queries used in this section. Experiment and try your own queries, executing them and evaluating the results.

Sorting and Grouping Output

Information is often most helpful when it is arranged and consolidated in prescribed ways. SQL provides mechanisms for sorting and grouping data in the SELECT statement to make the information as useful as possible.

Sorting Data   Once you have built a result set, you may wish to arrange the output in a specified manner. SQL does this with an ORDER BY clause in the SELECT statement. Any column found in the underlying data could be used to order data. For example, to select authors that live in California and sort the results of the authors query by last name, you might enter the following query.

```
SELECT *
FROM authors
WHERE state = 'CA'
ORDER BY au_lname
```

Data can also be sorted on more than one sort key. When using multiple keys, you will select one as the primary sort key. The secondary sort key will act as the "tie-breaker" for all like data sorted together under the primary sort key. If you have more than two sort keys in the SELECT statement, the next key in the list will be selected and the data will be sorted on that key. This process will continue until all sort keys have been used. To use the last name as the primary sort key and the first name as the secondary sort key, the query would look like the following.

```
SELECT *
FROM authors
WHERE state = 'CA'
ORDER BY au_lname, au_fname
```

Using Aggregate Functions   One way that we can group like data together is through the use of aggregate functions. Aggregates allow you to perform summary functions on your data such as summation or counting. Table 2.4 lists aggregate functions and their uses.

T A B L E 2.4 Transact SQL Aggregate Functions	**Aggregate**	**Description**
	SUM(expression)	Adds all non-null values in an expression
	AVG(expression)	Averages all non-null values in an expression
	COUNT(expression)	Counts all non-null values in an expression
	MIN(expression)	Returns the lowest value from an expression
	MAX(expression)	Returns the highest value from an expression

As an example, to count the publishers that have a state location listed in the database, you might use the first query below. To count all of the publishers, regardless of whether they have a state listed, you could use the second query below. Remember, aggregate functions skip nulls.

```
SELECT COUNT(state)
FROM publishers

SELECT COUNT(*)
FROM publishers
```

Grouping Data   Armed with the aggregate function, you can now group and subtotal data. For example, suppose that you wanted a list of all of the books in your database along with how many copies of each book has been sold. SQL provides the GROUP BY clause for this purpose.

When using GROUP BY, you will create a select list that has both aggregate and nonaggregate information. The nonaggregate data in the select list becomes the grouping criteria and is included in the GROUP BY clause. The query below is an example.

```
SELECT title_id, SUM(qty)
FROM sales
GROUP BY title_id
```

This creates a list of books organized by *title_id* along with the total number of copies of each book that has been sold. Additional aggregates and groups can be included if desired.

Any time that both aggregated data and nonaggregated data are included in the same select list, the query must have a GROUP BY clause that contains all nonaggregated data. ANSI SQL does not allow you to place expressions in the GROUP BY clause, only columns.

Another SQL query clause that is closely related to the GROUP BY clause is the HAVING clause. The HAVING clause behaves very much like the WHERE clause, except while the WHERE clause prevents individual rows from appearing in the result set based on the value of certain columns, the HAVING clause prevents groups from appearing in the result set based on the values of the aggregated data associated with the group.

As an example, suppose that in the previous query you only wanted to return those groups that have aggregate quantities greater than or equal to 40. The following query would give you the desired result.

```
SELECT title_id, SUM(qty)
FROM sales
GROUP BY title_id
HAVING SUM(qty)>=40
```

Modifying Data with SQL

In the previous section, you learned how to use the SQL language to retrieve data from a table. We can also use SQL to modify data in an existing table. There are three data modification statements in SQL, INSERT, UPDATE, and DELETE. They are quite easy to implement, and they are extremely powerful because they provide the flexibility needed to support even the most sophisticated database. In this section, we will look at each of these statements and their uses in a database application.

Inserting Data

SQL provides the INSERT statement to enter new data into a database. Although there are a few variations on the INSERT statement, the basic syntax appears as follows.

```
INSERT table_name
VALUES (value_list)
```

In the syntax listed above, the *value_list* must be provided in exactly the same order as the columns in the destination table. For example, if you wanted to enter a new record in the stored table using an INSERT statement, it would appear like the following query.

```
INSERT stores
VALUES ('2076','My Book Store', '32 East Way', 'Raytown',
  'UT', '84502')
```

You can also create a new row in the table without entering a value for every column. As long as the columns allow nulls or have default values associated with them enforced by the underlying data engine, you can provide a partial column list as follows.

```
INSERT stores (stor_id, stor_name)
VALUES ('2078','Your Book Store')
```

Updating Data

The UPDATE statement is used to make modifications to existing data. Its syntax differs somewhat from the INSERT statement because inserts take place one row at a time, while updates can occur column by column. This means that the syntax can be more verbose, but it is not inherently difficult to use. Following is the syntax of the UPDATE statement.

```
UPDATE table_name
SET column_name = expression
[WHERE condition]
```

The UPDATE statement can either change data in a table in total or based on specific conditions using the WHERE clause. For example, if you wanted to change every author's last name in the database to Smith, you might write a query like the following.

```
UPDATE authors
SET au_lname = 'Smith'
```

While this query would be quite effective, its results are not likely to be useful, and you will probably need to make changes to data on a much more selective basis. In our example, suppose that the author Albert Ringer has expressed an interest in having his name in the database changed so that Al is stored as his first name. The query to perform this action would look like this.

```
UPDATE authors
SET au_fname = 'Al'
WHERE au_lname = 'Ringer'
AND au_fname 'Albert'
```

In this query, it is important that the second statement in the WHERE clause checking the first name also be included. If this portion of the query is omitted, Anne Ringer would be terribly confused as to why everyone at the publishing house is calling her Al!

Remember that any number of values can be set in a single UPDATE statement as long as all of the changes correctly fall under the criteria provided by the WHERE clause. This eliminates the need to issue multiple UPDATE statements where one would suffice, thereby substantially increasing the performance of the overall operation.

Deleting Data

Like the UPDATE statement, the DELETE statement can selectively affect data based on criteria in a WHERE clause. This allows the deletion of any data in the table ranging from a single record to the entire table contents. The syntax of the DELETE statement looks like this.

```
DELETE table_name
[WHERE condition]
```

Using this syntax as the formula, the commands may look a little different from those that you might expect. For example, while it may logically appear that the following command would delete the entire authors table from the database, in reality the table remains and only the data is removed from the table.

```
DELETE authors
```

To drop a table from the database, the proper statement would be the DML command DROP TABLE.

Suppose that you only wanted to remove the authors from the database that have the last name of Ringer. In this case, the command would require a WHERE clause as in the following example.

```
DELETE authors
WHERE au_lname = 'Ringer'
```

Correlating Data with Join Statements

Microsoft Exam Objective

Write SQL statements that use joins to combine data from multiple tables.

In all of the previous examples, the SELECT or data modification statements affected only one table. The whole purpose for organizing data in a relational format is to remove redundancy by providing relationships *between* tables. For example, it is very likely that if you execute a query that requests sales information from the sales table, you will also want to extract information about the store that made the sale. While the sales table does include the *stor_id* column, this is probably not enough information.

A query of this nature is best satisfied with a JOIN statement. Joins define relationships between columns in different tables. Putting JOIN statements in queries allows you to select data in multiple tables at the same time.

Before we can look at the syntax and structure of the join, we must define some of the terms that we will use to describe standard join types. We will then apply this information to our queries.

Defining Join Types

Most database management systems require you to build your relationships as you request or query the data. This is usually done through a SQL statement. For example, if you are using Microsoft SQL Server and you want to find all book sales including the author ID, the query might look like the following. (Remember that the sales table does not include the *au_id* column.)

```
SELECT sales.*, titleauthor.au_id
FROM sales
INNER JOIN titleauthor
ON sales.title_id = titleauthor.title_id
```

In this example, the query extracts the *au_id* column from the titleauthor table and all of the information from the sales table. This type of join is called an *inner join*. You can create numerous types of joins as you build relationships into your databases. Some of these join types include:

- Inner join

- Left outer join

- Right outer join

- Full outer join

- Cross join

The type of JOIN statement you use when you relate two tables together can dramatically change the output of your query. Although the different join types may be confusing at first, they can often be the most elegant solutions to some fairly complex problems.

Inner Join An *inner join* relates two tables together and returns all records from each table that have a matching record in the other table. Figure 2.10 shows this in more detail. The two tables are being related in this example; however, the crossed-out records are not be returned because there is no matching record on the other side of the relationship.

F I G U R E 2.10

Inner join

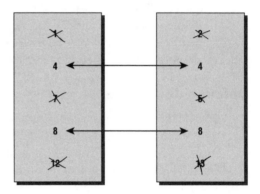

Left Outer Join In a *left outer join*, all of the records in the left table (the left table is listed first in the query) are returned as a result of the query, but only matching records are returned from the right table. Any records retrieved on the left side without matching records on the right simply place null values in the result set for that data which comes from the right table. Figure 2.11 illustrates a left outer join.

F I G U R E 2.11

Left outer join

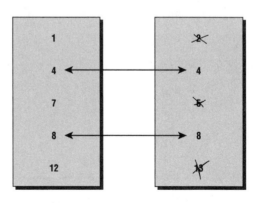

Right Outer Join   The *right outer join* is identical to the left outer join, only in reverse. Instead of retrieving all records from the left table, all records from the right table are retrieved, and only matching records are retrieved from the left table. Figure 2.12 illustrates a right outer join.

FIGURE 2.12

Right outer join

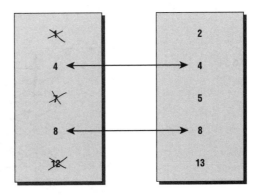

The only difference between a right and left outer join is how the query is written. For example, customer LEFT OUTER JOIN order is identical to order RIGHT OUTER JOIN customer.

Full Outer Join   A *full outer join* retrieves all records from both sides of the relationship, but for any record on either side that has no matching record, nulls are placed where the data from the other side would be entered. Figure 2.13 illustrates a full outer join.

FIGURE 2.13

Full outer join

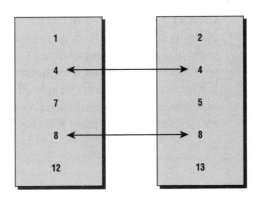

Cross Join A *cross join* is executed whenever two tables are related without providing a set of fields on which to relate. When this occurs, every possible relationship between the two tables is executed. This results in a Cartesian product, all possible combinations of all rows in the two tables. Note that this is different from a full outer join where a specific join field is provided. Figure 2.14 illustrates a cross join.

FIGURE 2.14

Cross join

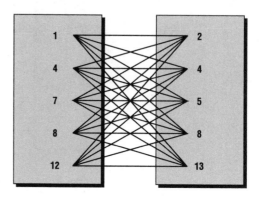

Cross joins are seldom useful in actual practice since they return all possible combinations of data and present no formal correlation of data; they are included here simply to complete the discussion. However, cross joins can be successfully used for generating large amounts of sample data for testing database performance.

Implementing Joins

Creating a query that uses a join statement is more an exercise in effective planning than programming. The database must be well normalized and planned, or the columns needed to make the joins may not exist. You must also decide exactly what information you are looking for and how to get it. If your data requirements include all the columns from one table, regardless of whether there is correlated data on the other side of the relationship, it is an indication that an outer join may be required.

When implementing joins, all of the join logic is placed in the FROM clause. This differs a little from the way that joins were handled in earlier versions of Microsoft SQL Server. Let's look again at the query that introduced this section.

```
SELECT sales.*, titleauthor.au_id
FROM sales
INNER JOIN titleauthor
ON sales.title_id = titleauthor.title_id
```

In this query, you will notice that the FROM clause introduces the first table in the join followed by the appropriate join operator. The list of valid operators is identical to the list of join types previously discussed. The following is a list of valid JOIN operators.

- INNER JOIN

- LEFT OUTER JOIN

- RIGHT OUTER JOIN

- FULL OUTER JOIN

- CROSS JOIN

The default JOIN operator is the INNER JOIN. If you simply use the word JOIN in your query without specifying the type of join desired, INNER JOIN will be used.

Joining Three or More Tables   To join more than two tables together, place another JOIN operator immediately following the link of the previous join. For example, suppose that you wanted to extract a list of authors with the last name of Ringer and the titles that they had written. This query requires a join between three tables, the authors, titles, and titleauthor tables. The query might look like the following.

```
SELECT *
FROM authors INNER JOIN titleauthor
   ON authors.au_id = titleauthor.au_id
INNER JOIN titles
   ON titles.title_id = titleauthor.title_id
WHERE authors.au_lname = 'Ringer'
```

Using Transactions

Microsoft ✓ *Exam* *Objective*   **Manage database transactions to ensure data consistency and recoverability.**

A transaction is a set of individual SQL statements that must execute as a single unit of work. In other words, a transaction defines a set of data modifications that must complete as a group. If an element of the group fails, the transaction must be rolled back. In today's client/server development environment, there are three different methods of implementing transactional behavior as a database.

- You can use the transaction features of the data engine (such as SQL Server) and write the transactional behavior in your stored procedures.

- You can use the transactional features of your client data access model. All data access models such as DAO, RDO, and ADO, as well as the ODBC API, provide support for transactional behavior.

- You can implement your data access logic in COM components and manage them through Microsoft Transaction Server. MTS supports transactions across components, making its transaction support very flexible.

We will address each of these approaches to transaction support when discussing its accompanying technology. In this section, we will focus on implementing transactions at the data engine level.

Implementing Transactions in SQL Server 7

Transaction support in SQL Server is provided through the use of three statements:

- BEGIN TRANSACTION

- COMMIT TRANSACTION

- ROLLBACK TRANSACTION

The BEGIN TRANSACTION statement starts the transaction. All of the statements following it are considered to be part of the same transaction. After opening a transaction, there are two ways to close it, commit or rollback. To commit a transaction means to save all of the changes permanently to the database. To rollback a transaction means to cancel all modifications and return the database to its original state.

Usually, transactions are allowed to commit as long as there is no error reported by the engine; however, if an error is reported, you can write your code to force a transaction to rollback. The code below illustrates a typical SQL Server transaction that supports both commit and rollback behaviors.

```
1  BEGIN TRANSACTION
2  DECLARE @ERR1 int
3  DECLARE @ERR2 int
4
5  DELETE newtable
6  SELECT @ERR1=@@Error
7  DELETE authors
8  SELECT @ERR2=@@ERROR
9
10 IF (@ERR1 <> 0)
11   ROLLBACK TRANSACTION
12 ELSE IF (@ERR2 <> 0)
13   ROLLBACK TRANSACTION
14 ELSE
15   COMMIT TRANSACTION
16
17 SELECT *
18 FROM newtable
```

The line numbers in the above example have been added for reference only. Do *not* put these line numbers in your SQL code.

Let's evaluate this code. Line 1 begins the transaction, followed by the declaration of two integer variables in lines 2 and 3. Line 5 deletes all of the rows from NewTable, the table that we created in Exercise 2.3. Following the deletion, the error status is saved into the first integer variable. This will be tested later; however, this statement should complete without error. Lines 7 and 8 repeat the process for the authors table, but this deletion should fail due to referential integrity violations. The error status is saved in the variable.

Line 10 tests the status of the first variable. If its value is anything other than 0, the transaction will rollback and continue to line 17. In this case, the value of the variable should be 0; this moves us to line 12 where the second variable is tested. In this case, the variable will contain the error code 547, a referential integrity error, thus forcing the transaction to rollback. If by chance both statements were able to complete without error, lines 14 and 15 would commit the transaction and save the changes in the database.

Lines 17 and 18 verify that the transaction did rollback. If you entered a couple of rows in NewTable in Exercise 2.3 as instructed, these rows should still be present in the table. Exercise 2.5 takes you through the process of creating and executing this transaction code in Microsoft SQL Server.

EXERCISE 2.5

Creating Transactions with Microsoft SQL Server 7

1. From the Windows Start menu, select Start ➣ Programs ➣ Microsoft SQL Server 7.0 ➣ Query Analyzer. In the SQL Server combo box, enter the name of your SQL Server. My example shows a server name of Server1. Use SQL Server authentication and enter a Login Name of **sa**. Leave the password blank. Click OK.

2. Open the Database list box at the top of the Query Analyzer window. Select pubs from the list. In the blank window, type the code from the preceding text (without the line numbers).

3. To execute the query, select Query ➤ Execute Query from the Query Analyzer menu. Evaluate the results. The following graphic shows the results of the query.

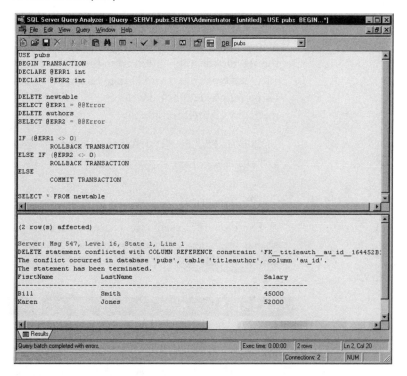

```
USE pubs
BEGIN TRANSACTION
DECLARE @ERR1 int
DECLARE @ERR2 int

DELETE newtable
SELECT @ERR1 = @@Error
DELETE authors
SELECT @ERR2 = @@Error

IF (@ERR1 <> 0)
        ROLLBACK TRANSACTION
ELSE IF (@ERR2 <> 0)
        ROLLBACK TRANSACTION
ELSE
        COMMIT TRANSACTION

SELECT * FROM newtable
```

```
(2 row(s) affected)

Server: Msg 547, Level 16, State 1, Line 1
DELETE statement conflicted with COLUMN REFERENCE constraint 'FK__titleauth__au_id__164452B
The conflict occurred in database 'pubs', table 'titleauthor', column 'au_id'.
The statement has been terminated.
FisrtName            LastName                              Salary
-------------------- ------------------------------------- ----------
Bill                 Smith                                 45000
Karen                Jones                                 52000
```

4. Note in the query results that the first delete completes without error, as shown by the statement that two rows are affected by the first query. However, because the second delete fails, the entire transaction is forced to rollback.

5. Close the Query Analyzer.

Creating Stored Procedures

Now that we have laid the foundation, we can look at the process of creating stored procedures in SQL Server. Like tables, stored procedures can be created from within the Visual Basic development environment.

Stored procedures give the database developer the ability to isolate data manipulation logic on the server. This abstracts the actual implementation of the server-side application from the client and business tier developers.

When creating a stored procedure in SQL Server, the syntax is as follows. Using the Visual Basic development environment, the basic structure is automatically created for you.

```
CREATE PROCEDURE procedure_name
Parameter_list
AS
SQL_statements
```

Exercise 2.6 presents the process of creating stored procedures from the Visual Basic development environment. In this exercise, we will create a simple stored procedure that returns a grouped list with aggregate values.

EXERCISE 2.6

Creating Stored Procedures

1. Open the datatier project, if necessary. Activate the Data View window by selecting View ➤ Data View window from the menu. Drill down into the pubs data connection so that the underlying folders are visible.

2. Drill down into the Stored Procedures folder and look at the list of stored procedures currently found inside the pubs database. Point to the Stored Procedures folder and click the right mouse button. Select New Stored Procedure from the pop-up menu.

3. Add stored procedure code in the window so that it looks like the following graphic.

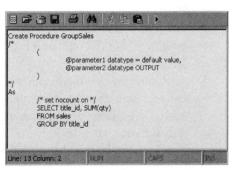

```
Create Procedure GroupSales
/*
        (
                @parameter1 datatype = default value,
                @parameter2 datatype OUTPUT
        )
*/
As

        /* set nocount on */
        SELECT title_id, SUM(qty)
        FROM sales
        GROUP BY title_id
```

Line: 13 Column: 2   NUM   CAPS   INS

4. On the New Stored Procedure toolbar, click the third button from the left (the blue cylinder icon). This will save the stored procedure to the pubs database. Close the New Stored Procedure window. You should now see the *GroupSales* stored procedure in the Data View window. Close the Data View window.

5. To test the stored procedure, open the SQL Server Query Analyzer. From the Windows Start menu, select Start ➤ Programs ➤ Microsoft SQL Server 7.0 ➤ Query Analyzer. In the SQL Server combo box, enter the name of your SQL Server. My example shows a server name of Server1. Use SQL Server authentication and enter a Login Name of **sa**. Leave the password blank. Click OK.

6. Open the Database list box at the top of the Query Analyzer window. Select pubs from the list. In the blank window, type the following code.

        EXEC GroupSales

7. To execute the query, select Query ➤ Execute Query from the Query Analyzer menu. Evaluate the results. Close the Query Analyzer.

Summary

In this chapter, we have investigated the factors involved in constructing the data tier of a multitier client/server application. It is impossible to over-emphasize the importance of the planning phase of this process, and significant attention has been paid in this chapter to normalization strategies and data structure.

Remember that the data tier serves as the foundation for your entire application, and it must be stable and efficient. Before Visual Basic 6, the data tier had to be implemented in other environments. As we have seen in this chapter, Visual Basic 6 provides numerous database features that simplify all aspects of database application development and make it easier than ever before.

Review Questions

1. If Table A, containing 25 records, and Table B, containing 50 records, are joined together with a cross join, how many records will be in the result set?

   A. 25

   B. 50

   C. 75

   D. 1250

2. If Table A, containing 25 records, and Table B, containing 50 records, are joined together with a right outer join, how many records will be in the result set? (Assume a one-to-one relationship exists.)

   A. 25

   B. 50

   C. 75

   D. 1250

3. If Table A, containing 25 records, and Table B, containing 50 records, are joined together with a left outer join, how many records will be in the result set? (Assume a one-to-one relationship exists.)

    A. 25

    B. 50

    C. 75

    D. 1250

4. A customer table contains a field identifying the employee number of an employee that is dedicated exclusively to servicing that customer's account. Which of the following statements is true concerning this scenario?

    A. Violation of first normal form

    B. Violation of second normal form

    C. Violation of third normal form

    D. No violation exists

5. In the same table as discussed in question 4, assume that a field has been added to the customer table that specifies the grade of the employee assigned to that customer. Which of the following statements is true concerning this scenario?

    A. Violation of first normal form

    B. Violation of second normal form

    C. Violation of third normal form

    D. No violation exists

6. A customer table has a field called *contact name* where the full name of the contact individual for that company is placed. Which of the following statements is true concerning this scenario?

    A. Violation of first normal form

    B. Violation of second normal form

    C. Violation of third normal form

    D. No violation exists

7. An order details table has a composite key of order number and product number. This table also contains a field that holds the customer number. Which of the following statements is true concerning this scenario?

    A. Violation of first normal form

    B. Violation of second normal form

    C. Violation of third normal form

    D. No violation exists

8. The field that identifies every record in the table as unique is called the

    A. Common Key

    B. Foreign Key

    C. Unique Key

    D. Primary Key

9. Which of the following is NOT a requirement of the Primary Key?

    A. It must be numeric.

    B. It must not allow nulls.

    C. It must be unique.

    D. It must be indexed.

10. Attributes of an entity are implemented as the:

    A. Rows of a table

    B. Tables of a database

    C. Columns of a table

    D. Key values in a table

11. Which of the following are advantages of using stored procedures in a database application? (Choose all that apply.)

   A. Abstraction of data access logic from the client and business tiers

   B. Interoperability among all popular relational database management systems

   C. Increased performance over submitting ad hoc queries to a database server

   D. Full support for advanced programming logic

12. Which of the following SQL WHERE clauses extracts rows from a table where the *lastname* column can be any number of characters but starts with the letter B?

   A. `WHERE lastname = 'B*'`

   B. `WHERE lastname = 'B_'`

   C. `WHERE lastname = 'B%'`

   D. `WHERE lastname = 'B?'`

13. Which of the following statements will drop the authors table entirely from the database?

   A. `TRUNCATE TABLE authors`

   B. `DROP TABLE authors`

   C. `DELETE authors`

   D. `DELETE TABLE authors`

14. The meaning of null is:

   A. Nothing

   B. Undefined

   C. Zero

   D. Empty

15. Which of the following is not a valid approach to enforcing database transactions?

A. Creating transactions at the data tier

B. Using Microsoft Transaction Server

C. Using the transaction support of a data access model

D. Storing data using a transacted file system

CHAPTER

3

Accessing Databases with the ActiveX Data Objects

With the rising popularity of distributed applications and the wide variety of data storage formats, a mechanism was needed to support, without bias, the plethora of data storage formats that have become so commonplace in the industry. As was noted in Chapter 1, the solution to this dilemma, OLE DB, brought a new approach to data access through COM interfaces.

Although OLE DB solved many of the common problems of data access, it also caused a problem of its own. OLE DB defines a set of low-level COM interfaces, so low-level, in fact, that they aren't even accessible from higher-level programming systems such as Visual Basic, VBA, and VBScript. The ActiveX Data Objects (ADO) solve this problem.

The purpose of ADO is to provide an accessible and intuitive interface for accessing data through OLE DB. In this chapter, you will:

- Explore the ADO model

- Implement the ADO Data Control

- Use SQL code with ADO in a Visual Basic application

- Call stored procedures with ADO

- Implement and manage cursors

- Manage data locking

No data tier is complete without a mechanism for accessing the data that is stored in the database. ADO allows the developer to implement SQL code either in the database as stored procedures or in the ADO code as a directly executed statement or a prepared statement. This chapter discusses both approaches.

ADO Basics

Like any other object model, your ability to successfully implement ADO in a distributed application is dependent on your knowledge of the object model and its associated properties and methods. In this section, you will explore the ADO model and learn how to navigate it. You will also implement the ADO Data Control, an ActiveX control that allows you to connect to a database from a Visual Basic form with little, if any, code.

After this discussion of ADO basics, you will be ready to move on to the more advanced sections of this chapter, including accessing and manipulating data with ADO and using stored procedures. Knowing how to use these techniques is critical when creating distributed applications; they make up a significant portion of the certification exams.

Getting Comfortable with the ADO Object Model

The Active Data Objects are arranged in a relational model, just like any other set of programmable objects. Upon first glance, however, you will notice something very different about the ADO model. Unlike other programmable object models, which rely very heavily on a hierarchy to provide order and structure, the ADO model is unusually flat and small, as illustrated in Figure 3.1. Note that unlike most other object models, there is more than one point of entry into the hierarchy, and that these entry points are essentially at peer with the other entry points in the hierarchy.

FIGURE 3.1

The ADO Model

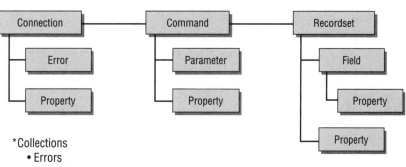

*Collections
- Errors
- Parameters
- Fields
- Properties

The reason that the ADO model is constructed so curiously has its roots in the technology that the model is designed to abstract. Remember that one of the hallmarks of OLE DB is its ability to access data in a variety of formats without a performance bias to one format over another. This means that access to a SQL-based database should be as efficient as access to a file-based database with the only difference being in the underlying data engine. If the ADO model is to provide an effective abstraction for OLE DB database access, it must be unbiased to data format, too.

Assume, for example, that the ADO model was constructed such that the Connection object was parent in the hierarchy to the Recordset object. This might be perfectly reasonable for a SQL-based database such as Microsoft SQL Server or Oracle, both of which require a connection to the server before a recordset can be generated. This, however, would show a bias against file-based data sources such as Microsoft Access or Microsoft FoxPro, neither of which require or even support a concept similar to the connection.

Under the ADO model, the Connection object plays a necessary role for SQL-based databases but is not required unless the underlying service provider requires the connection. If the OLE DB service provider does not require the connection, the developer can enter the model at the Recordset object without first instantiating a connection.

The ADO model consists of seven objects and four collections, each of which has very specific roles relating to the functionality of the service provider. Not every service provider will necessarily utilize every object in the model. The ADO objects are as follows.

Connection Creates and maintains a connection to a data source based on information that is proved when the connection is created. This information includes the connect string, username and password, cursor type and location, time-out values, etc.

Command Stores information about a SQL command or reference to a stored procedure. Command objects can be used to generate recordsets or to make data modifications. Although not required to issue a SQL statement to the database, the Command object can optimize this process, especially in cases where parameters or prepared statements are needed.

Recordset Holds all records returned from a database based on the results of a SQL call or a call to a stored procedure. The Recordset object is essentially a cursor to those records, providing the ability to scroll through the records as needed.

Error Contains information about a single data access error that has occurred when making a call to the database. The Error object contains all of the extended information about that error that is available from the OLE DB service provider.

Property Any characteristic of an ADO object used in program code. Properties fall into two categories: built-in and dynamic.

> **Built-in** Properties that are supported by ADO regardless of the service provider used to implement the object.

> **Dynamic** Properties that are implemented by the underlying service provider and that become accessible for any given object when using a specific service provider. Dynamic properties allow the ADO model to be extended by the service provider as needed to exploit the full functionality of the underlying database management system.

Parameter Stores all information relating to an individual parameter defined in a Command object. Most commonly used when implementing stored procedures in a data source using the Command object but can also be used when creating prepared statements in ADO.

Field Contains information relating to a single column of data in the current row of a recordset. The Field object not only contains the actual data for the field, but also all supporting information such as data type, size, and other properties explicitly defined by the service provider.

Some ADO documentation from Microsoft identifies the number of objects in the ADO model as eight rather than seven. The reason for this is that some of the documentation numbers the two different types of properties, built-in and dynamic, separately because of their unique implementations.

Along with the seven objects, the ADO model also contains four collections. A collection is a group of like objects that are related. For example, all of the controls on a Visual Basic form make up the Controls collection of the form. The collections supported by the ADO model are:

Errors Data access errors differ somewhat from other runtime errors in that data access errors can happen in groups. When a standard runtime error occurs, the application breaks on the first error that the application encounters. However, in a data access environment, it is often difficult to say exactly which error of many occurred first. For example, a single line of ADO code modifying a database can violate a number of rules or constraints all at the same time! If a single modification to a table violates both the uniqueness of a primary key and data referential integrity constraint, who is to say which error caused the system to break? For this reason, errors are aggregated into the Errors collection.

Fields   A single row in a recordset often contains multiple columns. All of the fields of a recordset are therefore aggregated into the Fields collection.

Parameters   It is very common for a single stored procedure or prepared statement to have multiple parameters that must be provided before the command can execute correctly. The Command object aggregates all of these into the Parameters collection, which, once loaded, will provide the information needed for the execution of the command.

Properties   Just like any other object, ADO objects have sets of properties. The Properties collection provides a method for enumerating a set of properties. Unlike the other collections, however, the Properties collections are available from a number of different contexts in the ADO model. Properties collections are provided for the Connection, Command, Recordset, and Field objects.

Implementing the ADO Data Control

Microsoft *Exam* *Objective*	**Access and manipulate a data source by using ADO and the ADO Data Control.**

The easiest way to implement the ActiveX Data Objects in your applications is through the ADO Data Control. This ActiveX control is a wrapper around ADO that makes it very easy to implement a simple data browser

and editor in your applications. Figure 3.2 shows a simple browser implemented with the ADO Data Control. The navigator buttons on the bottom
of the form represent the visual elements of the ADO Data Control.

F I G U R E   3.2

The ADO Data Control

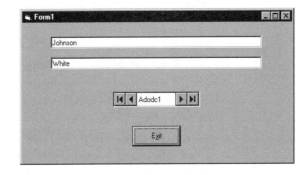

Although the ADO Data Control is extremely simple to implement, you
do give up some flexibility. Working with the ADO model through code
gives you much more control over your data. However, for prototyping and
simple interfaces, the ADO Data Control can provide a useful interface for
accomplishing the task quickly and easily.

Exercise 3.1 will walk you through the process of implementing the ADO
Data Control. If you have ever used the standard Microsoft Data Control or
the Remote Data Control, you will notice many similarities.

EXERCISE 3.1

Implementing the ADO Data Control

1. Start Visual Basic from the Start menu by selecting Start ➢ Programs ➢
   Microsoft Visual Studio 6.0 ➢ Microsoft Visual Basic 6.0. When prompted
   for a project template, click Standard EXE and click the Open button.

2. To add the Microsoft ADO Data Control to the toolbox, select Project ➢
   Components from the menu. In the alphabetical list of controls, locate
   Microsoft ADO Data Control 6.0 (OLE DB). Click the check box next to
   the reference to select it. Click the OK button.

3. In the toolbox, you should notice a new control in the lower-left corner. This is the ADO Data Control. The tooltip should read *adodc*. Place a data control in the form and two text boxes in the form. Use Figure 3.2 as an example.

4. Select the data control in the form. Press the F4 key to activate the Properties window. Set the CommandType to adCmdTable. Click the ConnectionString property. This should activate a builder button on the right side of the Properties window. Click the button to open a connection string builder.

5. Click the Use Connection String option button and click the Build button on the right side of the form. This will open the Data Link Properties window. From the list of service providers, Select Microsoft OLE DB provider for SQL Server. Click the Next button.

6. On the Connection tab, enter the name of your SQL Server in step 1. In step 2, click the option for Use a specific user name and password. Type **sa** for the username and leave the password blank. In step 3, select the pubs database from the drop-down list. Click the OK button.

7. Click the OK button in the Property Pages window to enter the new connection string in the Properties window. Scroll down the list of properties to locate the RecordSource property. Click the builder button.

8. In the Table or Stored Procedure list box, select the authors table. Click the OK button. You have now configured the ADO Data Control.

9. To bind the text boxes to the Data Control, click the first text box and set its DataSource property to adodc1. Set its DataField property to au_fname. Repeat for the second text box, selecting au_lname for the DataField.

10. Start the application by pressing the F8 key on your keyboard. Navigate through the recordset by clicking the navigation buttons on the ADO Data Control.

11. Exit the application by closing the form. Exit Visual Basic.

Implementing the ADO Model

Now that you are comfortable with the basic structure of the ADO model, let's implement the model by making some simple data access calls to our pubs database. This section will illustrate how we navigate the model to access data from a Visual Basic object or application.

As we discuss these techniques for accessing data with ADO, we will be using Visual Basic forms communicating with Microsoft SQL Server 7. Keep in mind, however, that this code will usually be placed in components rather than forms. Chapter 4 discusses this process in detail, but we must first be familiar with the structure of ADO code before we can place it effectively in the business tier.

Using the Connection Object

Before you can extract information from a SQL Server, you must first create a connection. All communication with the database goes through this connection. While it is possible in ADO to access a SQL Server without explicitly creating and using a Connection object, this does not mean that you are not using a connection. It simply means that you are not choosing to take advantage of the ability to control the connection through the ADO Connection object. Since connections are very resource-intensive on the server-side, the wise developer will always make the extra effort to control connection resources efficiently. This can provide a substantial boost to the performance of your application.

The Connection object supports many properties and methods, but the two most important methods are *Open* and *Close*. The Open method opens a connection between the data client and the OLE DB service provider, in this case SQL Server. This connection is created based on parameters that are provided in the Open statement such as a connection string, user ID, password, and other options. Many of these parameters, such as the connection string, can be established as properties before the connection is opened. The syntax of the Open method looks like this.

```
connection.Open [ConnectionString], [UserID], [Password],
[OpenOptions]
```

As you will notice, all of the parameters in the Open method are optional. The reason for this is that all of this information can be provided about the connection in different ways. For example, the connection string can be set using the ConnectionString property of the connection before calling the Open method. Likewise, the connection string provides support for the user ID and password as elements of the connection string. The OpenOptions parameter, which offers the developer support for more advanced features such as asynchronous connections, is always optional.

This means that there are many ways to open a connection. If your goal was to connect to a database called pubs on a SQL Server named Server1 using the login name of sa with a null password, the following code demonstrates different ways that this could be done.

```
' In General Declarations Section
Dim cn as ADODB.Connection

' In an Initialization event such as Form_Load
Set cn=New ADODB.Connection

' Creating the connection, method one
With cn
.ConnectionTimeout = 30
.CommandTimeOut = 30
.Provider = "sqloledb"
.ConnectionString = "server=server1;uid=sa;pwd="
.Open
.DefaultDatabase = "pubs"
End With

'Creating the connection, method two
With cn
.ConnectionTimeout = 30
.CommandTimeOut = 30
End With
Cn.Open "provider=sqloledb;server=server1;database=pubs",
"sa"
```

There is part of this connection string that could use some explanation, that is, the *provider*. The Provider parameter of the connection string indicates which OLE DB service provider the client will use to make contact with the database. Each service provider is identified by name, so all you have to do is to place the provider name in the appropriate parameter. The only difficult part is finding the name of the appropriate service provider. To make this task easier, Table 3.1 lists the service providers that Microsoft ships with Visual Studio 6 and their names as you will use them in your code.

T A B L E 3.1 OLE DB Service Provider Code Names	**Service Provider**	**Code Name**
	ODBC Databases	MSDASQL
	Microsoft Index Server	MSIDXS
	Microsoft Active Directory Service	ADSDSOObject
	Microsoft Jet Databases	Microsoft.Jet.OLEDB.3.51
	Microsoft SQL Server	SQLOLEDB
	Oracle Databases	MSDAORA

When you are finished with a connection, you should close it. This will prevent your application from being more resource intensive than necessary. This does not mean that you should close the connection after every request, however. Although connections are costly resources, it also takes a relatively long time to establish the connection. From a performance perspective, you should only close connections when the resource benefit of closing the connection outweighs the performance factor of re-opening the connection when necessary. To close a connection, use the Close method of the Connection object as in the following example. This assumes that *cn* is the name given to the object variable used to create the connection.

```
cn.Close
```

Although the Errors collection in ADO is associated with the Connection object, Chapter 12, *Error Handling in the Distributed Application*, discusses the implementation of this collection.

Armed with this information about the Connection object, you are now prepared to take a stab at it for yourself. Exercise 3.2 takes you through the process of establishing a connection using ADO. This exercise must be completed before moving on to other exercises in this chapter.

EXERCISE 3.2

Establishing a Connection Using ADO

1. Create a new folder on your hard drive to store the files that you will create for the project in this chapter. Call the folder **ADO**.

2. Start Visual Basic 6.0 and, when prompted for a New Project, select Standard EXE. Click the OK button to continue. The SQL Server must be running for this exercise. If it isn't running, the exercise will fail in step 7. In the Visual Basic Properties window, set the name property of Form1 to frmADO. Set the caption property to ADO Test Form. Add a label control to the form. Name the label lblMessage.

3. To make a reference to the ADO 2.0 type library in your application, click Project ➢ References from the Visual Basic menu. Scroll through the alphabetical list of type libraries until you find Microsoft ActiveX Data Objects 2.0 Library. Click the check box next to the library name and click OK.

4. Double-click the center of the form to expose the code module for the form. From the Object list box at the top-left side of the code window, select General. The Procedure list box in the upper right of the code window should now say Declarations. If this is not the case, select Declarations from the list. This point in the module is called the General Declarations section. In the future when you are asked to go to this point in the module, you will be instructed to navigate to the General Declarations section.

5. Type **Option Explicit** in the code window if it isn't already there. After the Option Explicit statement, declare a form-level called cn as an ADO connection by typing the following code.

```
Private cn As ADODB.Connection
```

6. From the Object list box, select Form. This should place you in the form load event. In this event, instantiate the Connection object by typing the following code. In place of *server1* in the ConnectionString property, enter the name of the SQL Server to which you are connecting.

```
Set cn = New ADODB.Connection
With cn
.ConnectionTimeout = 30
.CommandTimeOut = 30
.Provider = "sqloledb"
.ConnectionString = "server=server1;uid=sa;pwd="
.Open
.DefaultDatabase = "pubs"
End With
lblMessage.Caption = "Connection Established with " _
      + cn.DefaultDatabase
```

7. Select Unload from the procedure list box, navigating you to the Form_Unload event. To close the connection, put the following code in this event.

```
cn.Close
```

8. Test the application by hitting the F5 key on the keyboard to begin the application. The application should report no errors upon start-up and the form should look like the one pictured in the following graphic.

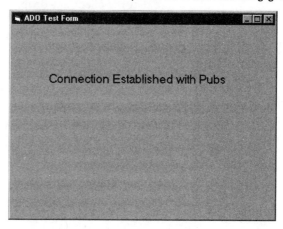

9. End the application by closing the form. Save the project in the ADO folder that you created in step 1. The filename for the form should be `frmADO.frm`, while the filename for the project should be `ADO.vbp`. Close Visual Basic after saving.

If you are running your SQL Server 7 on Windows NT 4, you can verify that the connection has been established with the server by following this procedure.

1. Open the Windows NT Performance Monitor by selecting Start ➢ Programs ➢ Administrative Tools ➢ Performance Monitor.

2. To add a SQL Server User Connections counter, click Edit ➢ Add to Chart from the menu. In the Object list box, select SQL Server: General Statistics. Select the User Connections counter and click the Add button in the upper-right corner of the dialog, then click the Done button. The line on the chart that you see informs you of the number of connections currently being made to the server. It is normal to see a couple of connections even when the server is not being accessed.

3. Open the ADO sample Visual Basic project that you just made and start the program running. This should make a connection to the database. Switch back to the performance monitor. The number of user connections should have increased by one.

4. Switch back to the Visual Basic application and stop it by closing the form. Exit Visual Basic. Switch back to the performance monitor and note that the client has dropped the connection.

Using the Recordset Object

Now that you are familiar with the process of creating connections, we are ready to move on to working with recordsets. This is, in many ways, the heart of what you will do with ADO. After all, what is the purpose of navigating a data access model if you never access data?

The Recordset object supports many properties and methods. Its list of properties and methods is very lengthy, primarily because the recordset level is where we do most of the work in a distributed application. Just like the Connection object, however, one of the most critical methods for the Recordset object is the Open method. The syntax of the Open method looks like this.

```
recordset.Open
[Source],[ActiveConnection],[CursorType],[LockType],[Options]
```

Source

The Source parameter indicates the SQL statement or other object that is the source of the recordset. Some of the possible values for this parameter include a SQL statement, the name of a table or stored procedure, or even the filename of a saved recordset. Some source types may or may not be supported, depending on the service provider.

In the previous chapter, we looked at the SELECT statement and learned many different ways that data could be retrieved and correlated with it. The source property of a recordset is one place that you can implement this code that you have learned.

ActiveConnection

If you have previously established a connection through the ADO Connection object, you can use the object variable that represents that connection in the ActiveConnection. The service provider will then use that connection for all communication with the server needed to create and maintain the recordset.

If a connection to the server has not been established, this parameter supports the use of a connection string that contains all of the information needed to connect to the server. The connection established using this approach is valid for the duration of the recordset only, and you cannot use it to open any other recordset or issue any other command.

Cursor Type

Microsoft ✓ Exam Objective

Retrieve and manipulate data by using different cursor types. Cursor types include forward-only, static, dynamic, and keyset.

This argument provides information to the service provider about which type of cursor the client application requests. There are four types of cursors that ADO supports; they differ primarily based on their concurrency with other recordsets open in the same database. Table 3.2 illustrates the different cursor types and the ADO constants used to request each cursor type.

T A B L E 3.2 Types of Cursors	**Cursor Type**	**ADO Constant**
	Forward-only	adOpenForwardOnly
	Static	adOpenKeyset
	Keyset	adOpenDynamic
	Dynamic	adOpenStatic

Forward-only cursors are limited in their ability to scroll through a recordset. In fact, this cursor type only allows the MoveNext recordset navigation method. This means that once you have scrolled past the record that you wish to view, you cannot go back to rebuilding the recordset. Another limitation of this recordset type is that it's read-only. If you wish to modify data, this is not the cursor type to choose.

With these restrictions, the forward-only cursor seems like it would never be the preferred cursor type. However, the forward-only cursor is extremely efficient. Since it never has to scroll backward, there is never any overhead to track where it has been, and since it is read-only, it doesn't have to maintain a dynamic link back to the data source. This is an excellent cursor to use for reporting and other types of one-way data-gathering activities. This cursor is the default in ADO.

The static cursor is also read-only, but it is fully scrollable, allowing the developer to go forward or backward through the data as needed. This cursor is also good for reporting, especially when the order of extracting the data is unknown until the time that the routine runs.

The keyset cursor is very popular for applications that require the ability to modify data and that don't need to be completely current with new data that is added to the database. The keyset cursor creates a set of keys upon creation of the cursor, one key per row in the underlying data source at the time the cursor is built. If, during the life of the cursor, any data changes within the keyset, the user of the cursor would see those changes. However, if any new data appears in the database after the cursor's creation, those rows would not appear in the recordset.

The dynamic cursor is fully concurrent, retrieving every record from the database whenever it receives the request. No keyset is built in advance. Any data in the database can be retrieved, no matter when it was added to the database.

Setting Cursor Location

Microsoft ✓ *Exam Objective* | **Retrieve and manipulate data by using different cursor locations. Cursor locations include client-side and server-side.**

Although there is no parameter in the Open statement to identify a cursor location, you can set this property in advance before issuing the Open method. This setting will specify where the cursor should be placed as the recordset opens. You can either set the cursor location to client-side or server-side. Each has its advantages and disadvantages.

A client-side cursor uses resources from the client workstation to maintain the cursor and the information that the cursor caches. Using client-side cursors can be very efficient in an environment where there are a large number of users, because every client is responsible for maintaining its own resources, thus eliminating the resource drain on the database server. The primary disadvantage to this cursor location is that client-side cursors can increase network traffic, since all of the communication between the database server and the cursor must go across the network. To request a client-side cursor, set the CursorLocation property to adUseClient before opening the recordset.

Server-side cursors use resources from the database server to manage cursors. In Microsoft SQL Server, server-side cursors are maintained in the tempdb database. If there are a large number of users, this type of cursor will adversely affect the performance of the rest of the database because of the additional demand placed on the I/O subsystem of the database server. The primary bottleneck on most database servers is I/O, so this can complicate the situation. However, server-side cursors are more responsive than client-side cursors. To request a server-side cursor, set the CursorLocation property to adUseServer before opening the recordset.

Other than the performance differences between them, there is virtually no difference in how you retrieve and manipulate data using client-side or server-side cursors. The ADO model abstracts these differences for you so that you can focus on the issue of interacting with your data without having to worry about implementation detail.

As you can see from this discussion, each of these cursor types has advantages and disadvantages, but the general tradeoff is one of concurrency versus overhead. The more concurrent a cursor is, the more resource intensive it is. For this reason, you should try to use the least concurrent cursor that you can without sacrificing the needs of your application.

Lock Type

Microsoft ✓ *Exam* *Objective*   **Use appropriate locking strategies to ensure data integrity. Locking strategies include read-only, pessimistic, optimistic, and batch optimistic.**

Through its service providers, ADO supports four different locking strategies. These strategies do not allow you to specify the granularity and type of lock; that task is the responsibility of the database management system. The ADO locking types allow you to specify the timing of the acquisition of these locks and how long they are held. Table 3.3 lists the four different locking approaches supported by ADO and the ADO constant that you will use in the Lock Type argument to request that type of lock.

T A B L E 3.3
ADO Lock Types

Lock Type	Constant
Read-only	adLockReadOnly
Pessimistic	adLockPessimistic
Optimistic	adLockOptimistic
Batch optimistic	adLockBatchOptimistic

If you do not set the Lock Type for the recordset, it will default to read-only. Read-only recordsets do not allow any data modifications to occur and are lower in resource consumption because no data modifications have to be tracked in the underlying record source.

All of the other lock types allow data modifications to take place. Pessimistic locking will lock the underlying rows in the record as soon as the client application modifies the recordset but before the application actually updates the record source. This prevents other users from attempting to modify the same rows while the first user is making their modifications.

The optimistic approach locks the underlying data when the client issues the Update method rather than upon data modification. This means that the database locks the rows for a shorter period, but it also means that some potential conflicts can arise since two users can attempt to modify the same rows at the same time. The update is granted to the user that issues the Update method first. The other user receives a runtime error.

The batch optimistic locking constant begins a special kind of update called a batch update. Using batch updates, the developer can write ADO code that issues changes to the database and even calls the Update method, but the results are not sent to the database server until the client calls the BatchUpdate method. Rows in the database are only locked during this BatchUpdate process.

Using the appropriate locking strategy is critical to the performance of any distributed application. While it is always beneficial to minimize the length of time that data locks, the resulting loss of performance due to contention may necessitate the use of a pessimistic locking structure.

Options

Also an Option argument, this parameter provides important information about the way that the rest of the open method executes. Table 3.4 lists some of the possible constants and their uses.

T A B L E 3.4 ADO Open Method Options	Constant	Use
	adCmdText	The argument in the Source parameter is text which should be interpreted as a command, i.e., SQL.
	adCmdTable	The argument in the Source parameter is a table.
	adCmdStoredProc	The argument in the Source parameter is a stored procedure.
	adExecuteAsync	The recordset will be built asynchronously.

Opening a Recordset

Using the Open method previously described, you can create a recordset for browsing or data modification. Assuming that you have an open connection represented by the object variable *cn*, you can open a recordset based on the authors table of the pubs database using the following statement. This statement assumes that you want to open a keyset cursor with a pessimistic lock type.

```
rs.Open "authors", cn, adOpenKeyset, adLockPessimistic,
adCmdTable
```

If you want to shorten the Open statement, you can also provide many of the parameters in advance in the same way that you did for the Connection object. The following code provides one possible example of this approach. This example also adds the CursorLocation property and sets this property to use server-side cursors.

```
With rs
.Source = "authors"
.ActiveConnection = cn
.CursorType = adOpenKeyset
.CursorLocation = adUseServer
.LockType = adLockPessimistic
.Open Options:=adCmdTable
End With
```

The example above uses a named argument with the Open method. Although the Options parameter is the last one in the parameters list, you can use it without providing any of the other parameters. The assignment operator for named arguments is a colon followed by an equal sign (=).

In addition to this approach, you can open a recordset using the Command object. This approach will be discussed in more detail later in this chapter.

Displaying Data in a Recordset

With the Recordset object, you can create a cursor that references rows in an underlying data source, but if you want to work with the data in the recordset, you must use the Field object. Fields in a recordset expose the data in the rows, including all of the special characteristics of each individual field.

Since there are usually many columns in a row, there is more than one field in the current record. These columns make up the Fields collection of the recordset. To retrieve data from a record, extract the member of the Fields collection that you wish to target by assigning its value to a variable or the appropriate display property of a control. The following code illustrates how the First Name and Last Name (stored in the fields *au_fname* and *au_lname* respectively) are extracted from the current row and placed into string variables.

```
Dim first as String
Dim last as String
first = rs.Fields("au_fname")
last = rs.Fields("au_lname")
```

You can also use a shorthand method of referencing elements of a collection by using an exclamation point (!) operator. This operator is called a *bang*. The purpose of the bang operator is to point directly to an element of a collection when the collection is understood. For example, the Recordset object contains two collections, the Properties collection and the Fields collection, but the default collection is Fields. This means that if you use the bang operator, ADO will assume that you wish to work with the Fields collection and allow you to reference the elements of this collection directly. The following example duplicates the functionality of the code above using the bang operator.

```
Dim first as String
Dim last as String
first = rs!au_fname
last = rs!au_lname
```

It's time to try your hand at creating recordsets. Exercise 3.3 adds to our previous application and creates a recordset based on data from the authors table. You will extract this data using a SQL statement.

EXERCISE 3.3

Creating a Recordset

1. Open the ADO project that you created in the previous exercise. Double-click the center of the form to open the code module for the form.

2. Navigate to the General Declarations section of the form. Under the statement that you used to declare the Connection object variable, declare an object variable for the Recordset object using the following code.

```
Dim rs as ADODB.Recordset
```

3. In the Object list box of the code window, select the form object. Make sure that the Procedure list box displays the Load event. Before the Set statement for the Connection object, declare a standard string variable called strSQL and assign a SQL statement to the string variable that will select the *au_fname* and *au_lname* columns from the authors table. You can accomplish this by typing the following code.

```
Dim strSQL as String
strSQL = "SELECT au_fname, au_lname FROM authors"
```

4. Underneath the Set statement for the Connection object, create a new Recordset object by using the following code.

```
Set rs = New ADODB.Recordset
```

5. Underneath the With block that you wrote to open the connection, create a With block that opens the recordset. Assume that you want a keyset cursor using pessimistic locking. Implement a server-side cursor. The completed block will look like the following example.

```
With rs
        .Source = strSQL
        .ActiveConnection = cn
        .CursorType = adOpenKeyset
        .CursorLocation = adUseServer
        .LockType = adLockPessimistic
        .Open Options:=adCmdText
End With
```

6. Change the caption of lblMessage to echo back to the user the first name of the first author in the database. Use the following code as an example.

```
lblMessage.Caption = "The author's name is " + rs!au_fname
```

7. For your reference, the entire Form_Load event should read as follows.

```
Dim strSQL As String
Set cn = New ADODB.Connection
Set rs = New ADODB.Recordset
strSQL = "SELECT au_fname, au_lname FROM authors"

With cn
    .ConnectionTimeout = 30
    .CommandTimeout = 30
    .Provider = "sqloledb"
    .ConnectionString = "server=server1;uid=sa;pwd="
    .Open
    .DefaultDatabase = "pubs"
End With
With rs
    .Source = strSQL
    .ActiveConnection = cn
    .CursorType = adOpenKeyset
    .CursorLocation = adUseServer
    .LockType = adLockPessimistic
    .Open Options:=adCmdText
End With
lblMessage.Caption = "The author's name is " + rs!au_fname
```

8. Navigate to the Form_Unload event. Above the code closing the connection, write a statement to close the recordset.

9. Hit the F5 key on your keyboard to start the application. The form should look like the graphic below.

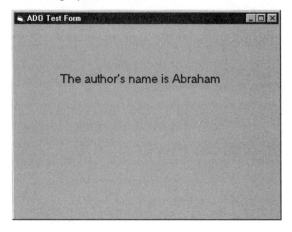

10. Close the form to end the application. Save the project and exit Visual Basic.

Now that you have created a recordset and can view the data in the current row, the next step is to navigate through the recordset. The ADO model provides four methods for the Recordset object to use in navigation, Move-First, MoveNext, MovePrevious, and MoveLast. These are the methods that you will use to scroll through a cursor.

WARNING

Each of the cursor types supports all of the navigation methods with the exception of the forward-only recordset, which only supports the MoveNext method.

You could navigate a recordset identified by the object variable *rs* by using the following code. The syntax is the same for the other move methods.

```
rs.MoveNext
```

Modifying Data through a Recordset

Just as with the SQL code discussed in the previous chapter, you can make three different modifications to databases, Insert, Update, and Delete. Each has a slightly different syntax, but they are somewhat similar to their corresponding SQL commands.

Updating Data

Updating data in an ADO recordset is just as simple as displaying data. The only difference is that instead of assigning the value of a field to a control or a variable, you will do it in reverse and assign the value of a control or variable to a field in a recordset. For example, look at the following code samples. The first example reads a field value into a variable, while the second example writes to the field.

```
' Read the value a field
first = rs!au_fname
' Write the value of a field
rs!au_lname = last
```

If you request a pessimistic lock when creating the recordset, the service provider locks the underlying rows in the data source at this point in the code.

Once modifications have been requested by assigning new values to the fields as in the example above, the service provider must update the data source before the changes are actually saved to the database. There are three ways to update a recordset.

1. Simply navigate to another record. The service provider calls an update as you leave the record.

2. Explicitly call the Update method of the recordset. This will update the records, but it will not change the current record.

3. Call an UpdateBatch method. This assumes that you created the recordset using a batch optimistic lock type. The batch optimistic lock allows you to make modifications on a number of rows without forcing you to write those changes to the recordset after every row. Simply issue an update or navigate as usual. When all of the modifications have completed, call the UpdateBatch method to write the entire batch to the recordset.

It is possible to cancel any data modification to the recordset that you have requested as long as you have not updated the recordset. Before the update, simply call the CancelUpdate method of the recordset. This cancels all data modifications on that record. If you are in batch update mode, you can cancel an entire batch by calling the CancelBatch method.

Inserting Data

The Recordset method used to insert a new record is AddNew. The AddNew method will add a new, empty record to the end of a recordset. Using the same approach as the Update method, you can then assign the value of a variable or control to the fields in the recordset that you wish to initialize. The insert is complete upon issuing the Update method or navigating to another record. The following example adds data into the *au_id*, *au_fname*, and *au_lname* fields in a new record in the authors table.

```
rs.Addnew
rs!au_id = '123-45-6789'
rs!au_fname = 'Joey'
rs!au_lname = 'Taylor'
rs.Update
```

Deleting Data

ADO supports the Delete method of a recordset to remove a row from the database. The syntax of this statement is as follows.

```
rs.Delete
```

Once a record has been deleted using the Delete method, that record is still the current record. You must navigate to another record before you attempt any other data extraction or modification. If you created the recordset using batch optimistic locking, the Delete method simply marks the record for deletion and does not actually delete the record until you call the Update-Batch method.

When making any data modifications, be sure to verify that the recordset can accept these changes or you will get an error. More than just making sure that you are using a keyset or dynamic cursor, you must also ensure that if you use a SQL statement to build the recordset, all of the necessary columns are included in the recordset and that the recordset does not represent a join between multiple tables. For example, if you build a recordset using only some of the columns from a table, you must include all of the required columns (those that do not accept nulls) in the recordset. Otherwise, you will not be able to use that recordset for inserts.

Exercise 3.4 walks you through the process of implementing data modifications through a recordset. You will change the *au_fname* field for the first record in the recordset.

EXERCISE 3.4

Modifying Data through a Recordset

1. Start Visual Basic and open the ADO project if necessary. Add a command button to the form. In the Properties window, set the Name property to **cmdUpdate**. Set the Caption property to **Update Name**.

2. Double-click the cmdUpdate button to open the code window for the form. You should be in the cmdUpdate_Click event. Add code to ask the user if they wish to continue with the update. If they answer yes, update the first record in the recordset to change the name Abraham to Abe. If the current name in the database is Abe then toggle the first name back to Abraham. Display the new record information in the Caption property of lblMessage. Use the following code as an example.

```
Dim intResponse As Integer
intResponse = MsgBox("Continue with the update?" _
    , vbQuestion + vbYesNo, "Warning")
If intResponse = vbNo Then Exit Sub
rs.MoveFirst
If rs!au_fname = "Abraham" Then
```

```
    rs!au_fname = "Abe"
ElseIf rs!au_fname = "Abe" Then
    rs!au_fname = "Abraham"
End If
rs.Update
lblMessage.Caption = "The author's name is " + rs!au_fname
```

3. Hit the F5 key on the keyboard to start the application. Click the command button and click the Yes button in the warning message to continue with the update. The name in the label should change. Click the command button again to repeat the test. This should change the name back.

4. Ensure that the first name of the author is left as Abraham. Close the form to exit the application. Save the project and exit Visual Basic.

Using the Command Object

Using the Recordset object, we executed a SQL command to send data back to the client application. While the Open method of the recordset gives you the ability to execute simple queries and stored procedures, it does have some limitations. If you want to use stored procedures or SQL commands that have parameters, you must use a Command object. In addition, if you wish to persist a SQL command by creating a prepared statement, you must use a Command object.

Table 3.5 lists the most common properties and methods associated with the Command object. Of these, the most critical is the Execute method, which executes the defined SQL statement or stored procedure through the service provider.

T A B L E 3.5 The ADO Command Object's Properties and Methods	Element	Type	Purpose
	ActiveConnection	Property	References a connection for command execution
	CommandText	Property	Sets the query or persisted database object that will be the source of the query

TABLE 3.5 *(cont.)*	Element	Type	Purpose
The ADO Command Object's Properties and Methods	CommandType	Property	Defines the type of object stated in the CommandText property. Identical to the Recordset property CommandType
	Prepared	Property	Indicates whether the command should be prepared and executed or executed directly
	CreateParameter	Method	Adds a parameter to the Parameters collection of the Command object
	Execute	Method	Executes the Command object

Although the syntax of the Execute method provides for Query parameters and an Options argument that allows you to set a command type, it is better if you provide these properties and parameters by setting the appropriate values before executing the command. The syntax is as follows.

```
command.Execute RecordsAffected, Parameters, Options
```

The RecordsAffected parameter is actually an Output parameter that supplies the number of recordsets that were affected by the execution of the command. To use this argument, simply provide an integer variable in the parameter location and read the value of this variable after the Command object executes. The sample code below illustrates one approach to executing a SQL command.

```
Dim cmd as ADODB.Command
Dim rs as ADODB.Recordset
Dim strSQL As String
Dim intRec As Integer
strSQL = "UPDATE authors SET au_lname = 'Jones' WHERE au_
lname = 'Ringer'"
With cmd
    .ActiveConnection = cn
    .CommandText = strSQL
    .CommandType = adCmdText
```

```
    .CommandTimeout = 30
    .Execute intRec
End With
MsgBox CStr(intRec) + " records were updated"
```

This example updates the authors table with a SQL UPDATE command. This task could have been completed using the recordset object, building a recordset with authors that have a last name of Ringer and resetting the last name to Jones on a record-by-record basis. The approach using the Command object is much more efficient, however. Instead of maintaining the additional overhead of a cursor, the SQL statement goes directly to the database and makes the required changes.

Using Parameters

To provide additional flexibility in implementation, commands often have parameters. These parameters allow the developer to capture input from the user about how the command will execute. For example, if you wanted to select author information from the pubs database but allow the user to select the last name of the desired author, you would have to create a separate query for each author and run the desired query as requested by the user. It is much easier to create a single query and provide a parameter for the *last name* field, which the user can provide when executing the query.

You provide parameters in a query by using the question mark (?) where variable information can be supplied. Any parameter supplied in this way becomes part of the Parameters collection of the Command object. By using this Parameters collection, you can load the parameters with values before the command is executed. The following example code demonstrates how you might do this.

```
Dim strSQL As String
strSQL = "SELECT * FROM authors WHERE au_lname = ?"
With cmd
    .ActiveConnection = cn
    .CommandText = strSQL
    .CommandType = adCmdText
End With

cmd.Parameters(0) = InputBox$("Enter Name to Find")
Set rs2 = cmd.Execute
```

```
Do Until rs2.EOF
    MsgBox rs2!au_fname + " " + rs2!au_lname
    rs2.MoveNext
Loop
MsgBox "End of List"
```

Direct Execution vs. Prepared Statements

Microsoft Exam Objective

Access and manipulate data by using the Execute Direct model.

WARNING   This exam objective is a bit misleading. ADO 2.0 does not support a method called Execute Direct. The intent of the objective is to ensure that you know how to do a direct execution against a database rather than a prepared statement. Direct execution is the default behavior.

The approach that we have used thus far to send SQL statements to the SQL Server has been a model called direct execution. This means that SQL Server simply accepts the query string from the client application and processes it directly with the assumption that the engine will only execute it once. SQL Server does not attempt to cache or otherwise preserve the statement for future use. As soon as it executes, the executable query is dropped and processing continues to the next statement.

This behavior is the default behavior in ADO, the assumption being that most SQL statements will be executed only once. Direct execution is more efficient when this assumption is correct because time is not wasted in processing and saving the query for future use.

Microsoft Exam Objective

Access and manipulate data by using the Prepare/Execute model.

There may be occasions when you will wish to repeat a statement many times. For example, perhaps you have a query that uses parameters, and you want the user to issue the statement to the database more than once. When this is the case, it may be more advantageous to cache or otherwise preserve the statement so that it can be reissued quickly and easily. A query that you cache in this way is called a prepared statement.

Prepared statements save a compiled copy of the statement on the database in temporary storage. This copy can then be used for every call. As soon as you destroy the object variable that references the prepared statement, the temporary object is dropped from the server.

You can create prepared statements in ADO by setting the prepared property of the Command object to true. This is the cue to the server to store a compiled temporary copy of the command for future use. While this process takes longer that simply executing a statement against the server directly, when repeated executions take place the extra time spent in preparation can be easily recovered with a few executions.

The following code example shows how you might implement a prepared statement. In this example, since we don't know the total number of iterations that the statement will repeat, we prepared the statement to make additional executions more efficient.

```
Dim cmd As ADODB.Command
Dim rs2 As ADODB.Recordset
Dim strSQL As String
Dim intResponse As Integer
Dim strName As String
strSQL = "SELECT Count(*) FROM authors WHERE au_lname = ?"
Set cmd = New ADODB.Command
With cmd
    .ActiveConnection = cn
    .CommandText = strSQL
    .CommandType = adCmdText
    .Prepared = True
End With
Do
    strName = InputBox$("Enter Name to Count")
    cmd.Parameters(0) = strName
    Set rs2 = cmd.Execute
```

```
      MsgBox "There are " + CStr(rs2.Fields(0)) + " authors in
the table " + _
            vbCrLf + "with the last name of " + strName
      intResponse = MsgBox("Count Again?",vbYesNo)
Loop While intResponse = vbYes
```

Using Stored Procedures

Microsoft ✓ *Exam Objective*

Access and manipulate data by using the Stored Procedures model.

- Use a stored procedure to return records to a Visual Basic application.

Up to this point, we have accessed the pubs database by placing the SQL statements in the ADO code. This code, located either in the client application or, preferably, a business object, is passed to the database server and parsed as the server receives the query. There are two disadvantages to this approach.

First, the developer of the business object or client application must be both very familiar with ADO, SQL code, and the mechanisms used to extract and modify information.

Second, since the query is written in ADO code instead of stored on the SQL Server, it must be parsed, resolved, and optimized with every execution. This can be a very time consuming process that must be repeated with every execution.

Using SQL Server stored procedures solves both of these problems. First, a developer who is responsible for creating business objects or client applications can focus on core competence. This means that the object developer can concentrate on creating great objects and not even know anything about SQL code. The only thing that the component developer must know is how to call a stored procedure with ADO. The implementation detail of the stored procedure is completely encapsulated from the developer.

While this benefit may seem insignificant at first, imagine that you have a large application with significant data query needs. If you have a developer on your staff that has extensive experience with SQL code, you wouldn't have your component developer writing all of your queries, and you would be much more likely to allow each developer to focus on their strengths. You would get a better product, and you would probably get it in a shorter period of time.

SQL Server stored procedures can also solve the performance problem caused by the reissuing of queries to the server repeatedly. Once a stored procedure runs on a SQL Server, it's stored in a memory area called the procedure cache. If the stored procedure ever runs again, it can be retrieved from the procedure cache; this is much faster than retrieving from disk or completely reprocessing the query.

By using prepared statements, you can greatly reduce the performance penalty for using ad hoc SQL statements in your application. However, to obtain maximum performance, stored procedures are preferred.

Stored procedures can be used for both selecting and modifying data. The process is much the same as the one that you have seen for using ad hoc SQL statements. You can use stored procedures with both the recordset and the Command objects. We will use the stored procedures created by the following SQL code as an example.

```
CREATE PROC authorlist
@lname varchar(40)
AS
SELECT au_lname, au_fname
FROM authors
WHERE au_lname = @lname
go

CREATE PROC authorlistfull
AS
SELECT au_lname, au_fname
FROM authors
```

The first stored procedure selects the first name and last name of any author whose last name is entered in place of the parameter called @lname. This is the only parameter in the stored procedure. The second procedure selects the first name and last name of every author in the database.

Stored Procedures and Recordsets

If the stored procedure has no parameters, you can place the name of the stored procedure in the Source argument of the Open method. By setting the Options argument to cmdStoredProc, this instructs the service provider to locate a stored procedure by that name and execute it. Unfortunately, if the stored procedure has parameters, this method will not work. The following code shows an example of this approach.

```
Dim rs2 As ADODB.Recordset
Set rs2 = New ADODB.Recordset
rs2.Open "authorlistfull", cn, adOpenKeyset, _
adLockPessimistic, adCmdStoredProc

Do While Not rs2.EOF
    MsgBox rs2!au_fname + " " + rs2!au_lname
    rs2.MoveNext
Loop
MsgBox "List Complete"
```

If the stored procedure has parameters, you can still execute the stored procedure with the Open method of the Recordset object. You will need to call the stored procedure with exactly the same syntax as would be required in SQL server, and you must set the Options argument to adCmdText. The following code illustrates this approach.

```
Dim rs2 As ADODB.Recordset
Set rs2 = New ADODB.Recordset
rs2.Open "Exec authorlist 'Ringer'", cn, adOpenKeyset, _
adLockPessimistic, adCmdText

Do While Not rs2.EOF
MsgBox rs2!au_fname + " " + rs2!au_lname
        rs2.MoveNext
Loop
MsgBox "List Complete"
```

Commands and Stored Procedures

To use stored procedures with a Command object, you follow a structure similar to that using the ad hoc SQL. Instead of using an ad hoc SQL statement as the CommandText, however, you use the name of the stored procedure. The following example illustrates the process with a stored procedure that has no parameters. Notice that to capture the resulting records, you will set a Recordset object equal to the execution of the stored procedure.

```
Dim rs2 As ADODB.Recordset
With cmd
    .ActiveConnection = cn
    .CommandText = "authorlistfull"
    .CommandType = adCmdStoredProc
End With
Set rs2 = cmd.Execute
Do While Not rs2.EOF
    MsgBox rs2!au_fname + " " + rs2!au_lname
    rs2.MoveNext
Loop
MsgBox "List Complete"
```

If you wish to implement parameters in your stored procedures through the Command object, you must add each parameter to the Parameters collection of the Command. This is a two-step process. First, you create the parameter and give it its value; next, you append the new parameter to the Parameters collection of the Command. The syntax of the CreateParameter method and the Append method are as follows.

```
Set parameter = command.CreateParameter (Name, Type,
Direction, Size, Value)
command.Parameters.Append parameter
```

The CreateParameter method of the Command object adds parameters in ADO that are designed to abstract the parameters in a SQL server stored procedure. The arguments in the CreateParameter method mimic the information that you provide about a parameter as you create a stored procedure in SQL Server.

The Name argument specifies the name of the parameter in the stored procedure. Type indicates the data type that the parameter assumes. Direction allows you to select between input or output parameters. If the data type of the parameter can vary in size, the Size argument specifies the actual size of the parameter. Lastly, the Value argument allows you to specify an initial value. You can always change this later. The following code illustrates one way that this scenario might be coded.

```
Dim cmd As ADODB.Command
Dim rs2 As ADODB.Recordset
Dim Param As ADODB.Parameter
Set cmd = New ADODB.Command
With cmd
    .ActiveConnection = cn
    .CommandText = "authorlist"
    .CommandType = adCmdStoredProc
End With
Set Param = cmd.CreateParameter("@lname", adChar, adParamInput, _
40, "Ringer")
cmd.Parameters.Append Param
Set rs2 = cmd.Execute
Do While Not rs2.EOF
    MsgBox rs2!au_fname + " " + rs2!au_lname
    rs2.MoveNext
Loop
MsgBox "List Complete"
Set cmd = Nothing
```

Microsoft ✓ *Exam Objective*

Access and manipulate data by using the Stored Procedures model.

- Use a stored procedure to execute a statement on a database.

When modifying data through stored procedures, you don't capture a recordset. As was discussed earlier, this approach is much more efficient than modifying data through a recordset using a cursor. Using a searched update in a stored procedure eliminates the need for very costly cursor overhead.

As an example, we will use the following stored procedure that inserts a new record into the publishers table. Note that parameters are provided for all columns in the publishers table.

```
CREATE PROC insertpub
@pub_id char(4),
@pub_namevarchar(40),
@cityvarchar(20),
@statechar(2),
@countryvarchar(30)
AS
INSERT publishers
VALUES
(
@pub_id,
@pub_name,
@city,
@state,
@country
)
```

 WARNING   The publishers table in the pubs database that ships with SQL Server 7 contains a check constraint on the *pub_id* column that restricts input to a four-digit string starting with "99". If you are following along with the examples in the book, be sure to enter a correct range of values or the entry will fail.

Although we used an insert operation in this example, you could also construct SQL Server stored procedures to handle updates and deletes in the same way by providing parameters to control the way that the procedure executes.

Calling this procedure is identical to the previous stored procedure example that we evaluated, with the exception of the fact that we are not building a recordset. You will not need an object variable to store a recordset. The following code illustrates how this call might take place.

```
Dim cmd As ADODB.Command
Dim Param As ADODB.Parameter
Set cmd = New ADODB.Command
With cmd
    .ActiveConnection = cn
    .CommandText = "insertpub"
    .CommandType = adCmdStoredProc
End With
Set Param = cmd.CreateParameter("@pub_id", adChar,
adParamInput, _
4, "9911")
cmd.Parameters.Append Param
Set Param = cmd.CreateParameter("@pub_name", adVarChar,
adParamInput, _
40, "Pub World")
cmd.Parameters.Append Param
Set Param = cmd.CreateParameter("@City", adVarChar,
adParamInput, _
20, "Newtown")
cmd.Parameters.Append Param
Set Param = cmd.CreateParameter("@state", adChar,
adParamInput, _
2, "DE")
cmd.Parameters.Append Param
Set Param = cmd.CreateParameter("@country", adVarChar,
adParamInput, _
30, "USA")
cmd.Parameters.Append Param
cmd.Execute
MsgBox "Record Added"
```

You will notice that in the code above, we are only declaring a single object variable for the parameter and using that variable to satisfy every parameter in the query. This common technique can save a lot of "virtual real estate" by recycling an object reference when we have exhausted the usefulness of its present reference.

Managing Multiple Recordsets

Occasionally a stored procedure will return more than one result set. This is especially common when a single set of parameters provided by a user can satisfy the data requirements for more than one result set. ADO differentiates between the multiple recordsets and allows you to navigate them as needed.

Take, for example, the following stored procedure. Although it returns two simple recordsets, there are two select statements, so you must treat them as separate recordsets.

```
CREATE PROC twocount
AS
SELECT Count(*) FROM authors
SELECT Count(*) FROM publishers
```

To navigate to the second recordset output by the stored procedure, you will use the NextRecordset method. This method allows you to set a new recordset to the second recordset exposed by the execution of the stored procedure. The following code illustrates how to use the NextRecordset method when navigating multiple recordsets.

```
Dim rs1 As ADODB.Recordset
Dim rs2 As ADODB.Recordset
Set rs1 = New ADODB.Recordset
Set rs2 = New ADODB.Recordset
rs1.Open "twocount", cn, adOpenKeyset, adLockPessimistic,
adCmdStoredProc
MsgBox "There are " + CStr(rs1.Fields(0)) + " rows in the
authors table"
Set rs2 = rs1.NextRecordset
MsgBox "There are " + CStr(rs2.Fields(0)) + " rows in the
publishers table"
```

Exercise 3.5 walks you through the process of implementing a solution with the Command object. This example will use an ad hoc query that returns multiple recordsets.

EXERCISE 3.5

Implementing the Command Object

1. Start Visual Basic and open the ADO project. Add a new command button under the Update Name command button. Set its Caption property to Count. Name the button cmdCount.

2. Write code into the click event of the command button that sends a query to the server through a Command object. The query should return the total number of authors in the authors table. Report the result back to the user in a message box. Use the code below as an example.

```
Dim strSQL As String
Dim rs1 As New ADODB.Recordset
Dim cmd As New ADODB.Command
strSQL = "SELECT COUNT(*) FROM authors"
With cmd
    .ActiveConnection = cn
    .CommandText = strSQL
    .CommandTimeout = 15
    .CommandType = adCmdText
End With
Set rs1 = cmd.Execute
MsgBox CStr(rs1.Fields(0)) + " rows in the authors table"
```

3. Start the application and click the Count button. Assuming that you have not added or deleted records from the authors table, the message box should report back 23 rows in the authors table.

4. Stop the application. Save the project and exit Visual Basic.

Summary

The Microsoft Active Data Objects represent the latest generation in data access interfaces. With ADO 2, this object model is finally becoming a complete implementation of its original version. ADO now supports even the most sophisticated data access features, including stored procedure access, prepared statements, multiple recordsets, and asynchronous query execution.

Visual Basic is a useful tool for writing many types of applications, yet it remains a tool primarily targeted at the implementation of data clients and business objects. For this type of work, Visual Basic is very well suited. ADO adds to the efficiency with which database applications can be implemented using Visual Basic 6.

This exam will place heavy emphasis on data access techniques. You should become very familiar with all of the techniques discussed in this chapter, especially focusing on the Visual Basic interaction with Microsoft's premier database management system, Microsoft SQL Server.

Review Questions

1. Which of the following is not an element of the ADO model?

   A. Database

   B. Error

   C. Connection

   D. Parameter

2. Which of the following ADO recordset types provides the greatest degree of concurrency?

   A. Static

   B. Forward-only

   C. Dynamic

   D. Keyset

3. Which of the following cannot be included in the Open method of the recordset?

  A. CursorType

  B. User Name

  C. CursorLocation

  D. LockType

4. Which of the following code examples will not read data from the *au_fname* column of a recordset represented by the object variable *rs*?

  A. `rs!au_lname`

  B. `rs(au_lname)`

  C. `rs.Fields("au_lname")`

  D. `rs.Fields("au_lname").Value`

5. Which of the following locking types will lock a recordset only during an Update process and not immediately when the data modifications are requested?

  A. Pessimistic

  B. Update

  C. Optimistic

  D. Batch optimistic

6. A prepared statement is:

  A. Query text cached on the client

  B. Query text cached on the server

  C. Compiled query cached on the client

  D. Compiled query cached on the server

7. Which symbol in an ADO query should you use to identify a parameter?

   A. !

   B. ^

   C. ?

   D. *

8. Which of the following will provide the best aggregate execution performance for a query that is not executed repeatedly?

   A. Direct execution

   B. Stored procedures

   C. Prepared statements

   D. ADO Data Control

9. Which method of the Recordset objects should you use to navigate multiple recordsets returned by a stored procedure?

   A. NewRecordset

   B. NavigateRecordset

   C. OpenFull

   D. NextRecordset

10. Which of the following scenarios will perform a direct execution of a Command object?

   A. The Execute method

   B. The Prepare method

   C. The ExecDirect method

   D. The Open method

11. Which of the following statements is capable of abandoning a series of modifications made to a recordset locked with a BatchOptimistic lock?

   A. CancelUpdate

   B. AbandonBatch

C. CancelBatchUpdate

D. CancelBatch

12. Which of the following approaches to data modifications is the least efficient?

A. Updating through a cursor using a recordset

B. A stored procedure

C. An update statement prepared and executed

D. An update statement executed directly

13. Which of the following is not an advantage of using stored procedures?

A. Developer focus on core competence

B. Increased execution performance over direct execution

C. Portability among various database server products

D. Well-defined methods for calling from ADO

14. An ADO dynamic property is:

A. A property that changes value at runtime

B. A value defined by the user

C. A property that dynamically resizes as needed to accommodate database parameters

D. A property implemented by the OLE DB service provider

15. Which of the following will not create a read-only recordset?

A. A lock type of read-only

B. A client-side cursor location

C. A forward-only cursor type

D. A static cursor type

CHAPTER

4

Designing and Implementing the Business Tier

In previous chapters, we addressed the general multitier architecture that we use in a distributed application. We addressed the role of components at the business tier and the importance that they play in a distributed application. Although you have studied how these components fit into the architecture, you have not really addressed the best way to create them.

In this chapter, you will look at components from the inside out by addressing the following topics:

- The basic terminology used in component development

- The evaluation and assembly of object hierarchies and organizations

- Creating basic object models

- Using ADO to implement a data access component

The first part of this chapter on terminology and structure will not be represented by questions on the exam. However, this information lays critical groundwork for the test subjects of creating and evaluating object models and implementing these models. If you already have a firm understanding of object-oriented analysis and design, you may want to skip ahead to the exam objectives later in this chapter. If not, you can start here at the beginning and explore this important topic.

In previous chapters, you learned about business objects and the part they play in multitier architecture. Although multitier database solutions represent a critical implementation of object-based development, this discussion is not limited solely to objects used in database solutions. The principles discussed here are relevant to any implementation of business objects.

Components Defined

To understand components and object-oriented programming, you need to understand some important terms that can be intimidating at first. Because the terminology is so important, the first part of this chapter will define some of those terms.

Component architecture terminology tends to form a pyramid. Understanding higher concepts depends on understanding the concepts below. We will begin by exploring the foundation and from there move toward the more exotic.

Classes

Classes are the formal definitions that provide the basis for all objects. Every *object* begins life as a class. The class code defines all the behaviors and attributes of the class. Therefore, the class is really nothing more than a collection of code that forms a template for the creation of other objects in our application.

More important than what classes are is what classes represent. A class may be a collection of code, but the fact that a class represents a physical object or process is what makes it so powerful. For example, a class could define everything about a real-world object such as a motor vehicle. It would have defined attributes such as wheels, an engine, doors, and other things that make up a motor vehicle.

One of the more powerful attributes of a class is the ability to base other classes on an existing class object. This ability relates to the concept of *inheritance,* which will be discussed later. If you have defined a general class such as "motor vehicle," you could use this class as the foundation for other classes, such as car or truck. Cars and trucks have a lot in common; those commonalties are defined in the general motor vehicle class. By basing the car and truck classes on this motor vehicle class, you do not need to redefine these attributes and behaviors in every single class.

However, cars and trucks also differ from each other. The parent class, motor vehicles, does not define these differences. Each respective class defines these behaviors and attributes as appropriate. The process of basing a new class object on an existing class is called *subclassing.*

Subclassing is an important element of object-oriented programming. It provides the foundation for building reusable code. Once defined, a parent class provides the starting point for the definition of all other objects that share those common behaviors and attributes.

Objects

An *object* is the implementation of a class. Remember that a class is a collection of code. This code acts as a template for creating an object. When we invoke the appropriate class function, an object is created based on the attributes and the behaviors of the class.

Every object has *interfaces*. An interface is the publicly exposed method, property, or function that the developer can use to manipulate an object. An interface actually provides a means by which the internal code of the object can execute without exposing all of the implementation detail to the consumer of the object.

According to object-oriented programming theory, every object must support four basic attributes:

- Abstraction

- Encapsulation

- Inheritance

- Polymorphism

These attributes are the reason object-oriented programming is so popular. Let's look at each of these concepts in more detail and see how they might affect the classes we create.

Abstraction

Abstraction is the ability to provide a virtual representation of a physical object or process. The previous example evaluated a class called "truck." The truck object created from this class represents an abstraction of all trucks on the road and emphasizes the similarities between them. Using the concept of abstraction, you can reference an object without needing to describe in detail every individual attribute of the object. Figure 4.1 illustrates this concept. In the diagram, we see that an object hierarchy refers to the truck on the right, but until properties of the hierarchy are defined, the model could actually refer to any truck on the road.

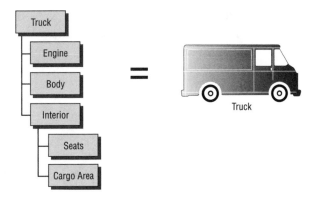

For example, you might be writing an application that interacts with a peripheral such as a printer. In order to work with the printer, you create an object that defines all of the attributes of the printer. The code inside the object does the physical interaction with the printer. When you write your application, you do not interact directly with the printer. The object has abstracted the printer for you so that all you have to do is interact with the object.

Encapsulation

Encapsulation is the ability of a class to hide its inner workings from the application that is implementing it. In other words, it allows a developer to define an object as a *black box,* meaning that the interfaces that the object exposes are well defined and public, and the actual implementation details of the object are hidden.

For example, you know how to drive a car. A car has defined interfaces such as a steering wheel, a gas pedal, a brake pedal, a clutch, and so on. You may not know exactly what happens in the engine when you press the clutch to the floor, but you do know that it behaves the same way every time. All you need to be concerned with is pressing the clutch at the right time to get the desired end result, which is to change gears.

Objects work the same way. Code defined by the class will execute when you set an attribute of an object. If you have an object that supports a color property and you want to set the color of the object to blue, you do not need to be concerned with how the color-change process happens. The class encapsulates this functionality. You only need to set the color property to blue to get a blue object.

Figure 4.2 illustrates this concept. The inner workings of the object are hidden from view, but interfaces exposed to the outside provide the mechanisms by which the object operates.

FIGURE 4.2

Encapsulation of object functionality

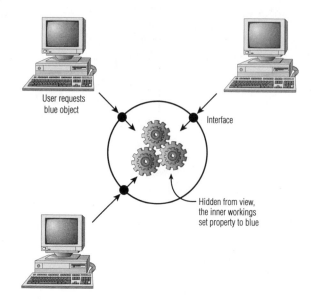

Inheritance

Inheritance is the ability to pass changes made to attributes and behaviors of parent classes to the subclasses whose foundation they provide. The principle of inheritance is extremely powerful when managing objects, because it guarantees that all objects in the same lineage will have consistently applied attributes from the parent classes. In other words, everything will always be the same.

Assume that our motor vehicle class specifies that every motor vehicle object has blue pinstripes. If the Car and Truck objects inherit from the motor vehicle, they also have blue pinstripes. This is because the parent defines this attribute for all subclassed objects.

Now change the attribute for the parent class. The motor vehicle class defines red pinstripes rather than blue. Because these subclassed objects inherit from the parent class, they now also have red pinstripes. Changing the attribute for the parent changes it for all objects descending from that parent.

Figure 4.3 illustrates the concept of inheritance. Objects built from child classes contain all of the attributes of the parent class that derived them. The child class can then extend these attributes by defining new attributes or redefining those inherited from the parent class.

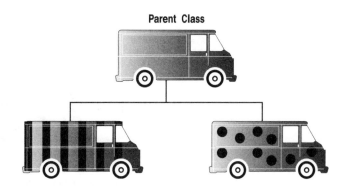

Parent Class

Polymorphism

The Greek root of *polymorphism* means "many forms." Polymorphism is the ability to implement interfaces generically in your applications without regard to the code in the class that implements the interface. In other words, you can have multiple classes that define the same interfaces; however, the actual code behind these interfaces may perform different tasks depending on which class is used. The application that calls the class object will not care as long as the interface remains constant. Therefore, the application can use objects of "many forms."

For example, when you arrive at the rental car counter at an airport with a reservation for a midsize vehicle, you could end up with a number of different models in that class. You probably don't care which model you get because your attitude toward these vehicles is *polymorphic*. You have defined an *interface* called "midsize car." Each of the cars in that classification support that interface, so you really don't care which car you get.

Figure 4.4 illustrates the concept of polymorphism. Although the inner workings of multiple components may be different, as long as the interfaces are consistently applied, the application can accept either.

FIGURE 4.4

Supporting
polymorphism

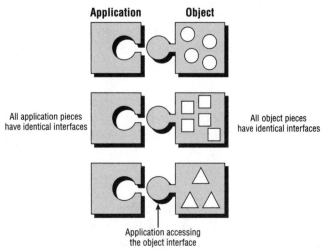

Application   Object

All application pieces
have identical interfaces

All object pieces
have identical interfaces

Application accessing
the object interface

**No matter what occurs inside the different objects,
the interfaces remain the same**.

Microsoft Visual Basic supports the principles of abstraction, encapsulation, and polymorphism in object development. Visual Basic 6.0 does not directly support inheritance, although there are a number of well-documented strategies for simulating interface inheritance in a Visual Basic object.

Components

There seems to be a fair amount of confusion about the difference between an object and a component. The difference is quite simple. An *object* is the implementation of a single class at runtime. A *component* is a compiled piece of code based on the aggregation of many classes.

The essential concept in that definition is that the component represents a *compiled entity*. When you want to use an object in an application, you must first install the component that provides the source for the object. For example, if you are creating an n-tier client/server application, you might create a set of classes that define the data access logic for the application. You can then compile these classes into a single component. This component is now ready for installation on any server in the enterprise that will host business processes.

Because components store multiple classes, you must include the ability to navigate in your components. You may not use all of the classes every time you create an application; however, the component must provide the ability to access any class object at any time necessary. To accomplish this, components often use hierarchies to arrange the classes they contain. These hierarchies give the developer the ability to use the object on whichever level is appropriate for the task at hand.

The hierarchy concept is a critical issue for component architectures because almost all components arrange classes in some kind of hierarchical relationship. The remainder of this chapter will focus on component hierarchies and their implementation.

In this chapter, the term *component hierarchy* refers to an organization of classes inside a component. The terms *object hierarchy* or *object model* also refer to a component hierarchy. When you see these terms, consider them synonymous.

Designing Components

T he best way to learn how to build object models is to evaluate existing models that are good examples of design. One object model recognized by many developers is the Microsoft JET Data Access Objects (DAO) model. The DAO model is a very typical object hierarchy. It defines objects and collections and arranges them in the logical structure needed to represent an abstraction of a database. Figure 4.5 illustrates an abbreviated version of this hierarchy.

If this is your first exposure to object models, Figure 4.5 will probably appear a bit redundant. For example, you see the word "workspaces" twice, once in reference to a collection and once for an object. The next section discusses the differences between collections and objects.

F I G U R E 4.5

The DAO object model

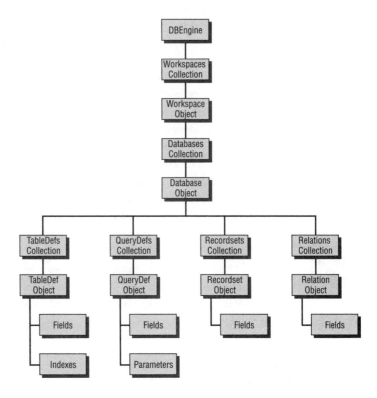

Collections and Objects

Collections represent groups of like objects. You can think of a collection as a container that holds zero or more objects of the same types. The membership of these collections is usually not fixed. The collection provides the developer with the interface to add and remove elements from the collection as necessary.

Collections may contain other objects, but in reality a collection is an object of its own. For example, you could say that a mailbox represents a collection of individual pieces of mail. You can add and remove mail from your mailbox at will. Notwithstanding this, the mailbox is an object as well. It has properties and methods the same as any other object, but the only way to get to the mail is to go through the Mailbox object.

Every collection has the capacity to support properties and methods. In addition, every collection must provide support for one property in particular, the count property. The count property is a read-only property that returns the total number of elements found in a collection. Armed with the count property, you can always identify the complete membership of any collection.

In addition to the count property, most collections also provide support for the *Add* and *Delete* methods. The collection uses methods for modifying the membership of a collection. If the collection does not support these methods, it must provide some other method to extend and remove membership to objects in the collection.

Collections contain objects. Collections and objects are based on classes, and you know that one class will not contain another class. The concept of containment is simulated by restricting the methods to create objects to the appropriate level in the hierarchy, therefore requiring us to navigate through the collection in order to add to it. The trick is really in how you write it.

A collection is a group of objects of the *same* type. If you prefer to think of this in terms of containment, then you can say that a collection contains objects of a single type or class.

You can extend this concept for objects. Although collections contain only objects of a single type, objects can contain collections. These collections can be of varying types. For example, Figure 4.6 illustrates a detailed view of the DAO TableDef object. This single object contains two collections: fields and indexes. Although these two collections reference two different types of objects, they are contained within a single object (the TableDef object).

The only way to access an index stored in a JET database is to go through the related TableDef object. Because every TableDef has its own collection of indexes, TableDef provides the necessary qualifier to identify the index with which you want to work. Exercise 4.1 will walk you through DAO collections using Microsoft Access 97. From this exercise, you will see the relationship between objects and collections and see their exposed development interfaces.

If the Control Wizard is enabled in your installation of Access 97, turn it off before continuing past step 3 of the exercise. With an Access form open in design view, locate the toolbox and click the button in the upper-right corner. This button will have a picture of a magic wand. The wizard is disengaged if the button doesn't look like it is depressed.

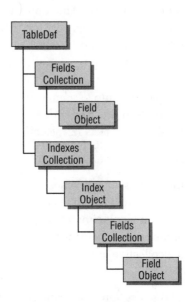

F I G U R E 4.6

The JET TableDef object with its collections

EXERCISE 4.1

Working with DAO Objects and Collections in Microsoft Access 97

1. Start Microsoft Access 97. When prompted for a database name, click the option for a blank database and click OK.

2. Save the database under the name Collect in a folder of your choice.

3. From the Database window in the center of your screen, click the Forms tab and click the New button on the right side of the screen. At the New Form dialog, select Design View and click OK.

4. In the center of this form, add a command button. Open the properties for the command button on the form by right-clicking your mouse and selecting properties from the pop-up menu. In the caption Property, type **Create Tables**. Close the Properties window.

5. Right-click again on the command button, this time selecting Build Event from the menu. When prompted for a builder type, select Code Builder and click OK. This should take you to the code for the Command click event.

6. Between the `Private Sub` and `End Sub` statements, enter the following code:

```
Dim db As Database, td As TableDef, fd As Field
Dim strTDName As String
strTDName = InputBox$("Enter a new TableDef name")
Set db = CurrentDb()
Set td = db.CreateTableDef(strTDName)
Set fd = td.CreateField("Field1", dbText)
td.Fields.Append fd
db.TableDefs.Append td
MsgBox Prompt:="Table Creation Complete", _
    Buttons:=vbOKOnly, _
    Title:="Create Table"
```

7. Close the code window and save the form by selecting File ➢ Save from the menu. Name the form **Create_Table**.

8. Place the form in form view by selecting View ➢ Form View from the menu. Click the Create Table button and enter a table name of your choice. You should receive a message stating that the creation is complete. Click OK to dismiss the message box.

9. Press the F11 key on your keyboard. This should bring the database window to the front. Click on the Tables tab. You should now see your table in the list.

10. Double-click your new table in the database window to open the table in datasheet view. Note the field that you created through code is called *Field1*.

11. Close the table and the form and exit Access.

If you look at the code that you typed in step 6, you should see very clearly the relationship between objects and collections. After referencing the Database object, you created the TableDef. Because the TableDef object is incomplete without at least one field, you then created the Field object. Before the process is finished, you must append each of the objects to their respective collections. The Field object is appended to the Fields collection of the TableDef, and the TableDef is appended to the TableDef collection of the database.

Designing Properties, Methods, and Events

Microsoft ✓ *Exam Objective*

Design the properties, methods, and events of components.

Object hierarchies are effective at describing the structure of components and the underlying objects that they represent, but they are not yet complete abstractions. Objects don't just sit idle; we create them so that they can perform tasks for us. Objects work through the implementation of properties, methods, and events. Before we continue, we should first define these terms.

Property   An attribute of an object. Properties can be read or write. Writing a value to a property sets the appropriate attribute of the underlying object.

Method   An action associated with an object. Methods allow objects to perform actions on other objects. Methods often provide redundant mechanisms for setting object properties.

Event   A message sent through the operating system that the object captures and to which it responds. Events allow points in the execution of an application for the execution of specific code routines.

In this section, we will look at the process of designing properties, methods, and events. Later in this chapter, we will see how they are implemented using Visual Basic.

Properties

Choose properties of your objects based on the elements of the underlying objects that you need to describe. If you are creating a component to abstract a database, you did some of the work when you normalized the database: You defined the entities by creating tables. The columns of these tables represent the attributes of these entities that you may wish to describe. Use this table structure as a starting point for your object model.

Although it may be tempting, it is often unnecessary to create a property for every column in the database. You should only create properties for the columns in your tables that you frequently use for searching, identifying, or manipulating your data source. You can access the other columns through generic methods that use the column names as arguments.

As an example, let's look at the publishers table in the pubs database. The structure of this table is shown below in Figure 4.7. This table has five columns, the *pub_id*, *pub_name*, *city*, *state*, and *country*. Depending on your business rules, you might create a read-only property of the Publisher object called *id* and a read/write property called pubname. In this case, the property name pubname might be used instead of a name property so as not to create a conflict with the general connotation of a name property.

FIGURE 4.7

The publishers table

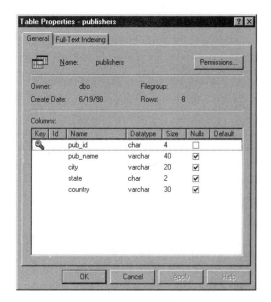

Methods

Methods allow us to perform actions based on the underlying objects. These object methods might perform changes to data on an individual row or even make modifications to table or database properties. The most common activities that you will want to abstract through methods are data modifications.

In Chapter 3, we created a stored procedure called *insertpub* that allowed us to insert a new row into the publishers table. As a reminder, the script used to create this stored procedure looked like this.

```
CREATE PROC insertpub
@pub_id char(4),
@pub_namevarchar(40),
@cityvarchar(20),
@statechar(2),
@countryvarchar(30)
AS
INSERT publishers
VALUES
(
@pub_id,
@pub_name,
@city,
@state,
@country
)
```

You will note that we carefully matched the parameter data types in the stored procedure with the data types used in the actual table. Since inserting data into the publishers table is an action that you take on the table, this action would be appropriately implemented as a method of the object. The method would provide all of the columns in the publishers table as arguments.

In addition to an Insert method, you might include other methods to change data in the table, delete rows, select an active row, extract data, etc. Often properties and methods can both be used to accomplish the same result. For example, if you wanted to change the name of a publisher in the table, you might design a read/write property called pubname. However, you could also design a method called UpdatePubName, accepting the new name as an argument. You could even provide both, giving your user a choice of implementation options.

Events

The events of an object allow the developer to identify when certain changes to the data environment occur and when data specific conditions exist. As an example, when abstracting a data table through a component, you might include a method to select an active row in the table. An event called *Change-Row* could provide a mechanism to inform the client application when a new row had been identified. This would be especially helpful if your object model provided the user with multiple ways to navigate from row to row.

Events can also be very useful in an environment where data must be accessed asynchronously. The advantage of asynchronous data access is that the component or client can continue with other tasks as the database performs the necessary data access function. A disadvantage, however, is that since the component or client is not tracking the status of the data task explicitly, you must find a way to inform the client or component that the task has completed. An event provides a very elegant way to support this application requirement.

The Nuts and Bolts

So what makes a good object model? This question has many different answers depending on whom you ask. Nevertheless, this section will attempt to arm you with a few basic principles that you can use when evaluating and designing object models.

Complete Abstraction

Recall that abstraction is defined as the ability to refer to a physical object in a virtual way. This ability is one of the primary yardsticks by which you can judge an object model.

The Microsoft Data Access Objects represent an abstraction of a JET data structure. This means that every element of that database is represented in some way in the object model. When evaluating object models, you must ensure that the object model represents all elements of the entity that you are trying to abstract.

For example, say you want to build an object model that abstracts a car. You might define certain objects such as the body, engine, interior, etc. As you go down the list of real objects in or on the car, you must represent these objects in your object model, or it will not be a complete abstraction.

Look at the Body object of your car. The body would support properties such as color or style for which the developer could provide a value. Other properties might be Boolean, such as a convertible property. True or false is the only way to answer whether or not the car is a convertible. Some of the properties in our example (such as style or convertible) are read-only. Once the car has been created, these properties are not readily changeable. Other properties (such as color) are read/write. You can certainly find someone who will paint your car for $99.95.

Our body object might also support certain methods. For example, a car with the convertible property set to True will probably support the Top-Up and Top-Down methods. When defining your hierarchies, consider the actions performed by or on your objects.

Properties or Collections?

Some objects in the real world pose some challenging categorization problems. Let's revisit our car example one more time. Every car (or at least every car the model will support) has four wheels. Classifying these Wheel objects presents an interesting situation. You could get the object model to work either by classifying them as individual wheel properties of the car or as a Wheels collection of the Car object.

In a situation such as this one, you should probably consider the collection option first and then put this new collection to some tests. You can take two perspectives on this issue: evaluate the collection based on its proposed number of members or judge the new collection based on the concept of fixed-collection membership.

Let's look at the size test first. When you work with properties of objects, you must refer to each of them individually. You can easily aggregate collections. For this reason, it is imperative that the group of objects represented by these properties is not so large that it is prohibitive and essentially nonfunctional. There is no firm cut-off point that determines when a group is too large to be a set of properties—that's really up to you as the creator of the object model. If the number of objects represented by these potential properties is not defined, consider what the average implementation will be.

If you, as the developer, determine that the number of properties that would have to be supported is too prohibitive to be effective, then you should create the model using a collection. If the element of the object with which you are working fails this test, there is no reason to continue. Simply create the element as a collection. In the example, four wheels are certainly not too many to support as properties, so you need to evaluate the next test.

The next test is simply a matter of identifying whether or not the number of elements in the group is fixed. Remember that every collection will support one property, the count property. This implies something very important about collections. Their membership is not usually fixed. You don't need to support a property to return the number of elements in a collection if you already know this information.

When you put wheels on a car through the fixed-membership test, it fails. There are a limited number of elements in the group, and there are a fixed number of these elements. Your conclusion should, therefore, be to create properties to represent the wheels. These properties might be named Left-FrontWheel, LeftBackWheel, and so forth.

Interface Exposure

Every object has interfaces. These interfaces allow us to do things with an object such as create it, destroy it, or otherwise manipulate it. Where these interfaces are visible is extremely critical for the proper management of the object. When you define the visibility of an interface, you are actually defining the *scope* of the procedure that supports that interface.

When scoping interfaces, Visual Basic 6 gives you three options. Each option determines where you can see the interface in your applications. Your options are:

- Public

- Friend

- Private

Public scope in an object means that the interface can be seen and used anywhere in the application. This includes within the class object itself, as well as the component that contains the object and the application that loads the component. You must include public interfaces in an object if you plan to control a particular object interface directly through code execution in the client application.

Friend scope in an object means that the interface is visible only within the object and the component that contains the object. Friend scoping is necessary if you want to use an object interface from another object in the component, but you do not want this interface to be visible from the client application that loads the component.

Private scope is the most restrictive. The interface is accessible only from within the object. It cannot be seen anywhere else in the application, neither in the component nor in the client application. Use private scope when you want to restrict the ability to call certain code anywhere outside of the object. This provides superior encapsulation of the object. Unless the object completely hides its implementation from external objects, the principle of encapsulation is being violated.

The different scoping options give the developer significant flexibility when defining object models because of the tight control the developer has over where each interface will be seen. It is not uncommon to see differently scoped interfaces in a single object or even objects that have no public interfaces at all. Figure 4.8 illustrates these different scoping options.

FIGURE 4.8

Scoping interfaces in an object

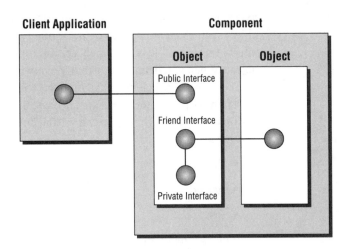

You can see an application of this concept by looking no further than your first exercise. The following listing contains a few lines of code from Exercise 4.1. Let's look at this code in more detail.

```
Dim db As Database, td As TableDef, fd As Field
Set db = CurrentDb()
Set td = db.CreateTableDef(strTDName)
Set fd = td.CreateField("Field1", dbText)
td.Fields.Append fd
db.TableDefs.Append td
```

The TableDef object in this example is of particular interest. Notice Line 3 in the code fragment. This code fragment creates a new TableDef object. Interestingly, you have not created the TableDef object directly; the code uses the CreateTableDef method of the Database object.

The TableDef object supports an interface for creation. Every object must be able to create and destroy itself when necessary. In this case, however, the scoping for the interface to create the object is a friend scoping. This means that the interface to create a TableDef object can only be accessed within the component, in this example, the DAO object library.

Because the interface to create a TableDef object is not directly accessible from a client application, the only way you can create a TableDef object is if another object in the component supplies a method by which to create a TableDef. This is exactly what you see in the previous code sample. The CreateTableDef method is actually a method of the Database object.

There is a very good reason for doing it this way. When you create a TableDef, it must be created within the context of a particular database. Because every database has its own TableDef collection, it is imperative that the database in question be fully qualified. To promote the concept of encapsulation (which states that you must hide this type of implementation detail from the user), the interface has been exposed through an alternate object.

Creating Object Models

Now that you know what makes a good object model, let's apply this knowledge. This section is just a long exercise, but its goal is to make you think about object hierarchies and how to create a good component architecture.

You already have the information necessary to start building simple hierarchies. There is no right or wrong answer to this exercise, and many different designs will provide the necessary functionality. Your task is to design a solution that meets all of the guidelines that have been discussed.

Although in practice you will probably build an object model to represent some sort of business process, we will start simply. You will build an object hierarchy based on a physical object that we can all imagine.

Exercise Scenario

You are working for WidgitCo, a high-tech electronics company that is devising stereo systems that can be controlled from a personal computer. To provide the most flexibility in their design work, WidgitCo wants to create an object model that represents the stereo system. In other words, the object model will abstract the stereo system itself. This object model should encapsulate all of the communication between the software application running on the PC and the stereo system itself. The model should be general enough so that multiple hardware systems can use the same object model.

WidgitCo has assigned you to create a basic hierarchical diagram of this model. You don't need to consider the implementation of each of these elements, such as public vs. friend interfaces and specific method functionality. Your only concern is with the basic object hierarchy and basic interfaces that they will support. As you consider this structure, you may want to follow these steps:

1. List all of the elements that make up the component that you are describing.

2. Look for common ground. See if some elements have commonalities that would make them appropriate to aggregate.

3. When you discover elements that you can aggregate, consider whether it would be best to represent them by using collections or properties of the parent element.

4. After arranging a basic hierarchy, consider what other properties and methods your objects should support.

Now, close the book, pull out a sheet of paper, and start writing. Make your object lists first and then start organizing the hierarchies. When you think you have a workable design, come back to this point in the book and we'll compare solutions.

Exercise Solution

Let's walk through a possible solution to the scenario. It is very important to understand that this is not the only possible solution; it is simply an example. Your design may vary significantly.

We will begin by listing all of the elements of a stereo system. Your stereo system may have additional elements or it may exclude some of these elements (such as a turntable). We will start with these elements:

- The entire system as a whole unit
- Speakers
- CD player
- Tuner
- Amplifier
- Cassette deck
- Turntable
- Wiring
- Remote control unit

The next step is to look for any commonalities that might exist among the elements listed. In this list, you can see an obvious opportunity for aggregation among all of the components. This would also provide the added advantage of allowing extensibility within the set of components, which is a requirement of our charter.

The next issue is whether we should implement these components as properties of a Stereo object or as a collection that the Stereo object contains. After we put the group of components through our test, we lean toward providing a collection rather than individual properties. Although the number of elements is not huge, it still may be large enough to cause problems if we use the property implementation. Also contributing to this conclusion is the fact that the number of elements in this aggregation is not fixed. We could have any number of elements, including multiple elements of the same type. Therefore, we will use a collection.

The list of elements that was the basis for our model includes a remote control unit. Because the PC application will not affect or control the remote control unit, we will eliminate it from the object model. We can substantiate this because our abstraction should be based only on those elements with which we intend to interface. If an object plays no part in the process, we can safely eliminate it from the model.

An object that exists in the real world can be safely eliminated from an abstracting object model if that object plays no purpose in the virtual application. However, you may want to include elements that you do not currently support to provide extensibility in your model.

We now have enough information to create a simple diagram illustrating our object model. Figure 4.9 represents a diagram based on the previous discussion.

FIGURE 4.9

The Stereo object model

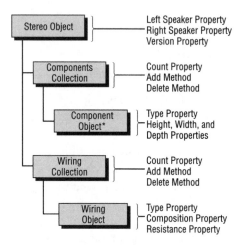

*Other properties of component objects will depend on the value provided for the type property.

As you look over this diagram, note some of the interfaces supported by these objects. Each of the collections supports the count property, as well as the Add and Delete methods. The process of adding or removing hardware might call these methods to ensure that the object model matches the physical hardware implementation. Also, note that the component object supports a type property. This value would be set based on the class of device, such as a tape deck or a CD player. Other properties of the component object would be specific to the class of device that it represents.

Although this object model is far from complete, it should give you a starting point from which to evaluate and create other object hierarchies. Consider the discussion points as you create your own hierarchies of objects.

Creating Components with Visual Basic 6

Microsoft ✓ ***Exam Objective***	**Create a COM component that implements business rules or logic. Components include DLLs, ActiveX controls, and active documents.**

Microsoft ✓ ***Exam Objective***	**Design Visual Basic components to access data from a database in a multi-tier application.**

Microsoft ✓ ***Exam Objective***	**Compile a project with class modules into a COM component.** ▪ Implement an object model within a COM component.

The remainder of this chapter covers all of the above exam objectives concurrently. However, only DLLs are covered in this chapter. ActiveX controls will be addressed in Chapter 6, and active documents will be discussed in Chapter 10. This chapter assumes a basic familiarity with component creation and emphasizes creating components specifically for a distributed application. For a basic discussion of component creation, consult *MCSD: Visual Basic 6.0 Desktop Applications Study Guide* (Sybex, 1999).

Now that we are familiar with the design stages of a component, we will create a simple data access component in Visual Basic 6. The exercises in this section will create a component with a single class designed to abstract the publishers table.

The Visual Basic Component Project

Every component in Visual Basic starts as a Visual Basic project. When you begin a new project in Visual Basic, you are presented with a list of project templates that provide the essential elements of applications, components, controls, and other Visual Basic compiled objects. COM objects in Visual Basic are generally created as one of the following project types.

- ActiveX EXE

- ActiveX DLL

- ActiveX Control

- ActiveX Document EXE

- ActiveX Document DLL

The difference between the EXE and DLL projects is primarily one of compiled component architecture rather than implementation. There are a few implementation differences, but they are relatively minor. As far as the component architecture is concerned, the EXE components load out-of-process while DLL components load in-process. This means that an EXE is more fault tolerant than a DLL, but the DLL can provide better performance.

When you create a new ActiveX DLL project, a class module will be provided for you automatically. Each class module represents a different object in our object model. You would add new class modules to the project for every new entity that you wish to abstract.

Project Properties

The project itself supports many properties that determine how the component loads and runs. Some of these properties are purely informational, while others are critical decisions that you must make to implement your component properly.

The three most important project properties for components are:

- Project Type

- Project Name
- Threading Model

Project Type

The project type property identifies what characteristics the compiled object will have. Visual Basic uses this setting to determine how the component should be compiled. You are free to change the project type at any time, no matter which project template you chose when the project was created.

Project Name

The project name property sets the value that will be used for the programmatic identifier in the Registry for each component. For example, if you had a project called Project1 and a class module named Class1, the programmatic identifier for that component would be Project1.Class1.

Microsoft ✓ **Exam** *Objective*   **Choose the appropriate threading model for a COM component.**

Threading Models

Before we can effectively discuss threading models, we should define some terms, primarily processes and threads. These concepts are central to a good understanding of the Windows operating system family.

A process is a Windows application loaded into memory, and it is really a container of sorts. A process is allocated 4GB of virtual memory, but this does not mean that every Windows application requires 4GB of memory in order to run. The space is virtual and can use hard drive space to simulate memory when necessary. The memory is split in half; 2GB is used by the system, and 2GB is used by the user program.

 Windows NT 4 Enterprise edition allows the 4GB memory space to be divided as 3GB for the user program and 1GB for the system. This provides additional memory capacity for large memory intensive applications and services such as Microsoft Exchange and SQL Server.

Each process contains resources that use this memory. One of the most important resources is called a thread. A thread is the smallest unit of execution that can be submitted to the processor. Threads have no resources or memory of their own. They get everything that they need to run from the process.

This means that processes don't actually process! Although it sounds a bit strange, a process is not a unit of execution. Only threads can be executed. This is why we sometimes refer to threads as *threads of execution.*

In the early days of Windows, i.e., prior to Windows 95 and Windows NT, all applications in the 16-bit world were single-threaded. This means that each process had only one thread of execution and all of the code for the process had to use that single thread. However, 32-bit architecture allows processes to create more than one thread.

There are two primary reasons why it might be desirable for a process to contain more than one thread. First, it allows activities to occur in the background, while other threads interact directly with the user. For example, Microsoft Word has a wonderful feature that I use daily. An automatic spell checker identifies misspelled words as I type by underlining them with a wavy red line. This happens because, as one thread of execution is handling the input into the keyboard, another thread is running behind checking my spelling against the dictionary. Microsoft Word is a single process, but separate threads perform different activities within that process.

Another reason that you might want a multithreaded application is to support multiple users. Suppose you created a component that you wanted to put on the network and allow many users to access from their client applications. If the component does not allow multiple threads to be created, each user will have to wait for the previous user to finish before starting the task that the component supports, or else it will have to keep track of what each user is doing so that it can perform the task simultaneously. This can create a real bottleneck in a multi-user application. Multithreaded components can allocate a thread to each user request, thus scheduling multiple threads to the processor and making the scenario much more efficient.

Visual Basic supports multithreaded applications through a model called *apartment threading*. All components in Visual Basic are either single-threaded or apartment-threaded.

Normally when a single-threaded component is loaded into memory, any global data that the object maintains is visible by all other users in the same process. This means that if one user makes a change to the global resources of that component, other users see the changes. To make this object available for multiple users, a sophisticated mechanism must be included in the component to keep the activities of every user separate so that the work of one user will not affect the work of another user.

Apartment threading solves this problem by confining threads in a component to operate in an "apartment" of virtual resources. Each thread is confined to its own apartment and is not aware of what the other threads are doing. When a client application calls a method of an object, the call is made through an isolated apartment. This eliminates the need to keep track of thread state and threading resources in the component code.

The primary reason for choosing the apartment threading model is when the object must be accessed by a multithreaded process or as a shared component from a number of clients. You usually would not design a data client to be explicitly multithread aware. However, Microsoft Transaction Server (MTS) can support this feature. MTS provides a multithread aware process environment that hosts apartment-threaded components, providing increased scalability of your business tier without the pain of writing multi-user components.

Single-threaded components in Visual Basic are actually apartment-threaded components limited to a single apartment.

Exercise 4.2 starts a project that we will use throughout this chapter to create a component. This component will interact with the SQL Server to provide access to the publishers table of the pubs database. In Exercise 4.2, you will start a new project and set project properties.

EXERCISE 4.2

Starting a Component Project

1. Create a folder on your hard drive to store the component files. Name the folder PubComp. Start Visual Basic. When prompted to select a project template, click ActiveX DLL and click Open.

2. From the Visual Basic menu, select Project ➤ Project1 Properties. Note that the Project Type is set to ActiveX DLL. This is because of the template that you selected when you began the project. Open the Project Type list box and note the other project types. Leave the setting at ActiveX DLL.

3. Note that the value in the Project Name text box is Project1. Delete this name and type **Pubs** in the Project Name text box.

EXERCISE 4.2 (CONTINUED)

4. At the bottom right of the dialog you will see the Threading Model list box. This should be set to Apartment Threaded. Open the list box to see the options, but leave the setting at Apartment Threaded.

5. To the left of the Threading Model list box is a check box labeled Unattended Execution. Selecting this check box increases the efficiency of the component but prevents the component from raising any dialogs or modal interactions with the user. Select this check box. The complete dialog should look like the following graphic. Click the OK button to close the dialog.

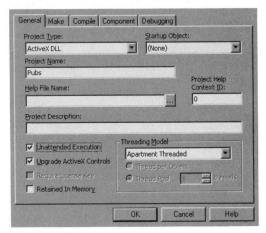

6. Since this component will access data from a SQL Server database using ADO, you must make a reference to the ADO object library. From the menu, select Project ≻ References. Select the check box next to Microsoft ActiveX Data Objects 2.0 Library. Click the OK button.

7. Save the project in the PubComp folder. Save the class module as Publisher.cls. Save the Project as Pubs.vbp. If prompted to add the project to SourceSafe, click No.

Class Properties

Microsoft Exam Objective

Compile a project with class modules into a COM component.

- Set properties to control the instancing of a class within a COM component.

The first step after starting a new project or adding a new class module is to set the properties of the class module. Unlike standard modules, class modules have properties that control instancing, data binding, etc. Class modules support the following properties.

- **Name**   The name of the class in the component hierarchy.

- **DataBindingBehavior**   Defines the component as a data consumer, indicating that it can be bound to a data source.

- **DataSourceBehavior**   Defines the component as a data source, indicating that it can provide data to other controls in an application.

- **Instancing**   Specifies whether a single instance of the component will service all client requests or whether multiple instances of the component will be loaded.

- **MTSTransactionMode**   Sets Microsoft Transaction Server transaction support properties for components designed to be implemented into a transaction server package.

- **Persistable**   Indicates whether data can be saved across instances of an object.

Controlling Instancing

Of the properties supported by the class module, the instancing property is one of the most important. This property identifies how and when the component will be loaded when the client requests component services. Table 4.1 lists the values associated with the instancing property and the component types that allow those values.

T A B L E 4.1: ActiveX Component Instancing Property Values

Value	ActiveX EXE	ActiveX DLL	ActiveX Control
Private	Supported	Supported	Supported
PublicNotCreatable	Supported	Supported	Supported
MultiUse	Supported	Supported	Not supported
GlobalMultiUse	Supported	Supported	Not supported
SingleUse	Supported	Not supported	Not supported
GlobalSingleUse	Supported	Not supported	Not supported

Private   A private class cannot be seen or manipulated from outside the component. Other classes inside the component can contain code to implement the features of a private class, but private classes cannot be manipulated by a component's client and are not documented in the type library of the component.

PublicNotCreatable   A PublicNotCreatable component exposes its properties and methods to external clients but does not support creation from the client. The class must be instantiated from within the component. This mechanism allows you to create dependent objects and object hierarchies.

MultiUse   A single instance of a MultiUse component can service all client requests. Only one instance will be loaded. If the component is compiled as an EXE, a single process is created for the component and all clients marshal their requests to that process. Components compiled as DLLs load a single instance in memory, but that instance is mapped into the address space of each client process.

GlobalMultiUse   Exactly like a MultiUse component in that properties and methods are accessible by external clients; however, those clients need not explicitly instantiate the component. The properties and methods are called as global functions and the component auto-instantiates when needed.

SingleUse   A SingleUse component requires a new instance of the component to be created whenever a new client requests that the object be instantiated. The ActiveX DLL, due to its architecture, does not support this option.

GlobalSingleUse   As with the GlobalMultiUse component, this component need not be formally instantiated by the client. The component will auto-instantiate when it is called.

In Exercise 4.3, you will continue to create the component that you started in Exercise 4.2 by setting properties of the class module.

EXERCISE 4.3

Setting Class Properties

1. Locate the Object list box at the top of the Properties window. Open the list box and select Class1 from the list.

2. Select the Name property. Enter the new name of **Publisher**.

3. Set the instancing property to MultiUse.

4. Save the project.

Preparing the Component Environment

Before you can start adding properties and methods to your class, you must consider the environment in which your component will run. Will you be accessing data from a data source? How will you handle errors in data access? What about business rule violations? You must answer these questions and plan for these issues in your component design. Let's look at two of these important issues, namely raising errors to report conditions beyond parameters and managing the environment for database access.

Raising Errors in a Component

Since you create a component to perform tasks such as enforcing business rules and accessing databases, you must have a mechanism of reporting unacceptable conditions to your client. For example, suppose that you want to create a component to enforce a business rule such as "Credit limits cannot be greater than $50,000." If the user attempts to write a value to a

CreditLimit column of a customer table that exceeds this amount, you must deny the attempt and relay this information to your client. The easiest way to do this is to raise a custom error in the component when the business rule has been violated.

To raise a custom error, simply use the Raise method of the Err object. The syntax is as follows.

```
Err.Raise number, source, description, helpfile, helpcontext
```

The number in a custom error raised from a component must be between 513 and 65,535. In addition, a constant value, vbObjectError, is added to the error number value to identify the error as coming from an external object and to push the error number out of the range of other valid error numbers.

As an example, suppose that you created a class module named Class1 as a member of a project called Project1, and you need to raise an error that identifies a duplicate key database condition in an underlying table. You might use the following syntax to raise the error. This example excludes the arguments for help support.

```
Err.Raise 513 + vbObjectError, "Project1.Class1", _

"Duplicate key not permitted"
```

When the error is trapped on the client side, you would trap for the error number plus the object error constant. Error handling in a distributed application is discussed at greater length in Chapter 12.

To implement business rules, our sample component will raise errors if certain conditions are not met. First, a custom error will be raised when the length of the *pub_id* supplied is not exactly four characters in length. Second, a custom error will be raised when a publisher number is provided to the component and that publisher number is not found in the database. Exercise 4.4 prepares for the error raising by declaring the appropriate constants. The errors will actually be raised in a later exercise.

EXERCISE 4.4

Adding the Constants to Support Object Errors

1. Start Visual Basic and open the Pubs project. Add a standard module to the project by selecting Project ➢ Add Module from the menu. In the Properties menu, name the module PubMod.

2. Declare a set of public constants in the General Declarations section of the module that will hold values for the error conditions raised by the component. Use error numbers 600 and 601. The constants should look something like the following examples.

```
' Declare Constants for Error Numbers
Public Const ERR_PUB_LEN = 600
Public Const ERR_PUB_NOVAL = 601
```

3. Declare two additional public constants that will store the description strings for the errors. Use the following as an example.

```
'Declare Constants for Error Descriptions
Public Const DESC_ERR_PUB_LEN = "The publisher number must
be exactly 4 characters in length"
Public Const DESC_ERR_PUB_NOVAL = "The publisher number
could not be found in the database"
```

4. Declare a final constant that stores the name of the class that is the source of the error. Use the form of project.class. An example is below.

```
'Declare Constant for Class Name
Public Const CLS_NAME = "pubs.publisher"
```

5. Save the project. Save the module as Pubs.bas.

Setting Up a Data Access Environment

When a component accesses data in a database, you must provide for various data access resources, such as making references to the appropriate object libraries and declaring object variables. Timing is all important when it comes to instantiating database resources such as connections and recordsets, so you want the application to be as responsive as possible and to hold open resources such as connections. However, you should be aware that there is an overhead price that you will pay for this performance benefit.

In our example, we have only one class in the component. We will therefore instantiate the connection when the class is instantiated and terminate the connection when the component is destroyed. Class modules provide two events that allow the developer to place code at the point that a class object is instantiated and terminated. These events are as follows.

Initialize Event fires as a new object is created.

Terminate Event fires as an object is destroyed.

Exercise 4.5 prepares the component for a data access task by creating and destroying an ADO connection in the initialize and terminate events.

EXERCISE 4.5

Creating a Connection in a Class Module

1. In the General Declarations section of the class module, insert a private object variable that declares an ADO Connection object. Use the following code as an example.

```
'Declare an ADO connection to access the pubs database
Private cn As ADODB.Connection
```

2. From the Object list box on the Code window, select the Class object. In the Procedure list box, select the Initialize event. Enter the following code to create a new connection. Note that this example uses a SQL Server name of Mobile1. You will need to substitute this with your server name.

```
Set cn = New ADODB.Connection
    With cn
        .ConnectionTimeout = 30
        .CommandTimeout = 30
        .Provider = "sqloledb"
        .ConnectionString = "server=mobile1;uid=sa;pwd="
        .Open
        .DefaultDatabase = "Pubs"
    End With
```

3. From the Procedure list box, select the Terminate event. Enter the following code to close and destroy the connection.

```
cn.Close
Set cn = Nothing
```

4. Save the project.

Adding Methods to a Component

The methods of an object are actions that can be performed on an object or actions that one object can perform on another object or the system. Methods are added to class modules by creating sub procedures or function procedures. Depending on how visible you want these methods to be, they can be scoped three different ways.

Public   Methods scoped as public are visible client applications making reference to the component as well as other classes defined in the component.

Friend   Methods scoped as friend are not visible to client applications but are visible to all class modules defined inside the component.

Private   Methods scoped as private are not visible to other classes defined inside the component and are only visible within the class in which they are defined.

Since you already know how to create sub and function procedures, creating methods should be quite familiar. Just like standard procedures, methods can accept arguments. These arguments can provide information to the method about how it will execute and affect underlying objects.

Our component might support methods such as SelectPub, ClearSelect, GetPub, and UpdateName. The SelectPub method selects an active row in the publishers table. The ClearSelect method clears this selection. The GetPub method retrieves the entire column set corresponding to the selected data row. The UpdateName method changes the *pub_name* column for the selected row.

The SelectPub Method

The SelectPub method will store in the component the *pub_id* value of the row with which the client wishes to work. The SelectPub method must be executed before any other properties and methods that affect a given data row can be accessed. The value entered by the user will be stored in a privately scoped member variable. Exercise 4.6 provides instructions on how to create the SelectPub method.

Creating the SelectPub Method

1. Activate the publisher class module by clicking the module name in the Project window and selecting the View Code option from the pop-up menu.

2. In the general declarations section of the class module, declare a private variable called mPubID that will store the active *pub_id* value from the table.

3. Insert a new procedure by selecting Tools ➤ Add Procedure from the menu. In the Name text box, type **SelectPub**. Set the procedure as a Public Sub and click the OK button.

4. Between the parentheses in the procedure name, add an argument for the method defined as a string. Pass this argument by value. The code below shows an example of the complete procedure name.

```
Public Sub SelectPub(ByVal PubID As String)
```

5. Add code to the procedure that creates a new ADO recordset object variable and a string variable to store a SQL string that will be used to access the database, as in the following example.

```
Dim rs As New ADODB.Recordset
Dim strSQL As String
```

6. Add code to the procedure that checks the number of characters in the PubID argument. Our business rule states that this value must be four characters in length. Raise an error and exit the method if this is not the case. Use the following code as an example.

```
If Len(PubID) <> 4 Then
    Err.Raise ERR_PUB_LEN + vbObjectError, _
        CLS_NAME, _
        DESC_ERR_PUB_LEN
    Exit Sub
End If
```

7. Add code to the procedure that creates a SQL string that counts the number of records in the database that match the PubID provided in the argument. Pass this SQL string to the server and capture the result in a recordset. Use the following code as an example.

```
strSQL = "Select Count(*) from publishers where pub_id =
'" _
    + PubID + "'"
With rs
    .Source = strSQL
    .ActiveConnection = cn
    .CursorType = adOpenStatic
    .CursorLocation = adUseServer
    .LockType = adLockReadOnly
    .Open Options:=adCmdText
End With
```

8. Add code to the procedure that checks the count value obtained from the database in the previous step. If the value is anything other than 1, raise the appropriate error and exit the method. Use the following code as an example.

```
If rs.Fields(0) <> 1 Then
    Err.Raise ERR_PUB_NOVAL + vbObjectError, _
        CLS_NAME, _
        DESC_ERR_PUB_NOVAL
    Exit Sub
End If
```

9. Add code to the procedure that closes and destroys the recordset. Also, store the PubID value in the private member variable declared in step 2. Use the following code as an example.

```
rs.Close
Set rs = Nothing
mPubID = PubID
```

10. Save the project

Adding Properties

Properties of a class abstract the characteristics of an object in real life. Every object can be described in terms of its properties. By making modifications to the properties defined in an object class, the actual object is also modified. For example, if you change the PubName property of the Publisher object, the data in the active row of the publishers table is also modified.

Adding properties to objects can be done in one of two ways. You can either create public variables in classes or create property procedures. Each approach has advantages and disadvantages.

Creating public variables of a class to implement properties of that class is a very simple technique to implement, but it suffers from one substantial disadvantage. Public variables can only store data in the component. It is impossible to perform any actions on an underlying object or perform any business rule enforcement. The property can appear in the type library of the component, but cannot have any substantive effect on an abstracted object. For this reason, using property procedures is generally preferred.

Although we are not finished creating all of our methods, we will now address the process of creating properties. This will allow us to work on properties and methods concurrently in later exercises. This is a common process, since properties and methods of objects are often closely related.

Using Property Procedures

There are three actions that you can take on properties. You can read them, write them, or set other object references through them. Because each of these three actions might result in varying behaviors, there are three separate property procedures that you can use to support each of these actions. These procedures are as follows.

Property Let   Executes when you write a value to a property.

Property Get   Executes when you read a value from a property.

Property Set   Executes when you set an object reference through a property by using a SET statement in the client. Similar in structure to the Property Let statement.

Just like methods, properties can be set to different scopes depending on the desired visibility. Public, friend, and private scope can each be used.

Each of these property procedures supports a slightly different structure. The Property Let statement requires a single argument, which is passed into the procedure as the value of the expression provided to the property. The following code example illustrates a Property Let called PubName, which writes the value provided by the user to the *pub_name* column of the publishers table. Notice how the argument called Name is used to set a value for the database.

```
Public Property Let PubName(Name As String)

Dim strSQL As String
Dim cmd As New ADODB.Command
If Len(Name) > 40 Then
    Err.Raise ERR_PUB_NAMELEN, _
        CLS_NAME, _
        DESC_ERR_PUB_NAMELEN
    Exit Property
End If
strSQL = "UPDATE publishers SET pub_name = '" _
    + Name + "' WHERE pub_id = '" + mPubID + "'"
With cmd
    .ActiveConnection = cn
    .CommandText = strSQL
    .CommandTimeout = 30
    .CommandType = adCmdText
    .Execute
End With
Set cmd = Nothing

End Property
```

The Property Get procedure reads a property value from the component. This procedure does not have any required arguments, but it does provide a return data type to strongly type the return value of the procedure. The return value of the property is indicated in a manner similar to a function; simply give a value to the property name inside of the procedure. The sample code below provides the Property Get side of the PubName property. Note how the property returns the column value through the property name.

```
Public Property Get PubName() As String

Dim strSQL As String
Dim rs As New ADODB.Recordset
strSQL = "SELECT pub_name FROM publishers where pub_id = '" _
    + mPubID + "'"
With rs
    .Source = strSQL
    .ActiveConnection = cn
    .CursorType = adOpenStatic
    .CursorLocation = adUseServer
    .LockType = adLockReadOnly
    .Open Options:=adCmdText
End With
PubName = rs!pub_name

End Property
```

In our sample publisher component, we might implement properties such as selected, ID, and PubName. The selected property is a Boolean property that identifies whether an active row has been identified. This is a read-only property. The ID property provides the value of the currently selected publisher ID. Since we have a business rule that prevents us from making modifications to the ID column, this property is also read-only. The PubName property provides the value of the *pub_name* column for the active row. This value is read/write at runtime.

Exercise 4.7 walks you through the process of adding the selected property and the ClearSelect method to the component. This Boolean property is read-only at runtime, so a public Property Let need not be implemented.

Adding the Selected Property

1. In the standard module, navigate to the General Declarations section. Add a private Boolean member variable called mSelected to store the selection status of the active data row in the publishers table. Use the following code as an example.

```
Public mSelected As Boolean
```

2. In the Publisher class module, create a public Property Get procedure called Selected that reads the value of this member variable and returns it as the value of the property.

```
Public Property Get Selected() As Boolean
    Selected = mSelected
End Property
```

3. In the SelectPub method, scroll to the end of the procedure. Immediately above the End Sub statement at the end of the procedure, add a line of code that sets the value of the mSelected member variable to true.

4. Create a new public sub procedure called ClearSelect. Add a line of code to the procedure that clears a string from the mPubID variable. Add another line of code that sets the value of the mSelected member variable to false. Use the following code as an example.

```
Public Sub ClearSelect()
    mPubID = vbNullString
    mSelected = False
End Sub
```

5. Save the project.

Adding Events

Events provide a method of signaling to the client application that an internal value or condition has been satisfied. For example, inside the SelectPub method, you could raise an event that signals to the client application that the current row selection has been changed. This would allow the developer to write code that takes a specific course of action whenever a change occurs in the current row.

Creating events occurs in two steps. First, you declare the event. This declaration is placed in the General Declarations section of a module. Declarations are scoped as public, indicating the public visibility of the event. When declaring an event, you can define parameters that the event captures and passes back to the client. The syntax of the declaration statement is as follows.

```
Public Event MyEvent(Param1 as String)
```

After declaring the event, you raise the event in the appropriate location to send the event signal back to the client application. Use the RaiseEvent statement to fire the event from the desired procedure or property. In the raise statement, you can also pass any desired values to the client through the parameters defined in the declaration statement.

```
RaiseEvent MyEvent('ParamVal')
```

Exercise 4.8 adds an event called SelectionChanged to the component. This event is fired in the SelectPub method, indicating that the current author selection has changed.

EXERCISE 4.8

Adding the SelectionChanged Event

1. In the General Declarations section of the Publisher class module, declare an event called SelectionChanged. Provide a parameter for the pub_id as a string so that the new pub_id, after the change has occurred, can be passed back to the client.

   ```
   Public Event SelectionChanged(PubID As String)
   ```

2. Locate the SelectPub method. Scroll to the end of the method and immediately before the End Sub statement, add a line of code that raises the SelectionChanged event. Pass the new pub_id back to the client by providing the value in the Event parameter. Use the following code as an example.

   ```
   RaiseEvent SelectionChanged(mPubID)
   ```

3. Save the project.

Compiling and Registering the Component

Microsoft
✓ ***Exam***
Objective

Register and unregister a COM component.

After completing the component project, it is time to compile the component. This process creates an ActiveX DLL that you can then reference from your client applications through COM. Compiling a component also registers the component on that machine. In addition, there are other methods that you can use to register the component, such as using the Package and Deployment Wizard and using the command line utility.

Before compiling your component, you should ensure that you have removed any unnecessary references to other components or controls. To compile, simply open the desired component project and choose Make DLL from the File menu. Exercise 4.9 walks you through the process of compiling a component.

EXERCISE 4.9

Compiling a Component

1. Open the Pubs project if it is not already open. From the Visual Basic menu select File ➤ Make Pubs.dll. Navigate to the desired location of the component and click OK. If there are any compile errors in your code, you will be informed of these at this point.

2. Verify that the component has been registered properly by checking the Windows Registry. To start the Registry Editor, select Start ➤ Run from the Windows start menu. Type **regedit** in the text box and click OK.

3. Go to Edit ➤ Find. Type **Pubs.Publisher** in the search box and click OK. When Regedit finds the appropriate key in the HKEY_CLASSES_ROOT portion of the Registry, expand the entry. The left list box will indicate the selection with an open folder icon. Expand the key by clicking the plus sign by the open folder. All interfaces should be in alphabetical order. When you locate the interface, expand the folder to reveal the clsid subkey. Your screen should now look like the one below, although the value for the clsid subkey will be different.

EXERCISE 4.9 (CONTINUED)

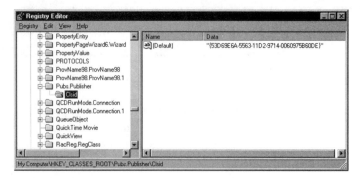

4. Close the Registry Editor.

Registering Components with the Command Line

In addition to the compile process, you can register and unregister components on any computer using a command called regsvr32.exe. All current
versions of the Windows operating system support this command. The
syntax is as follows.

```
Regsvr32 component_path [/U]
```

In the preceding syntax statement, if you omit the /U argument, the command will register the component. Including the switch causes the command
to unregister the component.

Using Visual Component Manager

Microsoft ✓ ***Exam*** ***Objective*** | **Use Visual Component Manager to manage components.**

The services provided by the Visual Component Manager are a very
welcome addition to the Visual Basic product. This utility allows the developer to publish, explore, and reuse Visual Basic components and interfaces,

which promotes the reuse of components, allowing you to import component elements into other applications as needed.

The Visual Component Manager is not actually a part of Visual Basic; it is an add-in. An add-in is an applet that is designed to interact with Visual Basic during the design phase of an application—think of it as an extension of the Visual Basic IDE. It offers services which are not found inherently in Visual Basic but which are important nonetheless. The Visual Component Manager supports three activities. They are:

Publishing   Storing components in a repository for future reference and inclusion in other projects

Locating   Finding components in the repository

Reusing   Inserting components into projects based on repository storage

The Visual Component Manager interface, illustrated in Figure 4.10, is a traditional Explorer-style interface. The tree view on the left side of the form contains a list of folders in which you can store your components. The built-in folders support all of the major objects that you can create using Microsoft Visual Studio. You can also add your own folders if desired.

FIGURE 4.10

The Visual Component Manager

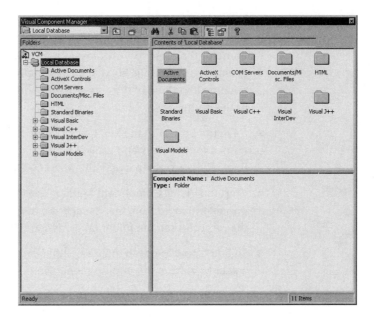

Publishing a Component

There are two primary ways to publish a component. If the source code for the component project is open in the Visual Basic IDE, you can click Tools ➤ Publish from the menu. This will present you with two options, Source Files and Build Outputs. The Source Files option publishes the source files of the current project in the repository. The Build Outputs option compiles the source files and publishes the results. You can also locate a component file in the Windows Explorer and drag the file into the appropriate folder in the Visual Component Manager interface.

Exercise 4.10 illustrates this process of publishing components with the Visual Component Manager. In this exercise, you will create and save a simple class and drag the file into the Visual Component Manager for publishing.

EXERCISE 4.10

Publishing Components with the Visual Component Manager

1. Create a new folder on your hard drive named VCM_proj. Inside this folder create two more folders, one called Source and another called Dest.

2. Start Visual Basic and select the ActiveX DLL template. Change the name of the class to VCMClass. Change the project name to VCM-Project. Add a public sub called TestMethod to the class. This will become a method of the class. Do not add any implementation code in the method.

3. Save the project in the \VCM_proj\Source folder. Use the default names for the class and project files. Close the project in the Visual Basic IDE and create a new Standard EXE project.

4. Start the Visual Component Manager by clicking View ➤ Visual Component Manager from the Visual Basic menu. Expand the tree view so that you can see the folder labeled Visual Basic.

5. To add a new folder to the tree, right click the Visual Basic folder and select New from the pop-up menu. Name the new folder ClassFiles.

6. Open the Windows Explorer and locate the contents of the \VCM_ proj\Source folder. Arrange the windows so that you can view both the new VCM folder and the Source folder contents in the Windows Explorer. Drag the VCMClass.cls file from the Windows Explorer into the ClassFiles folder in the Visual Component Manager. This will launch the wizard.

7. Fill out the Title and Properties dialog of the wizard so that it looks like the example illustrated in the graphic below. Click the Next button.

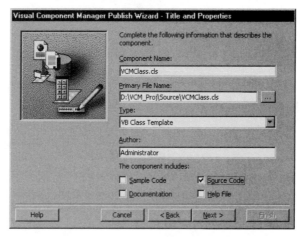

8. Add a short description of the component and click Next. The next screen will present you with a list of the files to be published. You should only see your class file in the list. This is sufficient, so click Next.

9. If any files need to be registered, this next screen will take care of that step. Since this is a source file and not a compiled object, this is not necessary, so click Next. Click the Finish button to complete the process. You will be returned to the VCM interface where you will see your newly published component.

10. Close the Visual Component Manager interface and exit Visual Basic.

Locating a Component

To locate a class in the repository, you can activate the Find dialog in the Visual Component Manager. You can access this dialog by clicking the toolbar button with the picture of the binoculars in the VCM toolbar. This dialog, pictured in Figure 4.11, gives you the ability to locate a component based on name, description, etc. Figure 4.11 illustrates the dialog after locating the VCMClass object in the repository.

FIGURE 4.11

Locating a component

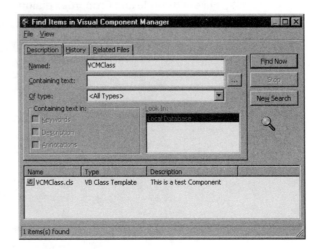

Reusing a Component

Using a component that has been published in a repository with the Visual Component Manager is a simple matter of opening the source for the receiving project and selecting Add to Project from the pop-up menu for the desired component. When it is imported, VCM even makes necessary changes to the properties of the imported object, as demonstrated in Exercise 4.11, which guides you through the process of importing a component into another project. As you will see, the process is very simple.

EXERCISE 4.11

Reusing a Component with Visual Component Manager

1. Start Visual Basic and create a new Standard EXE project. Open the Visual Component Manager interface by selecting View ➤ Visual Component Manager from the menu.

2. Locate the Visual Basic\ClassFiles folder in the VCM tree view. You should see your VCMClass.cls file published in that folder. Right-click on the icon for the VCMClass file and select Add to project from the pop-up menu.

3. You will receive an alert message that says that the class has been changed to private. This is because the source class was created in an ActiveX DLL project with the instancing property set to Multiuse, which means a public interface. Standard EXE projects cannot expose classes in that way and therefore have no instancing property, so the class is set to private. VCM does this for you. Click OK on the warning box.

4. Close the Visual Component Manager. You should now see that a new Class Modules folder has been added to the project window. If you look at the class module, you will see your TestMethod just as you created it.

5. Save the project in the \VCM_proj\Dest folder. You will notice that this project has its own distance file representing the VCMClass. This allows you to make changes to this class without disrupting any other projects.

6. Exit Visual Basic.

Summary

In this chapter, we looked at the foundations of object-based development and the process of creating components for a multitier application. Visual Basic makes this process very easy by providing convenient access to many tools needed to create and maintain component objects.

Components consist of one or more classes that abstract real objects and processes. Each class is defined with its supporting structure of properties, methods, and events. You create properties through the property procedures supplied by Visual Basic. Methods are supported through public sub and function procedures. Events must be declared first and are then raised in component code, providing a mechanism for passing values back to the client.

Components provide the needed layer of isolation between the data tier and the client application or presentation tier. By isolating business rules and data access logic in a component, the entire application is more maintainable through the distributed architecture.

Review Questions

1. Which principle of object design states that the implementation detail of the way an object works should be hidden from the developer?

   A. Abstraction

   B. Encapsulation

   C. Inheritance

   D. Polymorphism

2. Which principle of object design states that the object model should represent as closely as possible the object or process described in the real world?

   A. Abstraction

   B. Encapsulation

   C. Inheritance

   D. Polymorphism

3. Which principle of object design states that if multiple objects define the same interfaces, they can be implemented in the same way, regardless of their implementation methodology?

   A. Abstraction

   B. Encapsulation

   C. Inheritance

   D. Polymorphism

4. Which principle of object design states that a class has the ability to pass its attributes on to other classes by creating a subclass?

   A. Abstraction

   B. Encapsulation

   C. Inheritance

   D. Polymorphism

5. An interface that can be seen only in the class in which it is defined is scoped as:

   A. Public

   B. Private

   C. Friend

   D. Reserved

6. An interface that can be seen everywhere the component is referenced, including a client application, is scoped as:

   A. Public

   B. Private

   C. Friend

   D. Reserved

7. An interface that can be seen only within the object model or component in which it is defined is scoped as:

   A. Public

   B. Private

   C. Friend

   D. Reserved

8. Collections usually have fixed membership.

   A. True

   B. False

9. Which of the following properties or methods is not commonly supported by collections?

   A. Count

   B. Expand

   C. Add

   D. Delete

10. How many types of class objects can a single collection hold?

   A. 0

   B. 1

   C. 2

   D. 3

11. Which of the following procedure types will execute when you assign a value to a property of an object?

   A. Property Get

   B. Property Let

   C. Property Set

   D. Public Sub

12. Which of the following statements should you write in a procedure to cause the component to fire an event?

   A. RaiseEvent

   B. DeclareEvent

   C. FireEvent

   D. DoEvents

13. Which of the following constants should you add to a custom component error to identify the error to the client as coming from a
component object?

   A. objError

   B. vbClassError

   C. vbComponentError

   D. vbObjectError

14. The threading model that defines a set of isolated but identical processing spaces for thread execution is called:

   A. Multithreading

   B. Single threading

   C. Apartment threading

   D. Component threading

15. Which of the following compiled elements does not run in-process?

   A. ActiveX EXE

   B. ActiveX DLL

   C. ActiveX Control

   D. Standard DLL

CHAPTER

5

Creating ActiveX Controls

The addition of the ability to create ActiveX controls in Visual Basic 5.0 changed the perception of Visual Basic forever. This feature is extended in Visual Basic 6.0, adding more functionality and better performance. This chapter walks you through the process of creating ActiveX controls, including those that act as data sources and data consumers.

This chapter will first address the process of creating simple ActiveX controls, including adding properties, methods, and events. We will then look at the testing and debugging process for ActiveX controls followed by adding database features, including data binding and data source behaviors.

Like Chapter 4, *Designing and Implementing the Business Tier,* this chapter assumes basic exposure to creating ActiveX controls. Although we will review the basic process, this chapter is designed to be a refresher only. If you need additional information on these techniques, consult the companion volume to this book, *MCSD: Visual Basic 6.0 Desktop Application Study Guide,* also published by Sybex.

Creating Simple ActiveX Controls

An ActiveX control is a COM component that executes in-process within the client's address space. ActiveX controls usually provide a visual element to the user application as well as support custom methods and properties that pertain to the intended task of the control. In this section, we will look at the basics of creating ActiveX controls and their properties and methods.

The ActiveX Control Project

The ActiveX control template provides the basic structure of an ActiveX control project. This project provides all of the internal structure for an OCX file, the compiled version of an ActiveX control. While you do not have to code all of the intricate detail and COM interfaces of the ActiveX control, the template gives you a simple mechanism for adding properties, methods, and events to the control.

When you first create a new ActiveX control project, a single UserControl object is provided for you. Although the UserControl object is similar in appearance to a form, it is very different in structure. The UserControl object does not have a border like the form, so it eliminates properties such as BorderStyle that are normally associated with forms. Figure 5.1 illustrates the UserControl object. Note the differences in appearance when compared to the form.

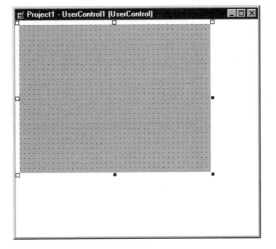

In terms of its event support, the UserControl object resembles a class module more than it does a form. While a form supports events such as Load and Unload, the UserControl object supports events like Initialize and Terminate. In addition, the UserControl also supports events that you can use to maintain the persistent nature of custom properties.

You save the UserControl in a project as a text file with a *.ctl extension. However, just like a form, the information in this text file is compiled into the

ActiveX control, eliminating the need to ship the UserControl file with the control. Just as you can define multiple classes in a component, you can also create multiple controls in an ActiveX control OCX file. It is actually a very common practice to group related controls together inside a single OCX.

Exercise 5.1 guides you through the process of creating a new ActiveX control project and setting project and control properties. The control that we will create is a set of custom feedback controls such as specialized text boxes, labels, and other convenient controls.

EXERCISE 5.1

Starting an ActiveX Control Project

1. Create a new folder on your hard disk in which to save project files. Call this folder CustomFeedback.

2. Start Visual Basic 6. When prompted for a project template, select ActiveX Control and click the OK button. You should now see a new UserControl object on the screen.

3. From the menu, select Project ➢ Project1 Properties to open the Project Properties window. In the Project Name text box, type **CustomFeed-back** and click the OK button. This will provide a library name for the OCX component.

4. In the Properties window, locate the name property for the UserControl. Change the name from UserControl1 to Clock.

5. Save the project files in the CustomFeedback folder.

Creating the Visual Interface

After creating the project, the first step is to create the visual interface of your control. There are two ways to create the visual elements of your control. You can:

1. Place existing controls on a user form, aggregating them together into a single control and modifying control behaviors. This type of control is often called an aggregate control.

2. Create a new control and visual interface from scratch. This is more challenging since, instead of relying on existing controls to provide the visual elements and visual behaviors, you must create them yourself. Because you must provide the code to draw these visual elements, this type of control is often called a user-drawn control.

Because of the complexity of user-drawn controls, this chapter will focus exclusively on aggregate controls.

You add existing ActiveX controls to a UserControl object in exactly the same way that you would add them to a form. You can set their design time properties in exactly the same manner, as well as set code for their event. These properties, methods, and events of the constituent controls of a User-Control are not automatically visible to the control's container, however. You must create custom properties, methods, and events to project these constituent behaviors outside of the UserControl. This will be addressed later in this chapter.

Sizing a Control

One of the important things to consider as you create the visual interface of your application is sizing the control. The UserControl object defines the default size of the ActiveX control in its container. Although you can create an interface that works perfectly with this default size, it is very likely that your user will require the ability to resize your control in its container.

To support control resizing, you can use the Resize event of the UserControl object to rearrange and resize the constituent controls as necessary. This can sometimes be a complex undertaking, performing constituent property modifications such as font changes and other attribute modifications as the User-Control object reaches certain thresholds.

Exercise 5.2 illustrates the process of adding constituent controls to a UserControl object and making the simple modifications required when the UserControl is resized in a client container.

EXERCISE 5.2

Adding and Managing Constituent Controls

1. Activate the Clock UserControl created in the previous exercise. Resize the UserControl to a height of 500 twips and a width of 3000 twips.

2. Add a label to the UserControl. Name the label lblClock. Remove the value from the caption property of the label. Set both the top and left properties to 0. Set the alignment property to Center. Set the Font property to 12 point bold.

3. Double-click the UserControl object to open the Code editor. Locate the Resize event of the user control. Write code to resize the label control to the scalewidth and scaleheight of the UserControl whenever the UserControl is resized in its container. Use the following code as an example.

```
Private Sub UserControl_Resize()
    lblClock.Width = UserControl.ScaleWidth
    lblClock.Height = UserControl.ScaleHeight
End Sub
```

4. In the Initialize event, add code to place the current time into the caption of the label. Use the following code as an example.

```
Private Sub UserControl_Initialize()
    lblClock.Caption = Time()
End Sub
```

5. Add a timer control to the form. Set the name property to tmrClock. Set the interval property to 1000. This will cause the timer to fire every second. In the Timer event of the timer control, add code to update the caption property of the label to the current time. Use the following code as an example.

```
Private Sub tmrClock_Timer()
    lblClock.Caption = Time()
End Sub
```

6. Save the CustomFeedback project.

Testing the Control

Microsoft ✓ ***Exam*** ***Objective***

Create ActiveX controls.

- Test and debug an ActiveX control.

Visual Basic makes it very easy to test an ActiveX control by creating a project group. A project group is a set of two or more projects running simultaneously within the Visual Basic IDE. To test an ActiveX control, simply add a new Standard EXE project to the project group. You can then test the ActiveX control on a form provided by the Standard EXE project without the need to compile the ActiveX control.

This process is also very helpful for debugging. Since the ActiveX control is not yet compiled, you can set break points and watch statements in the ActiveX control code, and the process will break inside the control as necessary.

Exercise 5.3 takes you through the process of implementing and testing the clock control on a standard form. Note particularly how the two projects interact together inside the Visual Basic IDE.

EXERCISE 5.3

Testing the Clock Control

1. Ensure that the CustomFeedback project is open in the Visual Basic 6.0 IDE. From the menu, select File ➤ Add Project. You should now see the list of project templates. Select Standard EXE and click Open.

2. Close the UserControl Designer window for the Clock control. You are not allowed to design and implement a control at the same time, so this designer must be closed before you can implement the control on the form.

3. You should see a new button in the toolbox of the Visual Basic IDE. Placing your pointer over the button should cause the tooltip to read Clock, as in the graphic below.

4. Double-click the Clock toolbox button to place the clock control in the center of the new form.

5. Change the width of the control in the form and notice how the time in the control recenters when you make the change.

6. In the Project window, you should now see both the CustomFeedback project as well as Project1, the Standard EXE project. The CustomFeedback project is visible in a bolder typeface than Project1 because it is currently set as the Start Up project. To make Project1 the Start Up, point to Project1 in the Project window and right-click. Select Set as Start Up from the pop-up menu.

7. To test the project at runtime, select Run ➢ Start from the menu. You should now see your clock running in the client form. Stop the form by selecting Run ➢ End from the menu.

8. To remove the Standard EXE from the project group, right-click Project1 in the Project window. Select Remove Project from the pop-up menu. When prompted to save the project files, click No.

EXERCISE 5.3 (CONTINUED)

9. Save the CustomFeedback project. If prompted to save the project group, save the * . vbg file in the same folder as the rest of your project files under the name Group1.vbg.

Adding Custom Properties, Methods, and Events

Just like the components that we discussed in the last chapter, ActiveX controls can also support custom properties, methods, and events. These custom elements are created in much the same way as they were with classes; however, because of the architecture of the control, providing persistence becomes an important element of this design.

In this section, we will discuss the process of adding custom methods, properties, and events to an ActiveX control. We will also discuss the life cycle of an ActiveX control and the part that this life cycle plays in proper property management.

Adding Methods

You add methods to an ActiveX control in exactly the same way as you do a component, through public sub and function procedures. Each procedure becomes an exposed method of the control.

For example, suppose that we wanted to add two methods to the Clock control, one to stop the clock and one to restart the clock. You could create two public sub procedures called StartClock and StopClock. Inside these procedures, you would disable and enable the timer control on the UserControl designer.

Note that you must control the timer through methods of the control. Since the timer itself is not publicly exposed to the client application, you must control the timer through the procedures, which then are exposed to the client as public elements of the control.

Exercise 5.4 guides you through the process of adding the StopClock and StartClock methods to the Clock control in the CustomFeedback project. Note how the timer is controlled through the public methods.

EXERCISE 5.4

Adding Methods to the Clock Control

1. Open the code module for the Clock control UserControl designer. Add a public sub called StartClock. In the code for the StartClock method, set the enabled property of the Timer control to true. Use the following code as an example.

```
Public Sub StartClock()
    tmrClock.Enabled = True
End Sub
```

2. Add another public sub called StopClock that sets the enabled property of the Timer control to false. Use the following code as an example.

```
Public Sub StopClock()
    tmrClock.Enabled = False
End Sub
```

3. Test the control by adding a Standard EXE to the project group. Create an instance of the Clock control on the form. Add two command buttons captioned Start and Stop. Code each button to call the StartClock and StopClock methods of the control respectively. Set the Standard EXE as the Start Up project. Start the application and test the buttons.

4. End the application and save the project group.

Adding Properties

Microsoft ✓ *Exam* *Objective*

Create ActiveX controls.

▪ Create an ActiveX control that exposes properties.

You will add custom properties to your control in the same way that you added properties to your components. Using property procedures, you can create custom attributes for your ActiveX control. You can also allow properties of the constituent controls contained in your custom control to be manipulated by creating custom properties that map to the constituent properties.

Also as with components, you will use the Property Let procedure to assign a value to a property and the Property Get procedure to retrieve a property value. These property procedures should be familiar to you already, having implemented them in your business tier components.

> If you are unfamiliar with the use of property procedures and have not yet reviewed Chapter 4 of this book, please do so before continuing.

Because the properties of constituent controls are not directly visible to the custom ActiveX control, you must add custom properties to the ActiveX control that allow you to manipulate the constituent objects. This will assist you in defining the properties and methods of your control.

For example, suppose you created a custom control with two constituent controls, both text boxes. You wish to give the user the ability to change the text in either constituent text box through custom ActiveX control properties. Suppose you intend to use the control to capture data input from the user such as a first name and a last name. You will include a command button that raises a message box echoing information back to the user. The ActiveX control designer might look like Figure 5.2.

FIGURE 5.2

A control designer with multiple constituent controls

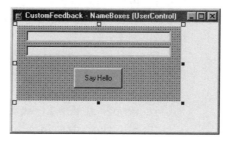

The control designer above implements essential property values as presented in Table 5.1.

T A B L E 5.1	Constituent Control	Property	Value
Properties of the Constituent Controls from Figure 5.2	Control	Name	NameBoxes
	First text box	Name	txtFirst
	First text box	Text	Null
	Second text box	Name	txtLast
	Second text box	Text	Null
	Command button	Name	cmdHello
	Command button	Caption	Say Hello

If you want to give the user of your custom control access to the text properties of the two text boxes in your control, you must create custom properties and perform the manipulation of the constituent control's properties inside these custom properties.

For example, you might create two custom properties called *FirstText* and *LastText* in your control. Inside the property procedures for these properties, you will read and write the text properties of the text boxes in the control designer. The following code illustrates how you might create the FirstText property.

```
Public Property Get FirstText() As String
        ' Returns the contents of the text box to the
property
    FirstText = txtFirst.Text
End Property

Public Property Let FirstText(FirstName As String)
    ' Sets the text in the text box based on the property
    txtFirst.Text = FirstName
    PropertyChanged FirstText
End Property
```

The PropertyChanged method of the UserControl object sends a notification to the ActiveX control's container, such as the form, that a property has been modified. This is necessary whenever you modify a property to keep the container's list of dirty property values coordinated with actual property activity.

If you were to test this control on a form at this point, the Properties window would reflect the new property just added in addition to all of the standard properties supported by an ActiveX control. Figure 5.3 illustrates how this Properties window might look. Notice the custom property called FirstText in the Properties window.

FIGURE 5.3

The NameBoxes
Properties window

Modifying Properties through Methods

Occasionally, you will wish to provide the user with the ability to change the properties of constituent controls through methods rather than actually making direct modifications to the properties. A good example of this behavior is the Move method of a Visual Basic form. The Move method has four arguments, namely left, top, width, and height. With the Move method, you can set all four of these form properties in one method call.

In our example, we may want to add a method called Clear. This method clears the contents of each of the constituent text boxes and informs the system that the FirstText and LastText properties have been changed. An example of this Clear method appears in the following code.

```
Public Sub Clear()
    txtFirst.Text = vbNullString
    txtLast.Text = vbNullString
    PropertyChanged FirstText
    PropertyChanged LastText
End Sub
```

Exercise 5.5 walks you through the process of creating a new ActiveX control project with the NameBoxes control described above. We will make future modifications to this control in later exercises.

EXERCISE 5.5

Creating ActiveX Controls with Properties

1. If it's not already running, start Visual Basic. When prompted for a project template type, select ActiveX Control and click Open. Change the name of the project to NameBoxes.

2. Add two text boxes and a command button to the UserControl designer as illustrated previously in Figure 5.2. Set properties of these constituent controls as described in Table 5.1.

3. Add a property called FirstText to the control by creating two property procedures that manipulate the text property of txtFirst. Use the following code as an example.

```
Public Property Let FirstText(FirstName As String)
    txtFirst.Text = FirstName
    PropertyChanged FirstText
End Property
Public Property Get FirstText() As String
    FirstText = txtFirst.Text
End Property
```

4. Repeat step 3, creating a new property called LastText that manipulates the text property of txtLast. Use the following code as an example.

```
Public Property Let LastText(LastName As String)
    txtLast.Text = LastName
    PropertyChanged LastText
End Property
Public Property Get LastText() As String
    LastText = txtLast.Text
End Property
```

5. Add a method of the control called Clear. In this method, clear the contents of the txtFirst and txtLast text boxes. Make sure that you write code to inform the container that these properties have changed. Use the following code as an example.

```
Public Sub Clear()
    txtFirst.Text = vbNullString
    txtLast.Text = vbNullString
    PropertyChanged FirstText
    PropertyChanged LastText
End Sub
```

6. Add code to the cmdHello command button click event that creates a message box saying hello to the individual named in the text boxes. If there is no entry in the text boxes, create a message box asking the user to enter data and try again. Use the following code as an example.

```
Private Sub cmdHello_Click()
    Dim strMessage As String
    If txtFirst.Text = vbNullString Then
        strMessage = "Please enter a first name!"
    ElseIf txtLast.Text = vbNullString Then
        strMessage = "Please enter a last name!"
    Else
        strMessage = "Hello there " + txtFirst.Text + _
            " " + txtLast.Text + "!"
    End If
    MsgBox strMessage
End Sub
```

7. To test the control, add a new Standard EXE project to the project group. Set the new Standard EXE project as the Start Up project. Create an instance of the new custom control on the form. Remember that you must close the form designer before you will be able to add the control to the form. Look at the Properties window for the new instance of the control that you created. You should see that the name of the control is NameBoxes1. Also note that there are two custom properties in this window called FirstText and LastText.

8. Run the project group and enter names in the text boxes. Click the Say Hello button and note the message box that is returned. Stop the application.

9. Below the custom control on the form designer, add another command button. Name this button cmdClear and set the caption to Clear. In the click event of this command button, call the Clear method of NameBoxes1. Use the following code as a guide.

```
Private Sub cmdClear_Click()
    NameBoxes1.Clear
End Sub
```

10. Run the application. Enter text in the two text boxes and click the clear button. The text should disappear. End the application.

11. In the Project window, right-click the Standard EXE project and select Remove Project from the menu. Do not save changes to the project. From the Visual Basic menu, select Project ➤ Project1 Properties. In the Project Name text box, type **DataControls**.

12. Create a directory on your hard disk called DataControls. Save the project in this directory. Do not save the group file.

The ActiveX Control Life Cycle

Microsoft ✔ *Exam Objective*

Create ActiveX controls.

- Use control events to save and load persistent properties.

Although it may appear that when you place a control on a form this control becomes a permanent part of that form, that is not actually the case. In reality, ActiveX controls continually go through a process of being destroyed and re-created. In addition, unlike standard applications that support only two distinct states, namely design-time and runtime, the ActiveX control supports three states.

Design-time   The state in which you create the control, designing all of its interface elements, properties, methods, and events. This state is similar to the design-time of a standard application.

Runtime   The state of the control when the container application is in runtime. The control code executes through its properties, methods, and events in this state. Both the control and the client are in runtime.

Implement-time   This state is unique to an ActiveX control. It is the state where the client application is in design mode but is implementing the ActiveX control previously created. This is actually a runtime state for the ActiveX control, as is illustrated in the previous exercise. Remember when you implemented the Clock control on the Standard form, the ActiveX control was actually running, although the Standard EXE project was in design-time. This can be verified by the fact that the clock was running even before the form entered runtime. This is also why you had to close the UserControl designer before you were able to implement the clock on the form.

WARNING   The term *implement-time* is not an official Microsoft term. It is a term that I use to describe this particular state of a control, but you will not see this term on the exam or in any official documentation. Microsoft has no official term for this state in which the ActiveX control is in runtime, but the application is in design-time. This state is distinct, however, because, in it, the control does not have the ability to execute methods or fire events (with the exception of a few specialized events that fire when the control changes states, as will be discussed later in this chapter).

As an application that contains an ActiveX control moves between implement-time and runtime, the instance of the control on the form is being destroyed and re-created. This means that any properties to which you give design-time value must be reset with those values as the new instance is created.

To make it easier, just remember that an instance of an ActiveX control is not able to withstand the transition between states. Every time the application moves from one state to another, any instance of an ActiveX control that is in that application must be destroyed and re-created in the new instance.

This destruction and re-creation means that any values associated with the custom properties of an ActiveX control are lost when the control changes states. Exercise 5.6 illustrates this behavior using the NameBoxes control created in the previous exercise.

EXERCISE 5.6

Monitoring Custom Properties Across States

1. If necessary, start Visual Basic and open the DataControls project created in the previous exercise. Add a Standard EXE project to the project group and open the form designer for Form1.

2. Add an instance of the NameBoxes control to the form. With the ActiveX control selected in the form, provide new values for the First-Text and LastText properties. You should see the values appear in the text boxes as you complete the entry in the Properties window.

3. In the Project window, set the new Standard EXE project as the Startup project. Run the project. Note that the values entered in the Properties window are no longer present.

4. End the project. Note again that the FirstText and LastText properties in the Properties window are empty. Remove the instance of the NameBoxes control from Form1.

5. Leave Visual Basic running with the project group intact in preparation for the next exercise.

To allow properties to be persistent across states in the control, certain events are fired as the control moves between application states and the control instances are created and destroyed. Table 5.2 illustrates the events that fire as the control moves through its life cycle. You can use these events to save and restore properties for each instance of the control.

T A B L E 5.2 Events in the ActiveX Control Life Cycle	**User Activity**	**Events**
	User adds a control to a form or designer. Control enters implement-time.	Initialize InitProperties Resize Paint
	Application executes. Control enters runtime.	WriteProperties Terminate Initialize Resize ReadProperties Paint
	Application terminates. Control re-enters implement-time.	Terminate Initialize Resize ReadProperties Paint
	Form designer containing the control is closed. Implement-time instance of the control is destroyed.	WriteProperties Terminate
	Compiled application executes. Runtime instance of the control is created.	Initialize ReadProperties Resize Paint

Using the PropertyBag

As we can see from the table above, certain events always take place as the ActiveX control moves between states. You can use some of these events, such as ReadProperties and WriteProperties, to save custom properties as the control moves between states. However, you must have somewhere that you can place these property values as the control is destroyed and is re-created.

Unlike the control, this location must be persistent across states and still be visible by the control.

To accomplish this, both the ReadProperties and WriteProperties events expose an object called the PropertyBag as a parameter passed into the event. The contents of the PropertyBag are persistent across all states of the control and specific to each instance of the control placed in the form. You read and write custom property values to the PropertyBag with the ReadProperty and WriteProperty methods of the PropertyBag object.

From the WriteProperties event, you can use the WriteProperty method to save custom property values before the change in states destroys the instance of the ActiveX control. The syntax of the WriteProperty method is as follows.

```
PropBag.WriteProperty (Name, Value[, DefaultValue])
```

While providing a default value is optional, using this parameter can make your application more efficient. When a default value is provided and the current property value is the same as the default, the value need not be written to the PropertyBag.

In our example, we have two properties, FirstText and LastText, that you must save before the control is destroyed. Using the WriteProperties event, you can save the custom property values into the PropertyBag as in the following example.

```
Private Sub UserControl_WriteProperties(PropBag As
PropertyBag)
    PropBag.WriteProperty "FirstText", txtFirst.Text,
vbNullString
    PropBag.WriteProperty "LastText", txtLast.Text,
vbNullString
End Sub
```

Once you have saved the properties in the PropertyBag, you can retrieve them after the form reinstantiates the control as the form enters runtime. You use the ReadProperties event for this task. When reading properties from the PropertyBag, you will set an internal variable or the appropriate constituent control property value equal to the custom property retrieved from the PropertyBag as seen in the following syntax.

```
Variable = object.ReadProperty (Name[, DefaultValue])
```

In our example, we must retrieve the saved custom property values from the PropertyBag and place them in the appropriate text boxes in our ActiveX control. The following code example illustrates how this can be done.

```
Private Sub UserControl_ReadProperties(PropBag As
PropertyBag)
    txtFirst.Text = PropBag.ReadProperty("FirstText",
vbNullString)
    txtLast.Text = PropBag.ReadProperty("LastText",
vbNullString)
End Sub
```

In Exercise 5.7, you will add the code to the ReadProperties and Write-Properties events to provide persistence for your custom properties in the NameBoxes control created in the previous exercise.

EXERCISE 5.7

Adding Property Persistence

1. From the Project window in Visual Basic, double-click the NameBoxes icon to activate control designer. Double-click the designer to activate the code window.

2. Navigate to the WriteProperties event of the UserControl object. Add the following code to the event to save the properties in the PropertyBag.

   ```
   PropBag.WriteProperty "FirstText", txtFirst.Text,
   vbNullString
   PropBag.WriteProperty "LastText", txtLast.Text,
   vbNullString
   ```

3. Navigate to the ReadProperties event and add the following code to read the property values from the PropertyBag into the appropriate text boxes.

   ```
   txtFirst.Text = PropBag.ReadProperty("FirstText",
   vbNullString)
   txtLast.Text = PropBag.ReadProperty("LastText",
   vbNullString)
   ```

4. Close the code window and the control designer. Place an instance of the control inside Form1. In the Properties window for the control, enter data for the FirstText and LastText properties.

5. Run the application. You should still see the values that you entered in the Text Boxes event though the control changed states. Make a change to one of the text boxes. End the application.

6. In the Properties window, you should still see the data that you originally entered into the Properties window rather than the changes that you made to the text box as the application was running. This is because the WriteProperties event does not occur as the application exits runtime.

7. Remove the instance of the NameBoxes control from the form and save the project. Leave the project open in Visual Basic in preparation for later exercises.

Adding Events

As with the components discussed in Chapter 4, custom controls can also recognize events. These events can be events that you fire from methods of your control, or they can be fired from within the events supported by constituent controls. Either way, the approach is the same.

Just as with components, to create custom events you will first declare the event from the General Declarations section of your control. You can then raise the event in the appropriate location in your control's code.

In our example, we have two text boxes called txtFirst and txtLast. Each of these text boxes supports a Change event. As with the properties of the custom control, these events are not directly accessible when the control is in implement-time or runtime. You must create custom events and fire these from the events of the constituent controls.

In this case, we might actually create two events, one when the txtFirst text box changes its contents and one when the txtLast text box changes. Exercise 5.8 implements these events in the NameBoxes control.

EXERCISE 5.8

Implementing Custom Events

1. Open the designer for the NameBoxes control and double-click to activate the code window. Navigate to the General Declarations Section of the code.

2. In the General Declarations section, declare two public events called FirstChange and LastChange respectively. Use the following code as an example.

```
Public Event FirstChange()
Public Event LastChange()
```

3. Navigate to the txtFirst_Change event. In this event, write code to inform the container that the FirstText property has changed and raise the FirstChange event. Use the following code as an example.

```
PropertyChanged FirstText
RaiseEvent FirstChange
```

4. Repeat for the txtLast_Change event. Write code to inform the container that the LastText property has changed and raise the LastChange event. Use the following code as an example.

```
PropertyChanged LastText
RaiseEvent LastChange
```

5. Close the code window and the control designer. Place an instance of the ActiveX control on the form from Project1. Double-click the control to open a code window for the form.

6. Navigate to the NameBoxes1_FirstChange event. Write code in this event to raise a message box stating that the event has been fired. Repeat the process for the NameBoxes1_LastChange event.

7. Run the application and enter a value in the first text box. The event will fire and raise the message box for you. Repeat for the second text box. This should again raise a message box for you.

8. Stop the application. In the NameBoxes1_FirstChange event, remove the message box statement. Repeat for the NameBoxes1_LastChange event. Remove the instance of the control from the form. Save the project.

Property Pages

Microsoft
✓ *Exam*
Objective

Create Active X Controls

- Create and enable Property Pages for an ActiveX control.

With the release of the Windows 95 interface, Microsoft introduced many new user interface design elements that added more functionality for the user. The goal of the revised user interface was to provide an environment where the user could interact with objects efficiently.

One problem with the pre-Windows 95 interface was that users weren't able to interact with objects using a single dialog box or menu. Very often, the user would have to open multiple dialogs or access multiple menus to work with a single object.

Property Pages were designed to handle this common complaint. A Property Page is a dialog that enumerates the properties of an object. Property Pages are often grouped together into sets of tabbed pages available from a single dialog box. Figure 5.4 illustrates the collection of Property Pages for the Microsoft Comm control. You would use this control to manipulate communications ports. To access Property Pages, you would typically click on the object with the right mouse button and select *Properties* from the popup menu.

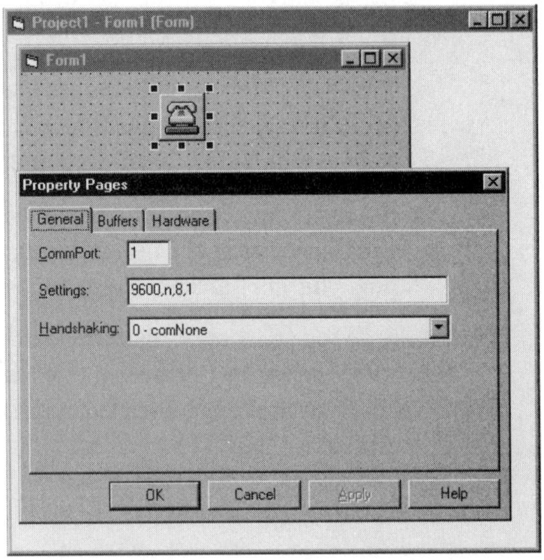

FIGURE 5.4

Property Pages for the
Microsoft Comm
control

Using the Property Page Wizard

The easiest way to add Property Pages to a Visual Basic project is with the Property Page Wizard. The wizard is an add-in to Visual Basic. Before you can use the wizard, you must load the add-in. To load the add-in, select Add-Ins ➤ Add-In Manager from the Visual Basic menu. This will present you with a list of available add-ins. Select the Property Page Wizard from the list and select the Loaded/Unloaded checkbox as pictured in Figure 5.5. After you select the OK button, the Property Page Wizard will be available in the Add-Ins menu.

FIGURE 5.5

The Add-In Manager

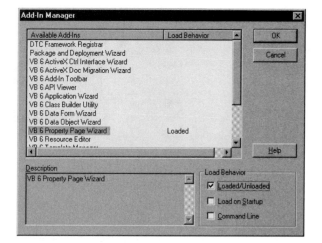

You will only be able to launch the Property Page Wizard if the active project contains a UserControl object.

The following set of figures illustrates the implementation of the Property Page Wizard using a simple custom ActiveX control as an example. This control consists of a text box placed on a UserControl object. Only one custom property, the text property, has been added. This property assigns the text of the text box to the text property of the ActiveX control.

The first form of the wizard is a simple introduction page informing you of the purpose of the wizard that you are running. If you don't want to see this form again, click the checkbox next to the statement, "Skip this screen in the future."

The next dialog allows us to add Property Pages for this control. Remember that a properties dialog usually consists of multiple pages, but in this example we will only add a single page. Click the Add button to add a Property Page. You will be asked to name the page, which for this example we have left at the default name of PropertyPage1. The completed dialog is illustrated in Figure 5.6

FIGURE 5.6

Adding Property
Pages with the wizard

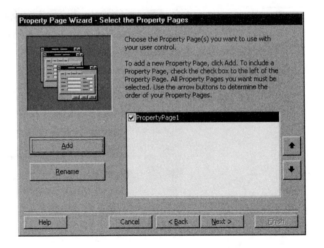

Clicking the Next button takes us to the Add Properties form. The list of available custom properties will be in the list box on the left of the form. To add support for this property to the Property Page, move the property from the left to the right by double-clicking or using the right arrow buttons in the center of the form. In our example, we have only one custom property, which has been added to the PropertyPage1 list on the right as illustrated in Figure 5.7.

Clicking the Next button will take you to the end of the Property Page wizard. The final form presents the Finish button that you will click when ready to complete building the Property Page. After completing the Property Page wizard, you should now see a Property Page listed in the Project window for the ActiveX control project.

FIGURE 5.7

Adding properties to
Property Pages

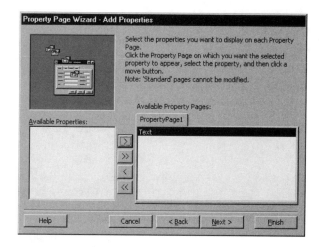

 To test your new Property Page, create an instance of the ActiveX control on a form and right-click to activate the popup menu. Select Properties from the menu. This will display your Property Page.

Using Built-In Property Pages

In our example, the wizard both created the Property Pages and connected them to the user control. In addition to your own custom Property Pages, you can also add support for some Property Pages that are built-in to Visual Basic. These are the StandardFont, StandardColor, StandardPicture, and StandardDataFormat.

To add these Property Pages to your project, access the properties of the UserControl object in the Properties window and locate the PropertyPages property. When the property is selected, a builder button appears on the right side of the text box next to the property as pictured in Figure 5.7. Click this button to access a dialog with a list of all the available Property Pages. Click on the checkbox next to the desired Property Pages to connect them to the control, as shown in Figure 5.8.

F I G U R E   5.8

The PropertyPages
property of the
UserControl

F I G U R E   5.9

Connecting
PropertyPages to a
UserControl

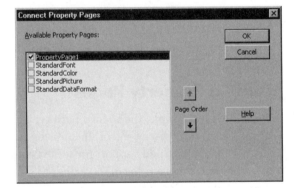

This form can also be used to enable other Property Pages for a UserControl
object. If you have many custom controls that use the same properties, you
might consider creating a common set of Property Pages and adding them
to each project. Once they have been added to the project, you can use the
Connect Property Pages dialog to enable them as needed.

ActiveX Controls and Data Binding

Numerous controls in Visual Basic support the ability to bind to data controls or data environments. This can be a very helpful feature, as it allows easy connectivity to all kinds of data storage.

Visual Basic 6.0 allows you to interact with data by providing this data binding in your own controls. Your controls can either act as data consumers or data providers. This means that you can either create controls that will be bound to data sources or you can create controls to which data consumers will be bound.

This section discusses the process of creating both data consumers and data providers. We will first address the issue of creating data consumers, sometimes known as data bound controls.

Creating Data Bound Controls

Microsoft ✓ *Exam* *Objective*

Create ActiveX controls.

- Enable the data-binding capabilities of an ActiveX control.

You can make an ActiveX control bindable to a data source by including the properties of the control you wish to be data bound in the DataBindings collection of the control. Every DataBindings collection has one property that is identified as the DataField property of the data bound control. After identifying this DataField property, you can add additional properties to the DataBindings collection of the control. This process is most easily accomplished by using the Procedure Attributes dialog pictured in Figure 5.10.

Figure 5.10 illustrates the appropriate Property Attributes dialog setting for adding the FirstText property to the DataBindings collection as the DataField property. You will notice that in the Data Binding section of the Procedure Attributes dialog, the property is identified as data bound and as the DataField property. You can only identify one property per control as the DataField property although the control can contain many data bound properties.

FIGURE 5.10

The Procedure
Attributes dialog

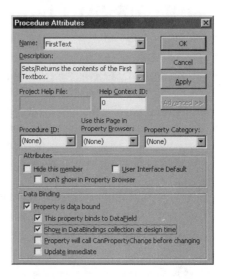

In addition to identifying the properties as data bound, some minor modifications must be made to the code that implements the properties. The Property Let procedure modifies the property value, and that property should now interact with the data provider. You must interrogate the data provider as to whether it will allow the new property value to be written to the underlying data source.

You can do this by calling the CanPropertyChange method from within the Property Let procedure. The result of this call will depend on the data provider, but calling the method allows the ActiveX control and the data provider to negotiate this update behavior with no more intervention on your part. The code below illustrates how you should do this.

```
If CanPropertyChange("FirstText") Then
    txtFirst.Text = FirstName
End If
```

Exercise 5.9 illustrates the process of adding two data bound properties to the NameBoxes control. The FirstText property will set as the DataField property and the LastText property will be added to the DataBindings collection through the Procedure Attributes dialog. You will then test this control using the ADO Data Control.

Implementing Data Binding

1. Open the designer for the NameBoxes control. From the Visual Basic menu, select Tools ➤ Procedure Attributes. Select the FirstText property from the Name list. Click the Advanced button to display the Data Binding section of the dialog.

2. Complete the dialog as pictured in Figure 5.4. After completing the dialog, select the LastText property from the Name list. Complete the dialog as pictured in the following graphic.

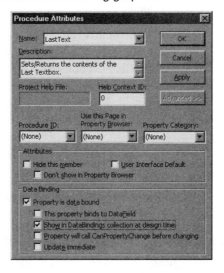

3. Click the OK button to save the Procedure attributes.

4. Open the code window for the control designer. Navigate to the Public Property Let FirstText procedure. Add the call to the CanProperty-Change method as illustrated in the following code.

```
If CanPropertyChange("FirstText") Then
    txtFirst.Text = FirstName
End If
```

5. Repeat the process by adding the call to the CanPropertyChange method in the Public Property Let LastText procedure.

6. Close the code window for the control and the control designer. Add a data control to the form. In the properties window, set the Database-Name property to `C:\Program Files\Microsoft Visual Studio\VB98\Nwind.mdb`. Set the RecordSource property to Employees.

7. Add an instance of the NameBoxes control to the form. Locate the DataBindings property in the Properties window. When you click on this property you will see a builder button (three dots) appear on the right of the property. Click this button to activate the Data Bindings dialog.

8. In the Property Name list box on the left of the dialog, select FirstText. On the right, open the Data Source list box and select Data1. In the Data Field list box select FirstName

9. Repeat the process for the LastText property. Select Data1 from the Data Source list and LastName from the Field List dialog. Click OK on the Data Bindings dialog.

10. Run the application. The NameBoxes control should display the data from the employees table in the Northwind database.

11. End the application and save the project. Close Visual Basic.

Creating a Data Provider Control

Microsoft ✓ ***Exam Objective***

Create ActiveX controls.

- Create an ActiveX control that is a data source.

Sometimes you may need your application to provide access to specific data sets. Rather than require your developer to implement ADO code or configure a standard data control, you can create your own data provider. To do this, you must place data access code inside an ActiveX control and set control properties to allow data clients to access data through the control.

An ActiveX control supports a property called DataSourceBehavior. By setting this property's value to vbDataSource, the control exposes data binding support and can act as the data source for a data bound control.

Since you already know the basis of ADO code, creating a data provider should look very familiar. Exercise 5.10 walks you through the process of creating a data provider control that accesses data from the pubs database on your SQL Server.

EXERCISE 5.10

Creating a Data Provider Control

1. Start Visual Basic and select the ActiveX control template when prompted. From the Properties window, set the DataSourceBehavior property to vbDataSource.

2. Double-click the control designer to open the code window for the control. Add a reference to the ActiveX Data Objects 2.0 library. From the Visual Basic menu, select Project ➤ References. Locate the Microsoft ActiveX Data Objects 2.0 Library from the list and click the check box to select this reference. Click OK to close the dialog.

3. Navigate to the General Declarations section of the control. Declare private variables for the Connection and Recordset objects. Use the following code as an example.

```
Private cn As ADODB.Connection
Private rs As ADODB.Recordset
```

4. Navigate to the UserControl_Initialize event. Write code in this event to connect to the data source and create a new recordset. The recordset should select all of the data from the authors table in the database. Use the following code as an example.

```
Set cn = New ADODB.Connection
Set rs = New ADODB.Recordset
With cn
.ConnectionTimeout = 30
.CommandTimeOut = 30
.Provider = "sqloledb"
.ConnectionString = "server=<your server>;uid=sa;pwd="
```

```
.Open
.DefaultDatabase = "Pubs"
End With
With rs
    .Source = "Authors"
    .ActiveConnection = cn
    .CursorType = adOpenKeyset
    .CursorLocation = adUseServer
    .LockType = adLockPessimistic
    .Open Options:=adCmdTable
End With
```

5. Navigate to the UserControl_GetDataMember event. Notice the parameters that are passed into the procedure. This procedure is executed whenever the bound control requests data. In this event, write code that sets the Data parameter equal to the recordset that you created in the previous step. Use the following code as an example.

```
Set Data = rs
```

6. Close the code window. Add four command buttons to the form. Name these buttons cmdFirst, cmdPrevious, cmdNext, and cmdLast. Arrange and caption them as illustrated in the following graphic. Reduce the size of the designer to fit the command buttons. Name the control Data_Authors.

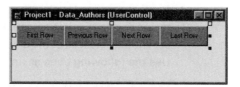

7. In the click event of the cmdFirst command button, write code to navigate to the first record of the recordset. Repeat for each button. Use the following code as an example.

```
Private Sub cmdFirst_Click()
    rs.MoveFirst
End Sub
```

```
Private Sub cmdLast_Click()
    rs.MoveLast
End Sub
Private Sub cmdNext_Click()
    rs.MoveNext
    If rs.EOF Then
        rs.MoveLast
    End If
End Sub
Private Sub cmdPrevious_Click()
    rs.MovePrevious
    If rs.BOF Then
        rs.MoveFirst
    End If
End Sub
```

8. Close the code window and the control designer. Add a new Standard EXE project to the project group and set it as the Start Up project. Add an instance of the Data_Authors control to the form.

9. Add a text box to the form. Set the DataSource property of the text box to Data_Authors1. Set the DataField property to au_fname.

10. Run the application. Click the buttons to navigate through the recordset. End the application and close Visual Basic.

Compiling Controls

When you compile an ActiveX control, the contents of the ActiveX control project are compiled into a file with an OCX extension. These controls can be used in Visual Basic applications, VBA applications, and Web pages whenever the services utilized by the controls are supported.

To compile the control, select File ➤ Make Project OCX from the Visual Basic menu. The resulting control is automatically registered with the computer upon which it is compiled. To distribute the control, use the Package & Deployment Wizard or a third party installation utility that will register the control with the local system.

Summary

In this chapter, we looked at the process of creating simple ActiveX controls. While this topic is primarily related to the design and implementation of desktop applications, there are times when you might wish to create custom controls for your Visual Basic client application.

We learned how to create controls that support custom properties and events. By providing custom properties and events in this way we can expose the attributes and events of underlying constituent controls that make up our custom object.

When data is required, the ActiveX control can be created to support either the data consumer or the data provider. While it may take a little bit of code to implement a robust control, ActiveX controls are easier than ever before to create, thanks to Visual Basic 6.0.

Review Questions

1. The Visual Basic project file that stores the design of a UserControl ends with which extension?

   A. .ctx

   B. .ocx

   C. .ctl

   D. .uct

2. Which event should you use to store property values into the PropertyBag?

   A. Terminate

   B. ReadProperties

   C. WriteProperties

   D. SaveProperties

3. Which of the following ActiveX control events does not occur as the application hosting the control is terminated?

A. Terminate

B. ReadProperties

C. WriteProperties

D. Resize

4. Which of the following situations would not cause the Initialize event of an ActiveX control to occur?

A. When a control is placed on a form at design-time

B. When a form designer containing a control is closed

C. When a compiled application containing a control executes

D. When an application terminates and re-enters design-time for the host application

5. Which of the following methods is used to inform an ActiveX control's container that one of its properties has been modified?

A. CanPropertyChange

B. PropertyModify

C. Property_Change

D. PropertyChanged

6. Which collection of an ActiveX control enumerates all of the properties that can be bound to a data source?

A. DataFields

B. DataMembers

C. DataBindings

D. DataProperties

7. Which event of an ActiveX control data provider runs every time a bound control extracts data through the provider?

A. GetDataMember

B. GetDataField

C. GetDataProperty

D. GetDataRow

8. Which event from the list below occurs only once in the entire life cycle of an ActiveX control?

A. Initialize

B. Resize

C. Terminate

D. InitProperties

9. Which parameter of the WriteProperty method can be omitted but should be included to increase the efficiency of the control?

A. Name

B. Value

C. PropBag

D. DefaultValue

10. Which method of an ActiveX control is used to interrogate a data provider for data update support?

A. CanPropertyUpdate

B. CanPropertyChange

C. PropertyModify

D. Updateable

11. Which event should be used to resize an ActiveX control as the user modifies the size of the control implementation on a form?

   A. Resize

   B. Paint

   C. Initialize

   D. SizeChanged

12. Which Visual Basic dialog box is used to expose the data binding in a data consumer control?

   A. DataBindings

   B. Data members

   C. Procedure bindings

   D. Procedure attributes

CHAPTER

6

Designing and Implementing the Presentation Tier

As highlighted in the first chapter of this book, a well-designed distributed application disperses both its logic and processing to other computers. The division is based upon a reasoned analysis of business process needs and resource opportunities. The presentation tier has several responsibilities. The central objective is to provide a local process that ensures valid and reliable data entry and retrieval.

The keys to implementing a functional data client are twofold: an intuitive and consistent user interface and certain data handling functions. This chapter will present the key skills needed to develop an effective presentation tier. In particular, this chapter will present the basic procedures to be followed in constructing the forms used in accessing remote data sources. Chapters 7 and 8 will cover the essential skills for connecting the client application with remote business objects and data stores.

Presentation Fundamentals: Forms, Controls, Events, and Data Display

We begin with the tools of generating the user interface: the forms, controls, and other visual elements that communicate context, meaning, and functionality to the user. Over the last ten years, the set of Windows-standard user-interface elements available to developers has increased dramatically. Each of these tools has strengths that set it apart when used for the right jobs. Carefully tailoring the user interface to the business needs of the application doesn't just improve the aesthetics of an application, it can also reduce errors in data entry and interpretation. Let's begin with the basics: a new form.

Working with Forms

Forms are the core of the visual interface. They are the screens shown in windows and dialog boxes. They are created at design time and then displayed to the user based on events in the program's operation. The contents and properties of forms can also be modified programmatically at runtime.

Adding Forms

Unlike the component projects described earlier, presentation tier projects are built on Standard EXE templates. To create a new Standard EXE project, launch Visual Basic. You will be presented with a series of templates to select from (see Figure 6.1). Exercise 6.1 takes you through the process of creating a new project.

F I G U R E 6.1

The New Project dialog

This initial form is set by default as the project's Startup Object. Since Visual Basic applications are event driven, one object has to be started when the application launches to set the stage for events to follow.

EXERCISE 6.1

Creating a New Project

1. To create a new Visual Basic EXE project, click Start ➤ Programs ➤ Microsoft Visual Studio 6.0 ➤ Microsoft Visual Basic 6.0.

EXERCISE 6.1 (CONTINUED)

2. In the New Project dialog, select Standard EXE and click OK. Your new project is created and displayed, beginning with a new blank form.

3. From the Project menu, select Project ➤ Project1 Properties.

4. In the Project Properties dialog, on the General tab, click the Project Name field, and replace Project1 by entering a name such as Royalties_Calc.

5. In the Project window, right-click Form1 and select Properties from the pop-up menu.

6. Click the Properties window to the right of the (Name) property, and type a form name such as frmAuthorsList.

Applications rarely have only one form. Most business needs are sufficiently complex to require grouping them by function on two or more forms. To allow your application to remain uncluttered and tailor screens to different functions, you will need to add additional forms to your project. Exercise 6.2 takes you through the steps of adding a second form to your project.

EXERCISE 6.2

Adding a Second Form

1. Open the Royalties_Calc project.

2. Select Project ➤ Add Form.

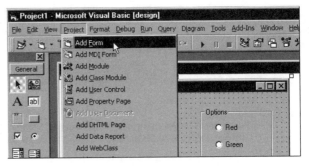

3. Rename the new form frmRoyaltiesCalc.

Forms should always be renamed immediately upon creation because all Form event procedures are coded to the form name. If the form is renamed after any events are coded, those procedures become orphaned.

Figure 6.2 shows the Project window for our royalties calculation application. Note that we have renamed the project and both of the forms. All Form events will now reference the new form names rather than Form1 and Form2.

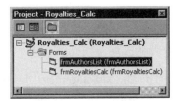

FIGURE 6.2

Royalties Calculator Project window

By convention, we have preceded our form names with the prefix "frm." This convention allows you to tell the difference in your code windows between forms, components, or other objects that might otherwise have similar names.

Multiple forms are loaded and managed programmatically. The primary methods used to initialize, open, and close a form inside a window or dialog include the Load and Unload statements and the Show and Hide methods of the Form object. We will discuss the use of these tools here, but we will not implement them in our sample application until we get further into the process of coding the functionality of the forms.

Opening and Closing Forms

To open a form procedurally, use the following code to call the Show method of the Form object. The code may be called in many ways, such as with the click event of a button on another form or by being called from a menu item.

```
frmNewForm.Show
```

The Load statement reads the form definition, initializes any variables associated with the form, and makes the form's methods and properties available to other parts of the running application. If not previously loaded, the Show method performs all actions of the Load statement, additionally opening a window for display of the form. The Load statement is called using the following code:

```
Load frmNewForm
```

Calling the Hide method of a form will close the window containing that form but leave the form and its variables in memory. The Hide method is functionally equivalent to setting the form's Visible property to False. To the user, the form appears to have been destroyed. The code to call this method is:

```
FrmNewForm.Hide
```

The Unload statement closes the form's window and removes the form and its variables from memory. The Unload statement is called using the following code:

```
Unload frmNewForm
```

Optionally, the keyword Me can be used to reference the current form. Using this syntax prevents incorrect references when multiple instances of the same form are running at the same time. The Me keyword is used in this way:

```
Unload me
```

Because unloading a form destroys all variables associated with the form, you should plan your design carefully to prevent the inadvertent deletion of variables that may be needed later. There are two primary means of preventing such problems. The easier but less efficient method is to consistently hide forms instead of unloading them. This will ensure that any needed variables are maintained; however, if a user later performs some operation that returns the screen, prior values will be returned (unless explicitly avoided by creating a new instance of the form). This may not be the intended result. This method also wastes resources, as the memory used by the form and its variables are never released. Repeatedly spawning new instances of forms or other objects without destroying previous instances is a very bad practice. The applications you write will require huge amounts of RAM and will eventually give the users "Out of Memory" messages.

The second means of supervising the timing of form unloading is to use the form's QueryUnload event. The QueryUnload event occurs when a form is unloaded, and it allows you to determine which technique was used to close the form and gives you time to cancel the Unload operation, if necessary.

Working with Controls

Blank forms are no more helpful than a command line interface. It is only when forms are combined with graphical objects and tools that forms become useful. Visual Basic comes with a number of standard controls that allow users to interact with data and application states.

Adding Controls to a Form

Microsoft
Exam
Objective

Implement navigational design.

- Add controls to forms.

You begin building the user interface elements by placing these controls on the forms you have created. Figure 6.3 shows the standard Visual Basic 6 toolbox from which you select controls.

FIGURE 6.3

The Visual Basic toolbox

There are two ways to add these controls to your forms. You can click a control in the toolbox to select it, then click and drag across the form to draw the outline of the control. Or, you can double-click on the toolbox control, which will automatically place an instance of the control in the center of the form. The double-click method is quicker to use, but requires manual resizing and placement on the form. Which method you use is essentially a matter of personal preference. Figures 6.4 and 6.5 illustrate the click-and-drag and double-click methods, respectively.

FIGURE 6.4

Clicking and dragging to place a control on a form

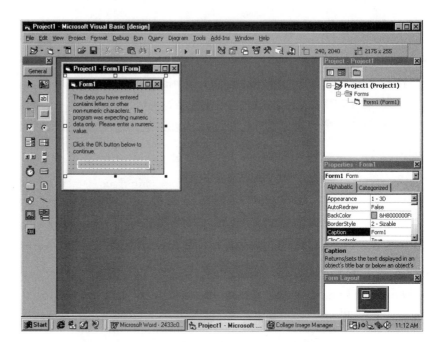

FIGURE 6.5

Double-clicking to place a control on a form

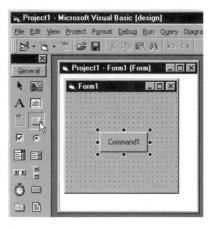

Using Custom Controls

One of the powerful features of Visual Basic is its ability to incorporate custom controls. You can give additional functionality to the Visual Basic environment by adding additional controls to the standard toolbox. Some of these controls are commercial products that you, as a developer, pay to use because they offer unique capabilities not natively supported in Visual Basic. Visual Basic also includes a variety of ActiveX controls that offer unique features for special needs. You may also build ActiveX controls yourself, combining native controls with your code to create a new visual object with custom characteristics and qualities. For more information on building custom ActiveX controls, see Chapter 5, *Creating ActiveX Controls*.

Microsoft ✓ ***Exam Objective***

Add an ActiveX control to the toolbox.

Adding custom ActiveX controls to the toolbox is a simple process requiring only that you open a dialog box showing the components installed on your system and select the components desired for inclusion in the toolbox. When the dialog is closed, the ActiveX controls are placed on the Visual Basic toolbox, and can be used on forms in the same general ways that other controls are used. Exercise 6.3 walks you through this process.

EXERCISE 6.3

Adding an ActiveX Control to the Toolbox

1. Either right-click the toolbox and select Components, or select Project ➢ Components.

2. In the Components dialog, select from the list of registered controls, and click to place a check mark in the box to the left of the control you wish to add.

EXERCISE 6.3 (CONTINUED)

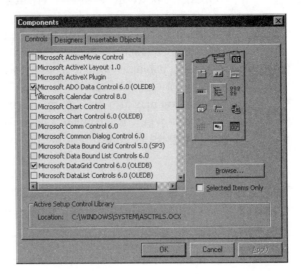

3. Click the OK button to return to the Visual Basic development environment.

If you cannot find the control you are looking for, it may not be installed on your system. If this is the case, follow the steps in Exercise 6.4 to add the needed control to your system registry.

The items available in the components dialog are a listing of all the ActiveX controls installed on your computer. In this case, *installed* means that the control has been registered with the registry on your computer. The registry is a database that is tightly integrated with the Windows 95 and Windows NT operating systems. Among its many responsibilities, the registry maintains a directory of COM components, making it possible to quickly generate a list of controls or find a specific control using COM's unique identifiers.

If the ActiveX control you need doesn't show up in the Controls dialog, you will need to register your control with the registry. Exercise 6.4 walks you through how to register a control.

EXERCISE 6.4

Registering an ActiveX Control

1. Ensure that the .ocx file you want to register has been copied to the local hard disk. Note the file's location (path).

2. Click Start ➢ Run.

3. In the Run dialog that appears, select the Regsvr32 utility and pass the full path to the .ocx file. This can be done in one of two ways:

   - Click the Browse button on the Run dialog and navigate to the .ocx file. When you have selected the desired file, click the Open button to place the literal path into your original Run dialog. Now position your cursor to the left of the Path statement and type **Regsvr32.exe**.

   - Directly call the utility and enter the full path. The path you type should look like this:

   ```
   regsvr32.exe "c:\Windows\system\Graph32.ocx"
   ```

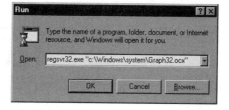

If you are more familiar with the DOS environment, the Regsvr32 utility can also be executed from a DOS command prompt. Remember to either type the full path of the .ocx file or issue the command for the utility from the ActiveX control's directory.

Setting Properties for Visual Basic Controls

Microsoft ✓ ***Exam*** ***Objective***

Implement navigational design.

- Set properties for controls.

Once each control has been placed on a form, its properties can be set and changed. Properties can include visual qualities like size, shape, and color, as well as programmatic qualities like name, data binding information, or how the control will respond to drag-and-drop operations. Properties can be set at design time using the Properties window (see Figure 6.6). This method works for all types of controls, but the specific properties available will change depending upon the control being examined.

FIGURE 6.6

The Properties window

A control's properties can also be set by your application's code at runtime. To set a control's properties, use statements of the form ObjectName.Property = NewValue. For instance, to set the Text property of a textbox control named txtName to "John," the following line of code can be used.

```
txtName.text = "John"
```

This code can be inserted into the click event of a command button or the Form_Load event of the form containing the control. The proper placement of the code depends upon the program execution needs of the application.

If you need to modify several properties of a single control, you can use the With statement for brevity and clarity. The code using the With statement looks like this:

```
With txtName
.Text = "John"
.Width = 2100
.HelpContextID = 57
.Height = 285
End With
```

Each different control type has its own set of properties. To illustrate some of the types of properties available, the following tables list the most commonly used properties of the most fundamental user-interface controls. Properties of the command button control are shown in Table 6.1, while Tables 6.2 and 6.3 list properties of the text box and label controls, respectively. Each property includes a brief description, and default settings, if they exist, are given.

Controls should be renamed shortly after placement on a form. When you script objects, programmatically set properties, or trap events, all code is dependent on the control's name property. If you rename the control after any coding of the control occurs, the prior code will be orphaned and moved to the General Declarations section of the Form module. The code will no longer be tied to the control it was written for.

T A B L E   6.1:   Commonly Used Properties of the Command Button Control

Property Name	Description
(Name)	Sets the programmatic or object name used within Visual Basic to identify the control to other objects. (Default: control type followed by counter [i.e., label1, label2])
Cancel	Setting this property to True maps the Esc key to activate the button. This is usually used for Cancel buttons on forms and dialogs and should only be set to True for one command button per form. (Default: False)
Caption	Holds the string to be printed on the button at runtime. (Default: initial button name)

T A B L E 6.1: Commonly Used Properties of the Command Button Control *(continued)*

Property Name	Description
Default	When the Default property is set to True, a command button becomes the default button on a form. The button's border is restyled to indicate that it will be activated if the Enter key is pressed. Must be set at design time. (Default: False)
Enabled	When set to False, dims a command button to gray and makes it unusable as a button. Contrast this with the Visible property. (Default: True)
Left	Allows you to assign or return the lateral placement of the left edge of the command button relative to the control's container, usually the hosting form or control. (Default: None)
Height	Specifies the linear difference between the top and bottom of the button.
Top	Sets the distance between the top of the form and the upper-inner boundary of the button. The bottom edge of a command button is specified by adding the value of the Top property to the value of the Height property. (Default: None)
Visible	When a button's Visible property is set to False, the button is hidden completely from the user. (Default: True)
Width	Specifies the distance between the left and right button boundaries. The right edge of a button is specified by adding the values of the Left and Width properties.

T A B L E 6.2: Commonly Used Properties of the Text Box Control

Property Name	Description
(Name)	Sets the programmatic name of the control. This name is used in code to reference the control, set properties, trap events, and call methods.
Alignment	Allows you to set the justification of text within the text box to Left, Center, or Right. (Default: Left Alignment)

T A B L E 6.2:   Commonly Used Properties of the Text Box Control *(continued)*

Property Name	Description
CausesValidation	Boolean property that determines whether the control's Validate event is fired when the control loses focus. (Default: True)
DataField	Allows you to set or return the specific field within a data member that a text box will be bound to. See DataSource and DataMember properties. (Default: None)
DataMember	Binds a Textbox control to a data member. Depending on the data source, a data member may represent a table, a data command, or a custom data subset. See DataSource property. (Default: None)
DataSource	Used to bind a Textbox control to a data source. See Chapter 7 for more information on the use of this and other data binding properties. (Default: None)
Enabled	Boolean property that sets the runtime activation status of the control. An enabled text box can be edited by the user. A disabled text box will not respond to any user-generated events. (Default: True)
Height	Specifies the vertical measure of a text box control. (Default: None)
Left	Returns or sets the distance between the internal left edge of a text box and the left edge of its container, usually a form or control. (Default: None)
MultiLine	Boolean property that sets or returns a parameter that specifies whether a Textbox control can accept and display multiple lines of text. Enables a basic word wrap functionality. (Default: False)
PasswordChar	Accepts one character and at runtime forces all characters to be displayed using the specified character. This functionality prevents prying eyes from reading passwords as they are typed. This feature is usually reserved for use in login dialogs or similar forms that require entry of a password. (Default: None)
ScrollBars	Allows you to set and return whether scrollbars are to be included with the textbox if the text should exceed the vertical space viewable within the textbox. Settings include vertical, horizontal, both, and none. (Default: 0-None)
Text	Contains the text entered or displayed in the edit area of a Textbox control. (Default: initial name of the control)

T A B L E 6.2:   Commonly Used Properties of the Text Box Control *(continued)*

Property Name	Description
Top	Returns or sets the distance between the top edge of a Textbox control and the top edge of its container. (Default: None)
Visible	Boolean property that will completely hide a text box from users' view when set to False. (Default: True)
Width	Returns or sets the distance between right and left boundaries of a Textbox control. (Default: None)

T A B L E 6.3:   Commonly Used Properties of the Label Control

Property Name	Description
(Name)	Sets the programmatic name of the control. This name is used in code to reference the control, set properties, trap events, and call methods.
AutoSize	Sets or retrieves the ability of a label control to resize to fit the contents of the Caption property. Boolean property. (Default: False)
Alignment	Allows you to set or retrieve the justification of text within the label to Left, Center, or Right. (Default: Left Alignment)
BackStyle	Sets or retrieves the background style of a label. There are two alternatives for this property, Opaque or Transparent. When set to Transparent, the background color and any graphics are visible behind the label. (Default: 1-Opaque)
BorderStyle	Sets or retrieves the border display setting. A label can have either no border or a fixed single border. If the BorderStyle is set to none, the caption of the label will appear to end users as contained within the form background itself. (Default: 0-None)
Caption	The text visible to users. This is the primary functional property of the Label control, as labels frequently do little other than provide static captions for other controls. (Default: default value of Name property)

T A B L E   6.3:   Commonly Used Properties of the Label Control *(continued)*

Property Name	Description
DataField	Allows you to set or return the specific field within a data member that a Label control will be bound to. See DataSource and DataMember properties. (Default: None)
DataMember	Binds a Label control to a data member. Depending on the data source, a data member may represent a table, a data command, or a custom data sub-set. See DataSource property. (Default: None)
DataSource	Used to bind a Label control to a data source. See Chapter 7 for more information on the use of this and other data binding properties. (Default: None)
Height	Specifies the vertical distance covered by the label. Often used in conjunction with the Top property to specify the location of the label bottom. (Default: None)
Left	Identifies the distance from the left edge of the Label control to the left edge of the label's container. (Default: None)
Top	A measure of the distance between the top of the Label control and the top of the label's container. (Default: None)
Visible	Specifies whether the Label control is visible or hidden to users. Boolean property. (Default: True)
Width	Specifies the difference between the right and left boundaries of the Label control. (Default: None)
WordWrap	Boolean property indicating whether a Label control with its AutoSize property set to True should expand horizontally or vertically to display the full text of its Caption property.

Figures 6.7 and 6.8 illustrate changes to some properties of the Command-Button, Label, and Textbox controls. Figure 6.7 shows a generic form with a series of controls. In this figure, all controls have been created using Visual Basic defaults.

FIGURE 6.7

A simple form with default properties

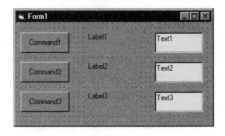

Figure 6.8 shows the same form after the following code has been executed in the Form Load event of the form.

```
Private Sub Form_Load()
Form1.Caption = "Form1 with Changes to Properties"

'Set properties for Command Buttons.
    'Command1.Default was set to True at Design Time.
Command2.Caption = "Button2"
Command3.Enabled = False

'Set properties for Labels.
Label2.Alignment = vbCenter
Label3.Alignment = vbRightJustify
Label2.BackStyle = vbTransparent
Label3.BorderStyle = vbFixedSingle

'Set properties for TextBoxes
Text1.Enabled = False
Text1.Text = "Not Editable"
Text2.PasswordChar = "*"
Text3.Visible = False
End Sub
```

FIGURE 6.8

Form from Figure 6.7 with modified properties

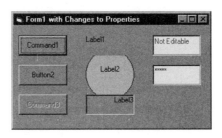

By defining user-interface controls as objects and exposing only explicit properties, methods, and events, Microsoft has reduced the level of control developers have over the interfaces of their applications. However, in establishing the specific types of controls that are available and the particular members exposed by each control, the Visual Basic development team has accomplished two very positive ends. First, by abstracting developers from much of the fine interface detail, development time is vastly reduced. Secondly, by automating much of the interface-building work beneath the surface of the Visual Basic development environment, they have passively enforced the standardized use of interface elements. This may seem to inhibit creativity on the part of independent developers (and perhaps it does to a small degree), but the benefit to users of a consistent and somewhat intuitive interface is tremendous.

We have discussed the basic tools used to build the rudiments of an application interface; forms, controls, and control properties. I will now discuss the glue that makes all of these pieces work together in your applications, namely, events.

Working with Events

One of the most fundamental abstractions in the Visual Basic environment is that code execution management is implemented in an event-driven paradigm. In other words, CPUs only know how to follow explicit linear sets of instructions. Historically, programming has involved creating these direct execution patterns. As computing has become more graphical and user-centric, this type of execution has come to involve numerous subroutines that watch for various user events to occur.

To make code more readable and reduce programming effort, Visual Basic provides all of the underlying functionality needed to monitor machine and user events. As a developer, all you have to do is script various events in conjunction with the controls already discussed.

Events are control-specific. In other words, events are not typically global, rather, they affect certain controls or objects. For instance, if a user clicks a mouse within an application window, that click event will be registered by the application as either a click event for the form or a click event for one of the controls on the form.

Event handling procedures can then be written to execute certain code when particular events are fired for specific forms or controls. Like controls' properties, events are tailored to the type of control. For instance, a command button has events that deal primarily with mouse, keyboard, and shifting focus, while text boxes include events that are useful in controlling program execution surrounding a text box (i.e., a Change event that is triggered when the Text property is changed, or a Validate event that can require a text box control to pass a validation test before focus can pass to another control). You can view the list of events available to a control by opening the Code Editor window, selecting the desired control in the Object drop-down list, and opening the Procedure drop-down list. See Exercise 6.5 below for a more detailed explanation.

In a Visual Basic application, only one control at a time can receive input from a user. This is referred to as *focus*. As a user clicks different controls or tabs through a form, the different controls receive and then lose focus. Each of these actions can trigger events if scripted by an event-handling procedure or event procedure.

For a description of how Windows operating systems generate Visual Basic events, see the article "How Windows Works: Windows, Events, and Messages" in the *Visual Basic MSDN* documentation.

Creating an Event Procedure

Microsoft ✓ ***Exam*** ***Objective***

Implement navigational design.

- Assign code to a control to respond to an event.

Exercise 6.5 gives the steps necessary to create an Event procedure. This particular Event procedure uses a Visual Basic built-in function that returns the current time from the system clock. The current time is placed in the Text property of a Text Box control.

EXERCISE 6.5

Creating an Event Procedure

1. Create a new Visual Basic project using the Standard EXE template.

2. On the default form (Form1), place one command button and one label control. Stretch the label control to a width of about 2 inches.

3. Double-click the command button to open the Code Editor window.

   Note that double-clicking the control created a simple Event procedure with the following lines of code:

   ```
   Private Sub Command2_Click()
   End Sub
   ```

   Similar Event procedures can be created manually by typing the code shown above, if necessary. You can also create Event procedures by selecting an object in the Object drop-down list, then the event of interest from the Procedures drop-down list.

4. Enter the following code. (If you renamed your controls as you created them, you'll need to adjust the control names in the code as necessary.)

   ```
   Private Sub Command1_Click()
   Label1.Font.Name = "Arial"
   Label1.Font.Bold = True
   Label1.Font.Size = 18
   Label1.Caption = Time()
   End Sub
   ```

   Your window should look similar to the following graphic.

5. Note the Object List box as identified by the floating tool tip. The Procedure drop-down list is located immediately to the right of the Object drop-down list box. Create an Event procedure for the label control by selecting Label1 from the Object drop-down list. The click event is the default event for that control, so it is created without further selection from the Procedures drop-down list.

6. From within the label click event, call the command button click event by typing the following:

```
Command1_Click
```

7. Save and test the application you have created.

You have created an application that prints the current time on a form when a command button is pressed. A Label control is used for display of the time but is otherwise invisible to the user. By calling the command button's click event procedure from the click event of the Label control, the time shown in the label can be updated by clicking either the command button or the label.

Of course, the click event of a command button is just the beginning. To create sophisticated applications that allow you to control the flow of execution while allowing users flexibility requires a wide variety of conditional events. Visual Basic provides a wealth of events to enhance your development. Understanding some of the more powerful events and when they occur will add significantly to the elegance of the user interfaces you build.

Using Form-Level Events

Microsoft ✓ *Exam* *Objective*

Write code that processes data entered on a form.

- Given a scenario, add code to the appropriate form event. Events include Initialize, Terminate, Load, Unload, QueryUnload, Activate, and Deactivate.

Multiform applications that allow users to interact with data and logic as needs arise create complex contexts for maintaining the status of an application. Form events offer special opportunities to developers. By being able to identify and manipulate unique application circumstances, Form events give control back to the developer. Table 6.4 presents a sampling of executive or administrative events used by forms. Each is supplemented with a short description.

T A B L E 6.4:   Form Events and When They Occur

Event Name	Description
Initialize	Event fires when the first reference is made to a property or event of the form. Occurs before the Load event. Can be helpful for setting initial values when this can be done prior to loading the form.
Load	Occurs as the form contents are loaded into memory. Often used to set properties of controls or the form itself just prior to showing the form.
Resize	Event occurs after the Load event but prior to painting the form. Also fires any time the form is resized in runtime service. This event is typically used for managing display aesthetics dependent on form dimensions. Size and shape of controls or the spacing between them may be recalculated as a function of new form dimensions.
Paint	Follows Resize events and occurs after all or part of a form has been moved or enlarged, or a covering form is moved. Only necessary when the AutoRedraw property has been set to False. Often used to force a redraw of graphics methods output. Because the Paint event follows all Resize events, care should be taken to not include actions that will cause object resizing. Otherwise, cascading or recursive events will occur, with the Paint event calling itself recursively until a stack overflow or similar error occurs.
Activate	Occurs when the form becomes the working window (in the foreground, with a highlighted title bar). This event happens only when moving focus within an application. The Activate event occurs before any control's GotFocus event. This event is useful for updating StatusBar or other application-level information when the active window changes.

T A B L E 6.4: Form Events and When They Occur *(continued)*

Event Name	Description
Deactivate	In contrast to the Activate event, occurs when a form passes focus to another form. Occurs after any contained control's Lostfocus event fires. The Deactivate event does not occur when unloading a form. This event can be useful for passing data to the new active window or otherwise ensuring consistent operation across forms.
QueryUnload	Traps calls to unload forms. Allows examination of the source of the Unload call. Often used to offer users the chance to save information before quitting or to cancel the Unload operation.
Unload	Occurs just before a form is removed from memory. Allows cancellation of the Unload operation. Allows prompting of users to save unchanged data before closing form. Unload events are indistinguishable by type or source.
Terminate	Occurs after the Unload event, when all references to a form instance have been removed from memory. Useful for maintenance tasks such as log entries or raising events based upon removal of a form.

Any given form in an application may use several of these administrative events or none of them. When necessary, however, these events allow developers to accurately anticipate a variety of possible execution scenarios and to handle them correctly.

Advanced Interface Controls

Visual Basic is designed to provide developers and end users with an environment that is fully integrated with the Win32 operating systems. A significant portion of this effort at integration includes providing the full spectrum of Windows interface tools. With the advent and maturing of the Windows 95 interface (now adopted in Windows NT 4), these tools include several rich tools for interacting with applications, the operating system, and the file system. The controls that provide these interface options deserve additional attention. These tools, the ListView, ImageList, Toolbar, and StatusBar controls, provide a level of interface sophistication that can set your applications apart from the rest. However, they require a little extra work to implement. In the following section, we will present each of these controls and their implementation details.

Microsoft ✓ *Exam* *Objective*

Create data input forms and dialog boxes.

- Display and manipulate data by using custom controls. Controls include **TreeView**, **ListView**, **ImageList**, **Toolbar**, and **StatusBar**.

Before any of these controls can be used, they must be added to the toolbox. For a review of the steps necessary to add a control to the toolbox, see Exercise 6.3. These and other Windows interface tools are contained in a single .ocx file. To add them all to your toolbox, open the Components dialog and select Microsoft Windows Common Controls 6.0. Figure 6.9 shows the Components dialog with this selection made. Once the dialog is accepted, the toolbox will have nine new controls available. See Figure 6.10 for an illustration of the newly populated toolbox.

FIGURE 6.9

The Components
dialog

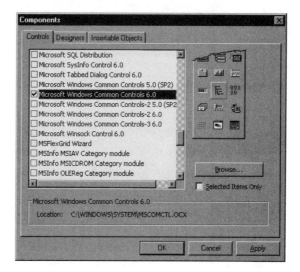

Displaying Information to Users with the StatusBar Control

The StatusBar is an important user feedback tool. It allows you, as a developer, to provide customized feedback on a continuing basis. A typical StatusBar, as implemented in Microsoft Word, is shown in Figure 6.11.

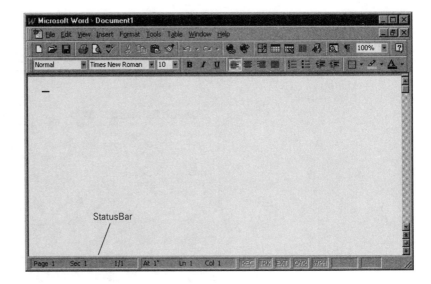

Placing the StatusBar control on your form requires only a simple double-click of the StatusBar icon in the toolbox. To add informational panels to your StatusBar, access the Property Pages for the StatusBar control. You can do this by either clicking the Custom property in the Properties window or right-clicking the StatusBar control and selecting Properties from the pop-up menu. The custom Property Pages are shown in Figure 6.12.

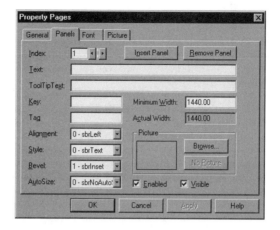

The StatusBar relies on the Panels collection to define the information to be shown. When a StatusBar control is placed on a form, the first panel is already created. Additional panels are created by clicking the Insert Panel button on the Panels tab of the StatusBar Property Pages.

Within each panel, you must specify whether you want to use one of the built-in panel functions or create custom panel information. The automatic functions are accessed by selecting one of the Style property options from the Panels tab. The built-in style options are described below.

sbrText   When this option is specified, the panel will display the Text property of the Panel object. The Text property can be filled in manually at design time or programmatically at runtime. If a bitmap has been placed in the Picture property, it will be shown as well.

sbrCaps   This style provides feedback to users regarding the status of the Caps Lock function. If the Caps Lock is active, the text "CAPS" is shown in the panel. If the Caps Lock function is off, then the "CAPS" text is shown dimmed.

sbrNum   This style allows users to monitor the status of the Num Lock function of their computer. Similar to the sbrCaps function, the text "NUM" is shown if Num Lock is on and is dimmed if Num Lock is off.

sbrIns   Similar to sbrCaps and sbrNum, this style shows "INS" when the computer's Insert function is active and is dimmed when the Insert function is inactive.

sbrScrl   This style shows "SCRL" to indicate the status of the computer's scroll lock function.

sbrDate   When this setting is selected, the panel displays the current date.

sbrTime   When this setting is selected, the panel displays the current time.

sbrKana   Displays "KANA" in the panel when a special setting is enabled for handling Katakana Japanese characters.

Other attributes and their optional settings that may be set for each panel include:

Alignment   Specifies whether text should be aligned to the left (default), right, or center of the panel.

Bevel   Specifies whether panels appear flat, indented (default), or raised.

Autosize   Returns or sets the width of a panel after a StatusBar control has been resized. Can be set to one of three options: expand panel to fit panel contents, expand to occupy any remaining space in the StatusBar, or fixed width.

Minimum Width   Sets the minimum width of a panel when panels are set to be automatically resized.

Key   A unique text string that allows each panel to be identified programmatically at runtime.

ToolTipText   Sets the string to be shown when the user hovers a mouse pointer over a panel of the StatusBar.

Enabled   Boolean property. If set to False, the panel contents are dimmed and unresponsive to user events.

Visible   Boolean property. If set to False, the panel disappears from the user's view; other panels absorb its space if so configured.

Now that we have covered the properties necessary to create a StatusBar, Exercise 6.6 presents the steps for adding a StatusBar to your application.

EXERCISE 6.6

Adding a StatusBar Control to Your Application

1. Start Visual Basic and create a new Standard EXE project.

2. Add Microsoft Windows Common Controls 6.0 to your toolbox.

3. Double-click the StatusBar icon on your toolbox to place a copy of the control at the bottom of your new form.

4. Right-click the StatusBar, and select Properties to access the Property Pages dialog for the StatusBar.

5. Click the Panels tab near the top of the form.

6. Click the Insert Panel button several times to create a total of six panels.

7. Using the table below, set properties for each of the six panels.

Panel Num.	Style	Key	MinWidth	Text	Autosize
1	sbrText	TestStatus		TestStatusText	sbrSpring
2	sbrDate	DateKey	750		
3	sbrTime	TimeKey	750		
4	sbrCaps	CapsKey	750		
5	sbrIns	InsKey	750		
6	sbrNum	NumKey	750		

8. Save and run your application.

9. Test the automatic panel styles by toggling the Caps, Insert, and Num Lock functions. Your application should look something like this.

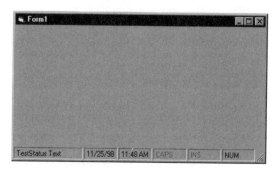

10. Resize the form while executing to test the panel width settings. All panels should be fixed except the text panel, which should expand to absorb any added screen width.

Updating the StatusBar at Runtime

The StatusBar control is heavily dependent upon the Panels collection, so any modifications to a running StatusBar will access the Panels collection, specifying the panel you want to modify and the property value to retrieve or set. Specifying the specific element desired from the collection is done through the key value assigned above, or through the index value assigned when the panel was created. Exercise 6.7 will update the text panel created in the sample StatusBar application.

EXERCISE 6.7

Modifying StatusBar Text at Runtime

1. Add a command button to the StatusBar sample application from Exercise 6.6.

2. Double-click the new command button to create a click event procedure.

3. Modify the click event procedure so that it looks like the following:

```
Private Sub Command1_Click()
Static count As Integer
count = count + 1
Form1.StatusBar1.Panels("Textkey").Text = _
    "Updated Value " & CStr(count)
End Sub
```

4. Save and run your application. Note that when you click the new command button, the text in Panel 1 of the StatusBar is updated.

Panels can be added to the StatusBar at runtime. In fact, the whole process of StatusBar creation can be delegated to runtime by creating the

Panels collection and setting all properties during the Form Load event. To add panels at runtime, simply call the Add method of the Panels collection. Use of the method call will look something like this:

```
Private Sub AddPanel()
Dim pnlAdd As Panel
Set pnlAdd = Form1.StatusBar1.Panels.Add
pnlAdd.Key = "FirstAddedPanel"
pnlAdd.Style = sbrText
pnlAdd.Text = "New Panel Text"
End Sub
```

The StatusBar can contain a maximum of 16 panels. If you try to create more than 16 panels, an error will occur.

The Panels collection also has Remove and Clear methods for additional functionality should you need to dynamically build or rebuild your Status-Bars. The Panels collection is "1-based" rather than "0-based." In other words, unlike most other collections, the first panel has an index number of 1 (one) rather than 0 (zero). If you try to access panel 0 in your code, a runtime error will occur. For more information on working with collections, see "Working with Collections" later in this chapter.

Configuring the ImageList Control for Use by Other Advanced Controls

The ImageList control is a facilitator control and is never seen by the end user. Its job is to store images that will be used by other controls at runtime. To configure the ImageList for use by other advanced controls, you just tell the ImageList control which images you want it to maintain and any unique identifying information you need each image to be associated with. The basic function of this control, if you haven't guessed by now, is to prevent reading images from disk every time they are needed. (It's also convenient because full paths are not required every time you need to reuse a bitmap.) See Exercise 6.8 for the steps to set up the ImageList control.

EXERCISE 6.8

Adding and Configuring the ImageList Control

1. Create a new Standard EXE project.

2. Add Microsoft Windows Common Controls 6.0 to the toolbox.

3. Double-click the ImageList Toolbox icon to place the control on your new Form1.

4. To begin configuring the control, right-click the control and select Properties from the pop-up menu.

5. You will be asked to identify the size of images this particular ImageList control will contain, 16 X 16, 32 X 32, 48 X 48, or custom. Select 16 X 16.

6. Clicking the Images tab provides the tools necessary to add images to the control.

7. Click the Insert Picture button and use the Open dialog box to locate the Open.bmp image file. This file is installed by Visual Basic, and can be found at: \Microsoft Visual Studio\Common\Graphics\Bit-maps\TlBr_W95\Open.bmp. File formats supported include BMP, JPG, GIF, ICO, and CUR.

8. Assign this image a key value such as Open; this name will be used in referencing the image from your code.

9. Repeat steps 7 and 8 to add New.bmp, Save.bmp, Print.bmp, Bld.bmp, Itl.bmp, and Undrln.bmp to the ImageList control. These images will be used below for building a toolbar.

10. Click OK to close the ImageList Property Pages.

Each ImageList can only contain images of a single size. If you need images of two sizes on the same form, you will need to create two separate Image-List controls.

Creating a Toolbar for Your Application

The use of a menu system to put commands within easy reach spurred the user interface revolution. The next significant step in making interfaces easier for users was the addition of application toolbars. Toolbars provide quick visual access to the most commonly used features of an application. When you build your application with Visual Basic, constructing toolbars is a relatively straightforward process. Exercise 6.9 presents the steps necessary to create a simple toolbar.

EXERCISE 6.9

Creating a Toolbar

1. Open the project created with Exercise 6.8. It should contain an ImageList control that has been configured to hold a series of file and formatting images.

2. Double-click the Toolbar icon on the Toolbox to place the control on your form.

3. Right-click the Toolbar control and select Properties from the pop-up menu.

4. The first step in configuring your Toolbar control is to set the Image-List property. Click the ImageList drop-down list box, and select the ImageList created earlier.

5. Next, click the Buttons tab. This tab provides the tools for setting most of the attributes of each Toolbar button.

6. Click the button labeled Insert to add a first Toolbar button.

7. In the Image field, type **New**. This will tie the New.bmp image in the ImageList to the new Toolbar button using the Key field of the Image-List control.

8. Set the key value for this button to **New**. You will use this key in scripting the button.

9. Repeat steps 6, 7, and 8 for each of the remaining images in the ImageList. Keys to be used include: Open, Save, Print, Bold, Italic, and Underline.

10. Click OK to close the Property Pages dialog and return to the form. Note the changes to the toolbar on your form.

The Allow Customize check box property allows end users to customize their toolbars to fit their needs. To deliver a polished application, you may want to add additional advanced or specialized toolbar functions beyond the defaults.

Your toolbar is now visually prepared, but the toolbar has no functionality. To activate the toolbar, you need to create a click event for the Toolbar object; because it is a single object, the toolbar only supports a single click event. To script the behavior of individual buttons on the toolbar, use a Select Case statement to capture which button was clicked. When you created the buttons, each button was given an index number and key. The Select Case statement, then, traps the index number or key of the button being clicked and will execute the code associated with that button. The code below shows an example of how this can be done using the buttons' key values.

```
Private Sub Toolbar1_Click(ByVal Button As Button)
    Select Case Button.Key
    Case "New"
        ' Call a function for creating a new document.
        NewDoc
    Case "Open"
        ' Call a function you have written to open a file.
        OpenFile
    Case "Save"
        ' Call your function for saving.
        Save
    End Select
End Sub
```

It is usually advisable to call functions from your Toolbar Select Case statement rather than writing code directly in the Toolbar click event procedure. Any code called in a function can easily be called from other parts of your application, enhancing flexibility and encouraging code reuse. Coding the event handling directly will render your code difficult to reuse.

Adding Windows Explorer-Like Functionality: The TreeView and ListView Controls

The TreeView and ListView controls allow you to implement information display services like those available in the Windows Explorer. Figure 6.13 shows the Explorer interface. The TreeView control allows you to create a hierarchical display similar to the left pane of the Explorer. This pane's primary strength is displaying relationships between entities and allowing interactive exploration of nested relationships.

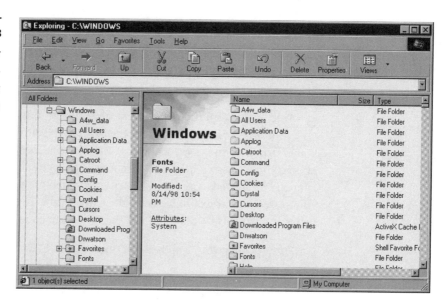

FIGURE 6.13

The Windows Explorer interface with Tree-View and ListView implementations

The TreeView and ListView controls are both written as tools for managing collections. Before discussing these controls, we will present a brief review of collections.

Working with Collections   Collections are by definition a group of objects that can be treated or handled as a group. These objects need not be identical in type, though they typically share some common characteristics. Common examples of collections in Visual Basic include the Forms collection, the group of forms currently loaded in an application, and the Control collection, the group of controls on each form.

The ability to systematically handle the various elements of a collection without explicitly identifying the number or identity of group members is a powerful tool for building flexible and reusable code. To loop through the members of a collection, use the For Each loop structure. For Each is a modification of the traditional For...Next loop and is used only in handling collections. The following code will loop through the controls on a form (including hidden controls like Timers and ImageLists), printing the name of the controls in the immediate window.

```
Private Sub Form_Load()
Dim myControl As Control
For Each myControl In Controls
Debug.Print myControl.Name
Next myControl
End Sub
```

Referencing a particular element of a collection is handled by identifying the root object and its collection, then specifying either the name of the item (as a string) or the element number. Where objects are included in collections, you will often need to reference the collection and the member object you are interested in as well as specifying which property or method you are interested in. For example, to set the value of the Text property of a certain control on a form, you could use the following code:

```
Form1.Controls("AppName").Text = App.EXEName
```

The value of this type of handling is apparent if you want to update similar controls across multiple forms. In this case, you can perform nested collection calls. We will work further with collections later in this chapter when we deal with dynamically modifying the Controls and Forms collections.

The TreeView control allows you to manage information with inherent relationships as a series of nodes. Every node hierarchy must begin with a root node. If we think of a corporate organization chart as an example of an information tree, the president or CEO would typically represent the root node. As related nodes branch out, the relationship between logical levels is described as a parent/child relationship. In the case of the organizational chart, the CEO/president is considered a parent node, while vice presidents and members of the board may be defined as child nodes. Nodes at the same logical level are handled by the TreeView control as members of a Node collection. A fully populated TreeView control actually defines a series of related collections. The TreeView control makes maneuvering through complex hierarchies like file systems more manageable for users.

Using the TreeView Control   The TreeView control has some parameters that can be set up at design time using visual tools. Much of the coding of the TreeView control, however, must be coded programmatically for runtime execution. Let's begin with the design time setup.

The initial task is to place an instance of the control on your form. You can then begin setting properties by right-clicking the control and selecting Properties. Figure 6.14 shows the Property Pages for the TreeView control.

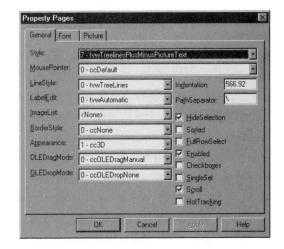

The TreeView control provides a great deal of customizability, and a full discussion of its features is beyond the scope of this chapter. The primary properties necessary for a basic implementation include:

ImageList   Allows you to bind the TreeView to an ImageList control. The ImageList will then provide the icons used by the TreeView to represent nodes.

Indentation   Allows customization of the horizontal distance that each logical level of the hierarchy is indented from its parent level.

LabelEdit   Specifies the editable status of node labels. If set to automatic, users can click and rename nodes. If set to manual, the process must be handled programmatically.

Sorted   Sets whether the nodes at the root level of the control should be sorted alphabetically by name. Can also be used to sort child node collections.

Style   Allows you to set the specific combination of visual cues to be presented by the TreeView control. Cues available include lines indicating relationships, the plus or minus box indicating whether subnodes are expanded or collapsed, pictures representing nodes, and text labels for the nodes. Optional values that can be selected for this property are:

   0 tvwTextOnly   Shows only the text of nodes.

   1 tvwPictureText   Uses text and images from ImageList.

   2 tvwPlusMinusText   Text and plus or minus boxes.

   3 tvwPlusPictureText   Includes images and plus or minus boxes with text.

   4 tvwTreeLinesText   Presents text for nodes, with lines showing relationships.

   5 tvwTreeLinesPictureText   Text and images like option 1, this time with relationship lines drawn.

   6 tvwTreeLinesPlusMinusText   Text and plus or minus boxes like option 2. This option includes relationship lines.

   7 tvwTreeLinesPlusMinusPicturesText   Includes all options: text, images, plus and minus boxes, and tree lines. This is the default style setting for new TreeView controls.

Once these basic definitions of the TreeView control have been made, you can begin to add nodes to the hierarchy. The TreeView control is instantiated as a series of related collections. The Nodes collections expose methods that are used as the basis for most coding of the control. These methods include an Add method, a Clear method, and a Remove method. These operations handle adding a node to a collection, clearing all nodes from a collection, and removing a single node, respectively.

The Add method will create a new node as part of a specified collection, and it will return a reference to that Node object. The method accepts up to six arguments (all optional except the text value). The formal syntax of the method, including arguments, is:

```
Object.Nodes.Add ([Relative], [Relationship], [Key], [Text],
[Image], [SelectedImage]).
```

The arguments are defined below:

Relative   References an existing node in the tree.

Relationship   Identifies the relationship between the node being created and the node identified as relative. The available options are:

tvwFirst   Places the new node before all other nodes at the level of the relative node.

tvwLast   Places the new node after all existing peer nodes to the relative node.

tvwNext   Places the new node into the collection just after the relative node (default).

tvwPrevious   Places the new node just before the node named as relative.

tvwChild   Creates the new node as a child node of the node referenced as relative.

Key   A user- or developer-defined name for use in future programmatic references to the node.

Text   The Screen value of the node. This value will be shown to users viewing the TreeView control.

Image and SelectedImage   Identifies images to be associated with nodes. Images can be read from disk or accessed from an ImageList control.

To actually call for the addition of nodes to a collection, use the following code:

```
TreeView1.Nodes.Add  , , "NodeKey", "NodeText"
```

In this case, the Relative and Relationship arguments are omitted because the node being created is to be a member of the Root Node collection. A fully defined call of the Add method might look like this:

```
Set NewNode = TreeView1.Nodes.Add "Languages", tvwChild, _
"English", "English", 1, 11
```

In this instance, we assume that 1 and 11 are valid index numbers for images in an ImageList control. The first number represents the image typically associated with the node, and the second number represents the image to be associated whenever the node is selected. The object reference returned by the Add method is passed to a variable for future use in defining or retrieving properties. Exercise 6.10 walks you through building a simple TreeView control.

EXERCISE 6.10

Adding a TreeView Control

1. Launch Visual Basic 6 and create a new project based on the Standard EXE template.

2. Select Project ➢ Components, and select Microsoft Windows Common Controls 6.0 from the Components dialog.

3. Double-click the ImageList control on the toolbar to place an instance of the control on your form.

4. Add the nethood.bmp and mycomp.bmp images to your ImageList control. You can find them in the \Microsoft VisualStudio\Common\ Graphics\Bitmaps\Outline\Nomask directory. Give the images key values of LAN and Computer, respectively.

5. Add the icon named net01.ico from the \Microsoft Visual Studio\Common\Graphics\Icons\Comm directory. Give it the key value of WAN. Review Exercise 6.8, if necessary.

6. Add a TreeView control to your form and resize if necessary to allow a good viewable area. Rename the TreeView control **tvwNetworkMap**.

7. Right-click the TreeView control, and select Properties from the pop-up menu.

8. On the Property Pages, General tab, select your ImageList control in the ImageList drop-down list box.

9. Click the OK button. Note that the ImageList control is bound to the TreeView control, and the image with index 1 has become the default icon for all sample nodes.

10. Begin the programmatic portion of the setup by defining the root node using the code below:

```
Private Sub Form_Load ()
Dim NetNode as Node
Set NetNode = tvwNetworkMap.Nodes.Add (, , "CorpWan", _
"Corporate Network", "WAN")
NetNode.Sorted = True
NetNode.Expanded = True
End Sub
```

11. Continue the Form Load event procedure, adding child nodes to the tree. The code is given here:

```
tvwNetworkMap.Nodes.Add "CorpWan", tvwChild, "SanFran", _
     "San Francisco", "LAN"
tvwNetworkMap.Nodes.Add "CorpWan", tvwChild, "NY", _
"New York", "LAN"
tvwNetworkMap.Nodes.Add "CorpWan", tvwChild, "SLC", _
"Salt Lake City", "LAN"
```

12. Continue to add code to the procedure to populate the LANs with users/computers.

```
tvwNetworkMap.Nodes.Add "SanFran", tvwChild, "FRogers", _
"Fred Rogers- IT", "Computer"
tvwNetworkMap.Nodes.Add "SanFran", tvwChild, "KTF", _
     "Kermit Frog- Sales", "Computer"
tvwNetworkMap.Nodes.Add "NY", tvwChild, "MDavis", _
"Miles Davis- HR", "Computer"
tvwNetworkMap.Nodes.Add "NY", tvwChild, "MCaine", _
"Michael Caine- Fabrication", "Computer"
tvwNetworkMap.Nodes.Add "SLC", tvwChild, "GPerlman", _
"Geoff Perlman- IT", "Computer"
tvwNetworkMap.Nodes.Add "SLC", tvwChild, "JKennedy"

"Jacqeline Kennedy- Foreign Affairs", "Computer"
```

13. Save and run the application. This is roughly how your form should appear when running (with all nodes expanded).

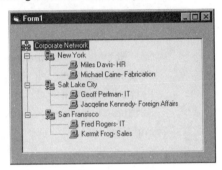

Using the ListView Control   It's traditional to use TreeView controls as navigational aids. Once you have navigated to the desired portion of the hierarchy, the ListView control can be used to display the nodes in the current collection.

To use the ListView control, you first add the control to the form in the same way the TreeView and ImageList controls were added. Initial configuration of the control is done through its Property Pages, as with the other controls (see Figure 6.15).

FIGURE 6.15

Property Pages for the ListView control

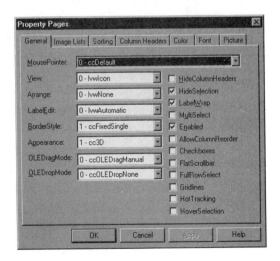

The ListView control is very powerful and has many configuration options. The list that follows includes the general types of settings available, with special comments on some specific properties. The Property Pages make properties available under the following tabbed pages:

General   Presents many of the properties that relate to the ListView control itself, such as the control's drag-and-drop modes and BorderStyle property. Additional properties worth special note are:

View   The ListView control supports four viewing formats. This property sets the default. You can change views at runtime, if desired. Options include viewing by small icon, by large icon, as a list, or as a report (in Windows Explorer, this view is called the Detail view). (Default: Large Icon view [lvwIcon])

Arrange   Allows you to set a default alignment. Options are align to the top, the left, or no alignment.

LabelEdit   Allows you to set in advance whether users will be able to automatically edit item labels (lvwAutomatic) or whether you will procedurally implement a manual item entry mechanism (lvwManual).

MultiSelect   Check box for setting whether multiple items can be selected by the user at runtime.

Image Lists   Exposes three properties to set bindings to ImageList controls for normal and small icon views and column headers.

Sorting   Allows you to set whether items will be sorted and, if so, on which key and in which direction (ascending or descending). If the SortKey property is set to 0 (the default), the text value of the item will be used. Other SortKey values represent subitem column numbers (described later).

Column Headers   When in Report view, the ListView control can present associated information alongside each item. These are displayed in columns. This tab of the Property Pages allows you to set values for the descriptive text and its alignment for the column header, the width of the column, and a Key value for referencing the column in code.

Color   Allows you to set the default background and foreground colors for the control.

Font   Sets the default font for the control.

Picture   Can be used to set a custom mouse pointer or an image to be placed in the background of the ListView control.

The only task remaining before we begin populating the Item collections of the control is to establish the column headers for the subitems we will use. To define these columns, select the Column Headers tab from the ListView control's Property Pages. Much as with the ImageList control, you add columns to the control by clicking the Insert Column button and configuring the parameters of that column. The only essential properties to modify are the Text and Key properties. The former is used to generate column headers when viewing the report, and the latter is used to refer to this column in code.

You can populate the ListView control directly from your code much as we did with the TreeView control. However, hard coding the values is somewhat unusual. The ListView control is more often used to present data from a database query or is used in conjunction with a TreeView to facilitate navigation. With this in mind, we will present the means by which the TreeView and ListView controls work together.

Binding TreeView and ListView Controls   The big question left remaining, then, is how do you get the TreeView control and the ListView control to work and play well together? Unfortunately, these controls require a good deal of coding, as you have seen. There are no fancy data binding tools for these controls. To update the items in the ListView control when a user clicks on some part of the TreeView, you, as the developer, must code the TreeView events to trap any user interaction and script the interaction with the ListView control.

The typical way of doing this is to place code in the Nodeclick event of the TreeView control. The Nodeclick event occurs anytime a user clicks on any node. The Nodeclick event procedures return, by default, a reference to the particular node that was clicked. In this event handler, then, you pass the referenced node as an argument to the Add method of the ListView control's List-Items collection. In this way, you are able to add the clicked node to the List-View control. To fully implement the traditional browser functionality, you will need to display, in the ListView, the child nodes of the referenced (clicked) TreeView node. This will be done with either nested For Each...Next loops, or a recursive operation that calls itself repetitively until all relevant nodes and collections have been processed.

See Exercise 6.11 for details on how to create a ListView control. This exercise will continue building the form begun in Exercise 6.10. We will add a ListView control to the form and populate it based on clicks in the TreeView control. The ListView control is quite powerful, allowing a good deal of customization, although this example will only build a simple prototype application for demonstration purposes. We encourage you to explore the abilities of the TreeView and ListView controls once you have completed the exercise.

Adding a ListView Control

1. Open the project saved at the end of Exercise 6.10.

2. Create a new ImageList control for 32 X 32 pixel images.

3. Add the nethood.bmp and mycomp.bmp images to your ImageList control. You can find them in the \Microsoft Visual Studio\Common\ Graphics\Bitmaps\Outline\Nomask directory. Give the images key values of LAN and Computer, respectively.

4. Also add the icon named net01.ico from the \Microsoft Visual Studio\Common\Graphics\Icons\Comm directory. Give it the Key value WAN. Review Exercise 6.8 if necessary.

5. Add a ListView control to the right side of the form. Rename it lvw-Network. You may have to expand the size of the form or adjust the TreeView control.

6. Right-click the ListView control and select Properties from the pop-up menu.

7. On the General tab, change the View field to **3 – lvwReport**.

8. On the Image Lists tab, set the ImageList for Normal icons to the new ImageList you just created.

9. On the Column Headers tab, click the Insert Column button, and use the following settings to configure the column:

   - Text: Name

   - Width: 4000

   - Key: Name

10. Leave other settings at their defaults, and close the Property Pages dialog.

11. Create a subprocedure called ScanNodes, and place the following code in it. This procedure will receive a reference to a node in the Tree-View and, based on that starting point, scan all descendant nodes for inclusion in the ListView control's ListItem collection.

```
Public Sub ScanNodes(aNode As Node)
Dim thisNode As Node
Dim i As Long
    lvwNetwork.ListItems.Add , , aNode.Text, aNode.Image
    If aNode.Children > 0 Then
        Set thisNode = aNode.Child
        For i = 1 To aNode.Children
            ScanNodes thisNode
            Set thisNode = thisNode.Next
        Next
    End If
End Sub
```

12. Enable the event handler for the TreeView's Nodeclick event with code to call the ScanNodes procedure. Use the code below:

```
Private Sub tvwNetworkMap_NodeClick (ByVal Node
        As MSComctlLib.Node)
lvwNetwork.ListItems.Clear
ScanNodes Node
End Sub
```

13. Add a command button to the form, and script the click event of the button to change views from Report view to Large Icon view and back. Use the following code:

```
Private Sub Command1_Click()
If (lvwNetwork.View = lvwIcon) then
    lvwNetwork.View = lvwReport
Else
    lvwNetwork.View = lvwIcon
End If
End Sub
```

EXERCISE 6.11 (CONTINUED)

14. Save and test your application. Your results should look like the graphic below. Click the command button to change the View property. Notice that in ListView mode, the cities are sorted alphabetically but users within a city are not. Sorting was only set as a property of the root node and applied to its child nodes.

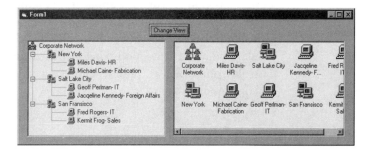

 You commonly use a ListView control in reporting data from a database. However, with the several new tools for binding controls to data sources in Visual Basic 6, it may be advisable to give serious thought to data bound ActiveX controls rather than ListView controls. The one notable advantage of using the ListView control is that once configured, the ListView offers an elegant solution for switching between view modes.

Thus far in this chapter, we have reviewed the basic tools for creating a user interface, including a few advanced ActiveX controls. In the next section, we will review programming approaches that can aid in creating powerful but flexible user services. In particular, we will discuss ways to adjust user services at runtime in order to adapt to multifaceted business needs.

Interactive Presentation Features

At first glance, the essentials of building a user interface are to create a series of forms, then connect those forms to the underlying mechanics (logic) of the application. Under this scenario, when you need a slightly different implementation of a form, you would make a second copy of the form and apply whatever changes were necessary. While this is a very workable solution for incidental needs, your application would quickly become bloated and consume huge amounts of resources if you needed to anticipate multiple variations on each form.

The available solution to this predicament is the ability to manipulate objects and collections at runtime so that you can customize the appearance and functionality of your application on the fly. We have already discussed the ways you can adjust the properties of individual controls and forms. We will now present the steps for modifying other interface elements. In particular, we will discuss modifying menus at runtime, adding and deleting controls from a form at runtime, and using collections to systematically modify controls and forms.

Working with Menus

We begin with a presentation on managing menus as a fundamental part of the user interface. An application's menu structure should be the central point of contact for most of an application's functions, so put some serious thought into designing the structure of your menu system. Menu items should be grouped in meaningful ways within menus, and the menus themselves should be logically unique. The menu structure should not detract from the usability of your application. It should, in fact, add to the intuitiveness of your program. Functions and their access should be apparent from the names and structure of your menus.

To add a menu to a form, just open the Menu Editor and begin adding menus and menu items. To open the Menu Editor, select Tools ➢ Menu Editor, or click the Menu Editor button on the toolbar (see Figure 6.16). Once the Menu Editor is open, you can begin building menus and menu items. Figure 6.17 illustrates the Menu Editor.

FIGURE 6.16

The Menu Editor
Toolbar button

The fundamentals of generating a menu include creating an item in the Menu Editor, setting name and caption properties, and assigning a location within the existing menu structure. Other settings can also be made here, some of which we will discuss shortly. The Name and Caption properties are set using the labeled text boxes. Placing a menu or menu item within the existing structure is accomplished through the use of the four arrow buttons near the middle-left of the Editor dialog. Horizontal placement, as managed through the right and left arrow buttons, controls the hierarchical placement of items. Items flush with the left edge of the window are set as menus. With each click of the right arrow, an item is nested more deeply within cascading menus. Moving an item vertically adjusts the item's location, either across the menu bar horizontally when moving between menus, or within a menu vertically.

When you indent an item relative to the item above it, the item above will shift from a menu item to the caption for a cascading menu. Menu captions and cascading menu captions can't be scripted themselves. If you plan to use cascading menus, plan ahead to include unscripted menu captions.

Exercise 6.12 shows the essential steps of building a working menu system. We will use this menu in later discussions on dynamically modifying menus.

EXERCISE 6.12

Creating a Basic Menu Structure

1. Launch Visual Basic and create a new Standard EXE project.

2. Open the Menu Editor using either the Menu Editor Toolbar button (refer to Figure 6.16) or select Tools ➤ Menu Editor.

3. Create a File menu with the following menu items: New, Open, and Exit.

4. Create an Edit menu with menu items for Cut, Copy, and Paste.

5. Create a Format menu with these menu items: Text, Paragraph, and Document.

6. Set the Text item above as a cascading menu caption by indenting menu items below it labeled Font, Bold, Italic, Underline, Double Underline, Strikethrough, and Small Caps. Provide a name for each item by adding "mnu" to the caption.

7. After the Small Caps item, insert a separator bar by creating a new menu item and placing a hyphen in the caption field. You will still need to give the separator a name.

8. Add a final item after the separator with Simple Menus as the caption.

9. Add a new menu labeled Help, with items labeled Topics and About.

10. Close the Menu Editor and click through the menu structure in design time to ensure that it is functioning as expected. If you start your application, the menu structure should look something like this.

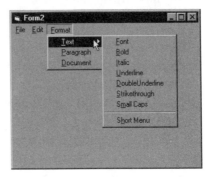

11. Save the project for use in a later exercise.

Microsoft ✔ *Exam Objective*

Implement navigational design.

- Dynamically modify the appearance of a menu.

Visual Basic treats each menu item as a named object. Each menu item has a click event, which is how you trigger code execution when the item is selected. Menus and menu items also have properties that can be set or retrieved at runtime. This is the most basic approach to dynamic modification of menus and menu items.

To modify the properties of a menu or menu item, simply use Visual Basic to set or retrieve the property as you would elsewhere. Namely, you reference the object (in this case, the menu or menu item) using the name you set in the Menu Editor, add a dot, and name the property to be set or retrieved. The menu properties you may find useful include: Caption, Checked, Enabled, and Visible.

The Caption property holds the value to be displayed in the application's menu structure. The Checked property indicates to the user that some application status is in effect because a check mark is placed next to a particular menu item. The Enabled property exposes the menu item to User events. When set to False, this property disables menu items, turning them gray and unclickable. The Visible property, when set to False, will completely hide menus or menu items from users.

To set a menu property, you create a traditional assignment equation of the form.

```
mnuEdit.Visible = False
```

Executing this command will remove the Edit menu from the user's menu bar. Exercise 6.13 demonstrates the process of making runtime modifications to a menu structure.

Implementation of the Checked property is not managed by Visual Basic. If you want to implement check marks in your menus as a status monitor, you will need to programmatically update the menu Check property at any point where that status may change.

EXERCISE 6.13

Modifying Menu Items at Runtime

1. Open the project created in Exercise 6.12.

2. Without running the application, select Format ➤ Text ➤ Short Menu. This will open the click event of the Short Menu item.

3. Script the Short Menu click event using the following code. This will change the list of visible menu items on the menu. It will also change the caption of the Short Menu item to cue users to reselect it to reset the menu.

```
Private Sub mnuShortMenu_Click()
If mnuShortMenu.Caption = "Short Menu" Then
    mnuShortMenu.Caption = "Long Menu"
Else
    mnuShortMenu.Caption = "Short Menu"
End If
mnuUnderline.Visible = Not mnuUnderline.Visible
mnuStrikethrough.Visible = Not mnuStrikethrough.Visible
mnuSmallCaps.Visible = Not mnuSmallCaps.Visible
End Sub
```

4. Save and test your application. Test the Short Menu menu item to see if it correctly resizes its own menu and renames itself.

Working with Object Collections and Arrays

Microsoft ✓ ***Exam*** ***Objective***

Implement navigational design.

- Create an application that adds and deletes menus at run time.

Up to this point, we have discussed only dynamic modification of the menu display at runtime. When using Visual Basic, you have additional opportunities to actually create and display menu items at runtime based on the circumstances of that moment. To do this, you must create a control array. A control array is a group of controls that are of the same type and share the same name. The individual instances of the control can have different properties, except for the Name property. These controls are distinguished from each other by the values of their Index property.

This test objective as worded is slightly deceptive. As a Visual Basic developer, you can show or hide menus at runtime. You can also create or delete menu *items* at runtime, but you cannot create menus at runtime.

To implement control arrays in Visual Basic, you create a control and set its Index value to 0. In the case of an array of menu items, you open the Menu Editor, create a menu item with the name of the control array you desire, and set the value of the Index property to 0. If desired, you can also create some or all of the additional control array elements at runtime (see the following warning). Then, to create additional controls as members of the control array, use the Load command, passing a new Index value to be used by the new control. When first created, new members of the control array will have properties identical to the Source control, so you may need to set properties procedurally before they are displayed. Properties that may need setting include Captions, physical location (for controls other than menu items), or Text properties. If you want to limit the number of controls that can be added to a control array, simply build code into your Load procedure to watch the size of your incrementing index number variable. Use a conditional statement to disallow calls to the Load event once a maximum number of controls has been created. Actually implementing a control array and adding a control will use code that looks something like this:

```
Count = Count + 1
Load mnuOption (Count)
MnuOption(Count).Caption = "Option #" & Count
```

To remove Control Array objects, use the Unload command, passing the Index value for the specific control you want to remove. Removing controls works in essentially the same way as loading new controls except that you decrement the counter. Be sure to use public variables for your counter variables unless you are sure that all adding and removing of controls will happen from the same procedure. The code for this functionality looks like this:

```
If (Count = 0) Then
Msgbox "Dynamic menu is empty. "
End If
Unload mnuOption (Count)
Count = Count - 1
```

Elements of a control array that were created at design time cannot be removed with the Unload command. Attempting to do so will return an error. You must create at least one menu item to create the array of controls, so if any design time-built items need to be removed from a menu, they should be hidden by setting their Visible properties to False. You should build conditional statements into your code that check for the removal of all dynamically created controls to avoid this problem.

When working with a control array, the individual controls don't act as unique objects. Rather, the array itself is the object that interacts. Because the array is the active object, the controls share the same name and also must share their Event procedures. The click event for a menu item control array is a single Event procedure, typically with a Select Case statement to allow trapping of the individual menu item that was clicked. Specifically, items are identified by their Index values. For instance, to open a recent file as listed in a Recent Items menu, the following code structure would be used:

```
Private Sub mnuRecent_Click(Index As Integer)
Select Case Index
    Case 0
        [code to open file in #0]
    Case 1
        [code to open file in #1]
End select
End Sub
```

Working with dynamic menus in this way presents unique challenges, and you must attend to two special issues. First, you must ensure that your Select

Case statement is able to handle all of the Index values it can receive. Index values that are not associated with an actual menu item are not a problem, as their Index values would never be called. The greater challenge is ensuring that you never have an Index value passed to the click event for which there is no matching Case statement. The safest way to handle this possibility is to carefully manage the Index values being assigned to new controls and limit the range and values assigned to the values for which there are Case evaluation statements.

The second challenge of event handling for menu control arrays is creating functional code to execute when you can't anticipate at design time what each menu item will represent at runtime. There are a variety of ways to handle this problem, one being to pass additional information to the menu item control array when the control instance is created. For instance, you can assign a custom value to the Tag property. You can then write a single event handler with variable execution based upon the Tag value that is associated with the Index value passed by the click event. Exercise 6.14 walks you through the process of creating and implementing dynamic menus.

EXERCISE 6.14

Building and Using Menus Dynamically

1. Open the project saved at the end of Exercise 6.13.

2. Add two command buttons and a text box to the form. Set the caption of Command1 to Add Menu. Set the caption of Command2 to Remove Menu.

3. Open the Menu Editor and add a fourth menu to the menu bar. Give it the caption Time. Set its name to mnuTimeSub, and set its Index property to 0.

4. Open the General Declarations section of the form module and declare a private variable named C as an integer.

5. Double-click the button with the Add Menu caption, and add the following code to its click event:

```
c = c + 1
Load mnuTimeSub(c)
mnuTimeSub(c).Caption = CStr(Time())
```

This will allow the button to cause the creation of new menu items.

EXERCISE 6.14 (CONTINUED)

6. Now add comparable code to the Remove Menu button. It should look like this:

```
If c <> 0 Then
Unload mnuTimeSub(c)
c = c - 1
End If
```

7. At design time, click Time ➤ Time. This will open the click event procedure for the menu control array for editing. Add code to the procedure to place the time saved in the clicked menu item into the Text property of the text box. The complete Event procedure should look like this:

```
Private Sub mnuTimeSub_Click(Index As Integer)
Text1.Text = mnuTimeSub(Index).Caption
End Sub
```

8. Save and test your application. Check to ensure that menu items are added and removed when the correct button is pushed, and that time stamps are transferred to the text box when a menu item is selected at runtime.

Microsoft
✓ Exam
Objective

Implement navigational design.

- Add a pop-up menu to an application.

While we are discussing the advanced use of menus to enhance the user services tier, we should mention the pop-up menu and its implementation. Pop-up menus provide an additional means of user interaction with the system. These menus appear on your form in response to the user right-clicking the mouse. Pop-up menus are best known for their use in providing context-sensitive help, but they can provide a series of other functions, including providing quick access to frequently- or probably-needed functions.

Pop-up menus are defined as traditional menus using the Menu Editor. If desired, pop-up menus can display menus already available as drop-down menus from the menu bar. However, it is more common to make functions available from pop-up menus that are not available in a comparable menu bar menu. To configure this type of operation, create a menu in the Menu Editor and uncheck the menu's Visible property. It will now fail to appear on the main menu. In the MouseUp event of the form (or any particular control on the form), trap for the use of the right mouse button. When this occurs, call the Pop-upMenu method of the form or control. The only argument necessary for the Pop-upMenu method is the name of the menu to be displayed. Exercise 6.15 demonstrates the use of pop-up menus.

EXERCISE 6.15

Creating a Pop-Up Menu

1. Open the project used in Exercise 6.14.

2. Create the following Form_MouseUp event procedure:

```
Private Sub Form_MouseUp(Button As Integer, _
 Shift As Integer, X As Single, Y As Single)
If Button = vbRightButton Then PopupMenu mnuTime
End Sub
```

3. Save and test the application by right-clicking the form after adding some time stamp menu items.

Microsoft
✓ *Exam*
Objective

Create data input forms and dialog boxes.

- Create an application that adds and deletes controls at run time.

Other controls can also be dynamically managed at runtime through the use of control arrays. Control arrays are a powerful tool that you can use throughout your presentation tier.

The most significant difference in implementation between menu item arrays and other control arrays is the way the array is initialized. When working with standard Visual Basic controls, arrays can be initialized in one of three ways:

- Setting a non-null Index value for any one control

- Manually setting two or more controls to the same name

- Copying a control and pasting that control back onto the same form

If you select either of the latter ways to create the array, a dialog will appear confirming that you wish to create a control array. Figure 6.18 shows the dialog.

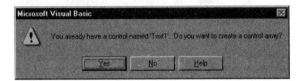

F I G U R E 6.18

Control Array
Confirmation dialog

Control arrays have four properties that you can use to customize your work with them. They primarily function to help you locate certain records and in the initialization of For each…Next loops. Those properties are:

Count   Returns the total number of elements in the array

Item   Allows you to reference a certain record in the array

LBound   Returns the lowest Index value present in the array

UBound   Returns the highest Index value present in the array

Controls (other than menu items) created using the Load command are not visible by default. Be sure to set their Visible properties to True.

As mentioned earlier in this chapter, there is a key difference between standard control arrays and menu item control arrays. Standard controls are much less rigidly constrained in their placement and physical size. When you add controls to a control array, you should procedurally manage issues such as ensuring that new controls are not merely placed on top of existing controls.

Most implementation details for nonmenu item control arrays are identical to those previously covered. The Load and Unload statements are still used to add and remove controls from the collection. Events are shared across all controls in the array. Where necessary, trapping for specific triggering controls is available.

Create data input forms and dialog boxes.

- Use the **Controls** collection to manipulate controls at run time.

Creating groups of controls is not particularly helpful if you don't have ways of managing the newly created objects. Because they were not available at design time, the specific functionality may not have been fully anticipated. Using collections allows for systematic handling of groups fo objects. As noted above, the general format looks something like this:

```
Private Sub Form_Load()
Dim myControl As Control
For Each myControl In Controls
Debug.Print myControl.Caption
Next myControl
End Sub
```

The problem with using this generic format is that controls may reside on the form which do not fit with the commands being executed. You can use the TypeOf keyword to check the type of a control before attempting to execute operations against it. For instance, if you want to place a call in a form's Resize event to systematically resize all command buttons to a certain height, you could address the form's Control collection with the following code to prevent unexpected results caused by incorrect property references:

```
If TypeOf MyControl Is CommandButton Then
MyControl.Height = 75
End If
```

This piece of code would find itself nestled within the For Each...Next loop.

Microsoft
✓ Exam
Objective

Create data input forms and dialog boxes.

▪ Use the **Forms** collection to manipulate forms at run time.

The same tools apply to the Forms collection. The Forms collection represents an application-wide, system-maintained list of all loaded forms in the application. The Forms collection has a few common uses worth mentioning here.

▪ Because it maintains a list of loaded forms and is aware of forms that are hidden, it can be helpful in scripting application shutdown. The Forms collection can be iterated through explicitly unloading each form after first saving data where necessary.

▪ It can be useful in making application-wide changes to settings like the default font on forms.

▪ It can be helpful in searching for specific forms that may or may not be open at various points in an application's operation.

The following code illustrates how the Forms collection can be used to systematically change the font of all Label and TextBox controls on all currently open forms. The technical name for the technique employed here is *nested enumeration*. Two separate For Each loops are used, one inside the other. The first loop moves through the Forms collection, and the inner loop executes once for each form. The inner loop moves through the controls on the current form.

```
Private Sub Command1_Click()
Dim myForm As Form
For Each myForm In Forms
    Dim myControl As Control
    For Each myControl In myForm.Controls
        If TypeOf myControl Is Label Or _
            TypeOf myControl Is TextBox Then
            myControl.Font.Name = "Comic Sans MS"
            myControl.Font.Size = 18
        End If
    Next myControl
Next myForm
End Sub
```

The TypeOf keyword is used to make sure that assignments to the Font property are only made to controls that contain a Font property.

Summary

In an n-tier application, the most visible aspect of good development is a user interface that provides an intuitive way for users to enter and retrieve data. Visual Basic 6 provides a wealth of tools for creating sophisticated data client applications. These tools include elegant controls for interacting with the user and mechanisms you can use to enforce data quality. By employing the methods reviewed in this chapter, you can create a successful first tier application that serves both of its primary functions: It acts as an intuitive user experience and provides reliable data handling. Without each of these functions, your client application would weaken the efficacy of the larger distributed architecture.

Review Questions

1. What behavior occurs when a command button's default property is set to True?

   A. When clicked, that button acts to accept any changes that have been made to data contained in the form.

   B. That button's click event will be fired if the Enter key is pressed, regardless of focus.

   C. That button will respond to the Cancel key being pressed.

   D. Any properties of that button not explicitly defined are set to True.

2. Presentation Tier applications are built using which Visual Basic template?

  A. Standard EXE

  B. ActiveX DLL

  C. ActiveX EXE

  D. ActiveX Control

3. Which property does every Visual Basic control contain?

  A. Text

  B. Caption

  C. Security

  D. Name

4. What are the two ways you can place a control on your form?

  A. Double-click the control's icon on the toolbox.

  B. Select the control from the Components dialog.

  C. Click the control's icon on the toolbox and drag the icon to your form.

  D. Click the control's icon on the toolbox, then click and drag across the form.

5. How do you add an ActiveX control to the toolbox?

  A. Drag the control's icon from the ActiveX button on the toolbar to the toolbox.

  B. Select Project ➤ Insert ActiveX Control from the menus.

  C. Register the control.

  D. Select the control from the Components dialog.

6. Which of the following is the correct syntax for registering an ActiveX control?

A. `Regserver32.exe c:\Windows\System\neat.ocx`

B. `Regsvr32.exe c:\Windows\System\neat.ocx`

C. `Regsvr32.exe neat.ocx`

D. `Regsvr32.exe /u c:\Windows\System\neat.ocx`

7. What happens when you register a component?

A. The component is copied to the Controls directory.

B. The component is installed onto your local hard disk, and the registry is updated to reflect its presence.

C. The registry is updated to reflect the presence of the control.

D. The licensing directory in the registry is checked for permission to use a component.

8. What does the ImageList control do?

A. It displays items in the ListItems collection in one of four views.

B. It displays the selected node(s) of the TreeView control.

C. It holds images in memory for use by the TreeView control.

D. It holds images in memory for other controls to use.

9. Which of the following uses the correct syntax for the Add method of the Nodes collection of the TreeView control?

A. tvwNetwork.Nodes.Add RootNode, tvwChild, NewChild, "The New Child"

B. tvwNetwork.Add "RootNode", tvwChild, "NewChild", "The New Child"

C. tvwNetwork.Nodes.Add (tvwChild, "RootNode", "NewChild", "The New Child")

D. None of the above

10. How do you program the ListView control to respond to clicks on the TreeView control?

   A. Script the TreeView_Changed event of the ListView control.

   B. Script the TreeView_Changed event of the ListItems collection.

   C. Place code in the TreeView_Clicked event of the ListView control.

   D. Place code in the NodeClicked event of the TreeView control.

11. How do arrays differ from collections? Select all that apply.

   A. Arrays require that all elements be of the same type.

   B. Collections allow the user to identify an object by its Index value.

   C. Menu items and other controls can be placed in arrays or collections.

   D. The For Each...Next statement is available for use in arrays.

12. Which of the following statements is false?

   A. Collections allow you to systematically manipulate objects.

   B. A control array has only one set of methods, but each control has its own properties.

   C. Controls in a control array must all have the same name, but a unique Index value.

   D. The Controls collection is created by dimensioning a variable of the type Collection.

13. How do you procedurally configure a pop-up menu?

   A. Call the Pop-upMenu method in the MouseUp event procedure, and pass a menu name.

   B. Create a root-level menu and set its visible property to False.

   C. Check the Pop-Up Menu Property check box in the Menu Editor.

   D. Place script in the RightMouseDown event that calls the Pop-up method of the desired menu.

CHAPTER

7

Creating a Data-Aware Client

While Visual Basic is quite capable of producing software across a wide spectrum of needs and uses, it has for several years been used primarily in the development of data client applications. In this book, we present specific tools that Visual Basic and the Microsoft BackOffice family of tools make available for building distributed applications. Given that context, one of the important tasks to be addressed in the planning and implementation of the user tier must be the use of user services in the gathering, maintenance, and display of data.

In this chapter, we will address these issues in two separate topics: ensuring data integrity and employing data binding. The former will present a number of specific tools at your disposal for controlling data quality, while the latter will review the several mechanisms available to developers for closely connecting data presentation tools and the underlying data they expose.

Ensuring User-Tier Data Integrity

When you take on the challenge of using user-tier software to support business needs and goals, you have two control mechanisms at your disposal: First, you can screen the data itself as it is entered and, second, you can validate it against a set of rules, confirming that the data complies with the necessary structure, form, and function. If you are able to consistently provide this service, the quality of the data collected will be much better. Because user services often encapsulate at least some business rules, you have the opportunity and responsibility to enforce consistency and *how* data is entered. If you also employ a strategy that restricts the *types* of data entered, you can quite closely regulate the reliability and validity of your data. We begin with a review of strategies for supporting the quality of data that is introduced to the business and data tiers. The two primary tools for maintaining the quality of data at entry are field- and form-level validation.

Microsoft
✓ *Exam*
Objective

Write code that validates user input.

- Create an application that verifies data entered at the field level and the form level by a user.

Field-Level Validation

The frontline defense against muddy data is often found in property settings on the very controls where the data is entered. This section will present several strategies for restricting data entry employing the following methods:

- Using the MaxLength property of TextBoxes
- Systematically modifying data entry using KeyPress events
- Trapping specific keys using KeyUp and KeyDown events
- Using the MaskEdit control

The MaxLength Property

Text boxes are quite commonly used to collect data. The TextBox control is a rather flexible object, allowing users great flexibility. Unfortunately, this flexibility often translates into poor implementation and meaningless data. However, the TextBox control does contain the MaxLength property, which allows you as the developer to set the maximum number of characters the TextBox can contain. While this is a crude measure, it does the job for basic functions. If an invalidly large number is attempted, the operation will fail, and the computer will beep. Because it is a fairly limited screening tool, we suggest that you use the MaxLength property primarily in conjunction with other data validation tools.

The KeyPress Event

The KeyPress event occurs whenever a printable character (or the Backspace or Enter key) is typed into the keyboard. The KeyPress event exposes the ASCII value of the keyboard event to the event handling procedure. By trapping these KeyAscii values and converting them to character values, you can enable a low level data validation tool. In essence, you will be individually checking each character typed for its appropriateness in the current control.

Because you return the KeyAscii value back to the Visual Basic application, you can use this event procedure to reject unwanted key values by setting KeyAscii values to 0 (or null) for those keys. You can also implement traditional character manipulation, such as converting characters to upper case, before returning to the KeyAscii value. If you need to trap the pressing of function keys, editing keys, or navigation keys, you will need to use the KeyUp or KeyDown events instead. These are presented below. The following code is an example of how to implement a KeyPress event procedure that validates individual characters.

```
Sub Text1_KeyPress(KeyAscii As Integer)
   'Only accept numeric characters.
   If Chr(KeyAscii) < "0" Or Chr(KeyAscii) > "9" Then
     KeyAscii = 0'Sets the character to null.
     Beep
   End If
End Sub
```

The KeyUp and KeyDown Events

The KeyUp and KeyDown events offer an even more powerful tool for trapping keyboard events. These events are triggered by *all* keyboard activity, not just the primary printable characters and a few additional keys. If you need to trap for the use of function keys, editing keys, or other non-printing ASCII characters, use the KeyUp or KeyDown events. The following code is an example of how to implement a KeyUp or KeyDown event in your application.

```
Sub Text1_KeyDown(KeyCode As Integer, Shift As Integer)
Select Case KeyCode
If vbKeyF1 or vbKeyF2 or vbKeyF3… Then
MsgBox "No Fkeys allowed."
End If
End Sub
```

The KeyPress event is more efficient and simpler to implement, so we recommend its use over the KeyUp or KeyDown events unless you need the special functionality these events provide.

Because keyboards can enter multiple characters by holding down a key, users can create multiple characters with only a single KeyUp event firing.

The MaskEdit Control

While the KeyPress, KeyUp, and KeyDown events offer an elegant character-based validation option, the MaskEdit control offers an even higher level of validation. The MaskEdit control is in many ways similar to a standard TextBox control. However, it has additional properties that allow it to provide data formatting and validation functions.

In particular, the Mask property allows you to specify the types of characters in certain orders or combinations that are allowed and raises a Validation-Error event if the Mask is violated. Aesthetically, the MaskEdit control also allows the user to view the data they are entering as it will appear after formatting. For instance, if the data for a particular field is to be formatted as a phone number, the input mask can be defined as (###) ###-####. In this case, the parentheses, space, and hyphen are literals. They are not saved with the data, but they are visual cues to the user of the form and format of the data. When using such a Mask, the user sees empty spaces within which to enter data. Figure 7.1 shows a MaskEdit control that is set to use the input mask just defined.

FIGURE 7.1

The input mask of a
MaskEdit control

The ValidationError event can be scripted to provide feedback to users about the particular data entry error that must be resolved. The following code shows how such an event might be coded.

```
Private Sub MaskEntry_ValidationError(InvalidText As String, _
                    StartPosition As Integer)
If StartPosition = mskID.MaxLength Then
Msgbox "Limit 10 digits"
Else
Msgbox "Digits Only"
End If
End Sub
```

This event procedure, combined with the special data-validating strengths of the MaskEdit control, allows you a good deal of control over both the type and quality of data being entered, as well as the feedback available to the user.

The MaskEdit control also offers additional features that make it a useful data entry validation tool. The control's Format property allows a format mask to be specified for use in displaying already-entered data. This allows you to enter data using the input mask, save the data without formatting, and display it later using a custom format.

The MaskEdit control's AutoTab property, when set to True, will set the focus to the next control in the form's Tab order when the final character of an input mask has been entered. For instance, when a user types the last character of a zip code into its field, the focus can automatically shift to the next data entry field, saving the effort of pressing the Tab key.

However, there is one particular twist to keep in mind if you decide to work with the MaskEdit control. In order to procedurally reset the value of the Text property of the control, you have to work procedurally around the mask, or you will reset it as well. In other words, you have two ways to reset the Text property of the control. The first way is to reset the Text property as you would normally, as shown in the following code.

```
mskInput.Text = ""
```

This clears the Mask property, which you will need to reset, as in the following code.

```
mskInput.Mask = "(###) ###-####"
```

The second way is to reset the Text property within the Mask in this way:

```
mskInput.Text = "(___) ___-____"
```

The MaskEdit control ships with the Professional Edition of Visual Basic but must be added to the ToolBar to make it available for use on your forms. To add the MaskEdit control to the Toolbar, select Project ➤ Components and check the item labeled Microsoft Masked Edit Control 6.0. Exercise 7.1 presents steps for implementing field-level validation of data.

EXERCISE 7.1

Field-Level Input Validation

1. Create a new project using the Standard EXE template.

2. Place a TextBox control on the form, and set its MaxLength property to 6.

3. Add the following code to the form module.

```
Sub Text1_KeyPress(KeyAscii As Integer)
'Only accept numeric characters
If Chr(KeyAscii) < "0" Or Chr(KeyAscii) > "9" Then
    KeyAscii = 0'Sets the character to null.
    Beep
End If
End Sub
```

4. Add the MaskEdit control to your ToolBox by selecting Project ➤ Components and checking the box next to Microsoft Masked Edit Control 6.0.

5. Place the MaskEdit control on your form, and click the Mask property in the Properties window. Type the following into the Property field: (###) ###-####.

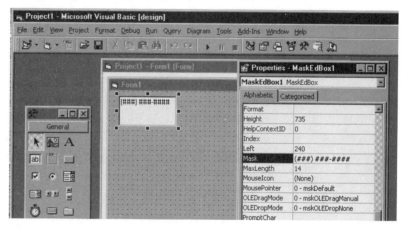

6. Save your work. Run the application, and test the validation tools by trying to type letters into the text box and typing more than six numeric digits into the text box.

7. Test the MaskEdit box by trying to enter letters instead of numbers into the phone number input mask.

If you procedurally access the Text property of the MaskEdit control, you will retrieve both the data and the mask. If you want to access the data without the mask information, use the ClipText property instead.

Form-Level Validation

Field-level validation offers a powerful solution for controlling the quality of data being entered. However, if you rely on it exclusively, you may allow other erroneous data to be saved. The primary weakness of field-level validation is that it can bypass fields where no data is entered or situations where data in two fields needs to be verified in relation to each other. Validating data at the form level addresses these problems nicely. Form-level validation is typically tied to the click event of the button used to accept or submit data entry.

Batch-Mode Validation

Form-level validation typically boils down to processing the field entries in a batch-mode fashion. At some point near the end of completing the form, a script is triggered. This script either directly examines each field for required properties, or uses the Controls collection to loop through properties on the form. The latter approach can be especially helpful if the form contains a control array with runtime-created controls. See Chapter 6 for more information on the use of looping in collections and the dynamic creation of controls. The following code shows the direct approach to batch-checking the validity of the fields on the present form. The Text controls on this form are bound to a data source, and all changes have already been saved elsewhere, so code unloads the form if no errors are found.

```
Private Sub cmdSubmit_Click()
  If txtFirstName.TEXT = "" Then
    MsgBox "You must provide a first name"
    txtFirstName.SetFocus
    Exit Sub
  ElseIf txtLastName.TEXT = "" Then
    MsgBox "You must provide a last name"
```

```
      txtLastName.SetFocus
      Exit Sub
   ElseIF txtAge.Text > 120 Then
      MsgBox "Age must be less than 120"
      TxtAge.SetFocus
   Else
      Unload Me
   End If
End Sub
```

Exercise 7.2 walks you through the building of a simple form with a series of data validation techniques as presented in this chapter. As you work through this exercise, keep in mind that data validation needs vary widely depending upon the business needs of your application, the complexity of the application, and the centrality of the application and its data to business functions. If you currently build Visual Basic applications, think about how you may implement these techniques to constrain the data entry procedures and increase the richness and accuracy of the data you collect.

EXERCISE 7.2

Testing Form-Level Validation

1. Open Visual Basic and create a new project using the Standard EXE template.

2. Name the project Chapter7.vbp.

3. Add the following three text boxes to the default form in your project: txtFirstName, txtLastName, and txtAge. Set the Text property of each to Null.

4. Place labels next to each text box to identify the data that will be entered into each of them.

5. Add a command button to the form. Name it cmdSubmit and assign it the caption Submit. Enter the code shown two paragraphs above as the click event for the Submit button you just entered.

6. Save and run the application. Your finished form should look something like the following graphic. Test its functionality by clicking Submit when one or more fields is empty. Note the behavior if multiple fields are empty. Note the use of Else If statements with non-mutually exclusive alternatives in creating this functionality. The primary goal is to notify the user and return focus, so multiple errors do not need to be trapped at once.

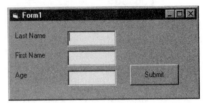

Modifying Forms or Controls Based on Input Values

Microsoft
✓ Exam
Objective

Write code that validates user input.

- Create an application that enables or disables controls based on input in fields.

At the beginning of this chapter we noted that in addition to controlling the quality of data collected, you can also control *how* the data is collected. There are a number of tools at your disposal for enforcing the implementation of business rules in the execution of your application and the collection and display of data. We will discuss the most relevant of these:

- Tab order and field validation
- Enabling program execution after validation

Tying Tab Order to Field Validation

We have already spoken a great deal about the techniques involved in validating individual fields. Another important quality of these techniques is that placing field-level validation code in the LostFocus event can allow you to return focus to the problematic control.

New to Visual Basic 6, the CausesValidation property and Validate event provide a more elegant way to implement this type of data validation. When configuring a form to enforce data validation, you set the CausesValidation property of all controls to True, with the exception of those controls used to provide assistance to the user. Setting this property to True on control X causes the Validate event of any control passing focus to control X to fire its Validate event. Execution returns to the previous control to process the Validate event procedure (if there is one). When configured in this way, users are forced to correctly enter data before moving to another data field, but they are still able to step outside the focus loop to obtain assistance if desired.

Tying Program Execution to Input Validation

Another way to modify the user experience is to mold the flow of execution by reigning in the freedoms of event-driven interfaces. In other words, you can enable and disable controls based on data validation. In its simplest form, this technique is used in disabling an OK button until all required fields are completed.

In Chapter 6, we presented some of the tools available for modifying the user interface at runtime. You can tie most or all of these techniques to data validation if needed. For instance, if you were collecting survey responses from the public, you could create command buttons on the fly, one for each response option after each question. Users then have only to click the button that represents "strongly agree" or "strongly disagree." The buttons, created as elements in a control array, each assign a unique corresponding value to the database. Using this model, data integrity is ensured by on-the-fly hard coding of values to response buttons. Exercise 7.3 walks you through the steps required to tie the enabling of an OK button to data validation code.

Disabling a Control Based on Validation

1. Open the Chapter7.vbp project.

2. Comment the click event of the Submit button (place single apostrophes before each line).

3. Create a new click event procedure for the Submit button that includes only the line Unload Me.

   We are now going to reverse the Validation method. Instead of only continuing when all entries are correct, we will prevent continuation as long as any fields are incorrect.

4. Create a Function named MyValidate. Place the following code in the procedure:

```
Private Sub MyValidate()
    If (txtLastName.Text = "") Or _
            (txtFirstName.Text = "") Or _
        Not IsNumeric(txtAge.Text) Then
            cmdSubmit.Enabled = False
    Else
    cmdSubmit.Enabled = True
    End If
```

5. Create a Change event for each of the three text boxes, and place a call to the new MyValidate function in each.

6. Insert the KeyPress monitoring code mentioned above in the KeyPress event of the txtAge control:

```
Sub TxtAge_KeyPress(KeyAscii As Integer)
'Only accept numeric characters
If Chr(KeyAscii) < "0" Or Chr(KeyAscii) > "9" Then
    KeyAscii = 0'Sets the character to null.
    Beep
End If
End Sub
```

7. From the Properties window, set the initial value of the Submit button's Enabled property to False.

8. Save and test the application.

   The form should prevent you from clicking the Submit button unless there is text entered in all three text boxes. The Age box will allow only numbers to be typed. The form with the Submit button disabled should look like the following graphic.

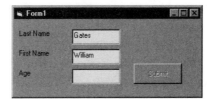

So far, this chapter has focused primarily on the input aspects of a data-aware client. Of course, being data aware is a two-way street. Databases are at least as concerned with returning and displaying data as with collecting it. The remainder of this chapter will focus on implementing the data binding tools included in Visual Basic to enable accurate and efficient display (with minimal programming) of underlying data sources.

Data Binding: Reaching Beyond the User Tier

The essence of a data client application is its ability to integrate smoothly into data-driven environment. With its new data binding tools, Visual Basic 6 joins the ranks of truly data-oriented development tools. A significant portion of this added data-awareness is across-the-board support for ADO and Microsoft's vision of Universal Data Access. (See Chapter 3, *Accessing Databases with the ActiveX Data Objects* for more information on Visual Basic's implementation of ADO).

Visual Basic 6 provides three ways for user interface elements of a client application to be tied to data elements: the ADO Data Control, the Visual Basic Data Environment, and data-aware classes. We will discuss each of these shortly. These ties, or bindings, represent dynamic connections between a certain control on a specific form, and a certain data source. As the current record in a recordset or cursor shifts, these changes are automatically reflected in the bound control.

Before we begin a discussion of the mechanisms for binding data to DataSource objects, we need to discuss what a data source is and how to configure them. A data source serves as a data middleman and represents the ideal of encapsulating data handling code, i.e., they are objects that are engineered specifically for the task of handling data. Data sources typically request data from a database and make the results available to bound controls.

Visual Basic Data Source Tools

Visual Basic 6 provides a series of different DataSource objects that you can use in your projects, depending on your needs and resources. The primary DataSource objects available are:

- The ADO Data Control

- The Visual Basic Data Environment

- Data-aware classes

We will briefly discuss each of these.

The simplest data source is the ADO Data Control. The ADO Data Control must be added to the toolbox and placed on a form to be used. To add the Data Control, select Project ➤ Components, then check the Microsoft ADO Data Control 6.0 (OLE DB). The control is placed on the toolbox and is now available for use. Place the control on your form.

To configure the Data Control, open the Property Page window, and access the ConnectionString property. Clicking the ellipsis button allows you to access the Custom Property Pages for the control. You will need to select a database access technology, either a data link file, an ODBC Data Source Name, or an OLE DB connection string. Figure 7.2 shows the first configuration dialog. Depending on which connection type you select, you will need to provide different information to connect to a database or other data source. The information needed may include information about the connection technology, user ID, or password. Depending upon the data source, you may have to set the Recordset property as well.

F I G U R E 7.2

Configuring the ADO
Data Control

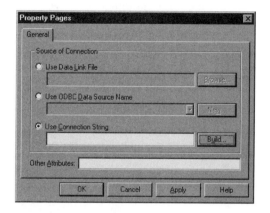

The Recordset property expects you to set a CommandType. For this property, you need to specify whether you will be generating a list of records based on a table in the database, a SQL query, a stored procedure, or other data command. After you select one of these, you will have to specify whatever additional settings are necessary to generate the query. When all dialogs have been dismissed, the ADO Data Control on your form holds a recordset based on the query information set. You can then bind series of controls to this object.

The Data Environment is a new object type that allows you to create Data-Source objects that you can interact with either through code or with bound controls. Whichever way you chose to interact with the Data Environment, it offers several advantages over the use of the ADO Data Control. The Data Environment is not a graphical control. It is an object (labeled as a Designer), which is included in the current project. This allows the Designer file to be reused across projects and makes the data source available throughout the project rather than containing the scope of the DataSource to a particular form, as the ADO Data Control does. The Data Environment also supports multifaceted data access. A single Data Environment object in a project can support multiple connection configurations and multiple data commands per connection.

The Data Environment is configured at design time by double-clicking the Data Environment in the Project Browser window. This will open the Data Environment window. You then right-click the default Connection object and select properties. In this way, you configure the Connection object to contact the data source. Once you right-click the Connection object, the connection is configured in an almost identical fashion to the ADO Data Control. Again, you will need to select between data access technologies: data link file, ODBC DSN, or OLE DB connection string. To select a recordset for passing to bound form controls, right-click the Connection object and select Add Command. Setting properties of the Data Command allows you to select a table of records, the return set from a stored procedure, or the results of an ad hoc SQL query. Figure 7.3. shows the Data Environment after a data command has been created.

FIGURE 7.3

The Data Environment window

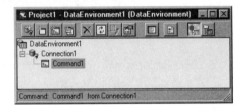

Exercise 7.4 demonstrates the steps to add a Data Environment, configure connection properties, and add a data command.

EXERCISE 7.4

Adding and Configuring the Data Environment

1. Create a new project using the Standard EXE template.

2. Name the project Databound.vbp, and the default form Databound.frm.

3. Select Project ➤ Add Data Environment.

4. To set the Data Link Properties, right-click the Connection1 Connection object that was created with the Data Environment. Select Properties from the pop-up menu to see the Data Link Properties dialog.

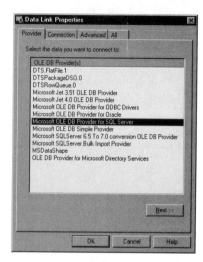

5. Select a data provider. Most commonly this will be either the OLE DB for ODBC Drivers, a Jet OLE DB provider, or OLE DB for SQL Server.

6. Click the Next button.

7. Depending on which provider you selected, you will be asked to answer several questions regarding connecting to a database. If you select OLE DB for SQL Server, you will be asked to provide the server name, login information, and database name. If you have SQL Server running on your machine, enter the name of your computer for the servername, **sa** for the userID, no password, and **pubs** for the initial database, as shown in the following graphic.

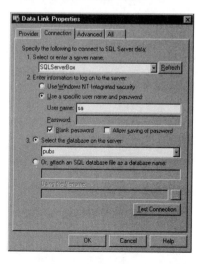

8. Click the Test Connection button to confirm correct configuration.

9. Right-click the Connection object and select Add Command from the pop-up menu.

10. Right-click the new command, and select Properties.

11. In the Command Properties dialog, select Table as the Database object, then next to Object Name select dbo.authors. Click OK.

The final type of data source at your disposal is a data-aware class. Classes can now be defined as either data sources or data consumers. To create a data source class, select Project ➤ Add Class Module, and select the DataSource Class template. Once the class file has been created, the only other mandatory operation is that you set the DataSourceBehavior property to vbDataSource. ADO code within the class can then connect to remote databases, returning recordsets to be served to other data consumers. These data-aware classes can serve as an independent data source to other forms and classes within the current project and to other projects once compiled. The class can be deployed as an application server if desired, though the preferred method of this implementation is through the use of a DLL and MTS.

Microsoft ✓ *Exam* *Objective*

Use data binding to display and manipulate data from a data source.

The three methods of binding controls to data sources include:

- Manually binding individual controls to a DataSource object

- Dragging a Command object from the Data Environment window to a form to create a series of bound controls

- Using the Data Form Wizard to create a data-aware form, complete with record navigation buttons

The rest of this chapter is dedicated to discussing these three means of connecting data sources and user interface controls.

Using Manually Bound Controls to Display Data

To bind a control to an existing data source is a relatively straightforward task. Most of the basic Visual Basic controls can be bound to data sources. Some of the qualifying controls include: TextBoxes, Labels, PictureBoxes, CheckBoxes, ListBoxes, ComboBoxes, and ImageBoxes. Setting data bindings for each of these is quite similar. To bind a TextBox control to a Data Environment and its Connection object, you have to set three properties of the TextBox control:

DataSource Property   This is set to the name of the data source, in this particular case, the name of the Data Environment.

DataMember Property   This is set to the name of the data command specifying the recordset to be used.

DataField Property   This property indicates which field in particular is bound to the single field of the text box.

While the binding process tends to be similar regardless of which type of display control is being bound, settings can vary slightly across data sources. For instance, the ADO Data Control does not expose a Data Member.

While this process is generally straightforward and simple, if you have to build a number of forms, or if your forms are complex, the process can become burdensome. To alleviate the monotony (and increased chance of error) that arises out of making systematic data bindings, there are two ways to automate the process. The next two sections discuss these methods.

Using the Data Environment to Connect to a Data Source

The new Data Environment tools of Visual Basic 6 provide a great labor-saving device in the creation of bound controls. Of course, this only works when you are using the Data Environment for binding, but in those cases it is a quick and painless way to generate forms and reports from existing recordsets and data structures.

To build bound controls from an existing Data Environment/Data Command, simply drag portions of the Data Command from the Data Environment window onto a form within the project. This is actually a group of features rather than one. If you right-click before dragging, you will be presented with a dialog asking whether you want to place individual controls (one record per form), a data-bound grid (multiple records per form), or a hierarchical flex grid (a combination of tree-view and data-bound grid controls). If you click the plus sign next to the Data Control icon to explode its contents, you can drag individual fields (or several at once) to the form. When dropped, Visual Basic draws the controls on the form, with all appropriate Binding properties already set. See Figure 7.4 for an illustration of the arrangement of windows and dialog that appears after right-dragging. Exercise 7.5 gives instructions for creating bound controls from a Data Command.

FIGURE 7.4

Data Command Auto Control Binding options

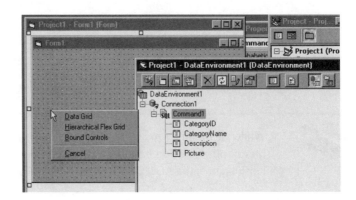

EXERCISE 7.5

Dragging a Data Command to Create Bound Controls

1. Return to the project you worked on in Exercise 7.4. Open the Data Environment window, if necessary, by clicking on the Data Environment designer in the Project Explorer window.

2. Drag the command object's icon to a blank form in the current project. New bound controls will automatically be generated based upon the fields in the Data Command.

3. Add a command button to the form with the following script in its click event (assuming you didn't change any default names):

```
DataEnvironment1.rsCommand1.MoveNext.
```

4. Run the application to test the bound controls. The finished product should look like the following graphic.

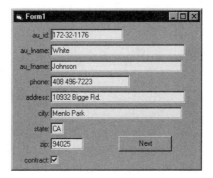

Using the Data Form Wizard to Create Forms with Bound Controls

As with many technologies, the Visual Basic Development Team has added a wizard for creating data forms with a minimum of user intervention. To access this wizard, use the Add-in Manager to load the Visual Basic 6.0 Data Form Wizard. The Data Form Wizard allows you to save wizard settings across sessions, to make building multiple forms easier.

Once you begin the wizard, you will be asked a series of questions. These include:

- Are you connecting to a local (Access) or ODBC database?

- What are the names of the DSN, user, password, and database?

- What type of data form? Single record per page? Grid?

- Which fields are to be shown, and from which table(s)?

- Which navigational controls would you like to include?

One downside of using the Data Form Wizard at the time of this writing is that the wizard has no facilities for working with OLE DB technologies. It is strictly geared around ODBC and Jet.

Summary

Data validation and data binding support Visual Basic's data handling, giving Visual Basic one of its greatest strengths: the ability to quickly create powerful data clients.

Data validation is used to ensure that errors are caught when data is entered so that corrections can be made to erroneous data. Data binding allows you to rapidly develop applications that display data from a recordset or database, saving you the effort of having to procedurally update the values displayed on forms.

By employing Visual Basic's data validation and data binding tools, you can create user-tier applications that develop quickly, while still maintaining the integrity of your data.

Review Questions

1. Which of the following cannot function as a data source?

   A. ADO Data Control

   B. MaskedEdit control

   C. Data-aware class

   D. DataEnvironment object

2. For which type of control would you not want to set the CausesValidation property to True?

   A. A command button labeled Help

   B. A command button labeled Validate

   C. The first text box on a form

   D. The last text box on a form

3. Which is not a property associated with data binding?

   A. DataSource

   B. DataMember

   C. DataFormat

   D. RecordSource

4. Which of the following events can tell whether a function key (e.g., F4) has been pressed?

   A. Change

   B. KeyUp

   C. KeyDown

   D. KeyPress

5. Which of the following is not a tool for validating data at entry?

   A. The MaskEdit format property

   B. The TextBox CausesValidation property

   C. LostFocus Event

   D. The TextBox MaxLength property

6. What does a data command do?

   A. Enforces data integrity

   B. Maintains data validity

   C. Defines the database interaction

   D. Defines the database query

7. You extract the value of the ClipText property of a MaskEdit control. What do you see?

A. The first five characters of information originally passed to the control

B. The last five characters originally passed to the control

C. The text that was originally typed into the service

D. The MaskEdit.text property with literals included

8. The Visual Basic 6.0 Data Form Wizard ignores which technology?

A. ADO

B. ODBC

C. Data-bound Grids

D. OLE DB

9. To automatically create data bindings, you can drag icons from the _____ to _____ .

A. Data View window – Form

B. ToolBox – Data View window

C. Data Environment window – Form

D. Toolbox – Form

CHAPTER

8

Calling COM Components

In Chapter 4 we discussed how COM components are created using Visual Basic 6, and we created components to implement our business tier. In the last few chapters, we have discussed the implementation of the presentation tier. To tie the presentation tier and the business tier together, you will call the components from your client applications. The mechanism that you will use to call these components is called *automation*.

In this chapter, we will look at how automation works. This will include a discussion of COM interfaces, especially those that support automation. We will explore the mechanisms behind automation calls, including the different approaches to binding. We will then look at the process of calling a COM component from a Visual Basic application or another component. Finally, we will investigate different approaches to enabling components to execute asynchronously using either component events or callback procedures.

Automation Basics

Automation (sometimes called OLE automation) is the process of calling the exposed methods of a component from a client application for the purpose of providing services to the client application. In Chapter 4, we discussed the process of creating components with Visual Basic 6. These components support automation through a set of methods provided by an interface called IDispatch.

As you will recall from our previous discussion, all COM objects support a concept called an interface. An interface is actually a binary standard calling point of a component. Interfaces have some qualities that suit them very well for objects in a distributed application.

- Interfaces are immutable. They cannot change once published.

- Interfaces can inherit from other interfaces, allowing modifications in a parent to change all child interfaces.

- Interfaces are standard. As long as a client knows that the interface supports COM, the calls made to the interface are standard and predictable.

With this set of assumptions, let's look specifically at the IDispatch interface.

Binding

The IDispatch interface supports automation. Whenever an automation call is made from a client to a component, the call is made through the IDispatch interface. To support automation, the IDispatch interface contains methods that carry out the work of calling the custom methods of the component. Which of these methods the IDispatch interface uses depends on the approach to binding that the component supports and the client requests.

 The IDispatch interface is marked private within the Visual Basic type library and is not directly accessible by an automation client. To use the IDispatch interface, you must use the Visual Basic automation functions that will be discussed later in this chapter.

Binding is the process of identifying to the automation client which custom methods of the component are supported and how these calls should be made. It is a necessary step in all automation calls, but different approaches to binding can significantly affect performance. There are two primary types of binding, *late binding* and *early binding*.

Late Binding

Late binding performs all binding activities at runtime. With every call to the component, the Visual Basic automation client makes a call to the IDispatch method called GetIDsOfNames and passes the name of the desired method. This will return to the client a value called a *dispatch ID* or DispID. The DispID is then passed back to the component through the Invoke function of the IDispatch interface. The Invoke function can then locate the method with the corresponding DispID and call that method.

As you can see, late binding requires numerous calls to the component for each call to a custom method. This is very inefficient, especially when using an out-of-process component packaged as an EXE. This is because each of the calls has to be marshaled across process boundaries, which can be a very slow process.

Early Binding

Visual Basic supports a more efficient approach to binding called early binding. During early binding, the automation client uses the type library provided by the component to compile direct references to the component within the automation client code. Exactly how this happens depends on the type of early binding used. There are two approaches to early binding, *DispID* binding and *vTable* binding.

DispID Binding   Using DispID binding, at compile time the automation client extracts the dispatch IDs from the type library of the component and compiles these dispatch IDs into the automation client code. This eliminates the need to call the GetIDsOfNames function of the IDispatch interface. When a call is made to the component, the dispatch ID compiled into the client is passed to the Invoke method of the IDispatch interface. Especially for out-of-process components, this can significantly increase the performance of the call because you only need one call from the client application to call the custom method of the component.

vTable Binding   vTable binding is more efficient than DispID binding. Instead of simply providing a dispatch ID that will provide lookup capability for locating the custom method, components that support vTable binding create a virtual table of custom methods. Each of these entries in the virtual table is actually a pointer to the corresponding custom method, making the access to the method very efficient. When the automation client is compiled, the address of the method's entry in the vTable is compiled into the code rather than the dispatch ID. This means that accessing the method is as simple as locating the entry in the virtual table and following the internal pointer to the custom method, which is much faster than using a DispID lookup.

When you use vTable binding to make a call to a custom method, you are not actually using the Invoke function of IDispatch. You are calling the method directly through this alternate interface provided by the virtual table.

The virtual table in the component is an example of a *dual interface*. If a method has a dual interface, this means that there is more than one way that the method can be called. In this case, the custom method can be called either through the Invoke method using the DispID, or directly using the vTable. Since the interfaces in the vTable inherit from the IDispatch interface, both are actually dual interfaces to the same internal function.

Components created in Visual Basic support early binding through vTable binding. This makes Visual Basic components as efficient as possible, since vTable binding requires virtually no processing overhead when making the function call, a very different scenario from late binding or DispID binding.

Calling COM Components

> ***Microsoft***
> ✓ ***Exam***
> ***Objective***
>
> **Instantiate and invoke a COM component.**
>
> - Create a Visual Basic client application that uses a COM component.

Now that we have seen the binding options available, let's look at how components are called from a Visual Basic automation client. We will start the discussion with an overview of object variables, which are an important part of the component equation. We will then look at the options available for calling a COM component from a Visual Basic automation client.

Object Variables

Visual Basic does not have any direct support for the programming concept of a pointer. A pointer is like a forwarding address. When an application accesses a pointer thinking that it is accessing the actual resource—an object or information—the pointer forwards the call to the location where the actual resource is located. Using pointers does not result in any significant increase in overhead, as the pointer is constructed to allow the application to access the resource directly.

Although Visual Basic does not have any direct support for pointers, it does support a structure called an *object variable*. An object variable works like a pointer in that the application uses the object variable to refer to an object in code. The object variable refers the application to the memory location where the actual resource is located. Object variables are very efficiently implemented in Visual Basic and provide an extremely useful mechanism for viewing and modifying object properties and calling object methods.

You create object variables in a similar fashion to the way you create standard variables, using declaration statements such as Dim, Public, or Private.

Remember that the declaration statements that you use and the location of the declaration will determine the scope of the variable. This is also true with object variables. Object variables declared locally will only be visible locally.

When declaring a standard variable, you also provide a data type. Object variables have no data types; however, they do have class names that must be used in place of the data type. Class names can be either very general or very specific. For example, suppose you have a Visual Basic form called Form1 and you wish to create an object variable to reference that form. The following list presents three declaration statements you could use, starting with a general statement and getting progressively more specific.

```
Dim frm as Object
Dim frm as Form
Dim frm as Form1
```

In the first statement, an object variable declared as object could actually mean any type of object. The second statement declares an object variable as class name of form, so it is more specific as to the type of object, but it does not completely identify the form in question. The final declaration specifically identifies the form named Form1 as the form with which you will work.

Object Variables and Binding

The method that you choose for declaring your object variables will determine the approach to binding that the application will use for that class of the component library. For example, if I use the statement `Dim frm as Object`, this will serve as the necessary declaration of the variable. However, since the specific class name is not known at compile time, the compiler must use late binding for all calls to the methods and properties of the object to which the object variable refers. Late binding is used whenever the class name provided in the code is:

- Variant
- Object
- Form
- Control

To enable early binding, you must specifically identify the specific object at the time that the variable is declared. For example, if you used the declaration `Dim frm as Form1`, the compiler can identify the class *Form1* at compile time and allow early binding to the form.

Visual Basic treats every individual Form and Control object as a separate class, inheriting from a base class of Form or Control. The form named Form1 is a unique class for the project in which it is defined and multiple instances can be created of the form or control within the project.

Exercise 8.1 walks you through the task of manipulating controls on a form through object variables. In this example, you will use the Controls collection of the form. You were introduced to this collection in Chapter 6. Through the collection, you will use an object variable to control the attributes of controls on a form.

EXERCISE 8.1

Using Object Variables

1. Start Visual Basic. When prompted for a project type, select the Standard EXE template and click OK. Add three text boxes and three command buttons to the form. Arrange them in a similar way to the following graphic.

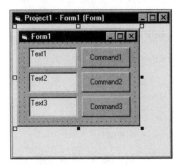

2. Navigate to the click event of the form. In this event, add code to iterate through the Controls collection, checking the class identity of each control. If the control is a command button, set the caption to **Command Caption**. If the control is a text box, set the text to **TextBox Text**. Use the following code as an example.

```
Private Sub Form_Click()
Dim ctl As Control
For Each ctl In Controls
    If TypeOf ctl Is CommandButton Then
        ctl.Caption = "Command Caption"
    ElseIf TypeOf ctl Is TextBox Then
        ctl.Text = "TextBox Text"
    End If
Next ctl
End Sub
```

3. Start the application and click in a blank area of the form not occupied by a text box or a command button. This will change the appropriate properties of the controls in the collection.

4. Close the application and exit Visual Basic.

Automating External Objects

Forms and controls are internal to the Visual Basic design environment, which makes them simpler to automate. When you automate an application or component that is external to Visual Basic, you must add a reference in Visual Basic to the type library that defines the object structure of the application or component. To make this reference, select Project ➤ References from the Visual Basic menu. This presents you with a list of all the type libraries registered on that computer. To add a reference, click the check box next to the library that you would like to use in your application. Figure 8.1 illustrates the References window in Visual Basic 6.

FIGURE 8.1

The Visual Basic
References window

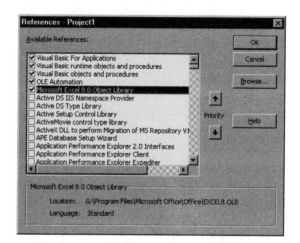

You will notice that in Figure 8.1, a reference has been added to the Microsoft Excel 8.0 Object Library. This is the type library that defines the object structure of the entire Excel object model for the client application. You will also notice that the bottom of the window displays the location of the object library file. This file ends with an .olb extension. Type libraries for larger applications are usually separate files ending with .olb or .tlb, while type libraries for smaller components are included within the .exe or .dll itself.

> The advantage of using type libraries is that, especially for larger applications that act as servers, the automation client can load the small type library file rather than the entire .exe to document the object model for early binding.

Instantiating Components

Once you have added a reference to the type library, you are ready to start writing automation code. There are numerous options available to instantiating a component. One of these involves the use of the Visual Basic keyword, *New*. The New keyword allows you to create a new instance of a class at the time that you declare the object variable or any other time of your choosing. Using the New keyword in the declaration statement is called auto-instantiation. You can also explicitly use the New keyword to control instantiation or use the CreateObject function provided by Visual Basic.

Auto-Instantiation   When declaring an object variable, you can use the New keyword to instantiate the object at that point. While this is not the most efficient method of instantiating an object, it does have the advantage of performing all of the necessary operations using a single line of code, the declaration statement. For example, assume that you have already added a reference to the type library for Microsoft Excel 8. The following code in the General Declarations section of a form creates a form-level object variable that references the Excel Application object. It also provides for the automatic instantiation of that object when needed.

```
Private xl as New Excel.Application
```

Controlling Instantiation with the New Keyword   Because of the extra overhead of auto-instantiation, you may wish to control your code a little more tightly by explicitly stating when the instantiation is to take place. This requires two steps, one to declare the object variable and another to instantiate the object with the New keyword. Since the instantiation is an executable statement, you cannot include the instantiation step in the General Declarations section of a form or a module.

To instantiate the object variable using the New keyword, you must use the *Set* statement. The Set statement is the mechanism through which the pointer to the actual object resource is established. This is also a distinction between using standard variables and using object variables. You would not use a Set statement when initializing a standard variable, but it is required when setting a pointer for an object variable. The following code example illustrates how the variable declaration statements and the Set statement are used together to instantiate an object variable.

```
' In the General Declarations section
Private xl as Excel.Application
' In an event or general procedure
Set xl = New Excel.Application
```

Using the CreateObject Function   Another option for object instantiation is the CreateObject function provided by Visual Basic. This function can be extremely convenient when automating older components and applications that do not support the New keyword. You use the CreateObject function with the Set statement much in the same way that you used the New keyword. The following code example illustrates how to perform this operation.

```
' In the General Declarations section
Private xl as Excel.Application
' In an event or general procedure
Set xl = CreateObject("Excel.Application")
```

Although they appear to behave very similarly, the New keyword and the CreateObject function are actually quite different in their internal mechanisms. Discussing the differences is beyond the scope of this book; however, you should be advised that in most cases where multiple instances are created from the same object class, the New keyword is the more efficient approach.

Terminating an Instance   Once you are finished with an instance of an object, you should release the pointer and recover its resources by terminating the instance. Once again, since you are using an object variable, you will need to use the Set statement to accomplish this. To terminate the instance, set the object variable to the keyword **Nothing**, as in the following example.

```
Set xl = Nothing
```

Calling Methods and Properties

Once the object has been instantiated and the object variable set, the object's properties and methods are accessible by the automation client. Using the object variable, the properties and methods of the class can be controlled directly. You use the object variable in the same way as any other named object inside of Visual Basic, such as a control or form. For example, once you have instantiated the Excel application, the program code is running in the background, but you do not see the Excel application on the screen. To make the application visible and bring it to the foreground, you use the *Visible* property of the Excel Application object as demonstrated in the following code.

```
Set xl = New Excel.Application
xl.Visible = True
```

As you can see, from this point forward the process of automation is essentially identical to using internal objects, calling their properties and methods. By providing an object variable as an established reference to an external object, all calls are automatically forwarded to the instantiated object and the desired services provided consequently. Exercise 8.2 walks you through the automation process of Microsoft Word 97. Using automation, you will instantiate the Microsoft Word application and enter text into the document.

WARNING This exercise will not work with versions of Microsoft Word earlier than version 8 (Office 97) because they do not support Visual Basic for Application. While you can still automate earlier versions of Word, you must do so using Word Basic.

EXERCISE 8.2

Automating Microsoft Word

1. Start Visual Basic, selecting the Standard EXE as your desired project template. Add a command button to Form1. Set the Caption property of the button to **Start Word** and the Name property to **cmdWord**. In the Project References dialog, add a reference to the Microsoft Word 8.0 Object Library.

2. In the general declarations section of Form1, declare a form level variable called **wd** as an object variable referencing the class Word .Application. Use the following declaration as an example.

```
Private wd as Word.Application
```

3. In the click event of the cmdWord command button, add code that instantiates the Word Application object using the New keyword. Set the Visible property to True for the application and add a new document to the documents collection of the application. Finally, using the Selection object of the Application model, use the TypeText method to enter the string **This is my first automation project** in the new document. Use the following code as a guide.

```
Set wd = New Word.Application
wd.Visible = True
wd.Documents.Add
wd.Selection.TypeText "This is my first automation project."
```

4. Start the application and click the command button. Microsoft Word will start, and the desired text will be entered into the document. Exit Microsoft Word and stop the application.

5. Experiment with the code by commenting out the last line and running the application again, exiting Word each time. Continue backward through the code, commenting out lines and running the application again to see the effect of the commented-out line.

6. When finished, exit Visual Basic and make sure that no instances of Microsoft Word are running.

Calling Custom Components

Although it is certainly nice to know how to automate full COM compliant applications such as Microsoft Word and Excel, your primary interest in a custom application is automating a custom built component. We did some component testing in Chapter 4 when we built the components, but we did not discuss the process and rationale to any extent. In this section, we will explore the use of custom components.

When you created component projects earlier, you provided a name for every class of the component project. In addition, you also provided a project name for the component project as a whole. This component project is often called a *library* and, therefore, the name of the project is the library name. The library name is the first name referenced in an automation instantiation or declaration. The second name is the class name. A dot (.) separates the library name from the class name in an instantiation or declaration, as in the following example.

```
Dim xl as Excel.Application
```

In this example, the name of the library is *Excel* while the name of the class is *Application*.

This combination of library name and class name separated by a dot is also known as the programmatic identifier and is recorded in the Windows Registry. Each programmatic identifier references a unique class ID, a 128-bit value stored in the Registry that identifies that interface as unique across all other interfaces.

When creating your own custom components, you provide a library name by setting the project name appropriately in the Project Properties dialog. This dialog is illustrated in Figure 8.2 and is accessed by selecting Project ➢ *ProjectName* Properties from the Visual Basic menu. The name of the project in this example is **TestCallProj**.

F I G U R E 8.2

The Project Properties dialog

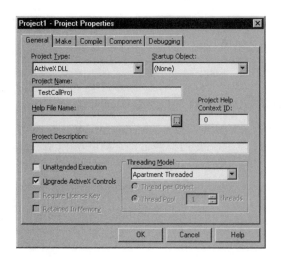

Each class name in the project must be unique and is set in the Visual Basic Properties window using the Name property for each class. This property setting, pictured in Figure 8.3, is the name that you will use as the class name when automating every component. The class name in this example is TestCallClass.

F I G U R E   8.3

Class Module Design-
Time properties

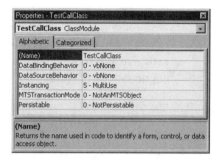

Once you determine the library name and class name of the desired class that you wish to automate, there is no difference between automating a custom component and any other Visual Basic object. You've already learned the basics of component creation from Chapter 4. Exercise 8.3 walks you through the process of creating and testing a simple component in process in the Visual Basic IDE. In this component, you will define a single class that will contain a single method called Flash, which will call a Win32 API called FlashWindow. Allow at least 20 minutes to complete this exercise.

EXERCISE 8.3

Creating and Calling Custom Components

1. Create a folder on your hard drive called TestCall. Inside the TestCall folder, create two more folders, one called client and one called component.

2. Start Visual Basic. When prompted for a project template, select ActiveX DLL and click the OK button. In the Project Properties dialog, name the project TestCallProj. Access this dialog by selecting Project ➤ *ProjectName* Properties from the Visual Basic menu. Enter the project name in the Project Name text box.

3. In the main Properties window, locate the properties for the Class1 class module. Change the Name property to read TestCallClass. The programmatic identifier of this class interface will therefore be TestCallProj.TestCallClass.

4. In the general declarations section of the class module, add a private declaration of the FlashWindow function of the Win32 API. The declaration is listed below for your reference. The declaration is case sensitive and should be entered on a single line unless you use a line continuation character.

```
Private Declare Function FlashWindow Lib "user32" _
    (ByVal hwnd As Long, ByVal bInvert As Long) As Long
```

5. Create a public subprocedure called Flash. Pass to this procedure a single argument called WHandle as a Long. In this procedure, call the FlashWindow function, passing the WHandle value in the hwnd parameter and a value of 1 in the bInvert parameter. Use the following procedure as a guide.

```
Public Sub Flash(WHandle As Long)
    FlashWindow WHandle, 1
End Sub
```

6. To test the component, add a new project to the project group. The use of project groups will be discussed in greater detail in Chapter 13. Add the project by selecting Project ➤ Add Project from the Visual Basic menu. When prompted for a project template, select Standard EXE from the list and select OK.

7. Set the Standard EXE (Project1) as the Start Up project by right-clicking Project1 in the Project window. Select Set as Start Up from the pop-up menu. Change the name of Project1 to ClientProject in the Project Properties dialog. Refer to step 2 if you are unsure of how to do this.

8. Set the name of Form1 in the ClientProject to frmClient. Add a command button to the form. Name the command button cmdFlash. Set the caption of the button to Flash Window.

9. Add a reference to the component project in the Project References dialog. To access this dialog, select Project ➤ References from the Visual Basic menu. Since TestCallProj is local to the project group, you should see the reference listed immediately under all selected references. Click the check box next to TestCallProj and click the OK button.

10. Add a timer control to the form. Name the timer tmrFlash. Set the Enabled property of the timer to False and the Interval property to 500. This will force the timer to fire every half second when the timer is enabled, but the timer will not be enabled by default.

11. In the click event of the cmdFlash button, write a single line of code that both enables the timer if it is currently disabled and does the reverse if needed. Use the following code as an example.

```
tmrFlash.Enabled = Not tmrFlash.Enabled
```

12. In the General Declarations section of frmClient, declare a Private object variable called obj as a new instance of TestCallProj.TestCallClass using auto-instantiation. Use the following code if needed.

```
Private obj As New TestCallProj.TestCallClass
```

13. In the Timer event of tmrFlash, call the Flash method of the object variable. Pass the window handle of the current window in the Whandle parameter, as in the following example.

```
obj.Flash Me.hWnd
```

14. *Very important:* Save your work before testing. If there are any errors in the Win32 API call, they will most likely result in a GPF and a loss of all of the work that you have done this far. Save the files with the following names and locations.

- TestCallClass.cls in \TestCall\Component

- TestCallProj.vbp in \TestCall\Component

- frmClient.frm in \TestCall\Client

- ClientProject.vbp in \TestCall\Client

- Group1.vbg in \TestCall

15. Start the application and click the FlashWindow button. This will flash the title bar of the form every half second. Click the button again to stop the flashing.

16. End the application and remove the ClientProject from the project group by right-clicking ClientProject in the Project window and selecting Remove Project from the pop-up menu. If prompted, save again.

17. To compile your ActiveX DLL project into a component, select File ➤ Make TestCallProj.dll from the Visual Basic menu. Compile this file in the \TestCall\Component folder. Using Windows Explorer, verify that the .dll file has been created by navigating to TestCall\ Component and viewing the contents of the folder.

18. If you do not see the .dll, check your Explorer options to verify that you are viewing all files. If the Active Desktop of Internet Explorer 4 has not been installed, these options can by accessed by selecting View ➤ Options in the Hidden Files group of the View tab. By default, .dll files are hidden from view.

19. Close the Windows Explorer and return to Visual Basic. Open the client project in the \TestCall\Client folder, replacing the TestCallProj project. If prompted, save the TestCallProj project.

20. In the client, select Project ➤ References from the Visual Basic menu. You will notice that the reference to TestCallProj is marked as MISS-ING. This is because you actually made a reference to the project running in the Visual Basic IDE and, now that the project is no longer running, the reference is no longer valid.

21. Remove the check mark next to the missing reference and scroll down to find the entry for TestCallProj. The list is sorted in alphabetical order. Place a check mark next to this entry. In the bottom of the dialog, the location should be reported as \TestCall\Component\TestCallProj .dll. Click OK.

22. All of the code used to automate the compiled .dll is exactly the same as the code used to automate the project running in the Visual Basic IDE. Only the reference must be updated. Start the client application and click the FlashWindow button. The title bar of the form will flash.

23. End the application and exit Visual Basic. Save the client project if prompted.

Communicating Asynchronously with Components

Microsoft ✔️ ***Exam Objective***

Instantiate and invoke a COM component.

- Create a Visual Basic application that handles events from a COM component.

Microsoft ✔️ ***Exam Objective***

Create call-back procedures to enable asynchronous processing between COM components and Visual Basic client applications.

One of the most empowering features of COM is the ability of components to execute asynchronously from the client application. This means that the client application can call a method of a component and wait for that component to complete in the background while the user of the client application continues with other activities. Notifications are then sent back to the client application when the background processing is complete.

There are two primary approaches that you can use for asynchronous processing. You can raise events in a component and then respond to those events in your client applications, or you can use callback procedures to communicate with the client. The latter approach requires some additional development work but provides the benefit of giving the developer greater control, not only of the communication from client to server, but also from server to client.

Using Events

As was briefly discussed in Chapter 4, Visual Basic allows you to add events to your components. These events can be raised at any location in the component code to provide notification to the client application that a process has completed or a threshold has been reached; or they can provide other notification required by your application model. In this section, we will discuss the process of including events in your component and responding to those events in your automation clients.

Adding Events to Components

Including an event in a component is a two-step process. First, you must declare the event, then you must raise the event. The event declaration takes place as a general declaration and is usually located in the General Declarations section of a class module. This declaration must be public and can include any parameters that the event will return to the client. The following example is a declaration of an event called *MyEvent*, which has a single parameter called *MyParam* returned as a long integer value.

```
Public Event MyEvent (MyParam as Long)
```

Once you have declared the event, you can raise the event at any time using the RaiseEvent statement. RaiseEvent will raise the event back to the client application and pass any values that you wish as the parameters of the event that you declared. The following sample code raises the event previously declared, passing a value back in the parameter.

```
RaiseEvent MyEvent(5)
```

To illustrate this process, Exercise 8.4 walks you through the task of creating a component that supports events. This component will simulate background processing by using a Win32 API function called Sleep. This function forces the thread to sleep for a certain amount of time, which is provided as an argument expressed in milliseconds. This component will force the thread to sleep for 10 milliseconds and then allow other foreground processing to take place. This process will be repeated one thousand times, totaling approximately 10 seconds of wait time. The procedure then raises the event back to the client application.

EXERCISE 8.4

Adding Events to a Component

1. Start Visual Basic. When prompted, select the ActiveX DLL template and click OK. Leave the project name as Project1 and the class name as class1.

2. In the General Declarations section of class1, add the API declaration for the Win32 API function Sleep as listed below. Note that the call is case sensitive and should be written on one line or with a line continuation character.

```
Private Declare Sub Sleep Lib "kernel32" _
    (ByVal dwMilliseconds As Long)
```

3. Below the API declaration, add a declaration for a public event called AsyncEvent. This event passes no parameters back to the client. Use the following code as an example.

```
Public Event AsyncEvent()
```

4. Create a public subprocedure called AsyncProc. This procedure accepts no parameters. In this procedure, write code that declares an integer counter variable and assigns the value of 0 to that variable. Within a loop, call the Sleep API function, using a value of 10 for the sleep duration argument. Following Sleep, allow foreground processing to continue by using the Visual Basic command DoEvents. Increment the counter by 1 and repeat the loop while the counter variable is less than 1000. Following the loop, raise the event. Use the following code as an example if needed.

```
Dim intSleepCount As Integer
intSleepCount = 0
Do While intSleepCount < 1000
    Sleep 10
    DoEvents
    intSleepCount = intSleepCount + 1
Loop
RaiseEvent AsyncEvent
```

5. Save the component in a location of your choice and leave the project open and Visual Basic running in preparation for the next exercise.

Calling Component Events

By default, an object variable declared to reference a custom class would not recognize the events raised by that component. If you wish to capture events in your client application that are raised by the components, you must use the WithEvents keyword when declaring the object variable. This keyword, positioned between the declaration statement (Public/Private) and the symbolic name of the variable, allows the client to be aware of the events raised by the components. The following code sample illustrates the use of the WithEvents keyword.

```
Private WithEvents MyVar as Project1.Class1
```

The WithEvents keyword is not supported in an auto-instantiation statement. You must use the Set statement with either the New keyword or the CreateObject function.

After you make the declaration of the object variable using the WithEvents keyword, you will notice that the Object list box of the Visual Basic code window contains a reference to the newly declared object variable. Figure 8.4 illustrates this. Selecting the object variable name from the procedure drop-down list exposes event templates for all of the declared events of the component. You will use these event templates to respond to the events raised from the component.

F I G U R E 8.4

Declaring an object variable using WithEvents

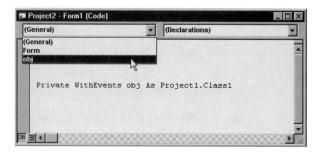

Exercise 8.5 explores this process of responding to events raised from components. In this exercise, you will declare an object variable using With-Events and respond to the AyncEvent event raised by the component.

Responding to Component Events

1. Visual Basic should be running with the Project1 ActiveX DLL project loaded. If not, start Visual Basic and open the project from its saved source.

2. Add a new project to the project group by selecting File ➤ Add Project from the Visual Basic menu. Select a Standard EXE project template.

3. Add two command buttons to Form1 of Project2. Select the first command button and set the Name property to cmdAsync and the Caption property to Call Async. Select the second command button, setting the Name property to cmdFore and the Caption property to Call Client Process.

4. Set a reference to Project1 from Project2 by selecting Project ➤ References from the menu. Locate the entry for Project1 immediately beneath the selected references. Click OK.

5. In the General Declarations section of Form1 in Project2, declare a Form level object variable as an instance of Class1 of Project1 using the WithEvents keyword, as in the following example.

```
Private WithEvents obj As Project1.Class1
```

6. In the Load event of Form1, set the object variable to a new instance of the class, as in the following code.

```
Set obj = New Project1.Class1
```

7. Open the Object drop-down list on the Code window for the form. Locate and select obj from the list. You should now be in the obj_ AsyncEvent procedure. Use the MsgBox statement to inform the user that the component event has fired.

8. In the click event of the cmdAync command button, call the AsyncProc method of the obj object. In the click event of the cmdFore command button, use the MsgBox statement to inform the user that a client event has occurred.

9. Set Project2 as the Start Up project. Since the next step will have you test the component which calls an API, you should save all of your work at this point. After saving, start the application and click the Call Async button. This starts the background processing of the component. Click the Call Client Process button to raise the local event. Move the form to a new location on the screen. Both of these are foreground activities that are independent of the background processing.

10. After a short time a message box will appear on the screen informing you that the background event has fired. Close the message box when it occurs and exit Visual Basic.

Using Callback Procedures

All of the COM calls that we have implemented up to this point have been client calls to a Component object. Custom events in a component are actually a departure from this process, but the complexities of the process are essentially hidden from you. When you declare an object variable using the WithEvents keyword, you are actually defining an interface in the client application through which the component can communicate back to the client. The process is abstracted from you, however. This means that you can't exercise a great deal of control over what happens on the client side when the component calls the client because you are limited to the code that you can place in the custom event procedure defined in the client.

Callback procedures remove this level of abstraction, allowing you more control over the communication between client and component, but also requiring you to write additional code to implement this functionality.

The key to callbacks in a Visual Basic application is the *Implements* keyword. This keyword allows a client class to implement all of the public members of the implemented class. For example, suppose you have a class compiled in a component that has one Public method called *Notify*. Using the Implements keyword in your client class, you could write the actual implementation code for this method in your client class. The advantage to this approach is that you can control every implementation of the component on the client side. This allows different clients to implement components differently and provides the client control that we discussed earlier.

Implementing callback procedures is a cooperative process between the component and the client. You must develop a component that defines the public interfaces. These can be fully implemented interfaces or they can be *abstract classes*, which are interfaces with no implementation code at all. An abstract class is created with a class module that defines all of the properties and methods of the class but does not have any implementation of them. The developer can then implement the interfaces in another class by referencing the abstract class with the Implements keyword and providing all of the implementation code in the class that implements the abstract class.

The Implements keyword can be used only within a class module. Only a class can implement the interfaces of another class. You can only implement the public members of that class, and you must implement *all* of the public members of that class.

Exercise 8.6 walks you through the process of a simple interface implementation project. This is a very simple structure. Interface implementation can be much more sophisticated than this example. Notice especially how the interfaces designed in the component look to the client class for implementation.

EXERCISE 8.6

Implementing Interfaces with Callback Procedures

1. Start Visual Basic. When prompted for a project template, select ActiveX DLL and click OK. This component will be your abstract class. From the Project Properties dialog, name the project CallBackComp.

2. In the Properties window, rename Class1 to IRemoteClass. The capital I is conventional to indicate a COM interface.

3. Add a public subprocedure called Method1 to the IRemoteClass module. This procedure should accept no arguments. Do not place any implementation code in this procedure. This completes your abstract class.

4. Add a new Standard EXE project to the project group. Name the project CallBackClient and set it as the Start Up project. Make a reference to the CallBackComp project in the Project References dialog.

5. Add a class module to the CallBackClient project by selecting Project ➤ Add Class Module from the menu. Select the standard Class Module template and click Open. Rename the module ClientClass.

6. In the General Declarations section of the ClientClass module, implement the IRemoteClass interface with the following statement.

```
Implements IRemoteClass
```

7. Open the Object drop-down list in the Code window. You should see IRemoteClass listed as an object. Select it from the list. You should now be in the IRemoteClass_Method1 procedure. This is the client implementation location of the abstract class defined in the component. Use the MsgBox statement in this procedure to notify the user that the remote class has been called. Close the Class Module window.

8. Go to the General Declarations section of Form1 in the CallBackClient project. Declare a private object variable called Robj as IRemoteClass and another called Lobj as ClientClass as in the following example.

```
Private Robj As IRemoteCLass
Private Lobj As ClientClass
```

9. In the Form Load event, set Lobj as a new instance of ClientClass. Then, to identify which client class should be called back when the remote class is called, set the Robj object variable to Lobj. This passes the reference of the ClientClass to IRemoteClass, which then completes the integration. Use the following code as a guide.

```
Set Lobj = New ClientClass
Set Robj = Lobj
```

10. Add a command button to the form. Leave the name and caption at their defaults. In the click event of the command button, call Method1 of Robj, the remote class.

11. Start the application and click the command button. Notice that although you have called the method of the remote class, the code that implements this method is in the client class.

12. End the application and close Visual Basic. Save your project if you wish.

Events vs. Callbacks

Now that you have been exposed to both approaches to the asynchronous processing of components, there is one remaining obvious question: Which approach applies to which situations? Each approach has advantages and disadvantages.

Events are very easy to implement and require minimal extra coding effort. They are also quite effective when there is no need to identify the specific client that is calling the component. Remember that events are like broadcast messages. The component raises them to the world at large and then completes its processing. There is no way for a component to respond based on the client's handling of an event, just as there is no way for the component to differentiate between clients.

The primary advantage of using callback procedures is that, unlike events, the component can identify each client application and respond accordingly. Control can be passed back and forth between the client and component as needed. In addition, the component can even respond to error conditions raised in the client application.

Callbacks do have their down side, however. The primary drawback of using callback procedures is the significantly increased effort that goes into developing applications using this approach. Nonetheless, if the additional flexibility of callback procedures is required according to your design specifications or is simply deemed worth the extra effort, callbacks are a good choice for asynchronous processing.

Summary

Calling COM components is very similar to calling standard Visual Basic objects. This behavior is by design, not by accident. As we have seen, components can be instantiated in a number of different ways, but once you have an object variable to work with, the process of calling a COM component is very familiar.

In this chapter, we have also evaluated different approaches to asynchronous processing. These included the use of events and callback procedures. As you saw in this discussion, events are much more easily implemented, but callback procedures offer a significantly greater amount of flexibility when you have a need to isolate the activity of specific client applications.

Review Questions

1. Which of the following COM interfaces supports automation?

A. Invoke

B. IUnknown

C. IDispatch

D. IDeclare

2. Which method of the IDispatch interface is avoided through DispID binding?

A. Invoke

B. GetTypeInfo

C. GetTypeInfoCount

D. GetIdsOfNames

3. Which of the following methods of the IDispatch interface is used when performing vTable binding?

A. GetIDsOfNames

B. Invoke

C. Both A and B

D. Neither A nor B

4. Which keyword is used when declaring a reference to an abstract class to support all of its public interfaces?

A. WithEvents

B. Public

C. Implements

D. ByVal

5. You are writing a component that performs some processing and then notifies a client application when the processing is complete. There is no need for the component to differentiate between client applications, nor will it continue processing after the client application's response to the notification, but you need the client to continue processing while waiting for a notification. Which technique should you use?

   A. Asynchronous processing with callbacks

   B. Asynchronous processing with events

   C. Synchronous processing with API calls

   D. Asynchronous processing using API

6. Which approach to binding will result in the best performance?

   A. Late binding

   B. DispID binding

   C. vTable binding

   D. All have identical performance

7. Which of the following is not an advantage of a type library?

   A. Usually smaller than the full component.

   B. Fully documents the component for early binding.

   C. Can be viewed by the Visual Basic object browser.

   D. When loaded, automation calls can execute without requiring the component to load.

8. Which of the following is the most efficient way to instantiate an object class when repeated instantiations will be made from the same class template?

   A. Auto-instantiation with the New keyword

   B. Using the New keyword with the Set statement

   C. Using the CreateObject function with the Set statement

   D. All of these methods offer generally the same performance

9. Which of the following declaration statements would result in late binding?

   A. Dim xl as Excel.Application

   B. Dim cmd as CommandButton

   C. Dim obj as Project1.Class1

   D. Dim frm as Form

10. Which of the following code statements terminates the instance of the object referenced in the object variable obj?

   A. Set obj = Nothing

   B. obj.Close

   C. Set obj = TerminateObject()

   D. obj.Terminate

CHAPTER

9

Using Microsoft
Transaction Server

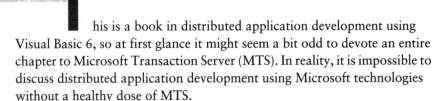

This is a book in distributed application development using Visual Basic 6, so at first glance it might seem a bit odd to devote an entire chapter to Microsoft Transaction Server (MTS). In reality, it is impossible to discuss distributed application development using Microsoft technologies without a healthy dose of MTS.

In this chapter, we will look at the process of installing and configuring the MTS service. We will use the MTS Explorer utility to manage the deployment and security of components running in the MTS environment. Finally, we will look at the process of client configuration for components deployed remotely under MTS.

Transaction Server Fundamentals

MTS is probably the most misnamed piece of software that Microsoft has ever shipped. The name seems to imply that its primary role is the management of transaction activity. In reality, MTS does this and much more. More accurately stated, MTS is a component management system, designed to aid in the transactional behavior, scalability, security, and deployment of components in a distributed application architecture. Let's look at some of the services that MTS provides.

Transaction Activity

A transaction is a group of data modifications that must complete on one or more data sources as a single unit of work. MTS can provide transaction support to ensure that MTS can provide transaction support to ensure that all of the requirements of a transaction are met. If all of the requirements of a transaction are not met, the transaction will fail to complete. MTS requires that all transactions adhere to the ACID test, a set of four general characteristics of transactions that must exist in order to complete the transaction. The ACID characteristics are as follows.

- Atomic

- Consistent

- Isolated

- Durable

Let's take a closer look at each of these characteristics.

Atomic

Atomicity is the all-or-nothing attribute of a transaction. Either the transaction will complete in its entirety, or it will fail in its entirety. No element of a transaction will complete without the rest of the transaction.

For example, suppose that you were writing an application to manage an airline frequent flyer program. When a member calls the service center to redeem frequent flyer points for a free ticket, you must take two steps. First, you must remove the points from the member's account, and then you must confirm their ticket on the desired flight. If one of these activities completes, they must both complete or the transaction will leave the data in an inconsistent state.

Consistent

A transaction is consistent if it resolves system and data state the same way every time and always leaves data in a state in which its integrity has been preserved. This concept is additional to the concept of the atomic transaction. Atomicity only defines the fact that the transaction will commit in its entirety, but it does not define how the individual transaction statements affect underlying data.

When a transaction is consistent, it means that the underlying work of the transaction is written in a way that always properly resolves data state. In our previous example of the frequent flyer transaction, just because the transaction completes in its entirely does not necessarily mean that the data is left in a consistent state. The actual work of the transaction is written to enforce that state.

Isolated

Isolation is the ability to hide the work performed by one transaction from all other transactions. To create a completely isolated transaction, this must be enforced at two levels; at the database level and inside the component.

At the database level, isolation means that the data modifications made by one transaction will not be read by other transactions until the modification has committed. This is called *dirty reading*. SQL Server enforces this behavior through a locking mechanism that places locks on pages as they are modified. These locks, called exclusive locks, are not compatible with any other locks, meaning that only the transaction that owns the lock can use the locked resource.

When SQL Server transactions read pages from a database, share locks placed on the resources prevent a read transaction from reading a resource that is in the process of being modified through another transaction. This allows all transactions on the server to be truly isolated.

At the component level, it is important that one client workstation connected to a component does not interfere with the work of another client connection to the same component. To accomplish this, components created for deployment in MTS should be compliant with the Apartment Threading model and must not preserve state information inside the component. More will be said concerning these requirements later in this chapter.

Durable

It is critical that once a transaction commits, the result of this transaction is a permanent modification to the database. It must be durable and fault tolerant to system failure. The support for this durability is provided primarily by the underlying data source.

SQL Server provides durability through its transaction log. The SQL Server transaction log is a write-ahead log, meaning that SQL Server writes all data modifications to the transaction log first before writing any data modifications to the database. This provides durability of the transaction because while the data changes might be stored in memory, the transaction log is stored on disk. If the system were to fail, all data modifications stored in memory would be lost. However, since the transaction log has a copy of all of these modifications, SQL Server can use this log to recover all of the data modifications and return the database to its original state.

Scalability

Scalability is defined as the ability of an application or system platform to allow a large number of users to connect to a system or application without a significant degradation in performance. Scalability is critical for distributed applications because the primary intent of a distributed application is to provide central application processing to a large number of users. If the application does not scale well, then the number of users could be seriously limited and the application would not fulfill its business purpose.

In the past, the most significant problem with scalability in a distributed application rested primarily with the business tier. Components created as single user components did not scale well because only one client request at a time could be executed by the component. This caused a consistent bottleneck in the distributed environment.

The problem could be resolved by creating components that could handle multiple users and user requests. This was a tedious task as much of the code written in the component was related more to threading and maintaining connection state information than was actually dedicated to the business purpose of the component.

MTS solves this problem by providing all of the internal "plumbing" necessary to scale a single user component. This allows the developer to focus on the core business problem rather than on the multi-user functionality of a component. As long as the component adheres to some simple standards, MTS can take care of the rest. The majority of MTS scalability support comes from three sources, apartment threading, just-in-time activation, and resource pooling.

Apartment Threading

A component contains many methods and resources that are accessible from client applications. However, in a single-threaded component, once a client connects to the component and automates it, only one thread execution is allowed to access the functionality of the component. This means that once a client automates an instance of a single threaded component another client can't use the component's resources. Either another instance of the component must be loaded or the client must simply wait for the component to become available.

The apartment threading model of components divides a component into apartments, each providing the functionality of a single method of the component. Although only one thread can execute inside of an apartment (i.e., method), every apartment gets its own thread, allowing multiple clients to use the component as long a they are using different methods of the component.

MTS manages the calls to the individual apartments of the component. The developer makes calls to the MTS components in exactly the same way as it makes calls to a single-threaded component. MTS manages the process of resolving these requests as well as the sometimes-complex process of one apartment calling another apartment.

Just-in-Time Activation

When working with standard components, a client application will create an instance of the component and hold that instance open during the process of working with the component. The component is held open and occupied through the duration of this entire cycle, which might include many method calls to the component. This means that the resources occupied by the component are held even during significant amounts of idle time.

When MTS manages components, a client call to create an instance of a component does not necessarily allocate those resources immediately. MTS will create an instance of the component only when necessary, preferring to route the request to other running instances of the component that are currently servicing other client requests. When components must be loaded or threads created, this will occur "just-in-time" to satisfy a client request. This mans that a component may actually be loaded and unloaded many times during the time that a client application presumably holds that component open.

Resource Pooling

Components use more resources than just memory. For a component to perform its work, it may need other resources such as threads and database connections. These resources can be very costly in terms of system resources.

For example, when a client application or component attempts to retrieve data from a database server such as Microsoft SQL Server, it must do so through a database connection. Since database connections require a lot of memory on the SQL Server, the number of connections is restricted by a server configuration. They are a very precious resource.

Unfortunately, clients rarely use database connections as efficiently as they should. To keep the application more responsive, database connections are often acquired early and released only when all database processing is complete. This means that the state of the database connection is often idle, wasting capacity that could be used by another client.

MTS manages all database connections as well as other resources, allowing them to be pooled and used more efficiently. Rather then each component requiring its own threads or database connections, these resources are managed by MTS, allocating them to components when needed, thus reducing idle time and increasing the maximum utilization of each resource.

Security

The work that some components do might be of a very sensitive nature. As a developer or a system administrator, you wouldn't want an unauthorized individual to gain access to the functionality of a sensitive component. For this reason, MTS implements its own security model that integrates with Windows NT security. This security model will be discussed at length later in this chapter.

Installing and Configuring MTS

Microsoft
Exam
Objective

Configure a server computer to run Microsoft Transaction Server (MTS).

- Install MTS.

MTS ships with Visual Studio 6 Enterprise Edition and installs with the BackOffice installer as part of the NT 4 Option Pack. You can also install MTS directly from the Windows NT 4 Option Pack cab files. If you don't have Visual Studio Enterprise Edition, you can download the Windows NT 4 Option Pack file from the Microsoft Web site. For this chapter, we will assume that you are using the Visual Studio Enterprise distribution of the Option Pack.

The full version of the Windows NT 4 Option Pack for NT Server is 87MB in size. This will take about 14 hours to download using a 28.8K connection.

Definitions

Before looking at the services provided by MTS in detail, we should first define a few terms that you will see in any discussion of MTS. These definitions will better acquaint you with the mechanisms that MTS uses to accomplish its tasks.

COM and DCOM

COM (Component Object Model) is simply a specification that describes the way that objects look on the outside and how they speak to each other programmatically. If an object is COM compliant, it will expose interfaces that can be used to access the functionality of the object.

Each interface contains methods. Some of these methods provide the functionality of the component. Other methods provide the ability to call other components or to expose additional functionality to callers. MTS components are COM compliant and are written as in-process objects. This means that when they are called by a client application, they run in a process environment provided by MTS, not their own process space.

While COM defines how objects relate to each other on a single machine, DCOM defines how this happens over a network. Networked components are essential for distributed applications, providing the ability to deploy components at a central location. This allows many client applications to share the functionality provided by the components. The goal of DCOM is to make this process essentially transparent for the developer.

Components

We normally define a component as a compiled EXE or DLL that contains related class definitions. The component in this definition provides the COM "wrapper" around the object classes.

In MTS, we use the term component a little differently. When you add a DLL to MTS, all of the public classes defined within the DLL are visible to MTS. Each of these classes is represented within the MTS Explorer as a different component. For this chapter, when we discuss the concept of a component, we will be referring to a class definition inside of a DLL that is installed in MTS. Each MTS component will define its own set of interfaces.

Packages

When DLLs are installed into the MTS environment, they are placed within packages. A package is actually an independent process space maintained by MTS that allows in-process objects to access the resources necessary to execute. A DLL in MTS can only be installed into one package. Packages are used to manage the security and the accessibility of the components that it contains.

Most MTS packages are user packages, meaning that they are created and defined explicitly by the user. However, MTS installs with two special packages called System and Utilities that are used to provide administrative functionality and transactional context.

Installing MTS

By accessing the NT 4 Option Pack installer, you can install MTS on your Windows NT Server. Exercise 9.1 walks you through the installation process.

EXERCISE 9.1

Installing MTS

1. Log on to your Windows NT Server as Administrator. Insert the Visual Studio 6.0 CD2 in your CD-ROM drive. Open My Computer or Windows Explorer and navigate to the location indicated in the following graphic.

2. Locate the Setup.exe file in the target folder on the CD and double click to begin the installation. The first screen you will see will be the introductory screen. Click Next to continue.

EXERCISE 9.1 (CONTINUED)

3. You must accept the license agreement before you will be allowed to continue with the installation. Click the Accept button to continue.

4. You will have the option of choosing a Typical, Minimum, or Custom install. Click Typical. This will install MTS as well as IIS 4 (which you will need for later chapters) and the Microsoft Index Server.

5. You will be prompted for the locations of the Internet Service managed directories. The defaults should be under C:\InetPub. Accept the defaults and click Next. Accept the default location for the mailroot directory and click Next. This should begin the installation.

6. When finished, you will be prompted to restart your computer. You must do this before the installation will be complete.

After installing Microsoft Transaction Server, you can access its administrative utilities by opening the Transaction Server Explorer. This utility is a snap-in to the Microsoft Management Console. All security and deployment functionality can be accessed through this utility.

To open the MTS Explorer, click Start ≻ Programs ≻ Windows NT 4 Option Pack ≻ Microsoft Transaction Server ≻ Transaction Server Explorer. Drill down into the Explorer window to expose the packages created in the default installation. This is pictured in Figure 9.1.

FIGURE 9.1

The MTS Explorer displaying a default installation

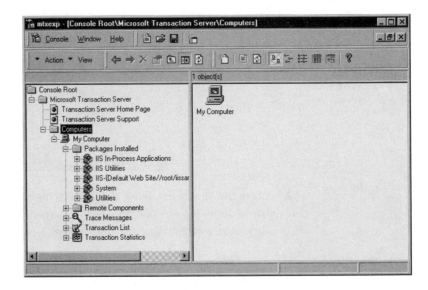

Managing MTS Security

Microsoft
Exam
Objective

Create a package by using the MTS Explorer.

- Assign names to packages.

While you can use the security mechanisms of the underlying data source to control all access to database information, this can sometimes pose some difficulties. The most significant difficulty is the inability of many relational database management systems to respond rapidly to changing requirements for database access.

For example, suppose that you had a corporate user account that had access to a SQL Server database. If you were to use the SQL Server security system to manage user rights in the server, the user would have to be added by the database administrator to the SQL Server access list. If the user leaves the company, the user must be removed from the access list. Now suppose that you have 1000 users accessing your server. As you can see, this would be a daunting task as well as repetitious, since the users must be maintained at the network level as well as the database server level.

The security model in SQL Server 7 facilitates this process much more efficiently by allowing the database administrator to provide database access to Windows NT groups directly without the need to add individual user accounts to the local access list.

The MTS security model simplifies this process by allowing the administrator to assign access for a Windows NT login or group to a component. At this point, the Windows NT user assumes the identity assigned to the component for all system authentication.

This means that as long as the SQL Server contains an account for the Windows NT user account assigned as the identity of the MTS package, any user that is allowed to access the contents of the component will be granted access to the SQL Server under the identity of the component. This simplifies security significantly; now an administrator must only ensure that permitted users and groups are granted access to the component.

Creating and Identifying Packages

You set the identity of the package by accessing the package properties. You can do this when you create the package or at any time thereafter. Figure 9.2 illustrates the Identity page of the package properties. In this example, the identity is set to a Windows NT user called TestPackUser.

WARNING To enable the MTS package to access all domain resources, the User account assigned to identify the MTS package should be a domain account rather than a local server account.

FIGURE 9.2

MTS Package Identity
Properties

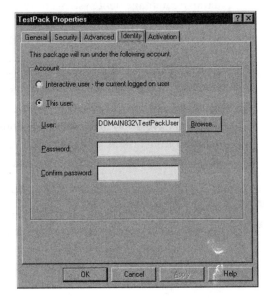

Exercise 9.2 takes you through the process of creating a package and assigning a Windows NT identity to the package. You will begin by creating a Windows NT user account that will be used to identify the package. You will then create a package and assign the Windows NT account to that package in the process.

EXERCISE 9.2

Creating Packages and Assigning Identity

1. To create a new Windows NT user account, open the Windows NT User Manager for Domains by clicking Start ➢ Programs ➢ Administrative Tools ➢ User Manager for Domains.

2. From the User Manager menu, click User ➢ New User. Create a new user named TestPackUser. Complete the New User form as pictured in the following graphic.

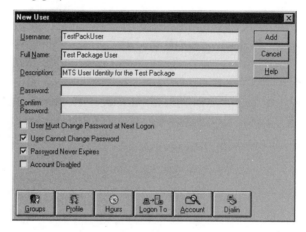

3. Click the Add button to add the user, then click Close. Close the User Manager for Domains.

4. Open the MTS Explorer by clicking Start ➢ Programs ➢ Windows NT 4 Option Pack ➢ Microsoft Transaction Server ➢ Transaction Server Explorer. Expand the tree view in the left pane of the Explorer until the Packages Installed folder appears beneath My Computer. Click to select the Packages Installed folder. Right-click the folder to display the pop-up menu. Click New ➢ Package.

5. In the Package Wizard dialog, click Create an empty package. Click the Next button.

6. Enter the name **TestPack** as the name of the new package. Click the Next button.

7. In the Identity dialog, click the Option button next to This User. Click the browse button (...) on the right side of the User text box. Select TestPackUser from the list. Click Add to add the user to the selected users list in the text box below. Click OK to accept the account. There will be no password unless you explicitly created one in step 2.

8. Click the Finish button to create the package. You should now see TestPack in the list of installed packages.

Working with Roles

Microsoft ✓ *Exam* *Objective*	**Use role-based security to limit use of an MTS package to specific users.** · Create roles. · Add users to roles.

Microsoft ✓ *Exam* *Objective*	**Create a package by using the MTS Explorer.** · Assign security to packages.

After you have created a package and set its identity, the next step in securing a package is to create roles associated with the package. A role is a collection of users that is defined at the package level as a set of potential users of the components that will be placed inside the package. Each component will be able to allow access to specific roles associated with the package, but is not required to do so. This provides user aggregation at the package level but implementation at the component level.

Roles are usually created by identifying specific security needs. Roles may be applied to some components, but not all. In addition, the developer of a component can allow a component to execute differently based on the role membership of the calling user.

After creating a role, Windows NT users and groups can be associated with the role. It is usually best to assign groups to MTS roles so that group membership can be maintained at the operating system level. This will provide no additional maintenance in MTS. Any user belonging to the group included within the role definition will be allowed to access any component that has granted access to that role.

Exercise 9.3 illustrates the process of creating MTS roles and adding Windows NT groups to the role membership. First, you will create a new user account and a new group. Next, you will add the user to the group. After creating the new MTS role, you will finally add the Windows NT group to the role, providing package access to the group.

EXERCISE 9.3

Adding MTS Roles and Mapping Windows NT Accounts

1. Start the User Manager for Domains. Create a new user account named TestUser. Leave the password null. Uncheck the option for User Must Change Password at Next Login. Set the option for Password Never Expires.

2. Add a new group by clicking User ➤ New Local Group from the User Manager menu. Name the Group TestGroup. Add TestUser to the group by clicking the Add button and selecting TestUser from the list. The completed dialog should resemble the graphic below.

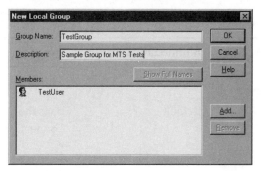

3. Give members of TestGroup the right to log on to the Windows NT Server locally. Select Policies ➤ User Rights from the menu. From the Right drop-down list, select Log on locally. To add TestGroup to the list associated with this right, click the Add button and select TestGroup from the list. Click the OK button to complete setting the User Rights. Close User Manager.

4. Open the MTS Explorer. Drill down through the tree view to locate the TestPack package. Expand the package to locate the Roles folder. Right-click the Roles folder and select New ➤ Role from the pop-up menu. Enter the name **TestRole** and click OK.

5. You should now see TestRole added to the left pane of the Explorer. Expand TestRole to reveal the Users folder. Select the Users folder and right-click. Select New ➤ User from the pop-up menu.

6. From the list that appears, select TestGroup. Click the Add button and OK to accept the selection. TestGroup should now appear as a member of the Users folder of the role.

To complete the process of setting security on packages, you will need to allow authorization checking on packages. Authorization checking provides two services.

1. Authorization checking ensures that only Windows NT users and groups are allowed to access components inside the MTS package.

2. The authorization checking options allow you to specify when the checking takes place. There are seven options for checking the identity of a user calling a component. Table 9.1 lists these options.

T A B L E 9.1	Authorization Option	Function
MTS Authorization Options	None	No verification of the user's identity is performed.
	Default	Uses the Windows NT default. This is identical to Connect.
	Connect	Verification is performed only when the user initially connects to the package.
	Call	Verification is performed for every call to an MTS package.

T A B L E 9.1 (cont.) MTS Authorization Options	**Authorization Option**	**Function**
	Packet	Verification is performed for every network packet received by the package.
	Packet Integrity	Uses packet authentication and additionally performs tampering checks on the packets.
	Packet Privacy	Uses packet integrity authentication and additionally adds increased package encryption.

To initiate package security, you must access the package properties and enable authorization checking. To access these properties, right-click the package in the MTS Explorer and select Properties from the pop-up menu. On the Security tab, check the option to enable authorization checking and select the desired authentication level from the list.

Securing the System Package

Microsoft ✓ **Exam Objective**

Configure a server computer to run Microsoft Transaction Server (MTS).

- Set up security on a system package.

To provide security for the administrative functionality of MTS, you must secure the built-in System package. Without providing security for this package, any NT Administrator user would have the ability to create and configure packages, including setting security on packages. To provide access to valid MTS administrators while restricting access to others, you can add the appropriate groups to the Administrators role that is built-in to the System package.

The process is simple, but important. First, you will create a Windows NT group that will contain all valid MTS administrative users. You will then add any valid MTS administrative users to the group that you just created.

Finally, in the MTS Explorer, you will first add the new Windows NT group as a member of the Administrator role and then initiate authorization checking in the security properties.

Do *not* enable authorization checking on the System package without first adding at least one Windows NT user account to the Administrator role. If there is no user associated with the Administrator role, there will be no way to access the administrative functionality of MTS and you will have to rein-stall Transaction Server to recover.

Exercise 9.4 takes you through the process of setting security on the System package. Be sure that you follow the steps exactly so that you do not run the risk of blocking your accounts from the MTS Explorer.

EXERCISE 9.4

Setting Security on the System Package

1. Open the User Manager for Domains. Create a new user account called MTSAdmin. Do not set a password for the account. Configure the account so that the password does not have to be changed at next login and that the password never expires.

2. Repeat step 1 adding a new User account called **NonMTSAdmin**. Con-figure this account identically to the account created in step 1.

3. Create a new local group called **MTSAdminGroup**. Make the Admin-istrator and MTSAdmin accounts members of the new group.

4. Set the user rights for the MTSAdmin and NonMTSAdmin accounts to enable them to log on locally to the Windows NT Server.

5. Open the MTS Explorer. Expand the tree view until you see the Roles folder for the System package. Inside the Roles folder you will see an Administrator role, expand this role to reveal the Users folder. Click on this folder to select it and then right-click the folder. Select New ➢ User from the pop-up menu.

6. From the list displayed, select the MTSAdminGroup. Click Add and then OK to accept the addition of the group. You should now be able to expand your MTS Explorer tree to resemble the following graphic.

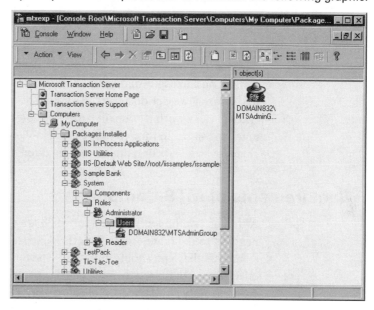

7. Be sure that the MTSAdminGroup has been properly added to the Administrator role before you continue with this step. Select the System package from the list of installed packages. Right-click the package and select Properties from the pop-up menu.

8. Click the Security tab and select the option to enable authorization checking. Click OK. You will receive a warning that confirms the fact that you have added your login account to the Administrator role. Click Yes to confirm.

9. Log off Windows NT and log in again as NonMTSAdmin. Open the MTS Explorer and expand the tree view to view the installed packages. You should get an error message when attempting to expand My Computer. This is because the account you are using does not have authorization for the System package.

10. Log off Windows NT and log in again as MTSAdmin. This time you should be able to expand the list view and explore the packages. Log off Windows NT and log in again as Administrator.

Creating Components for MTS

Microsoft ✓ ***Exam Objective***

Design and create components that will be used with MTS.

Y ou can use Visual Basic to create components that are deployed with Microsoft Transaction Server. Although there will be some minor differences in the way that you will create the components, the process is still very much the same. In this section, we will look at some of the requirements and characteristics of components designed for the MTS environment.

Requirements of MTS Components

Although components created for MTS are very similar to standard components as to the manner in which they expose their functionality, there are standards that you should follow to ensure that these components are as effective as possible. Adherence to these standards is very important to ensure a stable and effective business tier.

In-Process Objects   All MTS components must be compiled as DLLs since they will execute in-process under MTS.

Apartment Threading   MTS components should adhere to the apartment-threading model for maximum scalability under MTS. Although MTS can deploy single threaded objects, this greatly reduces the scalability of the component.

Stateless   MTS components should be stateless, meaning that each call to the component should be treated as an independent call that does not depend on any state data maintained in the component. Since the component dynamically loads and unloads without informing the user, maintaining state in the component is unreliable.

WARNING   One of the ways that components maintain state is with properties. Properties are designed to store data between component calls so that later calls can benefit from this state. For this reason, MTS components should not include properties. All calls to the component should be structured as methods and state data should maintained on the client rather than on the server.

Setting MTS Properties in Visual Basic

From within Visual Basic you can set the MTSTransactionMode property of a class to identify to MTS how this MTS component will participate in transactions. Not every MTS component will require or even support transactions. Although this seems a little strange at first, remember that MTS provides much more than just transaction control. It also provides object brokering, resource pooling, and other benefits to component developers. It is very possible that a developer might wish to take advantage of these features without necessarily providing transaction support.

The MTSTransactionMode property provides five options:

NotAnMTSObject   This class will not be deployed as an MTS object and provides no MTS support.

NoTransactions   This class exposes a valid MTS component but does not support MTS transactions.

RequiresTrasanction   This class exposes a valid MTS component and requires a transaction to execute. If the component is not created under the context of a current transaction, it will begin a new transaction.

UsesTransactions   This class exposes a valid MTS component that can function either with or without a current transaction.

RequiresNewTransaction   The MTS component requires a new transaction to begin whenever the component is called. This mode is common for components that enlist other components into transactions.

Setting the MTS TransactionMode property from within the Visual Basic class gives you the benefit of not having to set these properties from within the MTS Explorer when the component is installed. However, you can still choose a different level of transaction support for each class using MTS if you wish.

The Context Object

When a component is called under MTS, a corresponding Context object is created by the Transaction Server. The purpose of the Context object is to maintain the transactional and security context for the component call. When components are enlisted into a transaction, the Context object tracks the transactional status, reporting to MTS whether the transaction should complete in its entirety or abort.

You can think of the Context object as your mechanism to communicate with MTS from within your component code. Without the Context object, there is no way for the transaction to monitor the activity inside of the component.

Before you can call the methods of the Context object in the component code, you must first create an object variable and set that variable to an instance of the Context object. This will take place in every function call individually as you will not preserve the state of a Context object over multiple component calls. The sample code below illustrates this approach. Please note that the reference to the MTXAS library is not required if there is no other library referenced that contains a class called ObjectContext.

```
Dim ctxObject As MTXAS.ObjectContext
Set ctxObject = GetObjectContext()
```

Calling Other MTS Components

If you have the need, you can call other MTS components from within an MTS component. This common process allows a single component to enlist other components under the context of a single transaction. To do this, the CreateInstance method of the Context object is used.

Normally, when you wish to create a reference to an object using Visual Basic, you would use the CreateObject function. This function creates an instance of the object identified and returns a pointer to the instance of the object that is stored in an object variable. When using MTS components, the process is a little different. Instead of using the CreateObject method, you will use the CreateInstance method as shown in the following example. Note that ContextObject in this example would be the object variable of the Context object previously created.

```
Set ObjectVariable = ContextObject.CreateInstance
("ProjectName.ClassName")
```

Using this statement, you would now have an object variable inside your component code that you could use to manipulate the other component. If a transaction were active, this would enlist the new component into the transaction and monitor the status of that component, in addition to the initial component, before committing the transaction.

Testing for Role Membership

There may be occasions when the execution of the component will depend on the identity of the user calling the component. Since users are associated with roles to determine their level of access in an MTS package, we can use this package association to affect the execution of code within a package.

To do this, you will use the IsCallerInRole method of the Context object. This Boolean method accepts as an argument the name of a role associated with that package. The method returns a value of true if the user that is calling the component is associated with the role tested.

As an example, if you wanted to execute a certain block of code within a component if the caller is associated with the Managers role, you might use code like the following example.

```
If ctxObject.IsCallerInRole("Managers") Then
    'Process Here
End If
```

Reporting Transaction Status

One of the primary functions of MTS is to enforce distributed transactions from the component level. To do this, the component must have a way to communicate transactions status to the Context object. To support this ability, the Context object offers two methods.

SetComplete   Informs the Context object that the work of the component can complete without error.

SetAbort   Informs the Context object that an error has occurred and that the component cannot commit its portion of the transaction.

MTS monitors the context of every transaction. When all enlisted components report the ability to complete their work successfully, the transaction can commit. If one or more of the components report that an abort must take place, then all component activities abort, even if some could have completed their work without error.

The following code shows an example of how an MTS component might be structured to provide transactional status feedback to the Context object. Notice how the component completes normally as long as no errors occur; however, if the error handler is invoked, the component reports a request to abort the transaction to the Context object.

```
On Error GoTo err_TranExample
Dim ctxObject As MTxAS.ObjectContext
Set ctxObject = GetObjectContext()
'Data Access Code Here
If ctxObject.IsInTransaction Then _
    ctxObject.SetComplete

err_TranExample:
'All Error Resolution Code Here
If ctxObject.IsInTransaction Then _
    ctxObject.SetAbort
```

Using the Boolean method IsInTransaction of the Context object allows you to test the Context object for a current transaction before you call other transactions. This can be an important step if a component supports but does not require transactions since a transaction may not always be present when the component executes.

Adding Components to Packages

Microsoft ✓ *Exam Objective*

Add components to an MTS package.

- Set transactional properties of components.
- Set security properties of components.

After a component has been created and compiled into a DLL, that component must be added to an MTS package before MTS can manage it. You can take two different approaches to adding components to Microsoft Transaction Server. The first method uses the MTS menus.

In the MTS Explorer, you will drill down into the Explorer until you locate the Components folder of the package to which you wish to add the components. Right-click the folder and select New ➤ Component from the pop-up menu. You are given two options, one to install new components and the other to import components that have already been registered. The dialog is shown in Figure 9.3.

If you have copied the DLL to the computer and have not registered it yet, choose the first option to install a new component. This will register the component in the process of inserting it into the package. Click the Add Files button to locate the DLL that you wish to install. MTS will recognize the exposed classes and interfaces.

If the package has already been registered on the server, select the option to import components. You will be presented with a list of registered components. Select the one that you wish to add to your package and click the Finish button. This will install the MTS components into the package.

FIGURE 9.3

The Install Component
Options dialog

The other approach that you can use is drag and drop. Open the MTS Explorer and the Windows Explorer side by side, so that you can view them both on the screen. Drill down into the desired package so that the contents of the Components folder are visible in the right pane of the MTS Explorer. Drag the desired DLL from the Windows Explorer to the MTS Explorer as pictured in Figure 9.4.

FIGURE 9.4

Installing DLLs into
packages with
drag-and-drop

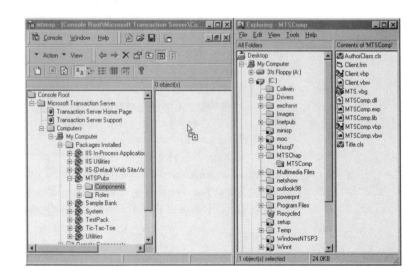

After the components are installed, you may wish to verify and set certain component properties. These properties can be accessed by clicking with your right mouse button on the component and selecting Properties from the pop-up menu. The two primary properties that you will manage in this window are the Transaction mode and Security.

In the Transaction tab, you will find four possible transaction states. These match the transaction states that we discussed earlier in our overview of the MTSTransactionMode property of Visual Basic. Figure 9.5 illustrates the Transaction tab of the Component Properties dialog.

FIGURE 9.5

Component transaction properties

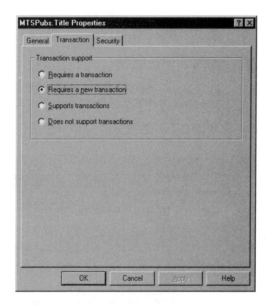

Microsoft ✓ **Exam** **Objective**

Use role-based security to limit the use of an MTS package to specific users.

- Assign roles to components or component interfaces.

The Security tab of the component properties contains a single option to enable authorization checking. If authorization checking is enabled for the package, you can choose whether to enforce authorization checking at the component level as well.

Also related to the security properties is the ability to associate certain roles with components in a package. If you allow authorization checking at the component level, you must add roles to the Role Membership folder of the component to identify those users that will be permitted to access the functionality of the component.

To add roles to the Role Membership folder of a component, select the folder and right-click. Select New ➤ Role from the pop-up menu. You will see a dialog with a list of roles that have been added to the current package. Select the role that you wish to add to the component list and click the OK button. Any members of this role will then be able to access the component.

Trying It Out

Exercise 9.5 takes you through the creation of a simple MTS component. This example does not enlist other components, but does require a transaction. If the data modifications fail, a run-time error will be raised and the transaction will fail to complete.

EXERCISE 9.5

Creating and Testing an MTS Component

1. Start Visual Basic. Select the ActiveX DLL from the template list. In the Project Properties dialog, set the name of the project to **MTSPubs**. Verify that the component is marked as Apartment Threaded. Set the Name property of Class1 to **Title**. Change the MTSTransactionMode property on the class to RequiresNewTransaction.

2. From the Project ➤ References menu, add references to the Microsoft ActiveX Data Objects 2.0 Library and the Microsoft Transaction Server Type Library.

3. Add a Public Function to the class named **UpdateTitleKey**. The function should accept three arguments called **OldValue**, **NewValue**, and **NewTitle**. All are string data types. The return value should be Boolean.

4. In the function, add code to capture the Context object. Connect to your SQL Server Data Source and execute two commands. One should update the title_id column of the titles table based on values provided for the new titled_id and the old title_id. The other should update the title column based on the title_id. Use the parameters of the function to provide values for these data modifications.

5. If the data modifications can complete without error, commit the transaction by using the SetComplete method of the Context object and set the return value of the function to true. If an error occurs, abort the transaction with the SetAbort method of the Context object and provide a return value of the function as false. The following code is an example of one possible structure of the function.

```
Public Function UpdateTitleKey(OldValue As String, _
        NewValue As String, _
        NewTitle As String) As Boolean
On Error GoTo Err_UpdateTitleKey
Dim cn As ADODB.Connection
Dim cmd As ADODB.Command
Dim ctxObject As MTxAS.ObjectContext
Dim strQuery1 As String
Dim strQuery2 As String
Set ctxObject = GetObjectContext()
Set cn = New ADODB.Connection
strQuery1 = "Update titles Set title='" + _
    NewTitle + "' WHERE title_id = '" + OldValue + "'"
strQuery2 = "Update titles Set title_id='" + _
    NewValue + "' WHERE title_id = '" + OldValue + "'"
'Establish a connection
With cn
    .Provider = "SQLOLEDB"
    .ConnectionString = "User ID=sa;Password=;" & _
                        "server=<your Server Name.;" & _
                        "initial catalog=pubs"
End With
```

```
cn.Open
'Execute Command
Set cmd = CreateObject("ADODB.Command")
With cmd
    .ActiveConnection = cn
    .CommandText = strQuery1
    .CommandType = adCmdText
    .Execute
End With
With cmd
    .ActiveConnection = cn
    .CommandText = strQuery2
    .CommandType = adCmdText
    .Execute
End With
ctxObject.SetComplete
UpdateTitleKey = True
Exit Function
Err_UpdateTitleKey:
ctxObject.SetAbort
UpdateTitleKey = False
End Function
```

6. Save the project files in a location of your choice. Save the class module as **Title.cls** and the project file as **MTSComp.vbp**. Make the MTSComp.DLL file by selecting File ➣ Make MTSComp.dll. Close Visual Basic.

7. Open the Microsoft Transaction Server Explorer. Create a new package called MTSPubs. Leave the identity as the interactive user. Drill down into the new package to the Components folder. Right-click the folder and from the pop-up menu, select New ➣ Component. Choose the option to install a component that is already registered.

8. From the list of programmatic identifiers that you see, select MTSPubs .Title from the list and click Finish. You should now see the new component in the Components folder of the package. Right-click the component and select Properties. Click the Transaction tab on the dialog. Ensure that the transaction attribute is set to Require a New Transaction.

9. To create a test client, start Visual Basic and select Standard EXE from the templates list. Add a reference to the MTSPubs DLL from the Project ➢ References menu. Add a command button to the form. On the click event of the command button, write code to call the Update-TitleKey method of MTSPubs.Title. Use the InputBox function to capture values from the user for the three parameters that need to be passed to the method. Raise a message box to inform the user if the transaction succeeded or failed based on the return value of the method. The code below shows a sample solution for the client code.

```
Private Sub Command1_Click()
Dim objMTS As New MTSPubs.Title
Dim strOldVal As String
Dim strNewVal As String
Dim strNewTitle As String
Dim blnReturn As Boolean
strOldVal = InputBox$("Enter Old Title Number")
strNewVal = InputBox$("Enter New Title Number")
strNewTitle = InputBox$("Enter New Title")
Me.MousePointer = vbHourglass
blnReturn = objMTS.UpdateTitleKey(strOldVal, strNewVal,
strNewTitle)
Me.MousePointer = vbDefault
Select Case blnReturn
    Case True
        MsgBox "Change Complete"
    Case False
        MsgBox "Error Occurred.  Change Aborted"
End Select
End Sub
```

10. To verify the data before and after the component executes, you will use the SQL Server Query Analyzer. Start the Query Analyzer by selecting Start ➤ Programs ➤ SQL Server 7.0 ➤ Query Analyzer. Enter and execute the following query.

    SELECT title_id, title FROM titles

11. Locate title number MC3026. You will change this number and title in the next step.

12. Start the client application and click the command button. Enter MC3036 for the old title number, MC3026 for the new title number and a title of your choice for the new title. You should be informed with a message box that the change was made.

13. Execute the above query again in the Query Analyzer to verify that the change was made to the database.

14. Run the client again. This time you will use a title_id that will fail the update because of a referential integrity violation. Use PC1035 for the old title_id, PC1036 for the new title_id, and any title of your choice.

15. This time the modification should fail. The change to the title could have taken place without error, but because the title modification was part of the same transaction as the title_id modification, the entire transaction failed to complete. Execute the query again to verify these results.

Working with Existing Packages

Microsoft ✓ *Exam Objective*

Create a package by using the MTS Explorer.

- Import existing packages

If you have created packages on a development server, you might wish to export these packages to a production server for implementation. This is a two step process of exporting the package into a file with a PAK extension followed by an import of the package on the destination server.

To export the package to a PAK file, drill down into the folder that contains the package that you want to export. Select the package you want to export. Right-click and select Export from the pop-up menu. In the Export Package dialog box, enter the path or browse for the folder where you want to create the package file. Type a pathname for the PAK file. Click Export to complete the process. The target folder will contain the PAK file as well as any required subcomponents.

Once the package has been exported, it can be imported back into another MTS installation by importing the PAK file. The easiest way to accomplish this is with the Package Import Wizard.

To access this wizard, select the Packages Installed folder underneath the target computer in the MTS Explorer. Right-click the folder and select New ➤ Package from the pop-up menu. Click the option to install a pre-built package.

In the resulting dialog, click the Add button and select the PAK file that you wish to import. This will add the package to the import list in the dialog. Click the Next button to advance to the next screen.

From the next screen, you will set the identity of the package. The last screen allows you to specify where the component files will be installed. Click the Finish button to complete the import.

Summary

Microsoft Transaction Server is a critical part of any distributed application using Microsoft technologies. MTS increases the scalability and ease of deployment of any multitier application.

Because all MTS components must be COM compliant, MTS is language neutral. MTS components can be created in any language that supports the creation of COM objects. These languages include Microsoft Visual Basic 6, Visual C++ 6, Visual J++ 6, and Visual FoxPro 6. This means that you can use the language with which you feel most comfortable to create your components.

MTS provides many services to an application. It is very important to remember that MTS is not simply a transactional management tool. Some of the additional services provided by MTS include object brokering, resource pooling, and security. With MTS support, your business tier is more stable, scalable, and manageable than ever.

Review Questions

1. Which of the following component threading models does Microsoft Transaction Server support? Choose two.

   A. Apartment threading

   B. Free threading

   C. Control threading

   D. Single threading

2. Which package authentication level should you use if you want to ensure the highest level of encryption available as the packets cross the network?

   A. Connect

   B. Packet Privacy

   C. Packet Integrity

   D. Call

3. Which of the following code examples would allow a user to access a component functionality only if the user was a member of a Windows NT group called Managers that is associated with the Admins role of a component?

   A. If IsCallerInGroup("Admins") Then

   B. If IsCallerInRole("Admins") Then

   C. If IsCallerInGroup("Managers") Then

   D. If IsCallerInRole("Managers") Then

4. Which of the following is a firm requirement of MTS components?

   A. They must be COM compliant.

   B. They must be apartment-threaded.

   C. They must be stateless.

   D. They must interact with a data source.

5. Which of the following methods is used to inform the Context object that a transaction must be canceled?

   A. CancelTran

   B. SetCancel

   C. SetAbort

   D. RollBack

6. You should avoid using properties in an MTS component because:

   A. MTS does not understand how properties are exposed.

   B. All properties are private interfaces.

   C. Properties execute differently than methods and can bypass MTS security.

   D. Properties usually maintain state on the server.

7. Which transaction setting is most appropriate for the root component that enlists other components into a transaction if the component is always and only used as a root component?

   A. Supports transactions

   B. Requires a transaction

   C. Requires a new transaction

   D. Does not support transactions

8. Which transaction setting is most appropriate for the root component that enlists other components into a transaction if the component is only occasionally used as a root component?

   A. Supports transactions

   B. Requires a transaction

   C. Requires a new transaction

   D. Does not support transactions

9. MTS objects must be packaged as

   A. In-process COM objects (DLLs)

   B. Standard DLLs

   C. Out-of-process DLLs (EXEs)

   D. PAK files

10. Which of the following statements is not true about the MTS security model?

   A. It is an optional service provided for the Administrator.

   B. It is integrated with the Windows NT security system.

   C. It uses the Context object to allow the component to query security status.

   D. It is never enabled when the object does not support transactions.

CHAPTER

10

Creating a Browser-Based Presentation Tier

Although the majority of all distributed applications are implemented using traditional Windows clients, Internet and intranet approaches are increasing in popularity. The distributed architecture actually lends itself very well to browser-based clients and can also increase your application's exposure to a much larger audience than can a traditional client application.

In this chapter, we will review basic HTML and VBScript structure and then discuss three different approaches to creating browser-based clients. First, we will look at the Active Server Pages (ASP) model. This approach allows the developer to create text files hosted on a Microsoft Internet Information Server (IIS); these text files contain Visual Basic script that can execute on the server and provide client services to the browser. We will then extend this model to discuss the implementation of an IIS Application that contains Visual Basic Web classes. Finally, we will explore active documents created with Visual Basic tools. These ActiveX documents are COM objects that can be hosted within an Internet Explorer (IE) browser. They allow you to create and deploy a browser client much in the same way as you would a traditional client.

HTML Overview

HTML, or HyperText Markup Language, is the formatting language of the Web. To effectively define what HTML is and the services that it offers to Web professionals, we must first define what HTML is not. HTML is not a programming language. There is no control of flow in HTML. There is no support for variables or other programming constructs.

As a markup language, HTML has more in common with other markup formats such as RTF (Rich Text Format) than it does with programming languages. The purpose of HTML is to provide instructions to Web browsers on how to display the files they download. There are some special extensions to HTML, such as Script, Object, and Applet tags that give a Web page author some programmability; however, HTML itself is not inherently a programmable environment.

HTML provides these instructions to Web browsers through elements called *tags*. An HTML tag is a note to the browser that it should handle the text inside of the tag in a particular way. However, not all browsers on the market today read every tag that can be placed into an HTML page. And, even if the tag is fully understood by a Web browser, it may not implement this tag in the same way as other browsers. This means that HTML does not define *exactly* how the page should be rendered, but rather *approximately* how the page should be rendered.

In this section, we will look at the most common tags that are used in HTML today, along with some of the special extensions that are supported by the Microsoft Internet Explorer. Tags can be divided into general categories, so we will deal with them categorically. In this section we will look at:

- Structure tags

- Formatting tags

- List tags

- Form tags

- Special tags

It is not the intent of this section to be a complete discussion of HTML, but rather to provide a consistent frame of reference for the remainder of this chapter. If you are experienced with HTML, you may choose to skip this section. If you require more detail concerning HTML, visit the Sybex Web site and search under HTML. There are many books available that can provide the level of detail that you need.

Structure Tags

Structure tags are those that define the layout of the HTML page. There are three primary structure tags. They are:

- <HTML> </HTML>

- <HEAD> </HEAD>

- <BODY> </BODY>

The <HTML> tag defines the scope of the entire HTML page. It is used to open the page and is found at the beginning of a page. The </HTML> tag is used to close the document and is found at the end of the HTML page. With most major browsers, this tag is optional and is not required, although it is usually included by convention for completeness. The other tags defined as structural tags are found within the HTML structure itself, so the <HTML> tags will usually be the first and last tags found in a Web page.

The <HEAD> tag defines the head section of an HTML page. It is within the head section that we place general information pertaining to the document as a whole. The title of the page and other special informational tags are usually found within the head section. Although not required, the head is the appropriate location for most general page information, and every page should include a head.

The <TITLE> tag is not technically a structure tag, but it is used within the header to identify the title of the page. This title will be displayed in the title bar of the browser in most browsers.

The bulk of the page is within the <BODY> tags. The body structure defines what the browser displays as the content of a Web page. The body section can contain many different nested tags within it, such as formatting tags, list tags, region tags, etc. Figures 10.1 and 10.2 illustrate how the <HTML>, <HEAD>, and <BODY> tags appear when implemented in a source file and how that source file would appear in Internet Explorer 4.

F I G U R E   10.1

Structure tags on a Web page

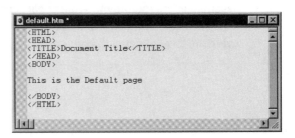

FIGURE 10.2

The source above
rendered in Internet
Explorer

Formatting Tags

There are many different tags that pertain to formatting. After all, this is what HTML was designed to accomplish. When formatting documents with HTML, most tags are approximate in their application. Different browsers may interpret these tags in different ways and thus display the text with slightly different formatting. Among these approximate tags are:

<EM>   Emphasis (displayed in IE as italic)

<CODE>   Sample code (displayed in IE as Courier font)

<STRONG>   Another approach to emphasis (displayed in IE as bold)

<BIG>   Displays text larger than normal

<SMALL>   Displays text smaller than normal

Some approximate tags are used to specify both font sizes and special characteristics. The set of heading tags, for example, displays up to sixth level headings in a format defined by the browser. These tags, <H1> through <H6>, are illustrated in Figure 10.3.

Other tags are very exact in their meaning. Some of these tags include:

<B>   Bold text

<I>   Italic text

<CENTER>   Center text or an embedded image

<FONT>   Can specify an absolute size ranging from 1 to 7 (3 is the default) or a relative size such as +1 or –1

<BASEFONT>   Sets the default font size for the page

FIGURE 10.3

Headings displayed in
Internet Explorer 4

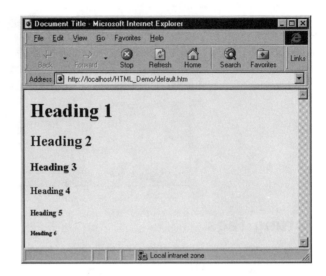

You can use all of these formatting tags with each other to display the page exactly how you wish. Figure 10.4 illustrates a sample Web page source using these formatting tags, and Figure 10.5 illustrates the same page displayed in Internet Explorer 4.

The <BR> tag that you see in this example is a line break. This will be explained in detail later in this chapter.

FIGURE 10.4

HTML source with
format tags

```
<HTML>
<HEAD>
<TITLE>Format Sample</TITLE>
</HEAD>
<BODY>

<BASEFONT SIZE=3>

<CENTER><FONT SIZE=+2>This text is centered and large</FONT>
<BR><BIG>This text is also centered and large</BIG>
<BR>This text is centered and normal</CENTER>

<BR><EM>This text is emphasized</EM>
<BR><I>This text is Italic</I>

</BODY>
</HTML>
```

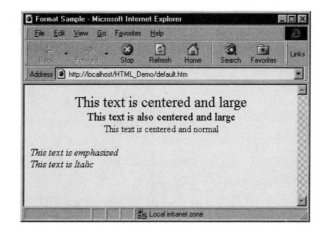

List Tags

HTML supports two general varieties of lists. *Ordered lists* are numbered
lists and *unordered lists* are bulleted. Lists are very simple to implement in
HTML. A list tag marks the beginning of the list and the end of the list.
Within a list, each item is marked with a tag that identifies the beginning of
a new list item. The list tags are as follows:

<OL>   Marks the beginning of an ordered list. Closed with the
</OL> tag.

<UL>   Marks the beginning of an unordered list. Closed with the
</UL> tag.

<LI>   Marks an individual list item. There is no close tag.

The sample code in Figures 10.6 and 10.7 show the implementation of an
ordered list.

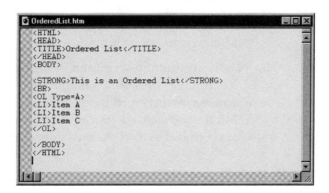

Form Tags

An HTML form is central to the ability of a Web page to provide the user with an interactive experience. It acts as a mechanism by which the browser packages values to send to a Web server for further processing. Once received by the server, a CGI, ISAPI, or other server-side application can process these values.

The form itself is marked with the form tags <FORM></FORM>. Within the form, each individual element is marked with a form field tag. This tag will differ depending on the type of form element displayed; the most common element is the <INPUT> tag.

The <FORM> tag supports various properties that define how the form will execute its task. Among these properties are:

ACTION Sets the URL of the process that will handle the form parameters. This is most commonly a CGI, Dynamic Link Library (DLL), or Active Server Page (ASP).

METHOD Defines how the form parameters will be sent to the destination URL. The most common methods are GET and POST.

NAME The name of the form. This is required if you intend to refer to the form from your client-side script.

Forms are made up of elements that define the parameters for the form. Each of these elements has a Name property that the form sends to the server to identify a context for each of these values. The form elements supported by HTML are very similar in structure and application to the common Windows-based controls. The most common form element tag is the <INPUT> tag, which supports a property called Type. Some of the values that the Type property supports include:

CHECKBOX   A checkbox is used to capture a Yes/No input.

RADIO   Option buttons used to capture a mutually exclusive choice.

TEXT   A text box for free-form input contained on one line.

RESET   A command button that will reset the values of all form elements contained in the form.

SUBMIT   A command button that will submit the contents of the form to the URL indicated in the Action property of the form.

BUTTON   A command button that will respond to client-side script through a click event.

HIDDEN   A control that is not visible to the user. Its value can be set through script and submitted with the other controls on the form.

In addition to the <INPUT> tag, other tags define elements used within forms. These tags include:

<TEXTAREA>   A text input across multiple lines and closed with the </TEXTAREA> tag. Includes parameters for the number of rows and columns.

<SELECT>   A list box that defines a list of items. A parameter is included to allow multiple items to be selected.

<OPTION>   An element within a <SELECT> list.

When used together appropriately, the elements within a form provide the ability to collect data in a manner that the user will find intuitive. Once the user clicks the Submit button on the form, the contents of the form will be submitted to the server in collection name/value pairs, one for each value accepted by a form element.

Although a single HTML page can contain multiple forms, each must contain its own Submit button or be able to initiate the submit process in some other way. Only the elements within the form that is submitted will be passed back to the URL, which is indicated by the Action property of the form. All other forms and form elements will be ignored.

Figure 10.8 illustrates a sample HTML source using a form and some form element tags. Figure 10.9 illustrates the same sample displayed in Internet Explorer 4.

F I G U R E   10.8

Using forms in an HTML page

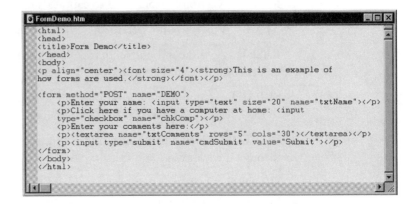

```
FormDemo.htm

<html>
<head>
<title>Form Demo</title>
</head>
<body>
<p align="center"><font size="4"><strong>This is an example of
how forms are used.</strong></font></p>

<form method="POST" name="DEMO">
    <p>Enter your name: <input type="text" size="20" name="txtName"></p>
    <p>Click here if you have a computer at home: <input
    type="checkbox" name="chkComp"></p>
    <p>Enter your comments here:</p>
    <p><textarea name="txtComments" rows="5" cols="30"></textarea></p>
    <p><input type="submit" name="cmdSubmit" value="Submit"></p>
</form>
</body>
</html>
```

F I G U R E   10.9

Above source displayed in Internet Explorer 4

Special Tags

Not all HTML tags fit into neat packages like the ones that we just discussed; many of them have unique applications. This section will address some of the most common special application tags supported by HTML or the Internet Explorer extensions to HTML.

Comments

There are two opening and closing tag sets used to mark comments in HTML. The <!-- and --> tags are used to begin and close comments in an HTML page. When used inside of a script tag, these comments prevent the script from displaying as text if the browser does not support the script used. The code sample below illustrates how to implement comments inside of a script.

```
<SCRIPT Language=vbscript>
<!--
Sub Hello()
MsgBox "Hello World"
End Sub
-->
</SCRIPT>
```

The other approach to implementing comments in an HTML page is through the <COMMENT> </COMMENT> tags. These tags will suppress all text within the tags, even if the intent of the text is to run as code inside of a script. As you use these tags in an HTML page, remember that this code and these comments will be visible to the user if they choose to view the source in their browser. To hide code completely from the user, it must run on the server. Active Server Pages can provide this functionality.

Paragraphs and Breaks

HTML ignores any carriage returns in an HTML page. If you wish to create a hard break between different sections of text, images, or other tags, you must include a tag that will force the break. There are two ways to accomplish this. A paragraph tag will provide the hard return but will also force a line space between the elements on both sides of the tag. The break tag will provide the hard return without the extra space.

Neither tag requires a closing element. To create a paragraph break, simply place the <P> tag where you wish the break to occur. Similarly, to create a break, place the <BR> tag where you wish the page break to take place.

The horizontal rule tag <HR> displays a horizontal line across the screen. This can be very useful to create a break between different areas of a single Web page. The <HR> tag supports a number of parameters that define its size, width, alignment, etc.

Hyperlinks

The primary reason the World Wide Web is so popular is because of its ease of use. It is very easy to navigate through the Web because HTML defines the ability to provide text and image pointers to other locations on the Web. The user can simply follow these links rather than be forced to type the address of every site to which they wish to navigate.

The tag used to provide any of these links is the anchor tag. This tag, expressed in the code as <A> </A>, supports a series of properties that define how each link behaves. The most important of these attributes is the HREF property, which defines the URL of the site to which the link refers. For example, if you wished to display the text "Go Visit Microsoft" as a link to the Microsoft Web site, the HTML would look like this:

```
<A HREF="http://www.microsoft.com">Go Visit Microsoft</A>
```

The term *anchor* tag refers to the ability of the tag to contain a name attribute. If the anchor is named, links can be made to this tag from elsewhere in the document.

Special Object Tags

There are two tags that are used to include executable objects in an HTML page, the <OBJECT> tag and the <APPLET> tag. These objects are not stored in HTML format, but rather are compiled into executable or interpretable formats that the browser can render appropriately, i.e., ActiveX controls and Java applets. A detailed discussion of the implementation of these tags is included in the "Implementing ActiveX Controls" section later in this chapter.

The <OBJECT> tag is supported natively only by the Microsoft Internet Explorer browser. If you wish your Web page to be completely compatible with all browsers, you must be very careful with the use of this tag. Providing alternate pages for non-Microsoft browsers is one way that this compatibility can be supported.

Special Tag Examples

Figure 10.10 presents source code of some of the most common special tags discussed in this section. The source is displayed in Internet Explorer 4 in Figure 10.11.

F I G U R E   10.10

HTML source with special tags

```
Tag Demo.htm *
<HTML>
<HEAD>
<TITLE>Tag Demo</TITLE>
</HEAD>
<BODY>

<CENTER><STRONG><BIG>This page contains tag samples</CENTER></STRONG></BIG>

<P>
This is text above a paragraph tag
<P>
This is text below a paragraph tag and above a break tag
<BR>
This is text below a break tag
<HR>
<P>
<A HREF="http://www.microsoft.com">This is a link to Microsoft</A>
<P>
<A HREF="http://www.sybex.com">This is a link to Sybex</A>
<P>
<Comment>This is a comment and will not be displayed in the browser</Comment>

<OBJECT ID="cmdTest" WIDTH=96 HEIGHT=32
  CLASSID="CLSID:D7053240-CE69-11CD-A777-00DD01143C57">
    <PARAM NAME="Caption" VALUE="ActiveX Control">
    <PARAM NAME="Size" VALUE="2540;846">
</OBJECT>
</BODY>
</HTML>
```

When testing your Web pages in a browser, it is very important to consider browser compatibility. If you wish to target your Web page to more than one browser, you must test your entire Web in every browser that you wish to support. If you have targeted your site to a specific browser, it is common courtesy to note this fact on the default page of your Web.

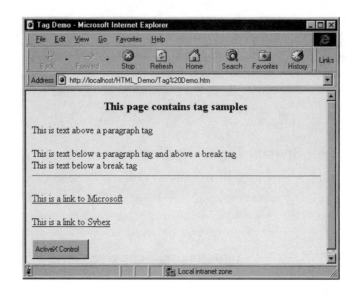

Using ActiveX Controls

Although HTML defines form elements used to take input from the user, these elements are often not flexible or robust enough to offer the interactive experience that today's users expect. There are different ways to bridge this gap between what HTML offers and what the users expect. One of the most robust solutions is the ActiveX control.

ActiveX controls are COM objects. COM defines a binary standard at which all objects and their containers can relate. As a COM object, the ActiveX control must have a COM container acting as host before the true power of the control can be exposed. Through this container, the properties, methods, and events defined by the object are exposed.

Microsoft Internet Explorer ships in other versions other than 32-bit windows (Unix, for example). Because of the binary standard defined by COM, ActiveX controls are multiplatform objects and can be supported in any container that supports COM objects, allowing ActiveX to act as a viable component of a solution under many different platform scenarios.

The Microsoft Internet Explorer provides the ability to execute ActiveX controls in a Web page through the <OBJECT> tag, a Microsoft Internet Explorer extension to HTML. In this section, we will examine the process by which ActiveX controls download from the Internet. We will then look at the <OBJECT> tag, the implementation of the ActiveX control on a Web page. Finally, we will explore some of the security issues surrounding the use of ActiveX controls.

Downloading ActiveX Controls

ActiveX controls are unlike other elements on a Web page. When ActiveX controls are downloaded from the Web, the are actually installed into the Windows Registry of the target computer. This extra step makes ActiveX controls very efficient because they do not have to download again once they are installed.

Figure 10.12 illustrates the basic process model of how ActiveX controls are downloaded to a browser machine from a Web page. In this diagram, you see that the local registry is consulted, before the control download begins, to identify whether or not the control has already been installed. If not, the control is downloaded from a location identified in the <OBJECT> tag.

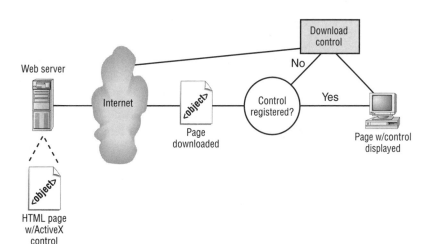

FIGURE 10.12

Downloading an ActiveX control from the Internet

Implementing ActiveX Controls

ActiveX controls are implemented through the <OBJECT> tag. This tag has many different properties. Among them are:

ID   The ID attribute exposes the name by which the control will be known on the Web page.

CLASSID   The ID number that the ActiveX controls write to the Windows registry. This 128-bit value is unique across all COM interfaces. If this value is found when the HTML page containing the control is downloaded, the control may be launched directly from the user's system.

CODEBASE   The codebase attribute identifies the URL from which the ActiveX control will be downloaded if necessary.

Let's look at the CLASSID attribute in more detail and see how it is implemented on a Web page. We will also perform an exercise covering the implementation of an ActiveX control.

CLASSID

Most of the attributes used in the <OBJECT> tag are quite intuitive, but the CLASSID can be a bit tricky. This attribute represents the CLASSID value that the control enters into the Windows Registry when it is installed. This CLASSID value is a 128-bit value that is a statistically unique identifier for a specific ActiveX control interface. The <OBJECT> tag must supply this value to identify the control that the developer desires.

There are a number of different ways to find and insert the appropriate CLASSID value into the <OBJECT> tag. When ActiveX controls were first introduced, the mechanism for inserting the CLASSID into the tag was quite painful. The developer would use a utility such as the Registry Editor to look up the CLASSID in the Windows registry. This would be copied from the registry and entered into the <OBJECT> tag.

Fortunately, the process is much easier now than it used to be. There are many tools that take the pain out of this process. Microsoft Front Page supports the insertion of ActiveX controls, as does Microsoft Visual InterDev.

Other <OBJECT> Attributes

Some of the attributes of the ActiveX control identify the control's placement and appearance on the Web page. These are optional attributes for most ActiveX controls but can be used to specify exact placement on the page. These attributes include:

WIDTH   The width of the control in the Web page

HEIGHT   The height of the control in the Web page

ALIGN   The alignment of the control

HSPACE   Spacing above and below the control

VSPACE   Spacing on the left or the right of the control

BORDER   Drawn border width around the control

There is another attribute that is integral to the functionality of an ActiveX control: the parameter attribute. Unlike the other attributes illustrated above, which supply only one value, the ActiveX control can support numerous parameters. To support this behavior, parameters are marked using <PARAM> tags that are embedded into the <OBJECT> tag. Each parameter has a name and a value.

Parameters used in the <PARAM> tags of an ActiveX control are the properties that would normally appear in the Properties window of Visual Basic for that control. The ActiveX control uses these parameters to describe the properties of a control and how the client browser will render it.

Figure 10.13 illustrates the HTML used for a Web page. Notice the implementation of the <PARAM> tags and how they set the properties of the ActiveX control.

F I G U R E   10.13

Implementing
<PARAM> tags

```
ActiveX.htm *
<HTML>
<HEAD>
<TITLE>Object Demo</TITLE>
</HEAD>
<BODY>


<OBJECT ID="UpDown1" WIDTH=16 HEIGHT=51
 CLASSID="CLSID:026371C0-1B7C-11CF-9D53-00AA003C9CB6">
    <PARAM NAME="_ExtentX" VALUE="423">
    <PARAM NAME="_ExtentY" VALUE="1323">
    <PARAM NAME="_Version" VALUE="327680">
    <PARAM NAME="Max" VALUE="100">
</OBJECT>

</BODY>
</HTML>
```

ActiveX Controls and Security

Since ActiveX controls are executable objects installed on a user's system, they have unlimited access to the resources on the user's computer. This poses an interesting security dilemma. ActiveX controls can solve many of the problems associated with creating dynamic Web pages, but the power that they provide to the developer can be dangerous to the user. How can users manage the security risks inherent in ActiveX controls?

Recognizing the potential dangers that malicious ActiveX controls provide, Microsoft has added security support into Internet Explorer to prevent unwanted and unauthorized downloads from the Internet or an intranet. Using the Security tab of the Internet Options dialog, the user can set Internet Explorer to various levels of security. Internet Explorer 4 supports either standard levels or custom security settings. Figure 10.14 illustrates the standard security options in the Internet Explorer 4 Internet Options dialog.

FIGURE 10.14

Security options in
Internet Explorer 4

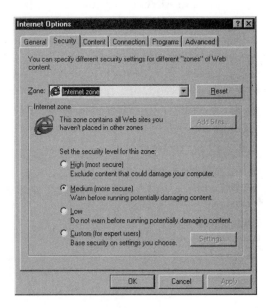

You will notice that the Internet Options Security tab has a drop-down list box at the top of the dialog. This list enumerates the various zones that

Internet Explorer supports. Different security settings can be configured for each zone. The zones supported are:

- Internet zone
- Local intranet zone
- Trusted sites zone
- Restricted sites zone

For both the trusted and restricted sites zones, the Add button shown in the dialog becomes active, allowing you to add the sites that qualify under these zone descriptions. In addition to the high, medium, and low security levels, each zone offers a custom setting that allows the user to specify exactly under which conditions an ActiveX control may be downloaded. Figure 10.15 illustrates the Security Settings dialog.

FIGURE 10.15

Custom Security Settings in Internet Explorer 4

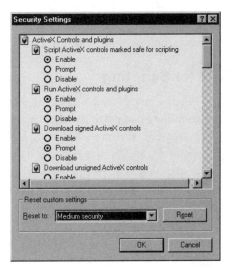

The custom Security Settings dialog in Internet Explorer 4 provides settings for three primary security issues relating to ActiveX controls. They control the browser's ability to download controls that have not been signed or marked safe for scripting or initializing. Let's look at each of these issues in more detail.

Signed ActiveX Controls

The only way to know for sure that any particular developer created an ActiveX control is if that control has been signed. Signing a control is a developer's stamp of authenticity, guaranteeing that the developer or company in question created the control. Note that this does not guarantee that the control is safe, only that the author of the control is the person or firm listed.

To get a digital signature, the developer must contact an independent certificate authority such as Verisign. The actual control being signed, as well as directory information about the developer, is sent to the certificate authority where this information is used to generate a digital certificate included with the control. The certificate guarantees that the developer or firm who has presented the control for a certificate is the party named on the certificate and that the controls have not been tampered with since the certificate was assigned.

If a user chooses to be prompted before downloading a control containing a digital certificate, they will be presented with the certificate in their browser. Depending on whether they trust the individual or firm named in the certificate, the user will choose whether to perform the download.

Safe for Scripting

When a developer compiles an ActiveX control and prepares it for distribution, they can mark the control as safe for certain activities. One of these activities is scripting. Scripting is the process of referring to the properties, methods, and events exposed by an ActiveX control from a scripting language such as VBScript or JavaScript.

When a developer marks a control as safe for scripting, it is a personal guarantee that the control cannot be manipulated on a user's machine in such a way that it would cause any damage to hardware or data. Note that, as is the case with code signing, this does not provide a complete guarantee to the user that the control will not be dangerous to the target computer. This guarantee only goes as far as the trust placed in the control developer by the user who is downloading the control.

Safe for Initializing

Most ActiveX controls support custom properties. The <PARAM> tags found in the Web page provide the initial implementation of some of these properties. After a Web page is first downloaded, but before it is actually initialized, these <PARAM> tags are read and the properties of the control are set to these initial values. Initialization of the control then takes place.

In addition to marking a control as safe for scripting, a developer can also mark a control as safe for initializing. This mark is the developer's personal guarantee that the range of values allowed for the parameters supported by the ActiveX control cannot cause any damage on the user's computer. Once again, there is no ironclad guarantee that this will be the case; the guarantee provided by the developer only goes as far as the user's trust in that developer or firm.

Implementing VBScript

The objects that you place into Web pages are not much help to you unless you can control them with some kind of programming environment. Programming code that you write in a Web page is added through the <SCRIPT> tag. There are two main types of script that you commonly see in Web pages today: JavaScript and VBScript.

JavaScript is based on the Java programming language and supports much of the same structure and syntax. The most popular browsers on the market today almost universally support JavaScript. Because JavaScript has the ability to cross the browser boundary, it is a very popular solution to the creation of interactive Web pages. In most browsers, including Microsoft Internet Explorer, if the developer does not explicitly state what type of script the Web page contains, the browser will assume it is JavaScript.

Although Microsoft does supply a JavaScript interpreter in the Internet Explorer browser, JavaScript is not strictly a Microsoft solution and, as such, is not covered in this exam.

VBScript is based on the Visual Basic language. It shares with Visual Basic the same syntax and structure used to create Visual Basic applications; however, it does not include all elements of Visual Basic. VBScript is optimized to download quickly and efficiently across the Internet and execute with very low overhead in the browser. If you are familiar with Visual Basic syntax, VBScript will look very familiar, and you will be writing effective VBScript code almost immediately.

All script must be contained within a <SCRIPT> </SCRIPT> tag set to execute. This tag supports only one attribute of note, the language attribute. By setting the language attribute of the tag to JavaScript or VBScript, you can select the type of script that you wish to use for your page. You can even use both types of script on the same page by explicitly defining the sections in which you write the script. If you do not specify which type of script you want, JavaScript will be the default.

In this section, we will look at the implementation of script through the <SCRIPT> tag. We will discuss the scope and visibility of script and look at the syntax of VBScript on a Web page.

 Although there is no exam objective dealing specifically with scripting, it is an important component of implementing an ActiveX or Java applet solution. You may see some scripting on your exam.

VBScript Structures

Like any programming language, VBScript defines certain keywords and structures that you will use to create your Web applications. If you are familiar with Visual Basic, most of these structures will look familiar. However, unlike in Visual Basic, there are restrictions placed on these structures. Pay attention to these limitations, because using the structures incorrectly will cause the script in your Web pages to fail.

Data Types

A data type defines the size and other characteristics of a piece of information. Data types are used most commonly when defining variables and other similar structure. While most programming languages define a number of different data types, VBScript defines only one, called the variant. The variant data type can accept any value that any of the standard Visual Basic data types support. It can accept strings, integers, and floating point numeric values.

VBScript also provides support for constants. A constant is like a variable in that it uses a symbolic name to reference a specific value, but unlike a variable, the value of a constant can't be changed. Constants are used when you have a fixed value that you wish to reference intuitively in your code rather than put the number in every place that it is used. Constants also give you the ability to change the implementation by modifying the constant rather than changing the code everywhere that it is implemented.

VBScript also supports variable arrays. An array is a group of variables that you reference with a single variable name. You differentiate between the variables by providing an index number to refer to the specific element of the array that you want. All arrays are 0-based in VBScript, so an array with index values ranging in index from 0 to 10 would have 11 elements in the array.

Scoping

The scope of variables refers to where they can be seen and accessed by the code in the Web page. There are two levels of scope supported by VBScript, local and script levels.

Inside a <SCRIPT> tag, you can define procedures that are called from script found elsewhere in the Web page. If a variable is defined within a procedure, it has local scope. This means that the variable is not visible outside of that procedure, and when the procedure completes its execution it releases all resources allocated to that variable.

When the variable is defined outside of a procedure, the variable has script level scope. Script level scope means that the variable is visible to any code in the Web page. It is not possible to define a variable to have scope outside of a single page when using client-side script. In the sample code below, the variable X has local scope, while the variable Y has script level scope.

```
<SCRIPT LANGUAGE=VBScript>
Dim Y
Y="Enter Your Name"
Sub Hello()
Dim X
X=InputBox(Y)
MsgBox X
End Sub
</SCRIPT>
```

Control of Flow

VBScript supports all of the standard Visual Basic control of flow statements. These include:

- If...Then...Else
- Select Case
- Do...Loop
- For...Next
- While...Wend

You are free to use any of these structures in your script; however, be aware that the While...Wend structure is provided for compatibility reasons only and offers no advantages over using the Do While...Loop structure. There is also a limitation in the Select Case structure in that it does not support cases using ranges of values. For this reason, no comparison operators such as greater than (>) or less than (<) can be used.

Error Handling

VBScript supports error handling but only through the On Error Resume Next statement. Unlike Visual Basic, Go To statements are not supported. Using the On Error Resume Next statement in code is often called *inline error handling*. Inline error handling means that instead of branching out to an error handler, the error is resolved within the script immediately after the error occurs.

If you suspect that a line of code that you have executed could possibly result in an error condition while you're using inline error handling, you should follow that code with an error check. VBScript provides support for error checking through the Err object. This object supports the following properties and methods:

Number property   The error number of the most recently generated error

Clear method   Resets the Number property of the Err object to 0

Raise method   Allows a specific error to be fired

Another element of VBScript that significantly aids in error recognition and debugging is the Option Explicit statement. Including the Option Explicit statement in your script forces you to declare all of your variables. Since Variant variables are auto-declared if you do not explicitly declare them, this can prevent some of the nastiest bugs, namely misspelled variables that are very hard to find. The sample code below illustrates how error handling is implemented with VBScript.

```
<SCRIPT LANGUAGE=VBSCRIPT>
Option Explicit
Sub ErrorSub()
On Error Resume Next
'A statement that may cause an error
```

```
If Err.Number<>0 then
MsgBox "Error Number " & Err.Number
Err.Clear
End If
End Sub
</SCRIPT>
```

Comments

You can use two different comment types inside your <SCRIPT> tags, VBScript comments and HTML comments. Visual Basic supports comments by using the single quote ('). Anything following this quote will be considered a comment to the end of the line.

HTML comments solve a problem that often presents itself with VBScript. If the browser does not recognize the <SCRIPT> tag, it will usually display the code as text rather than suppress it completely. To suppress script that may not be recognized, you can enclose the actual code inside the script tag within HTML comments. This is a standard practice that you should follow when putting any script into a Web page. The example code below illustrates how these different comments are used.

```
<SCRIPT LANGUAGE=VBSCRIPT>
<!--
Sub Comment()
Dim X
X=5
'This is a VBScript comment
End Sub
-->
</SCRIPT>
```

Using VBScript with Objects

The whole purpose of using VBScript in a Web page is to interact with objects such as ActiveX controls or Java applets. Through a scripting language, you have the ability to manipulate all of the properties and methods exposed by these objects. In addition, in the case of ActiveX controls and HTML controls, you can write script to respond to the events that are fired by these controls.

ActiveX controls allow the Web developer to write script code that responds to the events raised in the control. This makes the implementation of ActiveX controls very flexible. While Java applets can also recognize events, the response to those events must be compiled into the applet. Applets do not raise events that can be scripted from outside the applet.

There are three different object types for which a script can be written. These are the standard HTML control, the ActiveX control, and the Java applet. To write script to manipulate these objects, the objects must be identified by name. Every one of the object types identifies itself through some naming parameter in the objects tag.

HTML controls have an optional NAME parameter that identifies the control. Java applets also have a NAME parameter. ActiveX Controls use a parameter called ID to identify the control on the Web page.

Each object type has properties (parameters) that can be set by the user as the user interacts with the page. For example, in the case of the Microsoft Forms 2.0 Text Box ActiveX Control, properties such as Text, Left, and Top affect the position and contents of the text box.

Responding to Events

It is very important to have the ability to respond to the events fired by ActiveX and HTML controls. The four different ways that these events can be trapped are covered in this section. First, you can create an event procedure for every event that you wish to trap. This approach may look very familiar to experienced Visual Basic developers. In the example code below, if you assume that you have an HTML button control called cmdHello, the following code would run when you clicked the button in the Web page.

```
<SCRIPT LANGUAGE=VBSCRIPT>
Sub cmdHello_onClick()
MsgBox "Hello World"
End Sub
</SCRIPT>
```

You can also assign a procedure to an event of a control when the control is created. This method only works with HTML controls and is not a valid option for ActiveX controls. The code below demonstrates this implementation.

```
<SCRIPT LANGUAGE=VBSCRIPT>
Sub HelloWorld()
MsgBox "Hello World"
End Sub
</SCRIPT>
<INPUT TYPE=BUTTON NAME=cmdHello onClick="HelloWorld">
```

You also have the option of creating a different <SCRIPT> section for every control and event that you wish to code. This example works equally well with both HTML controls and ActiveX controls.

```
<SCRIPT LANGUAGE=VBSCRIPT FOR="cmdHello" EVENT="onClick")
MsgBox "Hello World"
</SCRIPT>
```

The last approach is to actually code the script into the object tag itself. Using this approach, you do not have a separate <SCRIPT> section. This may make the script easier to isolate, but it has the disadvantage of cluttering up the HTML source significantly. This approach is valid only for HTML controls.

```
<INPUT LANGUAGE=VBSCRIPT TYPE=BUTTON VALUE="Say Hello"
onClick="MsgBox 'Hello World'">
```

Working with Properties and Methods

An object on a Web page exposes its properties and methods for scripting as needed. VBScript accesses and manipulates the properties and methods of objects in exactly the same way as does Visual Basic. VBScript writes values to properties through the following syntax:

```
Object.Property = Expression
```

The expression indicated can be any valid expression, including a literal, a variable, or even a property of another object. VBScript reads property values by turning the syntax around and assigning the value of a property to a variable or some other process to capture the response.

When working with methods, there is no assignment operator. Methods are designed to act on an object rather than to provide a value to an object. The syntax for calling the method of an object is:

```
Object.Method [Arguments]
```

Methods may have one or more arguments that indicate how the method will be executed. While these arguments are not required, they are very common, as they further define the implementation of the object.

Creating Dynamic HTML Pages with Visual Basic

Microsoft ✓ *Exam* *Objective*

Create a Web page by using the DHTML Page Designer to dynamically change attributes of elements, change content, change styles, and position elements.

Although Visual Basic is primarily a development environment for full applications and components, you can create HTML pages with Visual Basic through the DHTML application template. With this tool, you can do all of your presentation tier development with Visual Basic.

Although the DHTML application object allows you to take advantage of Visual Basic functionality and design methods for HTML and DHTML pages, other tools such as Microsoft Visual InterDev might be better suited to the task of creating complex Web-based solutions. The Visual Basic solution works well for creating a browser-based solution that targets only Microsoft browsers or for creating collections of Web pages for simple deployment.

Dynamic HTML (DHTML) should not be thought of as a replacement for HTML, but rather as an extension to HTML. Although DHTML is not solely a Microsoft technology, all browsers that support DHTML (IE 4 and higher, Netscape 4 and higher) support slightly different flavors beyond the core functionality of DHTML.

The driving philosophy behind DHTML is to include the functional support for common browser behaviors inside the browser itself rather than inside downloadable components such as ActiveX controls or Java applets. The result is a Web page that contains in its text instructions to the browser about special animation effects, data binding behaviors, and other elements that formerly required downloadable components. This means that the Web pages are smaller that before and can download faster without sacrificing functionality.

One feature of the DHTML model is the expansion of the HTML object model. Before DHTML, only some HTML tags identified objects that could be scripted. These primarily included HTML elements such as forms and their controls. Using the DHTML model, other types of tags, such as structure tags and formatting tags, can be identified within the Web page, and the developer can write script code to affect these objects.

As an example, suppose that you defined a section of your Web page that you would use to display text; however, the text that is to be displayed changes depending on the location of the mouse pointer. Using HTML, you would have to redraw the entire page, but with DHTML, the change can be made within the browser and additional contact to the server is not required.

Exercise 10.1 illustrates the process of creating a DHTML page in Visual Basic 6.0. Although in this exercise you will create a single DHTML page, in most DHTML applications you will create many DHTML pages that relate to each other, as well as a COM component that downloads to the browser. This component provides additional functionality to the page beyond that provided by the DHTML model.

EXERCISE 10.1

Creating a DHTML Page

1. Start Visual Basic. From the templates list, select DHTML application and click Open.

2. In the Project window, drill down into the Designers folder. Double-click DHTMLPage1 to open the designer. The designer is divided into two panes. The pane on the left is a tree view of all of the objects recognized by the DHTML model. The pane on the right is a view of your Web page.

3. Click in the right pane and, at the cursor location, type **First Text**. Hit the Enter key. Type **Second Text** and hit the Enter key.

4. In the left pane, you should now see three items listed under the body. They should read (First Text), (Second Text), and (<FONT ...). Click, in the tree view, on the First Text item. In the Properties window, set the ID to idFirst.

EXERCISE 10.1 (CONTINUED)

5. In tree view, click the Second Text item and, in the Properties window, set the ID to idSecond.

6. Click the (<Font ...) item and, in the Properties window, set the ID to idPar.

7. Select the First Text item from the list again and right-click. Select View Code from the pop-up menu. In the Procedure drop-down list (right side), select the OnMouseOver event and enter the following code.

   ```
   idPar.innerText = "You are on the First Text item"
   ```

8. Select the OnMouseOut event for the same object and enter the following code.

   ```
   idPar.innerText = ""
   ```

9. From the Object drop-down list, select idSecond. Place similar code in the OnMouseOver and OnMouseOut events indicating that the user is on the Second Text item.

10. Click Run ➢ Start from the menu to start the application. When prompted for a start component, click the OK button to start the application as is. This will launch the Automation Manager and start Internet Explorer.

11. Move your mouse over the First Text item. You should see the text of the paragraph respond. As you move the pointer away, the text in the last block will disappear. Repeat this process for the Second Text item.

12. Close Internet Explorer, stop the Visual Basic application, and exit Visual Basic. If you see the Automation Manager on your taskbar, close this as well.

Creating Active Server Pages

Microsoft ✓ *Exam Objective*

Create dynamic Web pages by using Active Server Pages (ASP) and webclasses.

HTML is not a programming language, but rather a text markup language that allows a browser to render text appropriately inside a browser window. While some simple HTML controls are available to capture user input and DHTML extends this ability, HTML does not define any programming logic needed to manipulate and validate the data that the user has entered.

HTML does support a <SCRIPT> tag, within which we can include code written in a language such as VBScript or JavaScript. These scripting languages allow you to create programming logic such as validation procedures, conditional decision structures, and others. This code can be included in the HTML page itself. While the browser can interpret the script code, this can present three problems:

- Compatibility of your scripting language of choice with a particular target browser

- Longer delays for the user as the browser downloads and executes the script

- Security of script source code because any user can view the source in the browser at any time

The simplest solution to these problems is to move the programming logic from the browser to the server. If all of the program execution takes place on the server, script incompatibilities are not an issue because the client contains little or no script. In addition, download and browser execution times are cut because the programming remains on the server. Because the server simply returns the results of the programming logic and never exposes the programming directly, the user cannot see the script or code used to generate the result.

There are three primary approaches to moving the programming logic from the client to the server when using Microsoft Internet Information Server. The developer can:

- Implement a Common Gateway Interface (CGI) application on the server

- Create a custom Internet Information Server (ISAPI) application or ISAPI filter that executes on the server

- Use an existing ISAPI extension called Active Server Pages (ASP) to process HTML and script on the server

Server Process Architectures

When a Web application developer wishes to implement a server-side solution, there are two primary choices in terms of the implementation architecture, CGI and ISAPI. Each of these options has its own benefits and drawbacks. In this section, we will explore the architectural differences between CGI and ISAPI solutions.

CGI

The purpose of a CGI application is to capture and process values sent to the Internet server by an HTML form. These binary files are usually created in a language such as Perl or C++. Although it is beyond the scope of this chapter to discuss how to write a CGI application, we can evaluate the implementation of these tools.

A CGI application is a binary file with a *.cgi extension. This file is completely independent from the Internet server. Most Web application developers will create a directory in their Web called cgi-bin or something similar in which to place all CGI applications. Implementing a CGI application uses the ACTION parameter of the HTML form. The ACTION parameter is set to the location and name of the CGI application that you have designated to process the incoming data from the HTML form. Figure 10.16 illustrates this basic architecture.

F I G U R E 10.16

CGI architecture

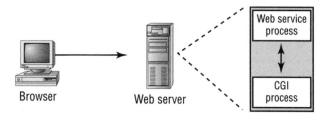

In this figure, the browser makes a request for a CGI service through an HTML form. The Web browser receives this request and passes the necessary parameters to the CGI, which is operating as an independent process on the Web server. Because the CGI is loaded in a separate process address space, it must provide a call-level interface to which the necessary parameters can be passed.

The CGI is responsible for processing the parameters and may provide additional information to the Web server, which can in turn be passed back to the browser. The key element of this architecture is that the CGI and the Web server are two separate processes, each maintaining its own resources and interfaces.

The most substantial advantage to CGI is that essentially every Web server on the market today supports it. Traditionally, if a Web application developer needs to process information on the server, CGI is the method of choice. This universal acceptance also implies that there is abundant documentation from both primary and third party sources on creating CGI applications.

Another advantage to CGI is that the applications are readily transferable from one Web application to another. If you have a need to implement identical services in another application on this or another Web server, the CGI application can be accessed by the new application easily and efficiently.

With all of the advantages of CGI, there are some problems, too. Because CGI applications run in a separate process address space, they can be slow when compared to the performance of other in-process models such as ISAPI applications and ISAPI filters.

Another potential problem with CGI solutions is that unless the developer is already familiar with a language that can be used to build CGI applications, such as Perl or C++, the learning curve can be very significant. This can be a problem when development time is at a minimum, as is the case with most Web development projects.

ISAPI

The Microsoft Internet Information Server is part of the Microsoft BackOffice suite of products. It supports a proprietary API known as the Internet Server API (ISAPI) that is used to develop server-side applications as extensions of the Internet Server Service. This approach differs significantly in architecture from the CGI solution. The ISAPI architecture is illustrated in Figure 10.17.

The primary difference between this architecture and CGI's is that, with ISAPI, the server-side application is actually part of the Internet Information Server (IIS) process address space. The application is not launched as a separate process. This architecture is possible because ISAPI applications are compiled as DLLs. When a 32-bit process uses a DLL, the DLL is loaded or its reference counter is increased and mapped to the process address space of the process that called it.

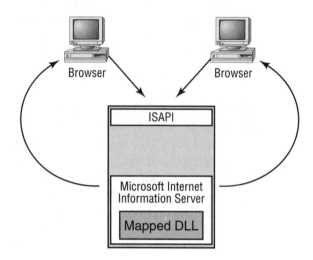

To access an ISAPI application, the HTML form's Action property is set to the location and name of the DLL. When the IIS receives this request, the DLL is loaded and mapped to the IIS process address space. IIS is then responsible for packaging the HTML response from the DLL and returning it to the browser. Upon completion, the DLL is unmapped and, if permitted by the recount, unloaded.

The primary advantage to this approach is that the architecture allows the use of an in-process component, potentially adding a significant performance boost to the application. It also allows for better use of server resources. The ISAPI application DLL needs to load only once to service all users.

If performance is ISAPI's main advantage, then portability is its main weakness. Although ISAPI applications can be easily ported from one Microsoft Internet Information Server to another, they are not usable on any other Web server. This is only a problem if you expect to support non-Microsoft Web servers, but if you only run IIS, the performance advantage is significant enough that you should use ISAPI wherever possible.

ISAPI also has the potential weakness of a learning curve. Most ISAPI applications are created in Visual C++. Unless the developer is already familiar with this language, it may be difficult to quickly implement effective ISAPI applications. This does not have to be a problem, however. Microsoft has created an ISAPI extension called Active Server Pages that allows the developer to utilize the advantages offered by ISAPI while writing code no more complex than HTML and script.

Active Server Pages (ASP)

When you install Active Server Pages (ASP) on a Microsoft Internet Information Server, you are actually installing an ISAPI extension. This extension is designed to extract HTML tags and script that have been explicitly marked for server-side processing. Active Server Pages prepares a properly formatted HTML file from the results of this server-side execution, which is then passed back to the browser.

Active Server Pages can be installed on all Microsoft Web Server products. This includes Peer Web Services for Windows NT Workstation and Personal Web Server for Windows 95.

One advantage of using Active Server Pages is that, unlike creating your own ISAPI applications, it requires no knowledge of programming languages such as C++. Armed with a knowledge of HTML and a scripting language such as VBScript, you are ready to start implementing server-side solutions.

Active Server Pages also provide full support for active scripting. Using a scripting language such as VBScript, Active Server Pages can be used to access external resources using OLE automation. These external resources can range from databases to your own business components.

Active Server Pages use VBScript by default. JavaScript can be used on an Active Server Page, but this is not a common practice. All of the illustrations and exercises in this chapter will assume the default of VBScript.

Understanding Active Server Pages

Before you can truly understand how the Active Server Pages extension works, you have to do a little background work on Internet communications. ASP is designed to blend functionally with HTTP, which is the application level protocol used for Web communications. The processes that browser and server computers implement when communicating across the Web are reflected in the ASP object model.

Internet Communications

Figure 10.18 illustrates the communication between client and server. After making an initial TCP connection, the browser sends an HTTP request message to the server in response to user actions in the browser such as clicking a hyperlink or the Submit button of an HTML form.

The server generates an HTTP response to the HTTP request. This HTTP response contains the resources that were requested by the browser or an error state indicating a reason why the resources could not be accessed. After returning the HTTP response message, the server closes the TCP connection.

FIGURE 10.18

Web communications between browser and server

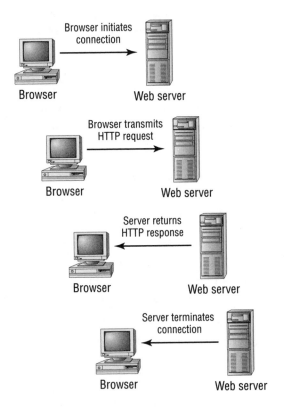

Browser initiates connection

Browser   Web server

Browser transmits HTTP request

Browser   Web server

Server returns HTTP response

Browser   Web server

Server terminates connection

Browser   Web server

The *Keep Alive* extension added to HTTP 1.1 allows a TCP connection to be maintained when the Web server would normally close it. This provides more responsiveness between the browser and the Web server, but it also increases the overhead on the Web server to maintain the open connection.

The HTTP Request   The HTTP request message is divided into two parts, the header and the body. While every HTTP request object has a header, not all will have a body. The HTTP request header contains fields that provide the server with information about the specific request. To give you an idea of the type of information the header contains, some of the fields are listed below:

Date   The date and time of the request

From   The Internet e-mail address of the user making the request

User-Agent   Details about the browser making the request

Location   The URL of the requested page

Other information found in the header of the HTTP request depends primarily on the Method property of the HTML form. You will recall that the HTML <FORM> tag supports, among others, the Method and Action properties. The Action property of the form indicates the target of the form. When the form fields are packaged for distribution to a Web server, it is the URL in the Action property that will process those values.

The Method property indicates how these values will be passed from browser to server. There are two primary settings for the Method property of the HTML form, Get and Post. The difference between these settings is based on the intent of the request and the amount of data being transferred from the browser to the server.

The Get method is usually associated with the process of retrieving data from a Web server. When the Method property of the form is set to Get, all values passed to the Web server are sent in the header of the HTTP request. There is usually no body to the request message when the Get method is used. Because of a 1K (1024) limit to the number of characters that can be sent in the HTTP request, the Get method is not appropriate for transmitting large amounts of data to a Web server.

The Post method is associated with a state change on the server or associated resource. For example, if you wish to enter a record into a database, it will change the state of the database, i.e., you are doing more than retrieving information, you are making a permanent change to the database. The Post method transmits its values to the Web server in the body of the HTTP request. There is no limit to the amount of information that can be transmitted in the body of an HTTP request.

The HTTP Response The content of the HTTP response message is usually the Web page that was requested by the HTTP request message. Like the request, the response message also has header and body portions. The header includes the status of the response, indicating the errors, if any, that have occurred.

The body of the response message is included if there is data to return to the browser. If the browser requested a Web page, the body of the response message would contain the requested Web page. In addition, this HTTP response message can contain a dynamically created HTML response. An HTML response is an HTML page that is sent back in the body of the HTTP response message. An HTML response can be created dynamically on the server by a server-side process such as a custom ISAPI application or an Active Server Page.

ASP and the HTML Response

Using the Active script in Active Server Pages, the browser can request information from a Web site or attempt to post information to a Web site. The Active Server Page is then responsible for creating the HTML response. Figure 10.19 illustrates how this process works using Active Server Pages.

FIGURE 10.19

Active Server Pages dynamically generate an HTML response

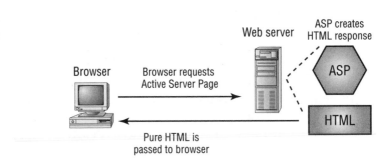

The ASP creates the HTML response by forcing code marked with the server-side script tags <%...%> to execute on the server. The result is placed into the HTML response in the same location as the server tags. All of the other information in the Web page is passed back as if it were a regular HTML Web page. There is nothing unique about an Active Server Page. It is a text file, just like a regular Web page, except that it is stored with an *.asp extension and contains server-side tags. The Active Server Pages ISAPI extension intercepts requests made for pages with the *.asp extension and looks for server-side execution tags.

Let's do a twist on the typical "Hello World" example using an Active Server Page. Instead of simply echoing, "Hello World" to the user, this example will pass back a different message depending on the time of day. Figure 10.20 shows code from an Active Server Page that will do this for us.

F I G U R E 10.20

An Active Server Page

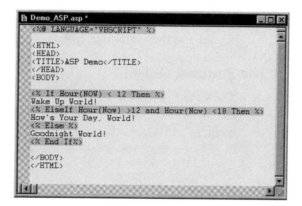

```
<%@ LANGUAGE="VBSCRIPT" %>

<HTML>
<HEAD>
<TITLE>ASP Demo</TITLE>
</HEAD>
<BODY>

<% If Hour(NOW) < 12 Then %>
Wake Up World!
<% ElseIf Hour(Now) >12 and Hour(Now) <18 Then %>
How's Your Day, World!
<% Else %>
Goodnight World!
<% End If%>

</BODY>
</HTML>
```

In this example, you will note that some of the HTML is enclosed inside server-side script tags. The execution of this server-side script determines which text string, which is not included inside the server-side script tags, will actually be displayed in the browser. By running the server-side script, the Active Server Page is actually creating an HTML response on the fly and returning that HTML response to the browser. The browser will see only the HTML, not the script that was used to create the HTML.

Implementing Active Server Pages

Now that you are comfortable with the basic paradigm under which ASP operates, you are prepared to more closely investigate the actual implementation of Active Server Pages. The ASP object model supports five main objects that closely follow the HTTP communication processes that were discussed earlier. These five objects are:

Request   Used to read the HTTP request

Response   Used to create the HTTP response

Server   Used to access server resources, including COM

Session   Used to hold user session state

Application   Used to hold application state

Working with these objects and their associated properties and methods is very similar to working with any object model. When using VBScript as the scripting language inside the ASP, the syntax is very similar to the syntax used in VB or VBA. In this section, we will look more closely at these ASP objects and their implementations.

The Request Object

The Request object is used to read an HTTP request message received from a browser. The properties and methods supported by the Request object are designed to extract information from the request message. The Request object supports a set of collections. We will look at four of them here:

- QueryString
- Form
- ServerVariables
- Cookies

QueryString   If the Web author has chosen to package the values in the HTML form using the Get method, those values are transmitted to the server in the header of the request message. The QueryString collection is used to extract these values from the header of this message.

Remember that every HTML form element supports a Name property. Only those form elements that are explicitly named using this property will have their values transmitted to the server when the Submit button is clicked. Thus, if the Get method of the form is used, these values pass to the server in the header of the HTTP request in the form of a name/value pair.

Reading these values out of the header is simply a matter of referencing the QueryString collection and then pulling the elements out by name. For example, suppose that you had two text input fields in an HTML form called First and Last to represent the first and last names of a client. The following code example would place the values provided for these fields in the variables First and Last.

```
<%
Dim First
Dim Last
First = Request.QueryString("First")
Last = Request.QueryString("Last")
%>
```

In the preceding code listing, you will notice that the server-side script tags are placed before and after the entire block of code. The Active Server Page ignores blank space just like a standard HTML page does. In this example, the variables First and Last could be evaluated inside server-side script as needed.

Form   The Form collection operates identically to the QueryString collection with the exception that the values are extracted from the body of the request rather than the head. Once again, values are placed into the body of the Request method in a name/value pair. The developer goes through the collection to extract the names and values necessary.

Sometimes an HTML control can pass back more than one value, such as a multiple select list. When this happens, the individual values are treated as arrays by the Request object. For example, assume that you have a multiple select list box in an HTML form called FavFood that allows a user to select their favorite foods. Multiple selections can be made. If the user selects two items from the list, they would be extracted from the collection using the following code:

```
<%
Dim Foods(1)
Foods(0)=Request.Form("FavFood")(0)
Foods(1)=Request.Form("FavFood")(1)
%>
```

The above code is also valid for the QueryString collection. Simply replace Form with QueryString in the code statements.

ServerVariables The ServerVariables collection represents the current state of the Web server and the information obtainable concerning the Web browser. Using the ServerVariables collection, you can evaluate many elements of your environment, from the screen resolution of the browser to the name of the server hosting the ASP. The code below illustrates how to work with the ServerVariables collection. This code retrieves the names for each of the ServerVaraibles supported. Figure 10.21 illustrates the results of this ASP request in Internet Explorer 4.

```
<% Dim X
For Each X in Request.ServerVariables %>
Name is <%= X %><BR>
<% Next %>
```

Use the <%= ... %> syntax rather than the <% ... %> syntax for server-side script when the code inside the script can be evaluated to a specific value and you wish to return this value to the HTML response.

F I G U R E 10.21

A list of valid server variable names

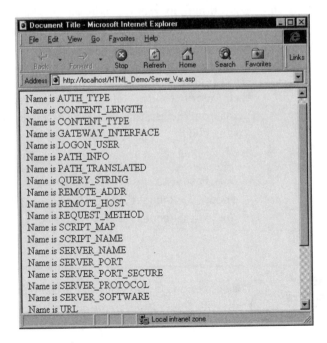

Cookies A cookie is a small file written to a specific directory of the user's system and is used by the Web application developer to store user settings for that user's next return to that Web site. You can consider a cookie to be the Web implementation of a private *.ini file; it saves a user's settings for future navigations to the site.

Cookies represent an interesting problem. Using cookies, a Web developer is allowed to read and write information directly from a user's computer. This poses a potential security hole. For this reason, most browsers allow a user either to be warned before accepting a cookie, or to simply deny all cookie writes to the user's system. This means that a developer can never be completely sure if code that is dependent on cookies will be totally reliable for all users.

There are two actions that you can take with a cookie. You can read from it or your can write to it. The Request object supports reading cookies, while the Response object supports writing to cookies. Cookies are associated with a single page. When a request is sent from the browser, it also contains any cookies associated with that page. All cookies are identified by name, so reading a cookie is only a matter of referring to that named element of the cookies collection. The code below illustrates how to read a cookie.

```
<%=Request.Cookies("UserName")%>
```

The Response Object

The Response object is used to dynamically create the HTML response that will be sent back to the browser. It can also be used to redirect the browser to another Web site when appropriate. The Response object supports specific properties and methods used to control the way that the response message is generated. The list of properties and methods includes:

- Buffer property
- Clear method
- Flush method
- Expires property
- Redirect method
- Write method

Using the Buffer   Under normal conditions, the response is sent directly to the requesting browser as soon as possible. This means that the process of sending the output may begin before the response has even been completely created. This is done to minimize lag time between the request and the response; however, the developer may wish to refrain from sending the response until the determination is made that the response can be created without error. For these cases, the developer can engage the buffer. Setting the Buffer property to True indicates that the contents will be buffered. The Flush method will output the buffer to the browser, and the Clear method will erase the contents of the buffer.

The Write Method   The Write method of the Response object is used to output information within server-side script tags to the HTML response. You will recall that in our earlier "Hello World" example, the server-side script tags were closed before the text strings were placed in the code. This is because anything included inside server-side script tags is assumed to be interpreted rather than being output directly. The Write method allows you to write the HTML response from within the server-side script.

Let's look at an example. When you looked at server variables earlier in this chapter, you saw the following code that listed the names of each variable.

```
<% Dim X
For Each X in Request.ServerVariables %>
Name is <%= X %><BR>
<% Next %>
```

Using the Write method, the same result could be created with the following code:

```
<% Dim X
For Each X in Request.ServerVariables
Response.write "Name is " + X + "<BR>"
Next %>
```

You will notice that this example does not close the server-side script tags before every text or HTML element needing output to the response. The Write method simply allows you to concatenate the text and HTML elements to the expressions needing evaluation.

The Redirect Method   The Redirect method of the Response object allows the developer to point the browser to a page other than the one originally requested by the browser. For example, suppose that you had a Web page that was available in either U.S. English or U.K. English. You could always ask your user which page they prefer and then provide links to those pages, or, using the Redirect method, you could redirect them automatically depending on the localization of the browser that they have installed. The following code supports this process.

```
<%
If Request.ServerVariables("HTTP_ACCEPT_LANGUAGE")="en-us"
Then
Response.Redirect "USEng.htm"
ElseIf Request.ServerVariables("HTTP_ACCEPT_LANGUAGE")="en-
uk" Then
Response.Redirect "UKEng.htm"
Else
Response.Redirect "NoSupport.htm"
End If
%>
```

Writing Cookies   Use the Cookies collection of the Response object to write a cookie to the user's computer. When an existing cookie is referenced, the value will be rewritten. If the cookie is new, it will be created for you on the user's computer. The following code sets a cookie called MCSD to the value of True.

```
<% Response.Cookies("MCSD") = "True" %>
```

Cookies are associated with specific Web pages by default. They are visible only within the Web page in which they are set. To increase the visibility of a cookie to include all pages of your Web, set the Path attribute as follows: `Response.Cookies("MCSD").Path = "/"`. The cookie will then be sent by the browser whenever it requests a page in your Web.

The Server Object

Active Server Pages support the ability to automate ActiveX Server components. These may be components supplied with Active Server Pages or IIS, such as the ActiveX Data Objects, or they may be objects of your own creation using Visual Basic or some other development tool capable of creating COM objects.

This process should look very familiar. For example, if you were writing an application in Visual Basic and wished to automate an object called Engine in the Library called Truck, the code would look like the following sample:

```
Dim EngObj as Truck.Engine
Set EngObj = CreateObject("Truck.Engine")
```

Using early binding, the object variable is declared as a Truck.Engine object and then set to a running instance of that object with the CreateObject function.

Using Active Server Pages changes a few elements of this implementation, but it is very similar in syntax. First, since variables in VBScript only support the variant data type, it is impossible to declare the variable as a Truck .Engine object. Second, when using Active Server Pages, CreateObject is not a function but rather a method of the Server object. Automating the same object using Active Server Pages would look like the following sample:

```
<%
Dim EngObj
Set EngObj = Server.CreateObject("Truck.Engine")
%>
```

With the exception of the placement of the server-side scripting tags, the code for the Active Server Page implementation and the standard Visual Basic approach are almost identical after the server component has been instanced. This introduces an exciting element of code and object reusability between your traditional client/server channel and your new Web-based channel.

An in-depth discussion of automation code and implementation can be found in Chapter 8. Review this chapter for more details on this process.

The Session Object

Traditionally, one of the most challenging problems of any Web development project is the inability to effectively allow persistence of information. Client-side script does not provide the ability to scope variables any greater than the page upon which they are declared. This can pose a problem if you wish to save information that will be referenced on other pages in your Web page. In the past, there were three ways to provide persistence in a Web application. You could:

- Use cookies

- Roll data forward

- Use a server-side database

Using cookies allows the developer to write information to the local hard drive of the browsing computer. This cookie can be pathed to be accessible from all pages in the Web. When a value must be referenced across pages, it is written to a cookie and then retrieved when appropriate. If the user refuses to accept the cookie, the persistence will be destroyed.

Rolling forward is the process of passing values from one page to another. Whenever a browser submits a request message, you can pass values in the header of the message and process them on the Web server, and the Web server can simply roll these values forward into the next Web page in a hidden control. This process can continue as long as necessary, but the obvious problem with it is the weight of pushing these values around from form to form.

The last approach is to create and configure a server-side database to store information persistently. By extracting unique information from each user making a connection, such as an Internet e-mail address, the database can store values on a user-by-user basis. The advantage to this approach is that the information can be persistent across connections. If a user leaves the site, the data will still be there on their return. On the other hand, there is a lot of work involved in setting up the database and writing the data access code inside a server-side process.

The Session object provided by the Active Server Pages model provides a more dynamic way to manage this persistence. Upon navigating to any Active Server Page in the Web site, a user is assigned a SessionID that identifies that user across all pages on the Web site. Active Server Pages store this SessionID as a memory-resident client-side cookie.

Even though this SessionID cookie is stored in memory rather than on the user's hard drive, the user must still accept this cookie before the SessionID will be active. If the user does not accept this cookie, the Session object will not be valid for that user.

The session begins when a user first navigates to an Active Server Page in the Web site. It can end in one of two ways. If the user logs no new activity to the site for the duration of the session time-out value, the session will terminate. The developer can also explicitly terminate a user session by calling the Abandon method of the Session object.

The default session time-out is 20 minutes. To change this value, you need to change a Registry key on the Web server. The key is HKEY_LOCAL_MACHINE\ System\CurrentControlSet\Serveices\W3SVC\ASP\Parameters\ SessionTimeout.

Through the Session object, persistent values can be created and stored. For example, suppose that you have a login form with a text input field called UserName. You wish to store this UserName in a session level variable so that it will be persistent across pages. Assuming that the Action property of the form was set to the Active Server Page that processes this form information and the METHOD is Get, the following code in the Active Server Page would create the persistent variable:

```
<% Session("UserName") = Request.QueryString("UserName") %>
```

If at any time you wish to immediately terminate a session, you can use the Abandon method of the Session object. The Abandon method will unconditionally terminate a session; however, if the same user navigates to another Active Sever Page in the Web site immediately thereafter, a new SessionID will be created and a new session will begin.

The Application Object

Just as the Session object allows persistence for users across pages, the Application object allows persistence across users for the entire application. There is a single Application object for every Web, which can be used to save values that are applicable to the Web as a whole. The Application object is created when the very first user navigates to an Active Server Page in the Web, and it terminates when the World Wide Web Publishing Service is shut down.

The Application object reads and writes variables in exactly the same way as the Session object. Application level variables are very helpful to track information such as hit counts, administrative data, and other information pertaining to the Web site as a whole. For example, if you want to retrieve the hit count for your Web and place that value into a page, the code might look like this:

```
This site has recorded <%= Application("hits") %> hits since
1/1/99
```

To keep the hit counter accurate, you would simply increment this Application variable every time a user navigated to your Web.

Since the Application object is valid for every user on your Web, there is a chance that more than one user might try to change the value of an Application variable at the same time. To circumvent this, the Application object can be locked to prevent any connection other than the one performing the locking operation from changing any Application values. If you want to increment your hit counter, the code might look like this:

```
<%
Application.Lock
Appication("hits") = Application("hits") + 1
Application.Unlock
%>
```

Using Global.asa

When you create a new Web on a Web server that has Active Server Pages installed, you should also create a file called Global.asa. If you are using a tool such as Microsoft Visual InterDev, this file will be created for you. The primary purpose of this file is to provide events for the Session and Application objects. You can write code in these events to allow custom handling of Session and Application startup and end. Figure 10.22 displays the default contents of the Global.asa file in the WordPad Editor.

F I G U R E   10.22

The default content of
the Global.asa file

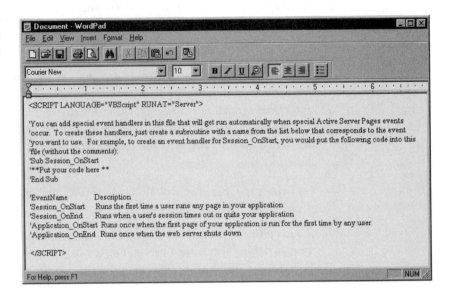

In Figure 10.22 the script tag includes a RUNAT parameter. This parameter
is set to the value "Server". This is an alternative to using server-side script
tags. If you have a large block of code that you wish to run at the server, this
format is often easier to maintain.

You will notice immediately from Figure 10.22 that the Global.asa file
is nothing more than comments, with the exception of the <SCRIPT> tags at
the top and bottom of the page. The comments provide instruction for the
implementation of the Global.asa file. According to the instructions, four
events are supported by Global.asa:

- Session_OnStart

- Session_OnEnd

- Application_OnStart

- Application_OnEnd

Applying these Session events is simply a matter of deciding what code you
want to run when a user first navigates to or leaves your site. The same can be

said concerning the Application events. For example, if you wanted to increment a hit counter when a user first navigates to your Web site, you could include the code to perform this operation in the Session_OnStart event.

IIS Applications and the WebClass

The Active Server Pages model adds a great deal of functionality to your applications, but since you must use a scripting language such as VBScript to provide the server-side functionality, you are somewhat limited in your ability to be very interactive. Formerly, the only way to harness the power of a full programming language in your server-side applications was to create a CGI application in a language like Perl or C++. You could also write directly to the Internet Server API (ISAPI) with C++ to create server-side processes. Although these approaches were very effective, the language learning curve made them accessible only to a handful of users.

The IIS Application in Visual Basic changes this. With IIS applications you have all of the functionality of an Active Server Pages application, and more. While you can still use the Active Server Pages object model in exactly the same way as previously described, the IIS application also allows you to perform server-side processing in a COM object that will run on the server. You can create this COM object with Visual Basic and use its services in all of the HTML objects that you will include in your Web-based application.

The COM object will be created by Visual Basic based on code located in a WebClass. Each IIS application has a WebClass that contains all of the functionality for the entire Web application. The WebClass is responsible for dynamically creating Web pages through the Active Server Pages model. This means that the client can be a browser of any type, since all the browser will ever receive from the WebClass is pure HTML.

Objects in an IIS Application

All objects in an IIS application fall into one of three categories:

- WebClass
- Custom WebItem
- HTML Template WebItem

The WebClass is the foundation for the IIS application. It defines the structure of the COM object that runs on the Internet Information Server. It also contains the definitions of the other two objects mentioned in the list above. Although there can be more than one WebClass per IIS application, a single WebClass is sufficient to define an entire Web-based application.

Every WebClass defines WebItems. A custom WebItem is one that you create in the IIS application. Every custom WebItem is a single Web page within your IIS application. Because you will be using the Active Server Pages model to create the Web pages, WebItems are implemented entirely through code rather than by using a graphical designer like a Visual Basic form.

If you have an existing HTML page that you would like to use as a foundation for building a new custom WebItem, you can import the Web page as an HTML Template WebItem. A Template WebItem can be sent to the browser in its entirety by the IIS application, and all of the objects and tags on a Template WebItem are available for you to reference in your custom WebItems. Figure 10.23 illustrates a WebClass window in Visual Basic with a custom WebItem called StartPage and an HTML Template WebItem called Books.

F I G U R E   10.23

A Visual Basic
WebClass

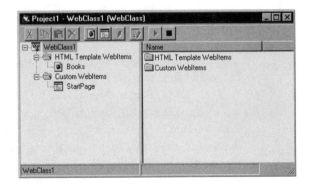

WebClass Events

Like any other Visual Basic object, WebClasses and WebItems recognize events. It is within these events that you write the code that creates the custom responses that are sent to the requesting client browser. Although the actual events are somewhat limited, the developer has more than enough control to respond to requests in a Web-based environment. Table 10.1 lists events, the objects with which they are associated, and the point at which the events fire.

	Event	Object	Timing
TABLE 10.1 IIS Application Events	Initialize	WebClass	Fires when the IIS application component first loads on the Web server
	Terminate	WebClass	Fires when the instance of the IIS application component is destroyed
	Start	WebClass	Fires when a user navigates to the ASP file created by Visual Basic at compile time
	Respond	WebItem	Fires in a WebItem when you navigate to that WebItem

When you compile an IIS application, the compiler creates an ASP file with the same name as the WebClass. This ASP file is the starting point for the Web application. When a browser navigates to this ASP file, the Start event of the WebClass will fire. Any code that is placed in the Start event will run. The Start event will usually contain setup code and instructions about where to navigate the user to continue the application.

The Respond event of a WebItem is called whenever a WebItem is requested inside an IIS application. In this Respond event, you will write the code that will define the HTML response back to the browser. You can use all of the objects in the Active Server Pages model, including the Response object, when creating your response. You can also write regular Visual Basic code to perform any additional server-side processing.

A Walk-Through of an IIS Application

The process of creating an IIS application is very similar to creating an ASP-based application. You start by getting out a yellow pad and pencil and planning the structure of your Web application. The application will probably not consist of just a couple of simple pages, but rather an interwoven "web" of items. You must first plan the contents and general flow of your application.

After your plan is complete, begin the IIS application with Visual Basic and add all of the WebItems to your WebClass. Every page in your plan will be represented by a single WebItem in your IIS WebClass. Just add and name the items first; you will add the code later. Make sure that you choose names that you will be comfortable with for a long time. After a WebItem is created, it is treated just like a Visual Basic form. If you change the name after adding code to the WebItem, all of the code will be moved to the General sections as general procedures and you will have to repopulate the code of your WebItem with these general procedures.

We will walk through an example of creating a simple IIS application in the following set of exercises beginning with Exercise 10.2. In our example, we will have a three-page Web application, a start page, and two details pages. Our Web application will navigate between these pages.

In order to do the exercises involving IIS applications, you must have IIS installed on a Windows NT computer or Personal Web Server on a Windows 95/98 computer. These can be found on the NT 4 Option Pack, which is the second CD in the Visual Studio 6.0 set.

EXERCISE 10.2

Starting an IIS Application

1. Start Visual Basic. From the list of project templates, select IIS Application and click OK to create the project. If you do not have a Web server installed, you will get error messages at this point. Select Project ➤ Properties from the menu and set the project name to IIS_Demo. Close the Properties window.

2. In the Project window, expand the Designers folder and double-click WebClass1. This will open the WebClass designer. Click in the left pane on WebClass1. You should now see the Web Class properties in the Properties window. Set the Name property and the NameInURL property both to SampleClass.

3. Point to SampleClass in the left pane of the Designer window and right-click. Select Add Custom WebItem from the pop-up menu. You should be able to type in the name next to the icon of the WebItem. Name the WebItem StartPage.

4. Repeat step 3 twice, creating WebItems named Details1 and Details2.

5. Save the project in a folder of your choosing. Leave Visual Basic running with the IIS_Demo project open for later exercises.

The next step in creating an IIS application is to navigate to the ASP file associated with the WebClass and create the response to be sent back to the browser when the IIS application begins. This point in time corresponds to the Start event of the WebClass. You may wish to execute some server-side code when the IIS application starts. This could include setting Session variables in your Active Server Pages environment or making calls to other server-resident components. In other situations, you may simply wish to navigate to a WebItem of your choice.

There are two ways to provide navigation in a WebClass or WebItem. You can use the NextItem property of the WebClass to identify the desired navigation target, or you can place a hyperlink in a WebItem that navigates to another WebItem. If you are creating a response to an initial application call, you may want to write code in the Start event that sends HTML to the browser. The HTML might render a startup screen and a set of hyperlinks to other pages. You can also simply point the browser to another Web item automatically without the browser being aware of the transition. To forward the browser to another WebItem automatically, you can use the NextItem method of the WebClass object. The following code example illustrates this approach.

```
Set NextItem = WebItem_Name
```

In Exercise 10.3, we will forward the browser directly to the StartPage WebItem by using the NextItem property. In a later exercise, we will add content to the StartPage WebItem.

EXERCISE 10.3

Handling the Start Event of a WebClass

1. In the left pane of the WebClass designer, double-click SampleClass to open the Code window. You will be taken to the Start event of the WebClass. In this event, you will see default code that used the Active Server Pages Response object to write an HTML response back to the browser. You will not be using this default response, so delete the code between the Sub and End Sub statements.

2. In the Start event of the WebClass, enter code that navigates the browser to the StartPage WebItem. Use the following code as an example.

```
Set NextItem = StartPage
```

3. Close the Code window for the WebClass and save the project. Leave Visual Basic running and the project open.

In the WebItems, we will use the Response object to indicate the structure of the Web page that you want sent back to the browser. Remember that the Response object is an abstraction of the HTTP Response message that is sent from the Web server to the browser application. By using the Write method of the Response object, you are structuring this HTTP response for the Web server to return to the browser. The sample code that follows demonstrates this approach.

```
With Response
    .Write "<HTML>"
    .Write "<TITLE>IIS_Demo Start Page</TITLE>"
    .Write "<BODY>"
    .Write "<B>Click below to go to the Sybex web</B>"
    .Write "<P><A HREF=http://www.sybex.com>Click Here!</
A></P>"
    .Write "</BODY></HTML>"
End With
```

To force the WebItem to render this output to the HTTP Response message, you must place this code within the Respond event of the WebItem. This event fires whenever the WebItem is called; it is the mechanism for allowing the code to execute before the response is sent back to the browser.

In our sample code, you will notice that a URL to a Web location is included in an anchor tag. You can use a similar mechanism to provide hyperlinks to other WebItems within your WebClass. The only problem with this approach is that the actual URL of the WebItem is not known as the application is developed. To solve this problem, the WebClass contains a method called URLFor. This method allows you to substitute the method call, providing the WebItem as a parameter, for the actual URL. The following code example creates a hyperlink that navigates to the Details1 WebItem using the URLFor method.

```
Response.Write "<A HREF=" & WebClass.URLFor(Details1) & _
    ">Click here for the first details page</A>"
```

This code creates a hyperlink in the calling page that navigates the browser to the Details1 page. The Respond event of the Details1 page then fires, rendering the intended contents of the Web page in the browser. Exercise 10.4 continues our example, creating hyperlinks in the StartPage that will navigate to the two details pages in our IIS application.

EXERCISE 10.4

Creating Hyperlinks in a WebItem

1. Double-click the StartPage WebItem in the WebClass designer to open the code window. In the Respond event of the StartPage, add code that creates two hyperlinks, one that will navigate to the Details1 page and another that will navigate to the Details2 page. Use the following code for reference.

```
With Response
    .Write "<A HREF=" & WebClass.URLFor(Details1) & _
        ">Click here for the first details page</A>"
    .Write "<P>"
    .Write "<A HREF=" & WebClass.URLFor(Details2) & _
        ">Click here for the second details page</A>"
End With
```

2. In the Respond events of the two details pages, write code that notifies the user of their current location, as in the following example.

```
Response.Write "You are viewing the first details page."
```

3. Save the project. From the Visual Basic menu, click Run ➢ Start to begin the application. Click OK to accept the current start conditions. If prompted for a virtual directory location, accept the default and continue. The Automation Manager will start, followed by Internet Explorer. You will navigate to the StartPage even though the address bar of Internet Explorer reads SampleClass.ASP.

4. Test the two hyperlinks. When finished, exit Internet Explorer and end the application. Save and close the project. Close the Automation Manager if it is still running.

Where WebClasses Fit

WebClasses act as an element of the presentation tier in a distributed application. Even though they are deployed on a central server, IIS applications created with Visual Basic are actually intended to define how information is returned to the browser. Although the resulting pages can contain client-side scripting, the browser is really nothing more than a remote rendering system and user interaction agent.

As you have seen from this short example, IIS applications and Web-Classes can leverage your existing experience with Active Server Pages and Visual Basic to provide very complete and flexible Web-based solutions while still maintaining browser compatibility. WebClasses allow the Web developer to harness the power of COM and the Visual Basic development environment to provide a full Web solution without the limitations of a traditional Web-based development environment.

Using Active Documents

Microsoft ✓ *Exam* *Objective*	**Create an active document.** • Use code within an active document to interact with a container application. • Navigate to other active documents

Microsoft ✓ *Exam* *Objective*	**Use an active document to present information within a Web browser.**

Active documents are applications that can run inside of the Internet Explorer browser or other container applications designed to host active documents. The active document model allows the developer to create applications using traditional design methods while still being able to implement that solution inside a Web browser. No knowledge of HTML is required because the active document is actually a COM object, not an HTML file.

When active document applications are compiled, a COM EXE or DLL is created along with the active documents that will contain the user interface. The COM server provides all of the supporting code to the documents that enable them to function correctly.

Creating Active Documents

You begin an active document project by selecting either the ActiveX Document EXE or ActiveX Document DLL template from the list of Visual Basic templates. The choice of a DLL or EXE depends on whether you prefer an in-process or out-of-process component to be downloaded to the client computer.

When you begin an active document project, you start with a single User-Document object. Although the UserDocument designer looks very much like a regular Visual Basic form, it packages its contents a bit differently. When compiled into an active document, the UserDocument requires the services of a host application, such as an Internet Explorer browser, in order to function.

Because of the architecture of active documents, only Web browsers that support ActiveX will be able to host the documents. This may affect your technology choices if browser compatibility is a very important design goal.

Adding controls to a UserDocument is the same as working with a form. Any standard or custom ActiveX controls can be placed within a UserDocument designer. In Exercise 10.5, you will place a data control into the UserDocument designer along with other data bound controls that will display the data.

EXERCISE 10.5

Designing an Active Document

1. Start Visual Basic. From the Template list displayed, select the ActiveX Document DLL project type and click OK. This will create an active document project with the supporting files compiled as an in-process COM object.

2. In the Project window, expand the UserDocuments folder to reveal the UserDocument designers in this project. Double-click the UserDocument1 designer to open it in the IDE.

3. In the Properties window, change the name of the UserDocument to DataDemo. Add two text boxes to the designer, placing one text box above the other. Name the top text box txtFirst and the bottom text box txtLast. Remove the default text from the text boxes.

4. Place a standard data control in the designer. Name the data control datNwind. The designer should now look similar to the example in the following graphic.

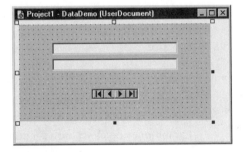

5. Set the DatabaseName property of the datNwind control to the path-name of the Northwind database that ships with Visual Basic 6. For a default installation of Visual Studio, which should be found in \Program Files\Microsoft Visual Studio\VB98\nwind.mdb, set the RecordSource property to Employees. This will configure the data control to use the Employees table of the Northwind database as the data source.

6. Set the DataSource properties of both the text boxes to reference the datNwind data control. Set the DataField property of the txtFirst text box to FirstName and the txtLast text box to LastName.

7. Save the project in a new folder of your choice. Use the default names of DataDemo.dob for the UserDocument designer and Project1.vbp for the project file.

8. To create the project DLL, select File ➢ Make Project1.dll from the menu. To test the project, start the Internet Explorer browser and navigate to the compiled active document. The name of this file is DataDemo.vbd. Note that the file extension is different that the designer extension of *.dob. The *.vbd file is a compiled object and is created as a result of making the project DLL. The following graphic illustrates the document rendered in the Internet Explorer browser.

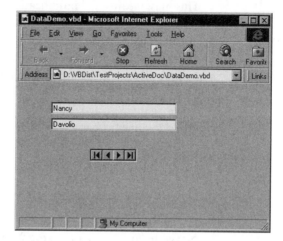

9. As you display the document in your browser, note that the navigation buttons on the data control are active and allow you to display the data in the browser. Also note that you were able to accomplish this without writing any Visual Basic code or HTML. Close your browser and the Visual Basic project, saving changes if necessary.

Coding the Active Document

Although our example of an active document did not require any code, if you desired to add code to the project, it would be structured as standard Visual Basic code. There are, however, two occasions when coding techniques particular to the active document environment must be used. These arise in navigation and container-related activities.

Navigating between Active Documents

In a standard Visual Basic application, you navigate between forms by using the Show and Hide methods of the forms. In addition, you have a great deal of control over the loading and unloading of the forms into memory through the Load and Unload statements. Since active documents must be hosted inside of a container application rather than as independent objects, you cannot use the same methods for form management that you can use with standard Visual Basic forms.

This may mean small modifications in the way that you write your user interface. In a standard Visual Basic application, forms often have elements of the interface that you use to close the form or exit an application. In a browser-based application using active documents, you never actually close a form specifically; you simply navigate to another form. For this reason, you must replace all of your standard form control code with navigation code.

To navigate in an active document, you will use the hyperlink property of the UserDocument object. The hyperlink supports three methods. They are:

GoForward   Moves to the next accessed Web resource. Works like the Forward button in a Web browser.

GoBack   Moves to the last accessed Web resources. Works like the Back button in a Web browser.

NavigateTo   Navigates to the Web resource indicated as the argument of the method. Used to navigate from an active document to any other Web resource including another active document.

The sample code below would navigate from the active document currently displayed in the browser to the Sybex Web site.

Note that the term *UserDocument* in this code context is used to provide a generic reference to the current UserDocument element. Its behavior is somewhat like the ME keyword used in a Visual Basic form.

```
UserDocument.Hyperlink.NavigateTo "http://www.sybex.com"
```

If you have multiple active documents located in the same directory on your Web server, you can use relative addressing to navigate between them. This eliminates the need to include a domain name and a resource path in your navigation statement. The following code example navigates to another active document called `reference.vbd`. It is assumed in this code that the new document lies in the same directory on the Web server as the document currently being displayed.

```
UserDocument.Hyperlink.NavigateTo "reference.vbd"
```

Remember that in an active document application, you will be simulating a true Web-based approach as much as possible. These navigation methods allow the developer to create a complete Web-based application using all of the features of Visual Basic, while maintaining the basic structure of a Web application.

Communicating with the Container

Every active document needs a container in order to be displayed. Microsoft currently ships a number of different active document containers. Although the container that everyone knows is the Internet Explorer Web browser, this is not the only active document container available. Each of the Microsoft Office products can host active documents and, in fact, the Microsoft Office Binder, one of the members of the Office suite, was actually the first active document container publicly released.

Because the document might behave differently depending on the type of container that is used as a host, it is sometimes necessary to query the container to identify its class.

The container is represented as the Parent property of the UserDocument object. Using the TypeName function, the developer can query the class of the container application. If the container application is Internet Explorer, then the TypeName function will return the text string IWebBrowserApp.

The following code example illustrates the process of querying the container to identify the class of the container. The label, lblContainer, will display a different caption depending on the container of the document.

```
Private Sub UserDocument_Initialize()
    If TypeName(UserDocument.Parent) = "IWebBrowserApp" Then
        lblContainer.Caption = "You are using a Web Browser"
    Else
        lblContainer.Caption = "You are not using a web
browser"
    End If
End Sub
```

Where Active Documents Fit

Although they might be considered too heavy for an Internet solution, in the case of an intranet, the active document approach to Web development gives the developer full access to the Visual Basic development environment without requiring the developer to learn any additional environments such as Active Server Pages or HTML. This means that the developer can apply what is known now rather than having to become fluent in other technologies to develop a Web-based application.

The largest single drawback to the active document approach to Web application development is the narrow scope of target browsers. This technology relies on the Internet Explorer browser and its supporting technologies, whereas other implementations, such as Active Server Pages and IIS applications, are browser-independent and provide a wider audience for the application.

Summary

The Internet is revolutionizing the way that applications are written. Even if the Internet is not the target of the application, Internet-related technologies such as Web browsers and Internet servers are changing the way that people interact with the world around them.

As we have seen from this chapter, Microsoft has supplied an extensive amount of support for Internet technologies in Visual Basic 6.0. In many ways, Visual Basic has been finely tuned to Internet implementations and technologies. With Visual Basic 6.0, you can create DHTML applications that execute completely on the browser and IIS applications that take advantage of Web server resources. Using active documents, you can even write Web-based applications without knowing any HTML at all, relying instead on a knowledge of Visual Basic development.

As Visual Basic continues to mature, Internet technologies will always be a high priority. The result will be two technologies that will grow and mature together. As the Internet expands, Visual Basic will certainly be there every step of the way.

Review Questions

1. Which of the following ASP objects should you use when constructing a message to send to a browser from a WebClass?

   A. Request

   B. Response

   C. Server

   D. Session

2. Which of the following technologies does not require Microsoft Internet Explorer in order to function?

   A. Visual Basic WebClass

   B. VBScript in an HTML page

   C. Active document

   D. Visual Basic DHTML application

3. Which event of an IIS application WebItem will fire when a request is made to load that WebItem from within the IIS application?

   A. Start

   B. Request

   C. Respond

   D. Navigate

4. Which of the following collections of the ASP Request object should the developer use to read the content of the body of an HTTP request message?

   A. Cookies

   B. Form

    C. QueryString

    D. ClientCertificate

5. Which method of the Response object is used in a WebClass to create the HTML response that is sent to the browser?

    A. Create

    B. Respond

    C. Navigate

    D. Write

6. Which of the following statements correctly identifies the class of an active document container as an Internet Explorer browser?

    A. TypeOf(UserDocument.Parent) = "ie4_browser"

    B. TypeName(UserDocument.Parent) = "ie4_browser"

    C. TypeOf(UserDocument.Parent) = "IWebBrowserApp"

    D. TypeName(UserDocument.Parent) = "IWebBrowserApp"

7. Which of the following is not a method of the hyperlink in an active document?

    A. GoTo

    B. GoBack

    C. GoForward

    D. NavigateTo

8. Which attribute of an HTML form defines whether form contents will be sent to the Web server in the head or the body of an HTTP request message?

    A. Put

    B. Action

C. Method

D. Value

9. Which of the following code element is not supported by VBScript?

A. Variant data type

B. Fixed arrays

C. GoTo statements

D. Event Recognition

10. When does a new session begin in an Active Server Pages application?

A. When a browser first accesses an HTML page in the Web

B. When a browser first accesses an ASP page in the Web

C. When the IIS Service starts on the Windows NT computer

D. Never; sessions are only supported by WebClasses.

11. If you do not specify which scripting language you wish to use in an HTML page, Microsoft Internet Explorer will default to:

A. VBScript

B. JavaScript

C. PerlScript

D. None, the <SCRIPT> tag will be ignored.

12. Which Active Server Pages object is used in the manipulating of cookies, either to read or to write?

A. Request

B. Response

C. Both

D. Neither, cookies are not supported in ASP

13. Which of the following events is not recognized by the WebClass?

   A. Initialize

   B. Terminate

   C. Start

   D. Respond

14. Which object in the Active Server Pages model is responsible for managing Session Start and End events?

   A. The Global.asa file

   B. The Session object

   C. Each ASP file manages its own Session events

   D. You must create a custom COM object to manage these events

15. When inserting an ActiveX control into a Web page using the <OBJECT> tag, which parameter of that tag identifies the control to the script on that page so that the control can be manipulated?

   A. ClassID

   B. Name

   C. ID

   D. CodeBase

CHAPTER

11

Creating Help Systems

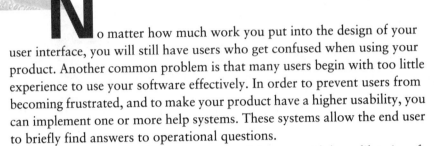

No matter how much work you put into the design of your user interface, you will still have users who get confused when using your product. Another common problem is that many users begin with too little experience to use your software effectively. In order to prevent users from becoming frustrated, and to make your product have a higher usability, you can implement one or more help systems. These systems allow the end user to briefly find answers to operational questions.

In some applications these systems are elaborate, with huge libraries of information available. In other applications, the help system is more focused. Visual Basic 6 is a prime example of the former. Visual Basic 6 ships with very extensive documentation in the form of the Microsoft Developer's Network Library. Topics covered in the documentation include programming concepts, information about the Windows operating system, and specifics for developing with Visual Basic. This model of documentation is appropriate because of the nature of the software package: Visual Basic is a development environment for knowledgeable developers, and it is a complex and powerful product.

In all likelihood, your own applications will be better served by a more concise help system that provides information about the general functions of the system and prompts regarding the functions of form elements. This chapter will lay out the basic skills and techniques used to add help systems to your applications. We will first review the planning stages of establishing help systems. Then we will present the techniques necessary to actually implement these features in your work.

HTML Help or WinHelp

For years now, Microsoft has promoted the use of the WinHelp system in its own and ISV-developed applications. In keeping with its recent push to integrate the Internet into all facets of its products, Microsoft has introduced a new paradigm for integrated help systems, HTML Help. HTML has distinct strengths as a format for support documentation. Perhaps the greatest strength HTML Help brings to software documentation is its roots in HTML. Building a technology on top of a cross-platform standard greatly simplifies the task of adapting existing documents from almost any platform. In fairness, Microsoft is not alone in its push to develop an HTML-based help strategy. While Microsoft has been developing its Microsoft HTML Help, Netscape Communications has also been working hard on its own standard, Netscape NetHelp.

The two fundamental differences in these models are similar to the differences between the companies' Web browsers. Netscape NetHelp provides more robust multiplatform support, including virtually every notable operating system. Microsoft HTML Help, on the other hand, is fundamentally aimed at the Windows platform, though the use of technologies based on open standards makes porting of help systems to other platforms feasible. The primary advantage of Microsoft HTML Help in this comparison is its support for use of Microsoft technologies like VBScript, ActiveX controls, and ActiveX documents. Because of its support for these Microsoft technologies, which are central to the effective use of Visual Basic, all further discussion of HTML Help will deal with the Microsoft implementation of this emerging technology.

While HTML Help is part of Microsoft's vision for the future of application development, support for WinHelp has been maintained in Visual Basic 6. You can still attach a WinHelp help file to your application, but the tools for creating WinHelp files are not shipped with the new version of Visual Basic.

Because HTML Help represents the growing edge of the online-support market, and because the exam objectives have explicitly identified the creation of HTML Help as a priority, creating WinHelp files will not be covered in this chapter. WinHelp files from older applications can still be used in revisions compiled under version 6 of Visual Basic. However, if you are developing a new application, the use of WinHelp is discouraged. The techniques necessary to use these old help files will be covered briefly under the "Converting WinHelp Projects" section below. All other information, examples, and exercises will assume the use of Microsoft HTML Help as the foundation of help systems.

Planning an Online Help System

As indicated above, the specific help system needs of an application depend on the level of complexity in the application and the technical sophistication of the end users. In our discussion of help system planning, we will discuss how these types of considerations, as well as the type of packaging and deployment, affect development plans.

Choosing a List of Topics

Having an elaborate help engine doesn't help a bit if the information a user needs is unavailable. One of the keys to creating a successful help system is generating a comprehensive set of information that the user can access as needed. To generate a comprehensive set of documentation, perform the following steps:

- Review each form in your application. Note each visible user-interface element. Each of these should have at least a simple explanation.

- Include items for each menu item in the application.

- Review your development plan for the application. List each major feature or concept, then review the document(s) again with this list of general concepts in mind. This time, scan for topics related to the major features. These subconcepts will become subtopics in your index.

- If you have begun formal documentation of the project, review the chapter headings or major structural divisions for topics that will need to be covered in the help system.

Creating HTML Files

HTML Help pages begin life as regular HTML files. All you need to do is go through the list of help topics you generated, writing general descriptive and technical background material as needed. You generate a single HTML file for each help topic previously identified. Because these pages are traditional HTML files, they can represent a compilation of text, graphics, sound, and video. Keep all of these files together so you can easily index them and create a Table of Contents. In order to provide a consistent interface across these pages, develop a series of templates upon which you can base other pages.

Because HTML is an open standard, you can generate the HTML topic files using any HTML editor or graphical Web page editor. However, the primary tool you will use in the creation of an HTML Help system is the Microsoft HTML Help Workshop. This piece of software handles the following tasks:

- Creation of skeleton HTML files for containing help content
- Direct HTML editing of files as they are built
- Creation and modification of the HTML Help Project File that manages the many individual HTML topic files
- Indexing of the collected topic files
- Generation of a Table of Contents

The HTML Help Workshop is not installed with the standard installation of Visual Basic. The setup program can be found on the *Visual Basic Installation* CD at: `D:\htmlhelp\htmlhelp.exe` (assuming that your CD-ROM drive is set as your D: drive). Alternately, the most recent version of this program should be available for download from `http://www.microsoft.com/workshop/author/htmlhelp/`.

NOTE

The help system that ships with Visual Basic 6 and Visual Studio 6 is the current MSDN Library. The library is very large and may be used either as a full or partial installation to your hard disk, or directly from the Installation CDs.

EXERCISE 11.1

Installing Microsoft HTML Help Workshop

1. Insert the Visual Basic 6.0 installation CD into your CD-ROM drive (or CD # 1 of the Visual Studio Suite).

2. Launch the Windows Explorer (or Windows NT Explorer if you are installing on a Windows NT machine).

3. Using the Explorer, navigate to the root directory of the installation CD, then open the HTMLHelp directory and double-click on the icon labeled `HTMLHelp.exe`.

EXERCISE 11.1 (CONTINUED)

4. Read and accept the End-User License Agreement.

5. Interact with the Setup Wizard to:

   - Set an installation directory

   - Specify complete or custom install

   - Add the HTML Help Workshop to the Start menu

   - Personalize the installation with your name

Once installed, you can use the HTML Help Workshop to generate help topic files. As mentioned above, it is a good idea to build template files upon which the individual topic files will be based. To build such a file, create a new file (of the HTML page type) and type or paste the formatted text into the body of the page.

For more information on the use of HTML Help Workshop, see the help file that accompanies HTML Help Workshop.

EXERCISE 11.2

Creating an HTML Topic Template

1. Launch HTML Help Workshop by selecting Start ➢ Programs ➢ HTML Help Workshop ➢ HTML Help Workshop.

2. Select the File ➢ New menu item (or click the New Item toolbar button).

3. From the dialog that appears, select HTML File and press the OK button.

4. Enter a title such as **_tmpConcept** in the HTML Title dialog box that appears, as shown in the following graphic.

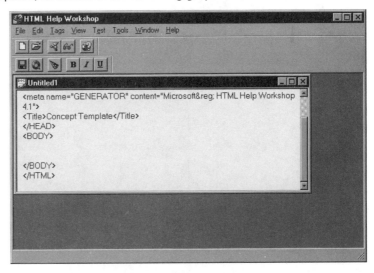

5. In the HTML file that is presented, lay out a general format to use in creating future HTML topic files. It may be helpful to create the actual HTML for the body of the template in a graphical HTML editor like Microsoft Front Page, as shown in the following graphic.

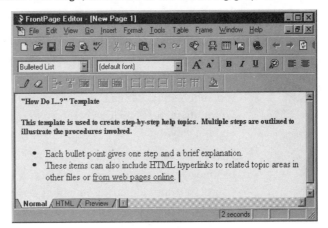

EXERCISE 11.2 (CONTINUED)

6. The HTML code generated in the template is shown in the following graphic. This code can then be used by HTML Help Workshop in generating help topic files.

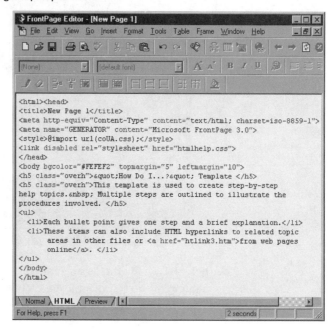

```
<html><head>
<title>New Page 1</title>
<meta http-equiv="Content-Type" content="text/html; charset=iso-8859-1">
<meta name="GENERATOR" content="Microsoft FrontPage 3.0">
<style>@import url(coUA.css);</style>
<link disabled rel="stylesheet" href="htmlhelp.css">
</head>
<body bgcolor="#FEFEF2" topmargin="5" leftmargin="10">
<h5 class="overh">&quot;How Do I...?&quot; Template </h5>
<h5 class="overh">This template is used to create step-by-step
help topics.  Multiple steps are outlined to illustrate the
procedures involved. </h5>
<ul>
  <li>Each bullet point gives one step and a brief explanation.</li>
  <li>These items can also include HTML hyperlinks to related topic
      areas in other files or <a href="htlink3.htm">from web pages
      online</a>. </li>
</ul>
</body>
</html>
```

Your topic files can contain more than plain help-oriented text. HTML Help Workshop ships with a basic image editing tool called HTML Help Image Editor. Its features include screen capturing, file editing, file converting, and file viewing.

Once you have generated templates for the general types of help files you plan to implement, you can generate topic files. Using the Windows Explorer, create copies of appropriate templates and modify them with the needed content.

As you build HTML topic pages, keep the following ideas in mind:

- Be as clear and brief as possible on individual topics. These tools are typically used by existing users who want a little prod in the right direction, not a long discussion.

- What you may miss in *depth* on any particular topic, make up for in *breadth*. Cover as many topics as you can imagine might be helpful.

- Take advantage of the fact that you are using HTML. A brief discussion of a topic with plenty of hyperlinks to related topics allows the user to determine the direction and depth of study. Using hyperlinks can also save you from having to duplicate information that is relevant to more than one primary topic.

The HTML Help Workshop ships with a thorough primer on coding in HTML. To access this reference, launch HTML Help Workshop, then select the Help ➤ HTML Tag Reference menu item.

Topic files are then added to HTML Help projects using HTML Help Workshop. We will discuss this below under the heading "Create a Project File."

Using Cascading Style Sheets to Format Help Systems

Template files provide a simple way of ensuring similarity in help system pages. For a more sophisticated and flexible means of controlling the presentation of these files, you can use Cascading Style Sheets (CSS). Cascading Style Sheets can define the style elements you use in HTML pages. The CSS page is referenced in each HTML page and, as the pages are rendered, the CSS is polled for layout and style information.

Perhaps the greatest advantage of using a CSS in laying out multiple HTML pages is the ability to quickly and consistently change style elements throughout a Web site. A process that might otherwise require you to manually modify each page requires only that you modify the CSS file.

If you decide to implement a CSS in your help system, the HTML Tag Reference contains a review of the syntax involved in implementing CSS sheets. Click the Help ➢ HTML Tag Reference menu item to access the tag reference.

If you have more advanced layout and formatting needs, Microsoft's Visual InterDev version 6 contains a robust interface for implementing CSS "themes" across multiple Web pages.

Implementing a Help System

We've now discussed many of the tasks necessary to prepare for the creation of an elegant help system. The remainder of this chapter will detail the measures needed to fully implement an interactive help system.

Using Microsoft HTML Help Workshop

The HTML Help Workshop that ships with Visual Basic is designed to pick up and run with the task of HTML Help development after the development of the help content pages. This one small utility manages several important functions, abstracting the details of the implementation from the developer.

Microsoft ✔ *Exam Objective*

Implement online user assistance in a distributed application.

- Create HTML Help for an application.

Using this utility application, we will proceed to develop an HTML Help application. The steps needed for this process are:

- Create a Table of Contents

- Create an Index File
- Create a Project File
- Convert WinHelp (if necessary)
- Add the HTML Help ActiveX control to the project
- Compile the HTML Help Project

After you complete these steps, the Package and Deployment Wizard will include the compiled help system in the deployment setup configuration. Your end users will have access to an integrated help system that allows hyperlinking of ideas within the text, context-sensitive assistance, and a searchable library of documentation.

Create a Table of Contents File

Microsoft's default HTML Help window contains several different views of the information available. These views are organized and exposed to the user with a tabbed-window interface. The Contents view provides the end user with a view of the information organized by logical groupings. The other two views are labeled Index and Search. These allow users to quickly find an indexed term or perform a full-text search of the entire help system.

The visual metaphor used in the Contents tab is that of books in a library. The user can select the major topic of interest (a book on a particular subject), then open the book to view chapters and topics within. See Figure 11.1 for an example of the Help screen with a tabbed contents window.

FIGURE 11.1

The Contents window

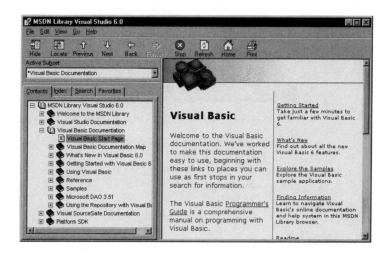

Building the Table of Contents involves identifying the topics to be included and organizing them logically. Each topic file to be included is represented by a heading or page alias. The order of these page aliases can be manipulated until a satisfactory logical order has been achieved. Re-ordering the items is accomplished with the use of arrow keys which can promote, demote, or relocate topics or headings.

Figure 11.2 shows a Table of Contents under development. Note the control buttons down the left side of the window. They allow the developer to view the properties of the contents file, add new headings and topics to the contents file, edit or delete the file references, and rearrange the order of table entries. The process of building these headings is somewhat similar to working in outline mode in either MS Word or PowerPoint. Exercise 11.3 gives the specific steps necessary to build your own Table of Contents.

FIGURE 11.2

A Table of Contents under development

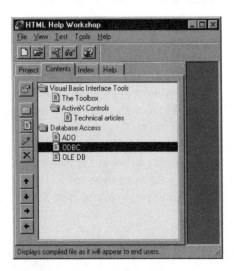

EXERCISE 11.3

Creating an HTML Help Table of Contents

1. Launch HTML Help Workshop.

2. Select File ➤ New, then click Table of Contents in the dialog that appears.

3. Use the Add a Heading and Add a Page buttons to add elements to the Table of Contents. For each heading or page you add, you must access the Table of Contents Entry dialog, as shown in the following graphic. For each entry, you must give an entry title and a file path or URL for the contents file. Type titles directly into the dialog. You can enter paths and URLs by browsing.

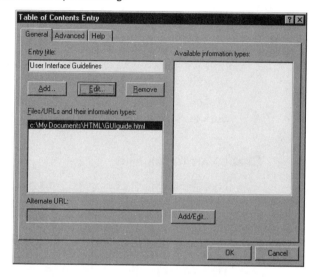

4. Once you have structured the concepts as desired, you can compile the contents table for use in the help system project file. To compile, select File ➤ Compile. You will be asked to provide a full path and name for the file to be created (.chn). To view the resulting contents structure, select View ➤ Compiled File... The following graphic shows how the resulting compiled contents window appears.

Note the differences between the two graphics in Exercise 11.3. The control buttons are missing from the compiled window, and the compiled window contains a traditional Windows Explorer-style tree structure. This tree structure will resemble the functionality of the contents window in the final help configuration.

WARNING   HTML Help Workshop is a new utility, developed for release with Visual Basic Version 6. Early revisions contain some missing features and may hang unexpectedly. For instance, in version 1.1, which shipped with the earliest copies of Visual Studio, attempting to access the Help tab of the Project window hangs the application, returning control to the user who Alt+Tabs away from HTML Help Workshop and then returns. We also received at least one "feature not yet implemented" warning. **Save your work often!**

Create an Index File

The index file, once compiled, will give functionality to the Index tab of the Help window. It will allow the end user to type in part or all of a word and find related help topics. Indexes work by creating a list of keywords that, upon lookup, will point to relevant topics.

There are two methods available for adding keywords to the index list. The first is very similar to the process for creating a Table of Contents. In HTML Help Workshop, you create a new file of type "index," then, in a dialog much like the Table of Contents Entry, you manually add keyword entries and their related page references. See Exercise 11.4 for details of the process.

EXERCISE 11.4

Creating an HTML Help Index File

1. Launch HTML Help Workshop.

2. Select File ➢ New, then click Index in the dialog that appears.

3. Using the Insert a Keyword button, add elements to the index. For each keyword to be added, you must access the Index Entry dialog. You can associate multiple topic files with a single keyword. In this case, merely open the existing keyword entry and add additional file associations. Each entry requires that an Entry Keyword be given, along with a file path or URL. Type keywords directly into the dialog. You can enter Paths and URLs by typing it directly or through browsing. The following graphic shows the Index Entry dialog.

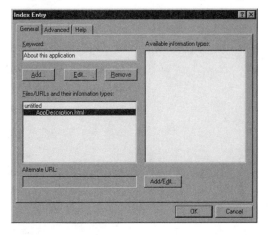

4. When you have completed this process, the Workshop Index tab will show the list of all subjects to be indexed, as in the following graphic.

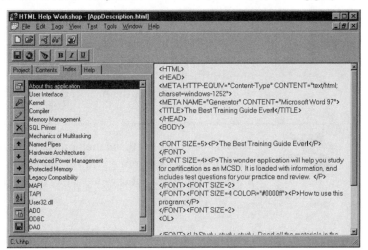

EXERCISE 11.4 (CONTINUED)

5. You then compile the list of index topics for use in the help system project file. To compile, select File ➤ Compile. You will be asked to provide a full path and name for the file to be created (.chn). To view the resulting contents structure, select View ➤ Compiled File... The following graphic shows how the resulting compiled index window appears.

The second method for generating an index can save some energy if you employ it while creating the help topic files. In this approach, the keywords are identified in the topic files, then HTML Help Workshop adds the keywords to the index as the project is compiled.

You can use either of these methods or a combination of both, though we recommend selecting one primary method. Mixing methods will create index files with potential redundancy or missing content.

There are two variations in how this tagging of files is accomplished. The first option is that you can add the code manually (usually as the files are created), using whatever tools you used to create the original HTML code. Alternatively, you can use the HTML Help Workshop to insert the code. Either variation simply inserts an <OBJECT> tag that contains an ActiveX class ID and sets the required keywords as parameters. Exercises 11.5 and 11.6 describe the exact procedures.

EXERCISE 11.5

Adding Keywords to the HTML Files at Content Creation for Generating Index Files

1. While each HTML topic file is open for editing in an HTML editor, simply insert the following object tag and parameters within the <BODY> section of the page.

```
<Object type="application/x-oleobject"
classid="clsid:1e2a7bd0-dab9-11d0-b93a-00c04fc99f9e">
<param name="Keyword" value="Keyword1">
<param name="Keyword" value="Keyword2">
</OBJECT>
```

2. Edit the value of the keyword tag above, inserting the actual keyword you want this particular page to be indexed by.

3. In the Compiler Information dialog that appears, select the Keyword tab and click the Add button to add new keywords. Multiple keywords can be added to a single page in one add operation by separating them with a semicolon.

EXERCISE 11.6

Using HTML Help Workshop to Add Keywords to the HTML Files in Order to Generate Index Files

1. Launch HTML Help Workshop, and open the HTML File to be modified.

2. Position your cursor within the <BODY> section of the page.

EXERCISE 11.6 (CONTINUED)

3. Select Edit ➤ Compiler Information.

4. In the Compiler Information dialog that appears, select the Keyword tab and click the Add button to add new keywords. Multiple keywords can be added to a single page in one add operation by separating them with a semicolon.

Once the keywords are prepared, either by placing object tags in the HTML pages or through the building of an index file, the final indexing functionality can be added to the project. If you had the index generated automatically by adding the <OBJECT> tag to your pages, you will need to make sure that the compiler switch is set to retrieve the keywords and build the index. You do this by first clicking the Change Project Options button on the Project tab window (see Figure 11.3). Next, from the Files tab of the Options window that appears, check the Include Keywords from HTML Files check box (see Figure 11.4).

F I G U R E   11.3

The Change Project
Options button

 When creating topics and an organizational structure for use with the default HTML Help viewer, tabs for contents index and search are automatically created for you. You can also build your own custom help viewer, but doing so is outside the scope of this chapter.

F I G U R E 11.4

The Include Keywords
from HTML Files
check box

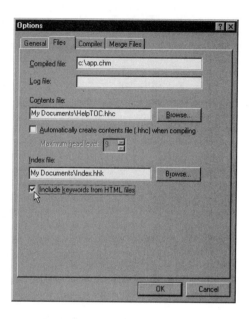

Create a Project File

Creating the project file is the last step in the process. The project file is created by the HTML Help Workshop application and serves as the organizational umbrella of the help application. Individual HTML topic files and their related graphics files are collected and associated with the project. The contents file (.hhc) and the index file (.hhk) are also included. Project files are referred to with a .hhp file extension while under construction. After compilation, the project file has a .chm extension.

To create a Project File, launch HTML Help Workshop, select File ➤ New, and press Project in the dialog box that appears (see Figure 11.5). Creating the Project File is just the beginning. As a content author for the help system, you must also add the HTML files you have created to the Project File. Figure 11.6 illustrates the Add/Remove file button through which the project is collected. Exercise 11.7 walks you through the whole process of creating a Project File and populating the project with HTML Help topic files.

F I G U R E 11.5

Choosing a type of
New file

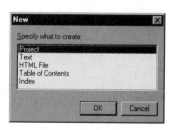

FIGURE 11.6

Adding a topic file to a
help project

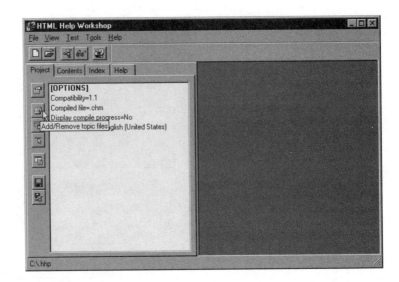

EXERCISE 11.7

Creating a Project File

1. Launch HTML Help Workshop by selecting Start ➤ Programs ➤ HTML Help Workshop ➤ HTML Help Workshop.

2. Select File ➤ New.

3. In the New dialog that appears, select the Project option (refer to Figure 11.8).

4. Click the Add/Remove button to add the individual HTML topic files you have created to the project (refer to Figure 11.9).

Compile Help Files

As indicated in Exercise 11.3 above, actually compiling the help system into a .chm file is relatively simple. You simply select File ➤ Compile, then provide a name and path for the finished file. Some project and compiler options can be configured by clicking on the Change Project Options button shown in Figure 11.3. For more information on the use of these custom settings, consult HTML Help Workshop Help. The only remaining tasks are to point the application at the help file and map certain controls to their respective help topics. These steps are covered below under the heading "Binding Forms and Controls to the HelpFile."

Converting WinHelp Projects

To ease the transition from the WinHelp engine to HTML Help, the HTML Help Workshop has a WinHelp project converter wizard. The wizard will automatically convert all RTF pages in the WinHelp project to HTML files, the .cnt file to a .hhc file, and the project file to a .hhp file. At this point, all you need to do to implement HTML Help is to generate an index file. Using the wizard, the transition from WinHelp to HTML Help can be a relatively painless operation for developers. Exercise 11.8 gives the steps to complete a conversion.

EXERCISE 11.8

Using the WinHelp Conversion Wizard

1. Launch the HTML Help Workshop and select File ➢ New.

2. In the dialog that appears select Project and click OK.

3. Click the Convert WinHelp check box to confirm your desire to convert WinHelp.

In the next dialog, you will also be asked to provide paths for the file you are converting and the one you are creating. Your new HTML Help Project will be built for you in the directory specified.

Binding Forms and Controls to the HelpFile

Microsoft ✓ *Exam Objective*

Implement online user assistance in a distributed application.

- Set appropriate properties to enable user assistance. Help properties include **HelpFile**, **HelpContextID**, and **WhatsThisHelp**.

Setting the HelpFile Property

In order to use the files you have created, you need to configure your application to use the help system. To initiate context-sensitive help, you must also set flags on individual controls to identify related topics to be presented. Exercise 11.9 gives the procedure for setting the HelpFile for an application.

EXERCISE 11.9

Setting the HelpFile Property of a Project

1. Open a new or existing project.

2. Open the Project Properties dialog box by selecting Project ➣ *project-name* Properties.

3. Select the General Tab to show the general project properties, as shown in the following graphic.

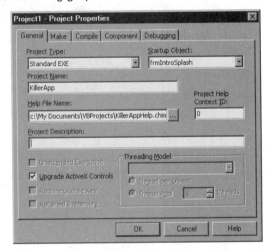

4. Identify the help file to be used. In the Help File Name field type either a full path or use the attached ellipsis button to browse to the file.

5. Close the Project Properties dialog box.

This method is most useful for design-time, as it assumes knowledge of the user's file system. Final production implementation of your help system is best accomplished using code like the following:

```
Private Sub StartupForm_Load()
App.HelpFile = App.Path & "\Help.chm"
End Sub
```

This script is placed in the load event of the project's initial form. Because it uses a relative path tied to the location of the application itself, the Help-File property is less vulnerable to unusual directory structures or applications that are moved after installation. The App object is a globally available object that exposes properties of the application itself. Here it is used to access the current application directory and to set the application's HelpFile property.

Help systems can also be built using object-oriented principles. Rather than a monolithic help system, a modular system may reduce development time and increase code reuse. Individual help files may accompany certain forms, and code components may contain their own help files. To reference different help system modules from within the application depending upon need, the above code can be called in subsequent form Load events or Class Initialization events, assigning new help files to the HelpFile property as needed.

Your application is now ready to provide global help to users. If the user presses the F1 key or selects either Contents or Index from the Help menu, they will be presented with the HTML Help environment.

The HelpFile property can be set for code component projects as well. If this is done and a Project Help ContextID is set, a specific help topic can be shown when a down-stream developer clicks the "?" button while your component's type library is selected in the Object Browser.

Context-Sensitive Help

For help support that is more responsive to the user's needs, a context-sensitive implementation can be used. Context-sensitive responsiveness in your help system requires that two steps be performed: forms and controls must have properties set to identify the particular help topic to be given, and the help file itself must be configured such that topics can be returned based upon the property values being sent from the application.

Setting the HelpContextID Property for Controls and Forms

As noted above, for the user to receive help that is related to the current user environment or operations, flags must be set that allow Visual Basic to make associations between controls and forms and the relevant help topics. These flags are actually the HelpContextID property of the respective forms or controls, and the actual ID number is of Long data type.

When these context assignments have been set and the help system activated, the help system will present the related help topic using the enabled HTML Help interface. As with setting the HelpFile property, there are two ways to set the HelpContextID property, either by using the Property window at design-time, or setting it procedurally at runtime. Exercise 11.10 shows how the HelpContextID property is set using the Properties window.

EXERCISE 11.10

Setting the HelpContextID Property from the Properties Window

1. Open a project containing forms and controls.

2. Select a form or control that you want to set the HelpContextID for.

3. In the Properties window, scroll if necessary to the HelpContextID property and double-click, as shown in the following graphic.

4. Type the Long number representing the HelpContextID into the empty box to the right of the property name.

5. Save changes to the application and test by setting focus to the form or control and pressing F1.

The HelpContextID can also be set programmatically at runtime. A traditional assignment statement will set this property. The following code makes the property assignment:

```
CmdSubmit.Text = 10000
```

The HelpContextID only works, of course, if topics in the compiled help file are mapped to equivalent ID tags. There are two ways to map ID numbers to the HTML Help topics. A header file written in C can be included in your project file which maps IDs to topics, or you can map topics yourself within Visual Basic. Exercise 11.11 shows the steps for the latter method of ID mapping.

Mapping HelpContextID Values for Help Topics

1. Launch HTML Help Workshop and open a project file.

2. Click the HTMLHelp API Information button.

3. Select the Alias tab and click the Add button to add an ID mapping, or alias.

4. In the Alias dialog, enter a HelpContextID and the HTML topic file that corresponds to that ID. The Alias dialog is shown in the following graphic.

5. Continue adding Aliases until all topic files and IDs have been mapped for the application.

Configuring "What's This" Help

An alternative to traditional context-sensitive help, What's This Help provides access to specific help content without the overhead of loading the HTML Help viewer. Configuring What's This Help is similar to configuring traditional context-sensitive help. Properties are set in similar ways, and both design-time and runtime methods are available. There are a few details of implementing What's This Help that require attention, however. Because the What's This button is inserted into windows' title bars when activated, the windows' Maximize and Minimize buttons must be removed. Additionally, the window's BorderStyle must be set to either Fixed Single or Sizable. The particular properties that must be set, and their respective values, are given in Table 11.1 below.

T A B L E 11.1	**Property**	**Value**
Property Settings to Enable What's This Help	WhatsThisHelpID (form or control)	<unique value for each form or control>
	MaxButton (form only)	False
	MinButton (form only)	False
	WhatsThisButton (form only)	True
	BorderStyle (form only)	1-Fixed Single or 2-Sizable

Just as context-sensitive help requires that help files be mapped to a Help-ContextID, WhatsThisHelp files must be assigned a WhatsThisHelpID value. What's This Help content, though, is stored in a text file named `cshelp.txt`. This file is then compiled within the regular help project.

What's This Help and context-sensitive HTML Help are mutually exclusive for individual forms and controls. When you enable What's This Help, activation of the HTML Help system is disabled for that form or control.

Passing Messages from Server Components to the User

Microsoft ✔ Exam Objective

Implement online user assistance in a distributed application.

- Implement messages from a server component to a user interface.

In addition to user-requested help systems, a client/server or multitier application may implement messaging from one user to another or from a server to an end user. Visual Basic 6 provides interfaces to the Microsoft Message Queue Server (MSMQ), which can be used to pass these types of system messages to the user.

Implementing MSMQ services involves creating an MSMQQueueInfo object and invoking the Receive method, which manages the tasks of reading any messages that are placed in the queue. Processing is asynchronous, so messages do not have to wait for existing processing to complete before being received. Exercise 11.12 shows the specific steps involved in preparing a client application to receive messages.

EXERCISE 11.12

Receiving MSMQ Messages in a Visual Basic 6 Client

1. Create a reference to the Microsoft Message Queue Object Library by selecting Project ➤ References and selecting the library from the list provided.

2. Instantiate the MSMQQueueInfo object, set the path for the Queue to receive, and run the Open method using the following code:

```
Dim QueueInfo As MSMQ.MSMQQueueInfo
Dim Queue as MSMQ.MSMQQueue
Set QueueInfo = New MSMQ.MSMQQueueInfo
QueueInfo.Pathname = "\\servername\queuename"
Set Queue = QueueInfo.Open(MQ_Receive_Access, MQ_Deny_None)
```

3. Invoke the Receive method using the following code:

```
Dim Qmsg as MSMQ.MSMQMessage
Set Qmsg = Queue.Receive(ReceiveTimeout:=1000)
```

4. Use code such as the following to gain access to the contents of the incoming messages.

```
Dim message as string
StringMSG = msmqmessage.Body
Msgbox ("incoming message", String,MSG)
```

5. If needed, you can execute the Close method of the MSMQQueue object. This is done by calling:

```
Queue.Close
```

6. Leaving the queue handler open will allow the client application to handle any future messages forwarded by the message queue.

Once the message has been received from the message queue, the contents of the message are stored in the MSMQQueue object. To present the message to the user, the properties of the object must be extracted and procedurally handled. Traditional dot-notation assignment statements can extract the message contents from the properties of the MSMQQueue object. For instance, the following code will extract the body of the message, placing the body contents into a text box control.

```
txtMessageBody.Text = Queue.Body
```

Summary

Providing an effective online help system can greatly enhance the usability of most applications. A good help system is also a sign of a polished development effort. Mastering the skills necessary to create an HTML Help system will aid you in passing the certification exam and rounding out your development skills.

Review Questions

1. What is the greatest advantage developers gain by using HTML Help instead of WinHelp?

   A. HTML Help is much easier to configure and use than WinHelp.

   B. The HTML Help engine is already installed on most PCs.

   C. Existing content is easily reused in help files.

   D. There is no advantage; WinHelp is a better technology.

2. HTML topic files can be created with which of the following tools? (Mark all that apply.)

   A. A text-based HTML editor

   B. A graphical HTML editor such as Microsoft Front Page

   C. Internet Explorer 4

   D. HTML Help Workshop

3. Where in an application can the HelpFile be specified?

   A. At design-time, in the App object

   B. At design-time, in a control's property window

   C. At runtime in the App.Helpfile property

   D. At runtime in the Project Properties dialog

4. Which of the following is not a file type found in an HTML Help File?

   A. `.hlp`

   B. `.hhk`

   C. `.hhc`

   D. `.chm`

5. When converting a WinHelp project to HTML Help using HTML Help Workshop WinHelp Converter Wizard, which of the following files is not created automatically?

   A. Project file

   B. Index file

   C. Contents file

   D. HTML topic files

6. What data type is the HelpContextID?

   A. String

   B. Integer

   C. Single

   D. Long

7. How are WhatsThisHelpIDs mapped to individual topics?

   A. What's This Help topics and their IDs are stored in a text file.

   B. IDs are mapped to topic files in a C header file that is included in the Project File.

   C. What's This Help uses the HTML Help topic mappings, and setting the WhatsThisHelp property to true overrides the regular context-sensitive help system.

   D. The help topics are stored locally, saved with each form or control.

8. Which of the following is a true statement?

    A. Pathname is a valid method of the MSMQMessage object.

    B. Receive is a valid method of the MSMQQueue object.

    C. The Close method of the MSMQQueue object should always be executed immediately following receipt of a message.

    D. Messages from the message queue are synchronous, meaning they will only be delivered after other pending events have completed.

9. Which of the following best describes the App object?

    A. It can be created as needed. It is used to bind a client application to a data source.

    B. It can be created as needed. It is used to set and retrieve properties of the current application.

    C. It is created automatically when an application is launched. It is used to set and retrieve properties of the current application.

    D. The App object provides an object handle for referencing component objects over a network.

CHAPTER

12

Error Handling in the Distributed Application

Unexpected occurrences are unfortunately all too common in sophisticated applications. To make it even more difficult, not everything that can go wrong in an application is actually your fault as a developer. For example, if your application prompts a user to insert a $3\frac{1}{2}$ inch floppy in the A: drive to read file information, and the user puts the disk in a $5\frac{1}{4}$ inch B: drive, this will cause a runtime error. Yet is this error really your fault?

Although you may not be directly responsible for the event that caused the error, it is certainly your responsibility to protect the user from making any mistakes that will cause the application to raise an exception. In a distributed application, this is complicated by the fact that an error can occur at any tier in the application.

This chapter discusses the process of adding error handling into a distributed application. Although some of these subjects are similar to standard desktop application error resolution, the distributed application complicates this process somewhat by requiring the components to forward errors back to the application. In addition, the ActiveX Data Object model supports an Errors collection. This collection is used to hold all data access errors and can be explored by the client application during the execution of the application. You might also have the need to resolve errors that take place in your SQL Server stored procedures. This chapter addresses these important elements of distributed application design.

Error Handling in the Client

Microsoft ✓ *Exam* *Objective* **Fix errors, and take measures to prevent future errors.**

Gracefully resolving errors is what separates a professional application from the crowd. It doesn't matter how many wonderful features your application provides if it won't stay up. Visual Basic provides the application developer with numerous features to aid in the effective resolution of errors in an application.

In this section, we will discuss some of the Visual Basic settings that specify how an application running in the Visual Basic IDE will respond to error conditions when they occur. We will then explore the Err object provided by Visual Basic to assist in the error handling activity.

Configuring Visual Basic for Error Handling

Visual Basic 6 supports three options for how error handling will take place in an application. Before you begin to implement error handling in your application, you should first verify that these options are set appropriately for your error-handling strategy. The options available are:

- Break on All Errors

- Break in Class Module

- Break on Unhandled Errors

These options are mutually exclusive. The options are found by going to the Visual Basic menu under Tools ➤ Options and selecting the General tab. Figure 12.1 illustrates this dialog. You set only one option, and it controls the error handling mode for all of the projects running in this Visual Basic IDE. This configuration will drastically change the way that your application responds to errors. Let's look at each of these options in more detail.

F I G U R E   12.1

The General Options dialog

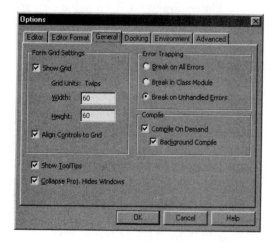

The configuration only affects error handling in the Visual Basic IDE. After the application has been compiled, all components will always pass their errors back to the calling application and the application will only break on unhandled errors.

Break on All Errors

This option states that the application will enter break mode whenever any error of any kind occurs. This will happen regardless of whether the application code has set an error trap. This can be very helpful to locate errors that might be hidden by an error trap that does not adequately handle the error.

Break in Class Module

This Error mode forces the application to break inside of a class module whenever you call a class module from your application. If no class module is called, then the break will occur in your client application code. This is the default error-handling mode for Visual Basic.

The benefit for allowing your application to break in the class module can be significant. If the system were not allowed to break in the class module, then the break would have to take place at the point at which the client application calls the component. This makes the problem difficult to locate because all you know is that an error has occurred in the component code without knowing exactly where that error occurred or which error occurred.

Break on Unhandled Errors

The option to break on unhandled errors allows the system to enter break mode whenever an error occurs outside of an error trap, but it does not allow a break inside a class module running in the Visual Basic IDE. Using this approach, the break always occurs in the calling application, never a component. The break could be triggered either by an error in the application code or an error in the component.

This is the mode that will be assumed after you have compiled the application and it executes outside of the Visual Basic IDE. When a break occurs in this mode in a compiled application, the break is fatal to the application, causing the process to end. In a production application, you never want this to happen, so this mode is helpful for identifying any locations in your code where an unhandled error might occur. At this point, it is essential to ensure that all of your errors are properly handled so that the application will not end unexpectedly on your user.

Identifying and Resolving Runtime Errors

Microsoft ✓ *Exam* *Objective*

Implement error handling for the user interface in distributed applications.

- Identify and trap run-time errors.

The trick to resolving runtime errors is identifying them when they occur and writing code to resolve the problem when the error arises. For example, assume that a user had begun a file I/O operation and intended to retrieve a file from a floppy disk. If the file requested is not present in the location indicated in the user action, a runtime error would occur. This error would have a number associated with it. In this case, the error number for a "file not found" error is 53. Table 12.1 lists some of the more common Visual Basic error numbers and their associated cause.

WARNING This following list is not a complete list of the errors supported by Visual Basic. All error numbers from 0 to 1000 are reserved for Visual Basic. Those error numbers that are not currently implemented are reserved for future use.

T A B L E 12.1 Common Visual Basic Error Numbers	**Error Number**	**Error Description**
	5	Invalid procedure call
	6	Overflow
	7	Out of memory
	9	Subscript out of range
	11	Divide by zero
	13	Type mismatch

T A B L E 12.1 *(cont.)*	**Error Number**	**Error Description**
Common Visual Basic Error Numbers	17	Can't perform requested operation
	20	Resume without error
	28	Out of stack space
	35	Sub, function, or property not defined
	48	Error in loading DLL
	53	File not found
	55	File already open
	58	File already exists
	61	Disk full
	67	Too many files
	71	Disk not ready
	76	Path not found
	91	Object variable or with block variable not set
	94	Invalid use of null
	337	Component not found
	360	Object already loaded
	423	Property or method not found
	430	Class doesn't support automation
	448	Named argument not found
	482	Printer error

Setting the Error Trap

The first step in managing runtime errors is setting the Error trap. This means that rather than simply allowing the runtime errors to halt the application, all errors will be intercepted by the Visual Basic application, giving you a chance to resolve them before they break the application.

To set an Error trap in a Visual Basic procedure, you will use the On Error GoTo statement. This statement is usually placed at the beginning of a procedure. When setting the Error trap, you will identify a point in the code to which the execution will branch when an error occurs. This section of code that resolves the error is called the *Error handler*.

Since Visual Basic does not directly support any type of centralized error handling, every procedure should contain an Error trap and an Error handler to resolve its own errors.

For example, if you wanted to create a procedure that set an Error trap that pointed to error handling code located at line label **ResolveError** further down in the procedure, the Error trap would look like the following example.

```
On Error GoTo ResolveError
```

This means that whenever an error occurs in that procedure, the code execution immediately branches to the line in the procedure labeled ResolveError. The Error handler then tests the error number and executes the section of code that is appropriate for that error number.

If you ever wish to turn off the Error handler after you have set the Error trap, simply use the statement On Error GoTo 0. This will disengage the Error trap. At this point, any runtime errors that occur in your application are critical.

A final mode of error handling is to deal with errors as they occur rather than to branch out to an Error handler. This approach is called *inline error handling* because you resolve the errors at the specific point of the error rather than taking the code to another point for error resolution. This approach will be covered in the "Handling Errors Inline" section later in this chapter.

Creating the Error Handler

The Error handler is the point in the procedure at which all errors are resolved. You identify this section of code with a line label that you reference from the Error trap. Every line label is identified in the code by following the label immediately with a colon (:). The Error handler will usually be the last section of code in a procedure and will be immediately preceded by an Exit Sub statement. This prevents the code execution from falling through to the Error handler. The following example illustrates the basic structure of a procedure in Visual Basic that contains an Error trap and an Error handler.

```
Sub TestErr()
On Error GoTo ResolveError
    ' Procedure Statements Here
Exit Sub
ResolveError:
    ' Error Handler Here
End Sub
```

Inside the Error handler, you will place a decision structure such as If … Else or Select Case to evaluate the error number. These structures must have a resolution path for all possible errors that could occur in that procedure.

Although you can use an If … Else statement, the Select Case is much more efficient and is preferred for this kind of extensive evaluation.

Using the Err Object Visual Basic provides an object called Err that you will use to test and respond to all attributes of an error. Table 12.2 lists some of the most common properties and methods of the Err object.

T A B L E 12.2 Common Properties and Methods of the Err Object	Property/Method	Description
	Number property	Returns the number associated with the most recently committed runtime error.
	Description property	Returns the descriptive text string associated with the most recently committed runtime error.

TABLE 12.2 *(cont.)*	**Property/Method**	**Description**
Common Properties and Methods of the Err Object	Clear method	Clears all attributes of the Err object including the Number and Description properties.
	Raise	Raises an Error condition which is trappable in an Error handler.

As you can see from the previous table, the simplest way to test for an error number is to use the Number property of the Err object. Suppose, for example, that in a particular procedure, the only two error conditions that you think might occur are Errors 53 (file not found) and 76 (path not found). You might create an Error handler that looks like the following example.

```
ResolveError:
Select Case Err.Number
    Case 53 'File not found
        ' Resolution Code Here
    Case 76 'Path not found
        ' Resolution Code Here
    Case Else
        ' Resolution Code Here
End Select
```

In the example above, the error number is tested in the Case statement and a separate block of resolution code executes when each error is raised. If an error occurs other than the two errors explicitly referenced, the final case might provide a notice to the user that an unknown error condition has occurred; this would allow a graceful exit from the application.

Other uses of the Err object include raising an error condition using the Raise method. This method can be very useful for testing and evaluation purposes. In addition, the Raise method supports the ability for a developer to raise user-defined errors. These errors, with numbers ranging from 513 to 65535, can be raised to signal a custom event in an application or component that is to be interpreted by the application as an error condition. The syntax of the Raise method is illustrated below.

```
Err.Raise number [, source [, description [, helpfile [,
helpcontext ]]]]
```

The Raise method has one required argument, which is the error number, and four optional arguments. Table 12.3 lists the arguments of the Raise method and their applications.

T A B L E 12.3 Arguments of the Raise method	**Argument**	**Usage**
	Number	Custom number to identify the error raised.
	Source	String identifying the application or component that is the source of the error, usually in the format *project.class*.
	Description	Text string providing a description of the custom error. If no description is provided, the generic description "Application-defined or object-defined error" is used.
	Helpfile	The pathname of an .hlp file that contains information about the error.
	HelpContext	The context ID of the appropriate help topic in the associated .hlp file. If omitted, the Error number is used.

Using the Resume Statement   Error handlers are generally not very useful if there is no way for the procedure to continue processing after the Error code has been executed. In Visual Basic, you should provide a Resume statement of some kind to identify to the procedure where you wish to resume processing after the Error code has executed. There are three valid resume statements:

Resume   The application resumes processing on the line of code that caused the error.

Resume Next   The application continues processing on the line of code following the line that caused the error.

Resume *line*   Execution continues at the point designated by the line label or line number indicated after the Resume statement.

Figure 12.2 illustrates the flow of each of these Resume methods. Each of these Resume statements returns control of the program to a different and distinct point in the code.

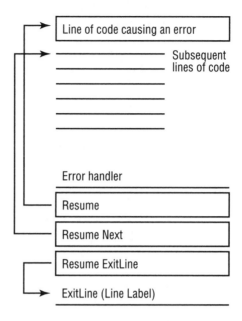

FIGURE 12.2

The flow of the
Resume statement

There is a requirement in error handling in Visual Basic that restricts the ease of centralized error handling frequently seen in other programming environments. This requirement is that the Resume statement in an Error handler and the point in the executing code to which you resume must be in the same procedure. This eliminates the option of creating a central Error procedure that contains all of the necessary Resume statements.

To extend our previous example, assume that our Error handler listed previously had the following requirements.

1. If the file is not found, prompt the user to insert media with the correct file and try the operation again.

2. If the path is not found, inform the user that the operation has been skipped and continue through the procedure.

3. If anything else occurs, inform the user than an unexpected error has occurred and exit the subprocedure.

To satisfy these requirements, the Error handler might look like the following example.

```
ResolveError:
Select Case Err.Number
    Case 53 'File not found
        ' Resolution Code Here
        Resume
    Case 76 'Path not found
        ' Resolution Code Here
        Resume Next
    Case Else
        ' Resolution Code Here
        Exit Sub
End Select
```

 When resuming out of an Error handler, the value of Err.Number is automatically set to 0. It is not necessary to execute an Err.Clear statement to accomplish this.

Error Handlers and the Call Stack

Remember that Visual Basic is a modular language. This means that it is not uncommon for an event procedure to call a general procedure, which in turn may call another general procedure, and so forth. This brings up the question of which Error handler will be used to resolve the errors found in a procedure.

The standard rule in this situation is that when available, the application will use the Error handler found in the local procedure first. If there is no Error handler in the local procedure or an error occurs or is raised within the Error handler, the error is passed up the call stack to the procedure that called the local procedure.

This process will continue until the application finds an Error handler that can resolve the error in question. If an Error handler is not found anywhere in the call stack, or if the error is continually raised in each Error handler, the Windows default action, Exit Process, will occur. This means that the application will end without notice.

Figure 12.3 illustrates the relationship between procedures in the error handling task. In Step 1, Sub A calls Sub B. An error occurs in Sub B, but because there is no Error handler in Sub B, the error is passed to Sub A in Step 2. Sub A has an Error handler and, in Step 3, successfully resolves the error and calls Sub B again. Sub A indicates the instruction to resume the execution of the code at the line that committed the error using the Resume statement. Since the Resume statement and the point in the code to which execution resumes must be in the same procedure, the resume cannot take place in Sub B. Instead, the resume occurs at the line of code that calls Sub B. The process then repeats.

FIGURE 12.3

Passing errors up the call stack

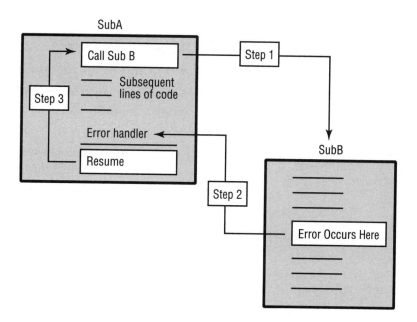

If you had used a Resume Next statement in Sub A instead of a Resume statement, the execution would have continued on the line of code following the call to Sub B.

As you can see from this example, the passing of errors up the call stack often does not have the desired effect. For this reason, you should include an

Error handler in every procedure. If you ever wish to pass any particular error up the call stack, simply raise the error again in the Error handler. Any error that occurs in an Error handler is automatically passed up the call stack to the calling procedure.

Completing the Error Handler

Now that we have addressed all of the major elements of an Error handler, we will construct a complete procedure, including error handling code. This procedure raises an error that will trigger the Error trap and place the execution into the Error handler. Exercise 12.1 walks you through this process.

EXERCISE 12.1

Creating an Error Handler in a Procedure

1. Start Visual Basic. Create a new Standard EXE project. Add a command button to Form1. Name the button cmdLocalError. Caption the button Local Error.

2. Double-click the button to access its click event. Enter code to prompt the user to enter an error number to raise. Raise the error indicated by the user input. Accomplish both of these tasks with a single statement. Following the error, create a message box indicating that the application is executing the line following the error raised.

3. Add an Error handler that resolves a type mismatch error (number 13) by creating a message box to inform the user of the type of error that has occurred. After this executes, resume the code back to the point of the error.

4. Add a generic handler that reports to the user through a message box that an unknown error has occurred. Force the code to immediately exit the procedure. The following code is an example of one possible coding of steps 2 through 4.

```
Private Sub cmdLocalError_Click()
  On Error GoTo ResolveError
  Err.Raise CInt(InputBox("Enter Error Number"))
  MsgBox "After Error"
Exit Sub
```

```
ResolveError:
  Select Case Err.Number
    Case 13 'Type Mismatch
      MsgBox "Type Mismatch Error Here"
      Resume
    Case Else
      MsgBox "Unknown Error"
      Exit Sub
End Select
End Sub
```

5. Run the application and click the Local Error button. When prompted for an error number, enter **13**. This will raise a type mismatch error. Click the OK button on the InputBox. You should now be in the Error handler and will see the message box indicating this. Click the OK button on the message box. You will be returned to the InputBox because your code specifies a Resume to the error condition. Enter any numeric value except for 13. You will be informed that an unknown error has occurred, and the procedure will end.

6. End the application. Save the form in a location of your choice under the name Form1.frm and the project as Errors.vbp. Leave Visual Basic running and the project loaded in preparation for the next exercise.

Handling Errors Inline

Microsoft ✓ ***Exam*** ***Objective***

Implement error handling for the user interface in distributed applications.

- Handle inline errors.

While the most common approach to resolving errors is through a complete error handling procedure, you may occasionally find it beneficial to handle errors as they occur in the code rather than branch off to an Error handler. This process is called inline error handling. The inline approach is similar to the branching approach in that you must set an Error trap in order to capture the errors as they occur. By contrast, however, instead of referring to an Error handler, you will deal with any errors directly.

The structure of the Error trap is a little different than the method previously discussed. Remember that in our discussion of Resume statements, we noted that when the Resume Next statement is used, the execution of the code returns to the line following the line that caused the error. Using this same logic, if you set the Error trap by using a Resume Next statement, the code execution will skip the line causing the error and continue to the next line of code. The following code illustrates this approach.

```
On Error Resume Next
```

When handling errors inline, you must resolve the errors as they occur and then clear the contents of the Err object so that no other inline Error handlers will respond to the error in question.

The following code illustrates the approach of using an inline error handling technique. The procedure contains a statement that might cause an error number 53 to occur. If so, error responses will fire. Otherwise the procedure will ignore the error handling code and continue.

```
Sub TestInline()
On Error Resume Next
' Error might occur at this point
  If Err.Number = 53 Then
    ' Resolve Error Here
    Err.Clear
  End If
' Procedure Continues
End Sub
```

Using inline approaches to error handling has both advantages and disadvantages. Some of the advantages include the ability to deal with errors as they occur rather than using elaborate branching schemes. Inline approaches also tend to simplify the approach to managing different responses to identical error conditions that might occur at different locations in the code.

Disadvantages also abound. First and foremost is the inability to perform any type of centralization of error handling. Although Visual Basic is already limited by design in the area of error handling centralization, using the inline approach to error handling makes centralization structurally impossible. This means that you have a tremendous amount of duplication of effort when managing errors.

Error Handling in the Component

Microsoft **Implement error handling for the user interface in distributed**
Exam **applications.**
Objective
- Determine how to send error information from a COM component to a client computer.

At the heart of error handling in the distributed application is the role of the component. You can manage errors in a component in exactly the same way as you do in a client application; however, the placement of the components offers you more choices for proper error management. There are essentially three roles that your components can take in the error handling task. These components can assume any combination of these roles simultaneously.

- The components can act independently, resolving their own errors internally and never communicating Error status to the client application.

- The components can pass their errors to the client application for resolution. The client application will handle the errors and interact with the component as needed.

- The component can raise custom errors indicating information about Error status inside the component.

In this section, we will explore each of these roles of the component in error handling. Remember that a single component may actually utilize all three of these approaches within its structure.

Creating Independent Components

Using this approach, the component resolves its own errors and is responsible for its own activities. This approach is very much like error handling from the client perspective that we discussed previously. The goal is to ensure that all errors are handled appropriately.

When using this approach to error handling, ensure that the error handling options are set to Break in Class Module. This will allow you to see the errors within the component and resolve them appropriately.

Although it may seem at first glance that this would be a desirable solution, it can be very limiting. Your client application often has an active interest in the activity and Error status of the components. While you may want your component to resolve some of its internal error conditions without client intervention, it is usually essential that the component communicate with the client application at some point. For this reason, this approach to error handling in a component is often used in tandem with the other two roles previously outlined.

Raising Standard Component Errors to the Client

Sometimes you may want the errors raised inside of a component to be passed back to the client application to be resolved there. This is very similar to the concept of passing an error up the call stack, which was discussed previously in this chapter (see Figure 12.3). If you fail to handle an error in a component, this will automatically be the result.

The key to using this method effectively is to provide the client with a method of determining where the error is coming from. To support this, the Err object has a *Source* property that identifies the project or component from which the error has originated. Using this property, you can customize your error response accordingly.

For example, if the error was raised in a component called "DataAccess," then this text string would be associated with the Source property of the Err object. Exercise 12.2 walks you through the process of investigating some of the useful elements of the Err object for distributed error handling.

EXERCISE 12.2

Raising Errors from a Component

1. Start Visual Basic, if it's not already running, and open the Errors.vbp project. To change the default break mode to break on all unhandled errors, select Tools ➤ Options from the menu. On the General tab, set the Error Trapping option to Break on Unhandled Errors. Click OK.

2. Add a new ActiveX DLL project to the project group by selecting File ➢ Add Project from the menu. Name the project ErrorComp and the class module ErrorClass.

3. To the ErrorClass module, add a Public Sub called ErrTest. In this procedure, raise a type mismatch error (13) using the following code.

```
Err.Raise 13
```

4. Close the code window for the component and open Form1 from the main project. Add a second command button to the form. Name the button cmdCallCompError. Caption the button Component Error.

5. Add a reference to the ErrorComp component by selecting it from the component list. To access this list, select Project ➢ References from the Visual Basic menu. In the General Declarations section of the form module, create a public object variable that instantiates the ErrorClass in the component. The following code provides an example.

```
Public obj As New ErrorComp.ErrorClass
```

6. In the click event of the command button, write code to activate inline error handling. Call the errTest method of the object. Create three message boxes that report back to the user the Number, Description, and Source of the error. Use the following code as an example.

```
On Error Resume Next
obj.errTest
MsgBox Err.Number
MsgBox Err.Description
MsgBox Err.Source
```

7. Run the application and click the Component Error button. You should see a sequence of three message boxes. Note the content of the third message box. It should read "ErrorComp", the name of the component project.

8. End the application and save the project group. Accept the default names for the component project and class files. Save the group under the name Errors.vbg. Leave Visual Basic running in preparation for later exercises.

Raising Custom Errors from a Component

One of the more useful features of the component in a distributed application is the ability to raise custom errors back to the client application. This allows the component to monitor its own internal status, only raising errors when the client application must be informed. The real advantage, however, is that the condition evaluated by the component might not actually constitute a Visual Basic runtime error condition. It might simply be a threshold that you wish to monitor inside your component, allowing the client application to act when necessary.

When raising your own custom errors from a component, as well as the error number, you need to provide an error description and a source string.

The description can be any string of your choice that effectively describes the condition being monitored inside the component. If you do not provide a string in the argument, then a default description of "Application-defined or object-defined error" is used by the system.

The Source property that we investigated in the previous exercise can also be customized. This argument should be expressed in the format of *project.class*. In our previous example, the Source property could be set to "ErrorComp.ErrorClass." This identifies with significant precision the source of the error.

When setting the error number for a custom error raised from a component or other automation object, you should add to the error number the intrinsic constant value of *vbObjectError*. Adding this constant to your error numbers forces your custom errors out of the range of the errors that might be used by the system and other client application elements.

WARNING Valid error numbers inside your component range from 0 to 65535; however, 0-512 are reserved for system errors. User-defined error numbers begin at 513.

As an example, we will assume that we are creating a component called Component1. To this component we add a Class module called Class1. This class contains a public subprocedure that compares an argument provided by the user to the data in the database looking for matching rows. When no match is found, we wish to raise a user-defined error numbered 65535. This error can then be trapped on the client and handled appropriately. The following code would raise this error from the component.

```
Err.Raise number:=vbObjectError + 65535, _
    Source:="Componenet1.Class1", _
    Description:="No Match Found"
```

Since the offset value of vbObjectError was used on the component side, it must also be used on the client side to ensure that the correct error has been extracted. The code below illustrates a fragment of an Error handler that responds to the error raised in the previous example.

```
Select Case Err.Number
    Case vbObjectError + 65535
        'Resolution Code Here
    Case Else
        'Resolution Code Here
End Select
```

In this section, we have seen how the component participates in the process of error handling in the distributed application. Remember that, generally speaking, handling errors inside a component is not significantly different from handling errors in the client application. The flexibility that custom errors can provide in a distributed application makes the entire management of a distributed application much simpler.

Using the ADO Errors Collection

Microsoft Exam Objective

Use the ADO Errors collection to handle database errors.

When errors occur in a database application, they may be more complex than simple runtime errors. When runtime errors occur, the application breaks at the first error encountered. By contrast, when a data error occurs, it could occur at the same point in time as other data errors.

For example, suppose that you attempted to enter a row into a database and this row violated numerous integrity settings on the table, such as a Primary Key violation, a business rule violation, and a referential integrity violation. Since any of these problems alone would prevent the row from being written to the database, it is a moot point to attempt to identify which of these violations occurred first. In fact, they should all be treated as equally obstructive.

Since the standard error handling approach can only deal with one error at a time, a different mechanism is required to effectively deal with groups of errors. Visual Basic already defines a standard construct called the collection that enables the developer to work with groups of objects. This same structure can be easily extended to work with groups of errors.

In the ADO hierarchy, the Errors collection is located under the Connection object. All database error conditions are returned to the Connection object and placed into the Errors collection. Iterating through this collection enables the developer to explore all of the errors that occurred as a result of the last error-generating database activity. Whenever a new error-generating database activity occurs, the Errors collection is automatically cleared of its previous contents and loaded with the new set of errors.

Examining the Errors Collection

Just like any other collection, the Errors collection supports a set of properties and methods that define how the developer interacts with the collection. For example, the Errors collection supports a property called Count that indicates the number of elements in the collection. In addition to the Count property, some of the more useful properties and methods of the Errors collection are listed in Table 12.4.

T A B L E 12.4 Common Properties and Methods of the Errors Collection	**Property/Method**	**Description**
	Count property	Returns the number of objects in the Errors collection.
	Item property	With an Index number, returns a reference to an element of the Errors collection.
	Clear method	Clears the contents of the Errors collection.

Like most collections, the majority of the functionality is provided at the object level. By iterating through the collection to identify the objects within, the individual Error objects can be examined as to their error number, status, and other identifying information. Table 12.5 lists the most common properties of the Error object.

T A B L E 12.5 Common Properties of the Error Object	**Property**	**Description**
	NativeError	The error number as reported by the data source. This value is database specific and, if used, requires modification if a different data source is used.
	Number	The ADO generated error number. This remains constant regardless of the data source used. However, this value provides less detailed error information than NativeError, as errors are commonly aggregated under ADO.
	Description	A text string associated with every error. This string often contains context-specific information about the database and tables involved in the error.
	Source	Returns the source of the error. This is usually the name of the OLE DB service provider.

Creating a Stored Procedure

Since we have determined that the most efficient approach to data access is through stored procedures, we will begin by looking at the error messages returned by stored procedures when they execute.

As an example, let's look at the authors table in the pubs database. The authors table is constrained by referential integrity to another table called titleauthor. This means that deleting a row from the authors table will cause a referential integrity error. Exercise 12.3 walks you through the process of creating a stored procedure in SQL Server that deletes a row from the authors table.

EXERCISE 12.3

Creating a Stored Procedure

1. Start the SQL Server 7.0 Query Analyzer by selecting Start ≻ Programs ≻ Microsoft SQL Server 7.0 ≻ Query Analyzer from the Windows menu. Enter the name of your server in the dialog. Choose SQL Server authentication and enter a Login Name of **sa** with no password. Click OK.

2. Enter the code that creates a stored procedure that deletes the record for Anne Ringer from the authors table. Use the following code as an example.

```
USE pubs
go
CREATE PROC del_ring
AS
DELETE authors
WHERE au_lname = 'Ringer'
  AND au_fname = 'Anne'
Go
```

3. Execute the script by selecting Query ≻ Execute Query from the menu. You should get "The command(s) completed successfully." as a response.

4. Open a new query window by selecting Query ≻ New Query from the menu. Enter the code to execute the stored procedure that you just created. Use the following code as an example.

```
EXEC del_ring
```

5. Execute the query. You should get an error message in response, informing you that the DELETE statement conflicts with a column reference to a foreign key. Note that the error number is 547.

6. Choose File ≻ Exit from the menu. When prompted, do not save changes.

Implementing the Errors Collection

Data errors can return entries to the Errors collection that cause runtime error conditions on the client, but warnings are also returned that do not cause runtime errors. For this reason, the Errors collection must be continually evaluated in your code at any point where you expect that a data access error could occur. For this reason, inline error handling approaches can be very convenient when managing the Errors collection.

To iterate through the Errors collection, you can use a For ... Next loop, using the number of elements of the collection as the iterative counter. You can also use the For Each ... Next structure to iterate through a collection. This structure is designed to handle collections and groups of objects, and it is usually easier to implement than the For ... Next loop. The code fragment below illustrates how this approach is used to iterate through collections of objects.

```
For Each ErrObj In Cn.Errors
    strErrMsg = "Native Error Number " +
CStr(ErrObj.NativeError)
    MsgBox strErrMsg
Next ErrObj
```

In Exercise 12.4, you will execute the stored procedure created in the previous exercise and examine the Error collection populated as a result of the stored procedure.

EXERCISE 12.4

Examining the Errors Collection

1. If not already running, start Visual Basic and open the Errors.vbg project group in the Visual Basic IDE. Since you will be implementing the ADO object model, you must make a reference to the library. From the menu, select Project ➤ References and select Microsoft ActiveX Data Objects 2.0 from the list. Click OK.

2. In the main project in the General Declarations section of Form 1, declare object variables as new instances of the ADO Command and Connection objects. The following code illustrates this.

```
Private Cn As New ADODB.Connection
Private cmd As New ADODB.Command
```

3. Add a new command button to the form. Name the button cmd-StoredProc. Caption the button Call Stored Proc.

4. In the click event of the command button, enable inline error handling. Write code that connects to SQL Server and creates a Command object that executes the stored procedure del_ring. After the stored procedure executes, iterate through the Errors collection and create a string that returns for each error the ordinal number of the error in the collection, the native error number, the source, and the description string. Display this information in a message box. Use the following code as an example.

```
Private Sub cmdStoredProc_Click()
On Error Resume Next
Dim strQuery As String
Dim strErrMsg As String
Dim i As Integer
strQuery = "del_ring"
With Cn
    .ConnectionTimeout = 30
    .CommandTimeout = 30
End With
Cn.Open "provider=sqloledb;server=server1;database=pubs","sa"
With cmd
    Set .ActiveConnection = Cn
    .CommandText = strQuery
    .CommandType = adCmdStoredProc
    .Execute
End With
For i = 0 To Cn.Errors.Count - 1
    strErrMsg = "Collection Element " + CStr(i) + vbCrLf
    strErrMsg = strErrMsg + "Error Number" +
CStr(Cn.Errors(i).NativeError) + vbCrLf
    strErrMsg = strErrMsg + "Source: " +
Cn.Errors(i).Source + vbCrLf
    strErrMsg = strErrMsg + Cn.Errors(i).Description
    MsgBox strErrMsg
Next i
End Sub
```

5. Run the application. Click the Stored Procedure button to call the procedure. The first message box should identify the error as number 547, the same error number seen in the SQL Server Query Analyzer. Advance through the message boxes, looking at the errors returned.

6. End the application and save the project group. Exit Visual Basic.

Summary

In this chapter, we have examined the process of error handling in a Visual Basic application. As we have seen, Visual Basic provides numerous features for the identification and resolution of error conditions. Using Visual Basic components, the process of creating a distributed application can be enhanced through the creation of user-defined errors and returning full control of error communication back to the client.

To ensure that all data errors are captured appropriately, the ActiveX Data Objects also implement the ADO Errors collection. This collection, located underneath the Connection object, contains all of the data errors that occurred as a result of the last error-generating data source activity. This collection provides indispensable information concerning the last error conditions that occurred in the data source.

It is impossible to overstate the importance of error handling in an application. When done correctly, you have effectively predicted all of the errors that could occur in the execution of your application. This will allow the application to remain functional, providing the maximum benefit to your users.

Review Questions

1. Which property of the Err object returns the numeric value associated with the most recent runtime error?

   A. Description

   B. Number

   C. NativeError

   D. Source

2. You are creating a client application that calls ActiveX DLLs. Which of the following properties of the Err object provides the name of a component that sends an error back to the client application?

   A. Number

   B. Description

   C. NativeError

   D. Source

3. How many error conditions can the Err object report at any single point in time?

   A. 0

   B. 1

   C. 65535

   D. Unlimited

4. Which of the following statements forces inline error handling?

   A. On Error GoTo *linelabel*

   B. On Error GoTo Inline

   C. On Error Resume Next

   D. On Error GoTo 0

5. Which of the following statements discontinues error trapping for a procedure?

   A. On Error GoTo *linelabel*

   B. On Error Resume Next

   C. Err.Stop

   D. On Error GoTo 0

6. You are creating an ActiveX component that raises user-defined errors. What is the valid range of error numbers that you can use for user-defined errors?

   A. 0 – 255

   B. 0 – 65535

   C. 0 – 1000

   D. 513 – 65535

7. You are creating an ActiveX component that raises user-defined errors. Which of the following statements correctly raises an error to the client with error number 20000?

   A. Err.Raise vbObjectError + 20000

   B. Err.Raise vbObjectError, 20000

   C. Err.Number = 20000

   D. Err.NativeError = vbObjectError + 20000

8. Which of the following is not a valid Resume statement in an Error handler?

   A. Resume

   B. Resume Next

   C. Resume Previous

   D. Resume line

9. Which property is associated with every collection defined by Visual Basic?

A. Clear

B. Count

C. Source

D. Number

10. Which ADO object acts as parent to the Errors collection in the ADO hierarchy?

A. Command

B. Recordset

C. Parameter

D. Connection

CHAPTER

13

Application Testing and Analysis

During the process of creating an application, whether it is a small desktop solution or a large distributed solution, you will eventually encounter some logical errors in your code. A *bug* is an error in the code that causes the application to behave in a manner that is unexpected and undesired. Bugs do not necessarily cause runtime errors, however. This means that they can be somewhat difficult to locate without some help.

Visual Basic provides a number of excellent debugging utilities that help you locate these errors when they occur. Since the errors might be located anywhere in the entire application from the presentation tier to the data tier, debugging a distributed application can be especially challenging.

This chapter is organized into two major sections. We will first look at the set of debugging tools that are available in the Visual Basic development system and discuss the appropriate application of each one. We will then evaluate how to use these tools for debugging a distributed application, which is a bit different from the approach that you might use to debugging a desktop application.

The Debug Tools

Visual Basic provides a complete set of debugging utilities designed to help you locate and resolve logic errors when they occur in your applications. These tools provide features such as the abilities to interact with your code at break-time, step through program code, and identify critical points in your code execution, such as when an expression value changes to a specific value.

In this section, we will look at the various elements of the Visual Basic debugging tool set and discuss their practical implementation. The tools that we will evaluate are:

- Break mode and stepping
- The Immediate window
- The Debug object
- Watch expressions
- The Locals window
- The Call Stack window

Entering Break Mode

The most basic element of debugging in SQL Server is break mode. This is a point in an application when an error occurs and the Visual Basic debugger is activated. Break mode does not cancel all previous program execution; it simply halts program execution. All variable and property values are retained. This gives you the ability to identify exactly what the current state of the system was at the time that the application error occurred.

If the Visual Basic IDE is in break mode, this is identified in the title bar of the main Visual Basic window. Depending on how break mode was initiated, you will also usually see a code window with a yellow bar on the line of code that caused the application to break. Figure 13.1 illustrates the Visual Basic design environment in break mode.

There are numerous ways for the application to enter break mode, including:

- Runtime errors
- Breakpoints
- Code statements, including:
  - Stop statement
  - Assert method of the Debug object
- Watch statements
- Manually entering debug mode from the Visual Basic IDE

We will look at each of these methods and their advantages and applications in some detail.

FIGURE 13.1

The Visual Basic IDE in break mode

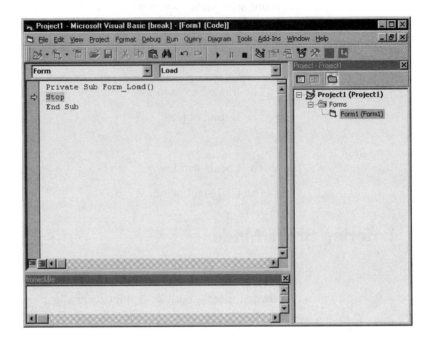

F I G U R E 13.1

The Visual Basic IDE in break mode

Manually Entering Break Mode

At any time during program execution, you can enter break mode by inter-acting with the Visual Basic IDE by using one of three methods. First, Visual Basic provides a keystroke combination of Ctrl+Break that will place the application into break mode.

This option is especially helpful for those times when your code enters an endlessly recursive loop. Ctrl+Break unconditionally halts all code execu-tion, permitting you to terminate an endless operation.

Another way to manually enter break mode is to select Run ➤ Break from the Visual Basic menu. The final method is to use the Break button on the toolbar. This is the button with two vertical bars, as shown in Figure 13.2.

F I G U R E 13.2

The Break button on the Visual Basic toolbar

Setting Breakpoints

Breakpoints are locations in your code that you identify as locations where you wish to halt execution. When the application encounters a breakpoint, the application halts unconditionally at that point and places the IDE in break mode for further debugging. Breakpoints are useful if you suspect that a problem exists in a particular section of your code. Rather than step through the entire procedure, you can set a breakpoint in your code and halt the code there.

Breakpoints can either be temporary or permanent. One way to create a temporary breakpoint is to use the Debug toolbar. On this toolbar, pictured in Figure 13.3, you will find a tool with a picture of a hand. Simply place the cursor in the line of code that you wish to break and click this button. A dark red bar will appear on the line. Click again to turn off the breakpoint.

F I G U R E   13.3

The Debug toolbar

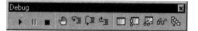

To activate the Debug toolbar, select View ➢ Toolbars ➢ Debug from the Visual Basic menu.

Figure 13.4 illustrates a code window with a breakpoint set. Notice the shaded bar on the line of code that is marked, as well as the large dot in the margin. If you wish, you can also use the margin to set the breakpoint. Simply point in the margin next to the line of code that you wish to set as a breakpoint. Click once to set the breakpoint. Click again to remove.

F I G U R E   13.4

A breakpoint in a code window

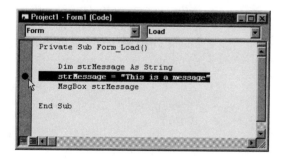

The breakpoints that you set in this manner are temporary in nature. They are not saved with the project and will be removed when the project is closed. If you wish to save breakpoints with a project, you must use a code statement. You can do this either by using the STOP statement or the Assert method of the Debug object.

The STOP statement will unconditionally halt execution of the code at the point of the statement. Since, by using the STOP statement, you are creating breakpoints that will not be removed when the project closes, you must be sure that you remove all STOP statements in your code before you compile the project. Otherwise, the STOP statement will force the application to end.

The debugging environment also provides a Debug object for special debugging activities. One of the methods of the Debug object is the Assert method. This method allows a conditional breakpoint to be created in your Visual Basic code. The Assert method requires one argument, a Boolean expression. Using the Assert method, you are asserting that the expression evaluates to true. If this is the case, the code will continue without breaking. If the expression does not evaluate to true, the code will break at the point of the Assert method.

Exercise 13.1 illustrates the use of the Assert method of the Debug object. In this exercise, you will request input from the user using a message box. Based on the response, the expression provided as the argument of the Assert method will evaluate to either true or false, causing the code to break at some points but not others.

EXERCISE 13.1

Using the Assert Method of the Debug Object

1. Start Visual Basic and select a Standard EXE from the project template list. In Form1, add a command button. Name the button cmdAssert and caption the button Test Assert.

2. In the click event for cmdAssert, write code that captures user input as a number ranging from 1 to 100. Using the Assert method of the Debug object, write a statement that will enter break mode if the value entered by the user is not a multiple of 7. Use the following code as an example.

```
Dim intResponse As Integer
intResponse = CInt(InputBox("Enter a number between 1 and 100"))
Debug.Assert (intResponse Mod 7 = 0)
```

3. Test the code by running the application. When prompted, enter a value that is a multiple of 7. The application should not break. Enter any other value. This should cause the application to enter break mode at that point.

4. End the application and close the project.

Since the Debug object is only active when the Visual Basic IDE is in use, you do not have to worry about removing the Debug.Assert statements from your code before you compile the project. Any references to the Debug object will automatically be removed for you.

Setting Watch Expressions

Microsoft ✓ *Exam* *Objective* | **Set watch expressions during program execution.**

Microsoft ✓ *Exam* *Objective* | **Given a scenario, define the scope of a watch variable.**

Another way to enter break mode is to define a watch expression. The Visual Basic debugger monitors a watch expression during the execution of the application. The system halts when the expression evaluates to true or when the expression value changes.

You can add a watch expression either during design mode or break mode. You cannot add a watch expression during runtime. To add a watch expression, select Debug ➤ Add Watch from the Visual Basic menu. This will present you with a dialog like the one pictured in Figure 13.5.

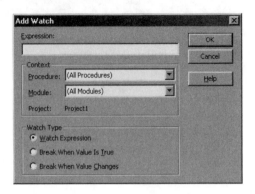

When completing the dialog, use the following information as a guide:

Expression   Text indicating the expression that you wish to watch. This expression can either be a Boolean expression in the format of X=10, or a simple expression such as a variable name or a property value such as txtName.text.

Context   This section of the dialog allows you to select the visibility of the expression that you wish to monitor. You can set both the module and procedure context of the watch. You should select the lowest context level possible with which you can still maintain appropriate scope.

Watch Type   Allows you to specify what will happen when the watch expression evaluates to a specific value. Your valid options are:

   Watch Expression   No action is taken. The value of the watch expression is merely monitored in the Watch window.

   Break When Value Is True   Places the application into break mode when the expression evaluates to true.

   Break When Value Changes   Places the application in break mode when the expression value is modified through any means.

Using watch expressions, you can locate the exact position of a problematic condition. For example, suppose that you have a procedure that makes a call to another function procedure called *selectval* in a module called *datacalls*. You seem to be getting a return value that you do not expect from the function, but you have no idea how this value is being calculated.

   The return value of the function is actually the Value property of a custom class called *dataclass*. You want to identify the exact point in time that the value is erroneously set to the unexpected value. Assume that the observed but undesired value is 5. We would set the watch expression values as follows:

- Expression: dataclass.value = 5
- Context:
  - Procedure = selectval
  - Module = datacalls
- Watch Type: Break When Value Is True

Exercise 13.2 illustrates the process of creating watch expressions in Visual Basic. In this exercise, you will set and edit watch expressions during the execution of a sample application.

EXERCISE 13.2

Creating Watch Expressions

1. Start Visual Basic if it is not already running. Create a new Standard EXE project when prompted for a project template. Add a command button to Form1. Name the button cmdTestWatch. Set the caption to Test Watch.

2. Double-click in the center of Form1 to open the code window. Add a new procedure to the form by selecting Tools ➢ Add Procedure from the menu. Set the procedure name to ReturnVal. Mark it as a Private Function procedure and click OK.

3. In the newly created procedure, set the return value data type to Integer as shown in the following example.

```
Private Function ReturnVal() As Integer
```

4. In the procedure, declare a variable called intReturn. Capture input from the user to set the variable value through an InputBox function. Set the return value of the function to the variable that you created. Use the following code as an example.

```
Private Function ReturnVal() As Integer
Dim intReturn As Integer
intReturn = CInt(InputBox("Enter a whole number"))
ReturnVal = intReturn
End Function
```

5. In the click event of cmdTestWatch, raise a message box that returns the value of the function back to the user. Use the following code as an example.

```
Dim intRVal As Integer
intRVal = ReturnVal
MsgBox "The Return Value is " & CStr(intRVal)
```

6. We will start by evaluating the return value of the function. To add the watch expression, select Debug ➢ Add Watch from the menu. Set the expression to ReturnVal = 5, the procedure to ReturnVal, the module to Form1, and the watch expression to Break When Value Is True. Click OK. To test, start the application and click the Test Watch button. Enter a value of 5 and click OK. The code should break at the End Function statement, immediately after the ReturnVal function is set to 5. This is not very helpful information, since you could have identified where this happens without setting a watch.

7. Hover your mouse pointer over the intReturn variable on the right side of the assignment. If there were more elaborate processing to this variable, you could use this method to locate the point in the code where the variable evaluates to 5.

8. End the application. In the Watch window, point to the watch expression that you added, right-click and select Edit Watch from the pop-up menu. Change the expression to intReturn = 5. Click OK.

9. Run the test again. This time the code should break after the InputBox statement, identifying the location that the variable evaluates to the value of 5.

10. End the application. Delete the watch expression by selecting the watch from the Watch window, right-click and select Delete Watch from the pop-up menu.

11. Save the project using names of your choice in a directory of your choice. Leave Visual Basic running with the project open.

Working in Break Mode

Once you have entered break mode, you have other tools available to assist you in your debugging efforts, including the following features:

- Stepping

- Immediate window

- Locals window

These tools can be used together to track and modify the specific program progression, property, and expression values. In this section, we will look at the application of these tools to properly monitor and modify expression flow.

Stepping Through Code

To monitor program flow interactively, you can step through your code one line at a time in break mode. You can use the step buttons on the Debug toolbar, the step options from the Visual Basic menu, or the shortcut keys for the step actions. Figure 13.6 illustrates the step icons and the shortcut keys that can be used to access this behavior.

The two options *Step Into* and *Step Over* behave identically except when a procedure is called in the code. When you call a procedure, the Step Into option will advance you into the called procedure and execute that procedure one line at a time. If you use the Step Over option, the called procedure is executed in its entirety in one step and you are advanced to the line of code after the procedure call.

Generally, you will want to debug your procedures from the bottom up, making sure that the called procedures are working correctly and then calling those procedures from other procedures or events. Using this approach, you will most likely step over the called procedures. If you know that they are working, there should be no need to execute them one line at a time.

As you are stepping, you can also reassign the next line of code to be executed. This allows you to repeat a given section of code repeatedly, testing under different assumptions. To do this, you will drag the yellow bar that represents the next line of code to be executed to a new location. When you step from that line, you will begin at the new location.

Figure 13.7 illustrates a code window in break mode. Notice that there is a highlighted bar indicating the line of code that will execute next. In the margin on the left side of this bar, there is an arrow. Dragging the arrow to another line of code will reassign the next executable line. As you drag, the pointer becomes a large right-pointing arrow with small arrows pointing up and down, as pictured in Figure 13.7.

F I G U R E   13.7

Relocating the execution point

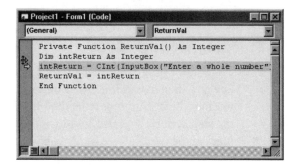

There may be times, however, when a called procedure must be executed within the context of a calling procedure. When this is a required element of testing, you can use the Step Into option to execute the called procedure one line at a time. Exercise 13.3 illustrates both of these approaches using the project that you created in the previous exercise.

EXERCISE 13.3

Stepping through Procedures

1. Using the project created in the previous exercise, navigate to the click event of the cmdTestWatch command button. Set a breakpoint on the line of code that reads `intRVal = ReturnVal`.

2. Start the application and click the Test Watch button. The application to break on the line of code is identified as the breakpoint.

3. To test the Step Into behavior, click the Step Into button on the Debug toolbar or press the F8 key. You should now be in the ReturnVal function. Continue stepping through the function until you step back into the calling procedure, answering any raised dialogs as necessary. End the application.

4. To illustrate the Step Out option, start the application and click on the Test Watch button. This will break the application again. Once more, click the Step Into button. This will advance you to the function. To the immediate right of the Step Over button on the Debug toolbar, you will see the Step Out button. This option will execute the remainder of a called procedure without stepping, returning control to the calling procedure. Click this button.

5. Immediately after clicking the Step Out button, you will see the Input-Box. Enter a number and click the OK button. You will be returned to the click event of the cmdTestWatch button. End the application.

6. To test the Step Over behavior, start the application and click the button. When the code breaks, click the Step Over button. This will execute the called function as a single step, raising the InputBox and returning you to the line following the procedure call.

7. Leave Visual Basic running with the test application open in preparation for the next exercise.

Using the Immediate Window

Microsoft
✓ *Exam*
Objective

Monitor the values of expressions and variables by using the Immediate window.

- Use the Immediate window to check or change values.

While in break mode, you can interact with your code using the Immediate window. The Immediate window allows you to read or modify the values of any write-enabled expression, including property values, variable values, etc.

This gives you the ability to test possible options and repeat the test numerous times without ever leaving the debug environment.

To read values from the Immediate window, you will use the Print statement. For example, if you want to see the value associated with the caption property of Form1, you would type the code `Print Form1.Caption` in the Immediate window and hit the Enter key. The result would look like the example in Figure 13.8.

FIGURE 13.8

The Immediate window

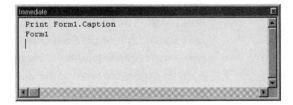

```
Immediate
Print Form1.Caption
Form1
```

As a shortcut, you can replace the command *Print* with a question mark (?). The question mark is shorthand for Print and will yield the same results.

If you need to set a property value or another expression value in the Immediate window, simply type the appropriate command in the Immediate window and press the Enter key. This will make the change to the executing application. For example, if you wanted to change the caption of Form1 to the text string *New Caption*, you need only enter the command `Form1.Caption = "New Caption"` in the Immediate window, and the change will be made.

Exercise 13.4 walks you through the process of monitoring and modifying values using the Immediate window. In this exercise, you will affect the values of variables as well as property values.

EXERCISE 13.4

Working with the Immediate Window

1. In the test application, the breakpoint should already be set from the previous exercises. If not, set the breakpoint in the click event of the cmdTestWatch button at the line of code that reads `intRVal = ReturnVal`.

2. Run the application and click on the Test Watch button. When the application breaks, activate the Immediate window. If you do not see the Immediate window on the screen, activate it by selecting View ➢ Immediate Window from the menu.

3. In the Immediate window, query the Caption property value of the active form by entering the following code.

```
? Me.Caption
```

4. To change the caption of the form, enter the command to make the modification in the Immediate window. Use the following code as an example.

```
Me.Caption = "New Caption"
```

5. Using the Step Into button, advance into the ReturnVal function. Continue advancing until the InputBox function is raised requesting input. Enter the value of 5 in the InputBox and click the OK button.

6. In the Immediate window, query the value of the intReturn variable by using the statement ? intReturn. This should return the value of 5.

7. Change the value of the variable to 6 by entering the statement intReturn=6. Continue stepping through the code until you see the message box raised by the click event of the command button. Because you changed the value of the variable before it was used to set the return value of the function, the message box should report that the returned value is 6.

8. Stop the application. Leave Visual Basic running with the test application open.

Using the Locals Window

Microsoft
✓ ***Exam***
Objective

Monitor the values of expressions and variables by using the Immediate window.

- Use the Locals window to check or change values.

The Locals window is a tool that the developer can use at break-time to explore the values of various application elements currently within scope. Those elements may include the properties of current objects, variables, and other application elements with value. The Locals window arranges these application elements in a hierarchical relationship depending on the natural container relationship between objects. This means that you would have to drill into a form to see references to a picture box on the form and into the picture box to see the command button contained inside the picture box.

Figure 13.9 illustrates the Locals window and the container relationship between objects. You will note that the current form is identified as Me. Listed underneath are all the attributes of the current form, including other collections contained inside the form.

FIGURE 13.9

The Locals window

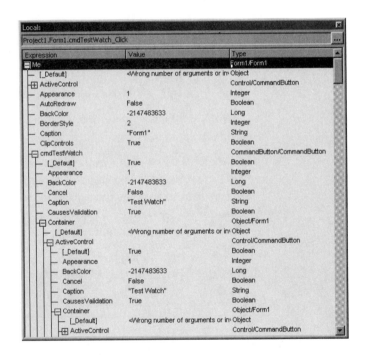

The Locals window is not only a handy tool for reading the values of properties and expression, it is also a very effective tool for modifying them. If you wish to make a change to a write-enabled value found inside the Locals window, simply click on the value that you wish to change, and you will enable the object for editing. Make a change to the value and the application will now reflect that modification.

The Locals window is also very effective for monitoring which values are currently within scope. If a value or expression that you expect to find is not present in the Locals window list, this is most likely an indicator that the element that you wish to find is not scoped properly for the current position of the application.

Exercise 13.6 walks you through the process of working with the Locals window. In this exercise, you will both read and write application values by using the Locals window.

Working with the Locals Window

1. Start the test application and click the Test Watch button. The application should break at the usual place. To activate the Locals window, select View ➤ Locals Window from the Visual Basic menu.

2. You should see two entries in the Locals window, ME and intRVal. There is a plus sign (+) next to the ME entry. Click this plus sign to expand the content of the current form.

3. In the list of values, locate the entry for Caption. The current entry should read "Form1". Locate the entry labeled Controls. This represents the Controls collection of the form. When you expand the Controls collection entry, you will find an entry labeled Item1. This represents the command button. Click the plus sign next to Item1 to view its values.

4. Scroll to the bottom of the list of attributes of the form until you find the entry for the width of the form. Click on the value associated with the width attribute. This should highlight this value for editing.

5. Enter the value **8000** for the width. You should see the results of the setting in the form. Experiment with other values, viewing the results on the form.

6. End the application. Leave Visual Basic running and the test project open.

The Callstack

Creating a good Visual Basic application can be a challenging process, but if you design a Visual Basic application correctly, it will be very modular in nature. Event procedures call general procedures, which may in turn call other general procedures many layers in depth. While this creates an environment that promotes the reusability of code within an application, the unexpected side effect is an application whose logic is sometimes difficult to follow.

When one procedure calls another and this process repeats itself many times, it does not take long to get hopelessly and completely lost. A road map, illustrating where you are and how you got where you are, can often help in the debugging process to identify your current location and how the code got to that point.

The road map provided by SQL Server is in the form of the callstack. The callstack shows you which procedure you are currently executing, as well as the sequence of procedures that brought you to that point. To activate the callstack, select View ➢ Call Stack on the Visual Basic menu. You can also use the Call Stack button on the extreme right of the Debug toolbar.

Figure 13.10 illustrates the Call Stack window. In this example, the procedure currently executing is procedure D. Procedure D is called by procedure C, and so forth. The process started with the click event of Form1.

FIGURE 13.10

The Call Stack window

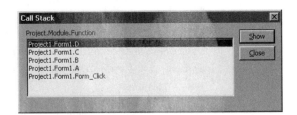

Debugging Distributed Application Elements

When an application is a self-contained desktop application, the debugging process is usually straightforward. Implementing some of the application logic into components may increase the reusability of the component code, but it also adds some complexity to the debugging environment.

In order to debug a Visual Basic application, it must be running in the Visual Basic IDE. Since the components will be ultimately packaged as separate files from the client application, more than one project is usually involved. In this section, we will revisit application testing using project groups and component projects.

Project Groups

When you need to test and debug multiple projects at the same time, you can use a project group to simplify the process. Opening multiple projects into the same instance of the Visual Basic IDE creates project groups. Project groups are saved as files with a *.vbg extension. Opening a project group will force all of the projects contained in the group to open into the same Visual Basic session. Figure 13.11 illustrates a project group containing two projects, a Standard EXE project and an ActiveX DLL project. The Standard EXE project is the Start Up project.

FIGURE 13.11

A Project Group

To create a project group, simply open a project in Visual Basic. Then add a second project group using File ➤ Add Project from the menu. It is very important that after opening the first project, you add all subsequent projects to the project group using the Add Project menu item. If you use the New Project or Open Project menu items, the existing project group will be replaced with the project that you requested.

Debugging Components and Controls

One of the advantages of using project groups for testing distributed applications is that you can test your client application and all of the component objects in the Visual Basic IDE before deploying them throughout the network. This enables you to correct functional and logic errors quickly and easily.

Since Microsoft Transaction Server implements single-user components, there is no substantial difference between creating a local component and a distributed component. This simplifies the testing process significantly.

Debugging Components

Using the project group, you can set breakpoints inside the DLL and call the DLL as you would normally. When you set a breakpoint in your DLL, the code execution will break at that point. This allows you to treat a component very much like a simple set of called functions. The debugging process is not very different.

In Chapter 12, you saw the error handling properties accessible from the Tools ➤ Options menu item on the General tab. These options are relevant only for error handling, not for setting breakpoints. When you set a breakpoint in a component procedure, the break will always occur exactly at the breakpoint in the component. The break will not be passed up to the client application.

Exercise 13.6 illustrates the process of debugging and breakpoint management in a Visual Basic component. This exercise will create a simple component and client application as two projects in a project group and force a break inside the component code.

EXERCISE 13.6

Component Debugging

1. Start Visual Basic if it's not already running. If a project is currently active in the Visual Basic IDE, close the project and create a new Standard EXE project.

2. Add a new ActiveX DLL project by selecting File ➤ Add Project from the Visual Basic menu. Select the ActiveX DLL template from the list and click OK. Ensure that the Standard EXE project is set as the Start Up project. If it is the Start Up project, the name of the project (Project1) should be in boldface in the Project window. If the Standard EXE project is not marked as the Start Up, right-click on the name of the project in the Project window and select Set as Start Up from the pop-up menu.

3. Open the code window for Class1 in the component project. Add a new public subprocedure to the project called Method1. In the code for Method1, raise a message box that informs the user that a call has been made to Method1 in Class1.

4. Activate the Standard EXE project in the project group by selecting Project1 in the Project window. Set a reference to the component project by selecting Project ➤ References from the Visual Basic menu. Click the check box next to Project2 in the references list and click OK.

5. Add a command button to Form1 of the Standard EXE project. In the click event of this command button, create an object variable called **obj**. Set the object variable to a new instance of Project2.Class1. Then call Method1 of the object variable. Use the following code as an example.

```
Dim obj As New Project2.Class1
obj.Method1
```

6. Start the application and click the command button to test the component. The command button should raise the message box called in the component code. Stop the application.

7. Open the code for Method1 of the component. Set a breakpoint in the message box call. Run the application and click the command button again. The application should enter break mode at the breakpoint in the component.

8. Stop the application. Click the Save button on the Visual Basic toolbar and save the project group in a location of your choice. Notice that you will be prompted to save each individual project as well as the project group file.

Debugging ActiveX Controls

Debugging ActiveX Controls in-process is very similar to debugging components. In fact, if you will recall our earlier discussion of ActiveX controls in Chapter 5, we used project groups to test those controls. To set breakpoints and step through control code, you must add the ActiveX control project to the project group. However, the way that you interact with the control is very similar in this debugging context is very similar to the method just described regarding components.

When debugging an ActiveX control, you will often be going back and forth between the control code and the client application code at design time. Remember that whenever you have the code module for a custom control open, any instance of that control that you have already implemented in a client form will be inaccessible until you close the code module for the control. Your visual cue that the control instance is inaccessible is a hatching pattern that Visual Basic will place over the instance of the control in the client form, as pictured in Figure 13.12.

F I G U R E 13.12

An inaccessible ActiveX Control instance in a client form

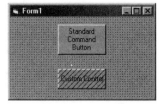

With the exception of these interactive behaviors, the behavior of ActiveX controls is practically identical to that of components, as far as debugging is concerned. Any breakpoints placed inside of an ActiveX control code module will force the code execution to break inside the control, thus allowing you to test the client application and a custom control in the same project group.

Although it is not actually included in the Visual Basic Distributed Applications exam, you should be aware that Microsoft ships a Transact SQL debugging utility that allows you to debug your SQL Server stored procedures from the Visual Basic IDE. This utility installs as a Visual Basic add-in. If you plan to implement a distributed solution using a SQL Server data tier, this utility might be a helpful addition to your debugging toolkit.

Summary

Although logical errors in an application can often be very difficult to locate in an application, the debugging tools that ship with Visual Basic 6 facilitate this process significantly. Using this set of utilities, you should be able to locate and resolve logical errors that interrupt the desired flow of your application.

One of the more important elements of a distributed application is the set of components that implement business rules and data access logic. Since MTS allows these components to be used as single-user objects, you can test these components very easily in the Visual Basic IDE using object groups.

The debug tools available include:

- Break mode and stepping
- The Immediate window
- The Debug object
- Watch expressions
- The Locals window
- The Call Stack window

Each of these tools has specific applications when locating and resolving logic errors in an application. Applying these tools successfully takes a little bit of practice, but it will soon become second nature to a seasoned developer.

Review Questions

1. Which of the following debug tools would you use to locate the specific point that a variable is set to an unexpected value?

   A. Breakpoint

   B. Watch expression

   C. Locals window

   D. Callstack

2. Which of the following could not be used to execute a conditional breakpoint?

   A. A STOP statement executed in a conditional IF block

   B. The Assert method of the Debug object

   C. A watch expression that breaks when an expression evaluates to true

   D. Setting a break in the Locals window

3. You need to monitor the value of a variable called *intReturn* that is private to a general procedure called *ReturnProc* in Form1. Which of the following would be the most efficient context for a watch expression?

   A. Form1, ReturnProc

   B. Form1, All procedures

   C. All modules, ReturnProc

   D. All modules, All procedures

4. You need to monitor the value of a variable called *intReturn* that is publicly declared in a module called *Module1*. The value of this variable is set and manipulated only in a procedure called *ReturnProc* in Form1 and read in other procedures in the application. Which of the following would be the most efficient context for a watch expression?

   A. Form1, ReturnProc

   B. Form1, All procedures

   C. Module1, ReturnProc

   D. Module1, All procedures

5. You need to monitor the value of a variable called *intReturn* that is publicly declared in a module called *Module1*. The value of this variable is set and manipulated in numerous procedures in the application. Which of the following would be the most efficient context for a watch expression?

   A. Form1, All procedures

   B. All Modules, All procedures

   C. Module1, ReturnProc

   D. Module1, All procedures

6. Which of the following debug tools would you use to locate your current position in a series of embedded procedure calls?

   A. Locals window

   B. Immediate window

   C. Callstack

   D. Debug object

7. Which of the following is not a valid watch expression setting?

   A. Watch expression

   B. Break When Value Is True

   C. Break When Expression Changes

   D. Break When Value Changes

8. Which of the following is not a valid stepping option?

   A. Step Around

   B. Step Into

   C. Step Over

   D. Step Out

9. Which of the following tools can be used to change the value of a variable or property during break mode of an application?

A. Watch window

B. Callstack

C. Locals window

D. Debug object

10. Which of the following project types cannot be included in a project group?

A. Standard EXE

B. ActiveX DLL

C. ActiveX Control

D. All of the above project types can be included in a project group

CHAPTER

14

Deploying a
Distributed Application

After you have completed developing your application, the task is not yet complete. The application must still be appropriately compiled, deployed, and maintained. For a distributed application, the deployment process requires extensive planning because of the many components and services that must be installed throughout the network to support the distributed solution.

In this chapter, we will evaluate the deployment and maintenance needs of a distributed application. The chapter begins with a discussion of the Visual Basic compiler and conditional compilation options. We will then discuss deployment media, methodology, and the use of the Visual Studio Package and Deployment Wizard for the deployment of all elements of a distributed application. These include the client applications, MTS components, Web pages, and other elements of a distributed application. We will also evaluate the appropriate configuration of DCOM in a distributed application network. Finally, we will look at the process of deploying application updates for client applications components, Web pages, and data elements.

Using the Visual Basic Compiler

Before an application element can be deployed, you must appropriately compile the element. Compilation is actually performed continually at different phases of the application development cycle. Every time you start an application in the Visual Basic IDE, it must be compiled before it can execute. In addition, the application or component must also be permanently compiled before it can be deployed.

In this section, we will look at the Visual Basic compile process. We will begin with a discussion of the action of the compiler during application design. We will then look at the process permanently compiling both client applications and components. We will complete this discussion by looking at conditional compilation processes in Visual Basic that allow us to perform different compiles depending on the value of the conditional compilation options.

Compiling at Design Time

One of the useful features of the Visual Basic design environment is the ability to compile projects temporarily as you test your applications. When you run a project, the project is actually compiling. You can control how this happens through the compile options located in the Visual Basic Options dialog. To access these options, Select Tools ➢ Options from the Visual Basic menu and select the General tab. Figure 14.1 illustrates this dialog.

FIGURE 14.1

The Visual Basic design environment compile options

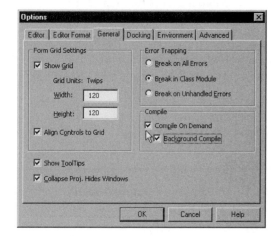

Figure 14.1 illustrates the default status for these settings. By default, Visual Basic performs a Compile On Demand. This means that as you start your project in the Visual Basic design environment, just enough of the project is compiled to get the application started. As you begin to use other features of your applications, they will also be compiled. With the Background Compile option also set, the Visual Basic compiler can also compile other portions of the application during idle time. These options allow the testing environment to be as responsive as possible.

This does not mean, however, that Compile On Demand can't also create some problems. When an application is compiled, some compile errors may be revealed. These are errors that may not be discovered until the application is physically compiled into a file (EXE, DLL, etc.). When you use Compile On Demand, these errors may not be revealed until later in the development process, perhaps even as late as the point of the actual file compilation.

To solve this problem, after you get to a testing point of your application, turn off the Compile On Demand option. This will force the entire application to compile when you run it within the Visual Basic IDE, thus revealing any compile errors whenever the application is run, rather than only when you access those offending features of the application.

Another solution to this approach is to start the application with a full compile rather than allowing a compile on demand. To access this feature when you run your project, select Run ➤ Start With Full Compile from the Visual Basic menu. This will force the entire project to compile and reveal the compile errors that may exist.

A final solution is to actually create the compiled file frequently throughout the development cycle of the application. Creating the EXE or DLL repeatedly throughout the application development cycle can often reveal important issues and errors that you should monitor throughout the application development process.

Compiling Project Files

Microsoft ✓ ***Exam Objective***   **Given a scenario, select the appropriate compiler options.**

When compiling project files, there are some choices that you will have to make concerning how you want the compile to take place. Visual Basic supports two general file formats. A project can either be compiled to Native Code or P-Code. Each format has its advantages and disadvantages.

Visual Basic P-Code (or *pseudo code*) is an intermediate step between a project text file and a native instruction set. When P-Code is processed, Visual Basic will perform a Compile On Demand, converting the P-Code instructions to a native set of instructions that can be executed by the processor. For the application to perform its work, calls must be made to the Visual Basic run-time library, provided in the file MSVBVM60.DLL (which must be shipped with every Visual Basic application). The most significant advantage of P-Code is that it tends to be smaller than a native code compile, thus it creates a smaller compiled file.

Native Code compiles skip the P-Code step by compiling an application directly to the native CPU instructions. Native compiles give the developer more optimization and debugging options than P-Code compiles and, in that regard, are often preferred. In addition to these advantages, since the native compile is made directly according to CPU instructions, it can perform much more quickly in processor-intensive situations such as extensive mathematical calculations.

Native code compiles still require the Visual Basic runtime library in order to function. You must ship the file MSVBVM60.DLL with every Visual Basic application, regardless of the compile approach used. The only occasion when you would not ship this file is when you can verify that the library is already installed and registered on every target machine.

To access the compiler options, select Project ➤ *Projectname* Properties from the Visual Basic menu. Clicking the Compile tab on the dialog presents the options pictured in Figure 14.2. These options control the type of compile as well as the options associated with a native compile.

F I G U R E 14.2

Project Compile
Options dialog

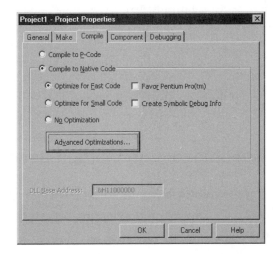

As you will see from Figure 14.2, there are numerous options available for native code compilation. Some options are available as Advanced Options by clicking the Advanced Options command button on the dialog. These should be used with care as they can have a destabilizing affect on the application. Table 14.1 elaborates on the standard options.

T A B L E 14.1 Native Compile Options	Option	Function
	Optimize for Fast Code	Optimizes for fast execution time.
	Optimize for Small Code	Optimizes for the smallest possible executable.
	No Optimization	Turns off all optimizations. Results in larger, slower executable.
	Favor Pentium Pro	Optimizes for Pentium Pro architecture. Will adversely affect performance on non-Pentium Pro machines.
	Create Symbolic Debug Info	Creates .pdb file that can be debugged with Visual C++ 5 or later.

Creating the Compiled File

After ensuring that the compiler options are set correctly, compile the project file. For standard client applications, this file will be an EXE, while for components, this can be either an EXE or a DLL. Remember that for an MTS implemented component, you must package the component as a DLL.

To create the compiled file, select File ➤ Make *Projectname* {EXE | DLL} from the Visual Basic menu. This will compile the project, report any detected compile errors, and create the EXE or DLL in the target location.

Using Conditional Compilation Constants

Microsoft ✓ ***Exam*** ***Objective***   **Control an application by using conditional compilation.**

There may be times when you want a single source file to compile differently, depending on variables external to the application. For example, assume that you are targeting a single application to two different locales. Rather than developing and maintaining multiple projects and source code, you want to create and maintain a single set of source files. This will make the updating of an application significantly easier than using multiple source files.

One of the approaches that you can take to this situation is to use conditional compilation. Assume that you wanted to compile two versions of the application, one using U.S. English and another using Latin American Spanish. In your code, you can declare conditional compilation constants and use these constants to determine which blocks of code compile into your application.

To implement this approach, you will use the Conditional Compilation Block statements provided by Visual Basic. These variations of the traditional If … Else structure all begin with a pound sign (#). Assuming, therefore, that you wanted to support these two languages, you can use a Conditional Compilation Block as shown in the following example.

```
#If conUSEng Then
    MsgBox "Good Morning"
#Else
    MsgBox "Buenos Días"
#End If
```

In this example, if the conditional compilation constant evaluates to true, the U.S. English version of the message box is used. Otherwise the Spanish version compiles into the code.

To specify an appropriate value for the conditional compilation constant, place the constant in the Conditional Compilation Arguments text box in the Project Properties dialog. To activate this dialog, select Project ➤ *Project-name* Properties from the Visual Basic menu and select the Make tab. This dialog is illustrated in Figure 14.3.

If you used more than one Conditional Compilation argument in your application, place them all in the dialog as one string. Simply separate each constant/value pair with a colon(:). Also note that the Visual Basic intrinsic constant True evaluates to –1, which is why that value is used in this example.

F I G U R E   14.3

A declared Conditional
Compilation argument

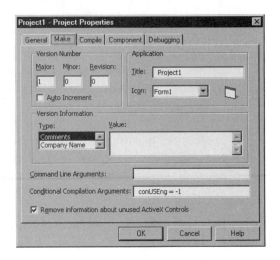

Although there are other ways to accomplish this task, the conditional compilation approach does offer two distinct advantages. First, it creates a smaller executable because only needed code is compiled in the application. Second, it allows you to control the compilation from a location outside of the source code. This means that you won't need to make any modifications to the source code to compile the application under a different set of instructions.

Exercise 14.1 walks you through the process of creating a conditional compile. In this exercise, you will use a Conditional Compilation Block in your code and set a Conditional Compilation argument in the Project Properties dialog. Changing the value of the argument will change the way that the code executes.

EXERCISE 14.1

Using Conditional Compile

1. Start Visual Basic. When prompted for a project type, select Standard EXE and click OK. Add a command button to the form. Name the button cmdHello. Clear the caption property so that the button has no caption.

2. Double-click the form to open the Form Load event in the code window. If a constant called *conUSEng* evaluates to true, write code that uses a Conditional Compilation Block to set the button's caption to Hello. If not, then set the caption to Hola for a Spanish language distribution. The following code provides an example.

```
#If conUSEng Then
    cmdHello.Caption = "Hello"
#Else
    cmdHello.Caption = "Hola"
#End If
```

3. Navigate to the click event of the cmdHello command button. Using a similar approach, create a Conditional Compilation Block that creates a message box that says **Good Morning** when the U.S. English constant is used; otherwise, have the message box respond read **Buenos Días**. Use the following code as an example.

```
#If conUSEng Then
    MsgBox "Good Morning"
#Else
    MsgBox "Buenos Días"
#End If
```

4. Open the Project Properties by selecting Project ➤ Project1 Properties from the Visual Basic menu. Click the Make tab on the dialog. In the Conditional Compilation Arguments text box, type **conUSEng = -1**.

5. Click OK to close the dialog and run the application. The caption of the command button should be the English version. Click the button to raise the message box. The message box should also be displayed in English.

6. Stop the application and open the Project1 Properties window again. Change the value of the conUSEng constant to 0 (zero). Run the application again. This time, all of the Spanish strings should be displayed.

7. End the application and close the project. Save it if you wish.

Compiling from the Command Line

You do not have to compile an application from the Visual Basic IDE. You can also use a command line to perform the compile. The command line uses the existing settings in the Make tab of the project properties. You can also provide additional arguments through the use of command line switches.

To perform a command line compile, simply navigate to the folder where Visual Basic is installed and use the VB6.exe command with the switches in Table 14.2. These switches give you additional flexibility for the treatment of error condition and provisions for Command Line arguments and Conditional Compilation arguments.

You can substitute a *groupname* for a *projectname* in any of the following switches that accept a *Projectname* argument.

T A B L E 14.2 Command Line Compile Switches	**Switch**	**Use**
	{/m | /make} *projectname*	Indicates the location of the project file to be compiled.
	{/r | /run} *projectname*	Compiles the project and runs it.
	/runexit	Compiles and runs the project. Visual Basic exits when returned to design mode.
	/out *filename*	When using /make or /runexit, indicates an error file location where all compile errors will be written.
	/outdir *path*	Indicates path location of the /out file.
	{/d | /D} *Constant=value*	Indicates Conditional Compilation arguments and their values. Separate multiple constant/value pairs with a colon (:).
	{/c | /cmd} *argument*	Indicates any Command Line argument to be used. Must be the last switch in the command.

Deployment Media and Methods

One of the main questions that must be answered in application deployment is how the application will be delivered to the clients and servers needed to run the application. Part of the issue regarding the physical medium used to install the application is the size of the application. If an application is large, many forms of media can be eliminated because using them to copy large volumes of data is not convenient. Even though the network may seem like a useful way to distribute large applications, network bandwidth limitations or network connection reliability may prevent you from relying on the network for deployment. In short, there is no easy answer to the question of how to deploy an application. The advantages and disadvantages of each type of deployment medium are discussed in the following sections.

Floppy Disk Deployment

Microsoft ✓ *Exam* *Objective*

Plan and implement floppy disk-based deployment or compact disc-based deployment for a distributed application.

For many years, commercial software was distributed on floppy disks. In prior years, PC-based programs were very small because of the limitations of DOS programs and the size of hard drives. Recently, floppy disks have been used less as the size of programs has grown, as hard drive capacity has increased, and as new media (such as CD-ROMs) have developed to store larger programs. However, using floppy disks to distribute software still has many advantages.

The application's size is an obvious limitation when floppy disks are used to distribute applications. Because a single high-density floppy can hold only 1.44MB of data, using floppy disks to distribute applications larger than 5–10 MB is not very practical. You certainly can spread application files across multiple disks, but asking installers to swap out disk after disk during the installation process is not reasonable.

You can, however, overcome the size limitations of recordable media. Disk-based storage solutions, such as Iomega Jaz drives and ZIP drives, allow much larger files (up to 2GB for Jaz drives) to be written to one disk. However, these disks cannot be used in standard floppy drives, and the installer must have a ZIP drive or a Jaz drive to read these disks. You can obtain external versions of these drives to allow one drive to be used on multiple machines; however, this method can become very impractical if you are deploying an application to many machines.

One advantage to using a floppy disk to distribute applications is that the hardware needed to read the medium is available on virtually every PC. You don't need to worry about the hardware's compatibility or availability. Also, floppy disks are easily duplicated. Swapping floppy disks in and out of a PC as you duplicate them may seem cumbersome, but duplicators that hold a stack of disks and repeatedly duplicate the same disks are available to make the task less tedious.

Floppy disk size can limit the solutions you use to deploy an application. For many installations, the easiest way to deploy an application is to create a self-extracting executable that runs the installation process. The maximum size of the floppy disk limits the size of an executable that you can fit on a single floppy. This may force you to break the application into multiple files, which must be installed through an installation program that guides the installer through the process of swapping disks. Creating this type of installation program may involve more work than storing all the files on one disk or CD-ROM.

Installation programs should automate the process as much as possible. CD-ROMs work well because you can place AutoRun files on them that will start the install when inserted on a Windows 95/98 or Windows NT machine. If the process is automated, it will run the complete installation without user intervention. You can also configure the BIOS to boot from the CD so that the installation begins at boot time.

Floppy disks can be configured to start a process at boot time. The standard AUTOEXEC.BAT and CONFIG.SYS files can contain commands to begin the installation and guide the user through the installation process, even through disk changes. However, this method doesn't work if the application must work with the operating system to write configuration settings to the Registry or to modify other system settings. The operating system on a bootable disk would be on the disk, so the operating system on the hard drive would not execute if you used this method to install an application. Windows 95/98 and Windows NT don't support the concept of an

AutoPlay floppy disk, so you really can't use a floppy disk to automatically start an installation once the operating system has booted. The installer must execute a command on the floppy disk to start the installation. Even though the rest of the installation can be automated (except for disk changes), the floppy disk will not meet your needs if you want a completely automated installation.

Another benefit to using floppy disks to deploy an application is portability. Once an application is copied to disks, it can be sent to other installations without requiring network or Internet connections. Because the files used to install the application never cross the network, you don't have to worry about network bandwidth limitations or the reliability of network connections. And once the disks are made, they are available as a backup for the application, even if the network goes down or the file server hosting the application is not available.

However, the very mechanism used to distribute applications via disks is one of its weaknesses. Should updates or corrections be needed for an application, new disks must be created, duplicated, and distributed. The installation process must then be completed again, with floppy-based installations completed at each computer. The ease of performing maintenance and updates should also be considered in choosing floppy disks (or other removable disks) as the physical medium for an application deployment.

When networks were not as widespread as they are today, data and applications were typically propagated through some sort of portable medium, such as a floppy disk. Networks were designed to centrally locate resources and make them easily accessible to everyone. In most cases, using a network is the preferred alternative because you don't have to worry about duplicating and distributing the software. However, you must still plan the installation on the network in order to minimize the impact on network traffic.

CD-ROM Deployment

Distributing applications with CD-ROMs has many of the same benefits and limitations as using floppy disks, but the size limitations aren't as severe because of the CD-ROM's greater capacity. Most commercial software is currently released on CD-ROM. Even very large applications can fit on one or two CD-ROMs, considerably reducing the amount of media that must be duplicated. Because so many programs are distributed with this medium, installers and users should already be accustomed to this form of distribution.

A CD-ROM can contain approximately 600MB of data. After file compression, one CD-ROM should be able to hold more than 1GB of original data. Using DVD-ROM alternatives, you can store many gigabytes of data on a single disk, although this standard has not yet achieved widespread adoption. In most cases, you should be able to fit your application on a single CD-ROM.

As with floppy disks, the CD-ROM drive needed to read this medium is available on most PCs. Although CD-ROM drives aren't found on older PCs, they can be added quite easily. Duplicating an application is easy with a CD-ROM burner; however, this process isn't very fast for large volumes of data. The inexpensive CD-ROM burners that are available for home and business use aren't designed for fast duplication of a high volume of disks. If you only need to burn a few copies of a CD-ROM, these recording devices may be suitable. If you need to create many copies of the CD-ROM, you should purchase a high-volume duplicating device, which is considerably more expensive than a standard CD-ROM burner.

CD-ROMs can be used to completely automate an installation. Windows 95/98 and Windows NT both support AutoPlay CD-ROMs. You can make the CD-ROM initiate the installation process as soon as the user inserts the CD-ROM into the drive. You can also add bootable information to the CD-ROM so that the user can start the installation upon booting up the computer.

Like a floppy disk, a CD-ROM distributed application is very portable. You can send CD-ROMs to remote sites that don't have a connection to the main network. Because your application will probably fit on one CD-ROM, there shouldn't be too much to send. However, you may need to create multiple copies of the installation CD-ROM, one for each user or installer. If you must rely on specialized installers to deploy the application, it can be a slow process for these installers to install the application one computer at a time.

If you need to update or modify an application, you must again create and duplicate new CD-ROMs and send these to each of the locations using the applications. The installers must then go to each computer and install the upgrades or patches. In many environments, such as in large installations, the time lag in deploying applications in this manner is not acceptable.

Burning large numbers of CD-ROMs can be a very slow process. For large distributions, you can contract a software duplication company to burn the CD-ROMs—just make sure you allow enough time for the duplication.

Network Deployment

Microsoft ✓ *Exam* *Objective*

Plan and implement a network-based deployment for a distributed application.

Deploying applications over a network bypasses many of the problems inherent in removable media (disks and CD-ROMs) deployment. Size is an issue with network deployment, and bandwidth, speed, and reliability of the network connections must all be considered when designing this type of deployment.

A network deployment can take one of two forms. The first method is to simply use the network as a method to deliver the application files to the client. The application files reside on a file server, and when the client initiates the installation, the files are downloaded and installed to the client. The second method is to create a network installation where only a few files are copied to the client. Each time the client executes the application, the necessary application files are downloaded to the client's RAM. Very few files are written to the client, so the initial network traffic isn't much of an issue. However, the network is utilized each time the client executes the application, which can put a strain on network bandwidth.

A number of issues must be considered if network deployment is to work effectively. First, you must make sure the network will support the traffic needed to distribute the application files to the clients. If the installation will be initiated by the users, either through manually starting the application or through automated means (such as through a logon script), you must account for network traffic during busy periods and working hours. If deployment can be scheduled for off-peak hours (by using installers or automated processes such as Systems Management Server), then bandwidth won't be as much of a consideration.

When planning for bandwidth, you must account for WAN links between different sites on the network. If all of the clients receiving the application reside on a LAN, then the speed of the network connection isn't much of an issue. But if you have sites separated by slower WAN links, you have much less bandwidth to play with. You may have to deploy to those sites through removable media or create a staging server at those sites where the application can be downloaded once to the staging server and then installed by the clients on their own LAN from the staging server.

The bandwidth used to deploy the application will vary greatly depending on the type of network deployment you choose. If you plan to install the application on the client hard drive, the network will be used only once for each installation. You should be able to schedule this deployment during off-peak hours, so you can limit the impact on the network. If you decide to create a network installation, then bandwidth will be used each time the client executes the application.

Because the application will normally be used during peak hours, network traffic can increase significantly. A single client can access the application several times during one day, dramatically increasing the traffic needed to support a network application over a client-based application. You must also make sure there are an adequate number of servers to provide the application should one of the servers or network links go down. Because the clients are relying on network servers to provide the application, that application must be available when the clients execute it or the functionality of the application will be severely compromised.

Solving the bandwidth problems due to a network deployment includes scheduling the installation for off-peak hours, putting a distribution server on each subnet, and phasing in the deployment.

In spite of the traffic generated by deploying a network-based application, this deployment method has a number of benefits. Because the files are stored on centralized servers and fewer copies must be modified, updating or patching applications is easier. Rollouts are also much quicker using this method. You don't have to install the application on as many machines (just the network servers), and because you can use the network to transfer the files to the servers, you don't have to make duplicates and send them to the installers.

The traffic generated by networked applications can also be minimized. You can create more application servers and spread the load among them. When creating these servers, you should usually place them on the segment where the clients are located. Then requests for the application can be handled on the local segment without passing any network traffic on through the routers to other segments of the network. Based on consultation with the network administrator, you must decide whether the benefits of a network-based application outweigh the work (and possible additional hardware) necessary to reduce the impact on the network by deploying this application.

You must also work with the network administrator to plan the placement of files for a client-based installation. Even though the files will travel over the network once before they are written to the client hard drive, you must still plan for servers to contain these files that are readily available to clients. Again, you can place files on servers that are on the same segment as the client. Updating installations using this method is not as easy as installing a copy of the application on every client hard drive. However, you can use the same method to deploy upgrades (that is, place the files on a server and have the clients initiate the upgrade process).

This upgrade is still easier than using removable media. The source files for the application reside on only a few servers, so you simply have to upgrade the files on those servers. You must then ensure that the upgrades are made on all the client computers in an efficient manner so that all the copies of the application are on the same version. Using a network installation product like SMS can help automate the installation and upgrade process and ease the task of tracking the clients as they are upgraded.

NOTE

Although it is very unlikely that you will encounter any exam questions relating to the Systems Management Server and its deployment functionality, you should be aware that the Microsoft SMS tool, part of the Microsoft BackOffice suite of products, can aid you significantly in a network deployment model. Using SMS, you can schedule installation and upgrade jobs throughout the network.

Internet Deployment

Microsoft ✓ *Exam* *Objective*

Plan and implement a Web-based deployment for a distributed application.

Deploying traditional Win32 applications over the Internet is similar to deploying them over the network. Basically, the Web server fulfills the function of the network file server. When a client connects to the Web server and selects the appropriate link, the application files are downloaded and installed on the client. Using a Web server for network-based applications is not very feasible. The Internet doesn't provide the high-speed reliable links needed to download an application to the client each time it is executed.

Although Internet files are typically located on a single Web server, you may have to plan for some redundancy in deploying applications over the Internet. You must plan for excessive traffic on the Web server that is providing the application files. If the server becomes overwhelmed with client access, the application may not deploy in a timely manner. If you depend on users to initiate the installation, they may quit after trying unsuccessfully to connect to the Web server.

Not only do you need to be concerned about availability and reliability, you must also plan for security. You may not want unauthorized users to access an application. If you use the Internet to deploy applications, everyone on the Web is a potential unauthorized user. If you invoke a security method like NT Challenge/Response, you must also account for the slower Web server connection because the client must be verified for each accessed Web page.

You can use Microsoft Proxy Server or some other firewall server to protect the files and your other network servers. Another alternative is to use an Internet Service Provider (ISP) to provide the Web server that will host the application. This would not expose your network to any outside access (although you would need to verify that the security methods employed by the ISP were adequate to protect your application).

If you use the Internet to deploy an application, you must also create the necessary Web pages to drive the installation. These Web pages may simply call a script you have already created to install the application. However, you must make sure that all of the files are in a path on the Web server that can be located by the clients and easily downloaded. Using the Internet is probably the most useful when installing applications at remote sites that don't have a connection with the rest of the network. But because of security concerns and Internet reliability, you can choose to deploy applications to those sites using removable media.

Internet Deployment for Web-Based Applications

With regard to Web-based applications, the deployment process is conceptually very different. Your concern is not deploying a Win32 executable to many individual desktops, but providing a set of HTML pages, Active Server Pages, and other supporting elements to the Web server. Unlike a Win32 application deployment process, the clients do not need to run any type of setup utility to install the application to the local machines. Only a browser is needed for the user to interact with the application.

There are many mechanisms that you can use to copy Web-application elements to your Web server for deployment. These include the Visual Basic Package and Deployment Wizard, publishing your Web using the Microsoft Front Page server extensions on the Web server, and even traditional FTP methods. The use of the Package and Deployment Wizard will be discussed in greater detail in the next section.

Deploying Updates

Microsoft ✓ *Exam* *Objective*	**Deploy application updates for distributed applications.**

Deploying application updates is similar to deploying full applications and brings up the same concerns as standard application deployment. However, one of the primary goals of the distributed architecture is to reduce the overhead involved in deploying updates to an application.

Remember that if a distributed application is correctly planned and developed, the most volatile elements of the application will be located in components or scripts that are very easily modified. In our present business environment, it is critical that an application remains as adaptive as possible to a changing business climate and changing needs. By designing an application to host its most volatile elements in centralized locations, you increase the application's ability to adapt to the changing environment. You might call this technological evolution: Only those applications able to adapt quickly and successfully will survive as others become obsolete.

One of the greatest strengths of COM is its *versioning*. Recall from our earlier discussion of COM that all interfaces are considered immutable. We cannot add, delete, or modify these interfaces in anyway without re-versioning the component. However, by adding interfaces to an existing component, new features can be supported without destroying the compatibility for older applications. Of course, you can always upgrade the internal workings of a component. As long as you do not modify the public interfaces, there should be no compatibility issues.

The data tie follows the same general rules. By updating the stored procedures that make up the data-processing tier, you can upgrade an application quickly and easily without requiring a full redeployment. However, as with components, it is very important that you do not modify any of the existing parameters—either with regard to their expected data types, orders, or other requirements.

Using the Package and Deployment Wizard

Microsoft ✓ ***Exam Objective***

Use the Package and Deployment Wizard to create a setup program that installs a distributed application, registers the COM components, and allows for uninstall.

The Visual Basic Package and Deployment Wizard is an upgraded tool to replace the old Visual Basic Setup utility. The Package and Deployment Wizard allows the developer to create custom setup scripts, creating `.cab` files and a custom setup utility. It can also deploy these setup packages to a floppy disk or other removable media, a network deployment location, or a Web server for a Web-based deployment.

In this section, we will look at the Package and Deployment Wizard as a utility for creating deployment packages. These packages allow the developer to install client applications, client components, and even distributed components. We will first look at the process of managing a simple setup package. Then we will look at the deployment options, including the deployment of distributed components and Web-application elements.

Creating a Setup Program

After the development of your project is complete and the application and/ or components have been compiled, it is time to package and deploy the application. Packaging and deployment can be aided significantly with the Visual Basic Package and Deployment Wizard. In this section, we will look at the process of creating a simple application package. This package will contain a setup utility along with the .cab files that contain the application elements. By executing the setup program that results, all installation requirements will be fulfilled, including installing and registering of all COM components used in the application.

To start the Package and Deployment Wizard, from the Windows desktop, click Start ➢ Programs ➢ Microsoft Visual Studio 6.0 ➢ Microsoft Visual Studio 6.0 Tools ➢ Package & Deployment Wizard. The first form of the wizard, pictured in Figure 14.4, allows the user to select the Visual Basic project to be packaged or deployed. This form also allows a selection of either the packaging or deployment functionality of the wizard. To create a setup package, enter the location of the Visual Basic project file in the Select Project text box and click the Package button.

FIGURE 14.4

The initial screen of the Package and Deployment Wizard

If you have already built a setup package for a particular project file in the past, you will see an additional screen at this point that allows you to select the previously created package script for modification. If you want to start from the beginning again, select None from the Packaging script list box.

After clicking the Package button, you will see a form that allows you to select the type of package that you want to create. This form is pictured in Figure 14.5. Your options will include a Standard Setup Package and a Dependency File. Use the Standard Setup Package option to create a setup program will all supporting .cab files. If you only need to generate a list of the files that are dependency requirements of the Visual Basic project, then select Dependency File. A setup program with .cab files will not be generated.

FIGURE 14.5

Selecting the type of package

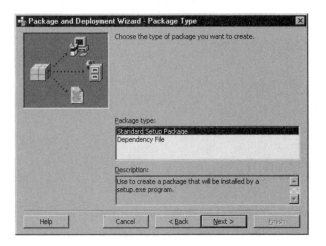

After clicking the Next button, select a location for the setup package files. This can either be located on a local drive or on a visible network location. To point to a network location, click the Network button in the Package Folder dialog illustrated in Figure 14.6. You can also create a new folder at this point by clicking the New Folder button on the dialog. The wizard will create a folder called Package under the location that you select. The package files will be written to this location.

WARNING   The location that you indicate here should be the working folder for maintaining the setup program. This should not be the location from which the deployment will be accessed. You will use the Deployment functionality later to copy the necessary files to a network or other location for deployment to target machines.

FIGURE 14.6

Selecting a file location for the package

NOTE   After you click the Next button, you may be presented with a dialog that warns you of files for which dependency information cannot be located. This is not an error message, only a warning. If you have referenced any COM components in your application, the wizard will not be able to identify any files upon which the components depend. You will have to include these manually.

The next form of the wizard reports the files that will be included in the setup package. In this list you will see your project executable as well as any other files upon which the executable depends. If you have any other files that you need to ship with the application, such as graphics, COM components, .dll files or any other file dependencies that the wizard was not able to detect, add them to the file list at this time. To do this, click the Add button in the Included Files dialog pictured in Figure 14.7. This will open a browser window you can use to navigate to the desired files.

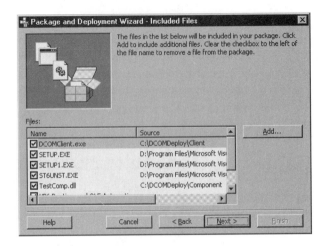

The next screen of the wizard allows you to specify how the .cab files are to be broken up for deployment. If you intend to deploy the application via a network or on a single CD-ROM, you will most likely need to select the option for a single .cab file. However, if you choose to deploy on floppies or expect that the total cab size will exceed the storage capacity of your target deployment media, you will need to break this up into multiple .cab files.

Figure 14.8 illustrates the Cab Options dialog. Note that the Cab Size list box is a drop-down list, not a combo box. This means that you must select the desired cab size from the options listed. You cannot specify your own custom cab size in this form.

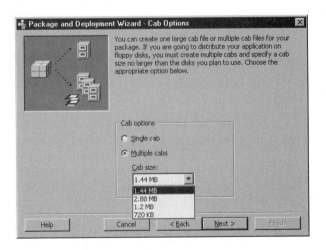

The next form of the wizard allows you to specify the title of the application that will be displayed in the setup program dialogs. Figure 14.9 illustrates this configuration dialog, and Figure 14.10 illustrates the fist screen of an actual installation with the title application property that was configured in Figure 14.9.

FIGURE 14.9

The Installation Title dialog

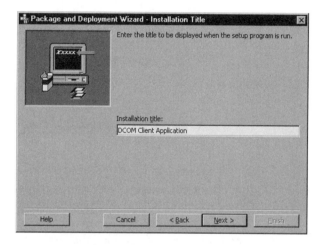

FIGURE 14.10

A running setup using the previously configured installation title

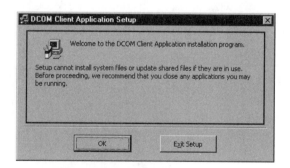

The next form of the wizard specifies the location and organization of the Windows Start Menu shortcuts for this application. By default, a single shortcut is provided in a single program group. This shortcut points to the installed location of the application executable. To add another group or shortcut to the menu structure, click the New Group and New Item buttons located in the Start Menu Items dialog pictured in Figure 14.11. You can also change the attributes of any element in the menu structure by selecting that element in the tree view on the left of the dialog and clicking the Properties button on the right.

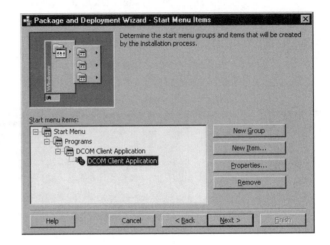

Often, some of the components of an application will be shared across multiple applications. These shared items can be marked as such so that when you uninstall an application, the user will be prompted before shared items are removed. This is a safety feature that prevents the removal of one application from destroying the installation of another.

Figure 14.12 illustrates the Shared Files dialog, the next form in the wizard. Using this dialog, check the boxes to identify any components in your application that should be treated as shared items.

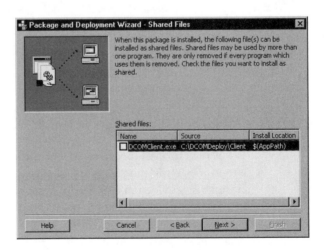

When Windows applications install, files are usually copied to many different locations. The setup program copies some files to the newly created application folder, but other files may be copied to alternate locations such as the Windows, System, and Common Files folders. The Install Locations Dialog, pictured in Figure 14.13, allows you to target individual application components to an installation location of your choice.

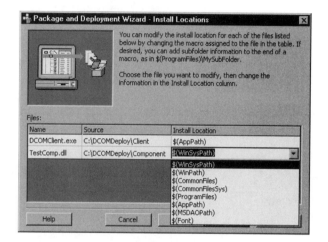

To install to a custom location, type the location in the Install Location column of the dialog grid. For example, if you wanted to install a set of graphics files into a Graphics folder located under the application folder, modify the Install Location value for those files to read $(AppPath)/ Graphics.

The last form in the wizard, pictured in Figure 14.14, allows you to save these setup settings for future use under the name specified in the text box. When you run the wizard for a Visual Basic project file for which you have previously created a setup script, you will be prompted to select the name of a setup script from the drop-down list, pictured in Figure 14.15.

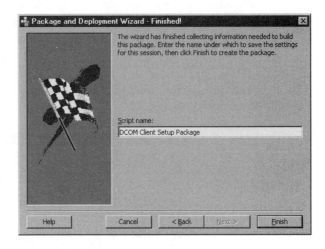

Final wizard
dialog

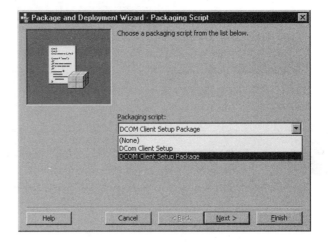

F I G U R E   14.15

Selecting a previously
saved setup script

Uninstallation

The Microsoft Windows 95/98 and Windows NT logo program requires that
all applications installed on a Windows operating system be able to be uninstalled if necessary. Not only is it necessary for your application to carry the
logo, it is also a feature that users expect. Fortunately, the Visual Basic Package
and Deployment Wizard automatically satisfies this requirement for you.

Applications are uninstalled through the Add/Remove Programs applet in the Windows control panel. By opening this applet, you can select the application that you want to uninstall from the list and walk through the dialogs to perform the operation. This will remove the installation files and directory as well as the Start Menu shortcuts that reference these items.

If you marked some of the application elements as shared elements, during the uninstallation process you will be prompted to indicate your preference for removing these files. If other applications other than the one that you are uninstalling depend on this shared file, you should not remove it.

Component Setup

If you are creating a setup program designed to install a component to a server machine or a client application that references a component packaged as an out-of-process server (EXE), you may be asked whether the application or component must support DCOM. DCOM, or the Distributed Component Object Model, is the mechanism used to allow clients and components to communicate over networks. Using DCOM, a client is able to access a component across a network transparently. The application calls the component no differently than if the component is local.

Additionally, DCOM provides support for component security. The network administrator can configure access to the component that allows all clients to create the Remote object, or controls the access based on an Access Control List (ACL), which is a list of Windows NT accounts that are allowed to access a particular resource. You can also assign an identity to a component, allowing the component to act under the context of a single Windows NT account.

If the client application and the component will execute on two different computers, you will need to ship some supporting DCOM files with the client or component. These include the DCOM security providers, the automation manager utility, and other elements required to implement DCOM in your solution.

If you are deploying components under Microsoft Transaction Server, DCOM will be used to allow the client application to access the MTS component.

Deploying a Setup Package

Any existing setup package can be deployed using the deployment functionality of the wizard. This portion of the wizard copies the setup package to a network location, Web folder, or if the setup is broken into multiple `.cab` files, a set of floppy disks for a floppy-based deployment. Users can then access the setup package at its deployed location to perform the installation. The figures that follow illustrate the deployment forms of the wizard. The process starts with the initial form pictured earlier in Figure 14.4. To access the deployment functionality of the wizard, click the Deploy button.

The initial screen of the deployment process allows you to select a setup package for deployment. All of the setup packages that you have created using the wizard will be listed in the drop-down list of the dialog pictured in Figure 14.16. You must create the setup package before you use the deployment portion of the wizard.

FIGURE 14.16

Selecting a setup package to deploy

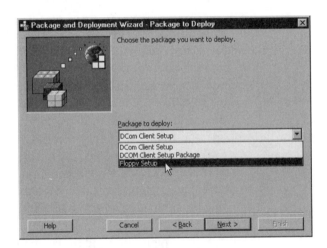

The next screen of the deployment process allows you to select a form of deployment. This form, pictured in Figure 14.17, offers three choices. You can either perform a floppy-based, network-based, or Web-based deployment. The other forms in the wizard will depend on the selection made here.

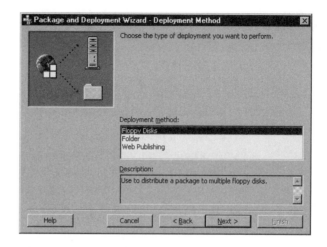

Floppy-Based Deployment

If you select the option for deployment on floppy disks, you must provide the
location of the desired floppy drive. The form illustrated in Figure 14.18 will
offer you a choice of all of the write-enabled and removable media options
available on the local machine. If you have Iomega ZIP or JAZ drives,
SyQuest drives or other large capacity removable media options, you will see
them in the drop-down list.

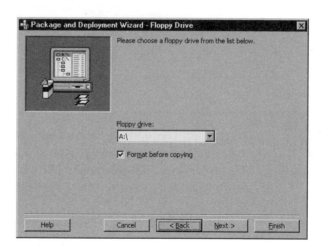

Unless you can verify that the target media is formatted appropriately, select the Format before copying check box in the dialog. This will ensure a clean copy.

Network-Based Deployment

In the case of a network deployment strategy, the Package and Deployment Wizard will copy the setup package to a network location of your choice. This dialog, pictured in Figure 14.19, allows you to select a local drive, mapped network drive, or shared network location. After navigating to the desired location, create a new folder directly from this screen.

FIGURE 14.19

Selecting a network deployment location

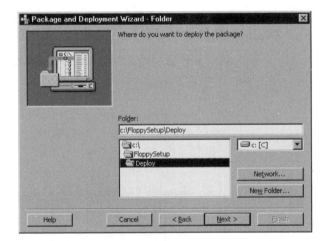

When using a network deployment approach, you must have write access to the folder that will act as the target for the deployment. Also remember that all users installing the application based on this package must have read access to the folder in which the setup package has been deployed.

Web-Based Deployment

In the case of a Web-based deployment, the Package and Deployment Wizard will present options as to which files must be deployed and the location on the Web server that will host the setup package. Figures 14.20 and 14.21 illustrate the Items to Deploy form that will be raised if a Web-based deployment is selected. The first form pictured in Figure 14.20 lists only those setup package elements that you will need to ship to make the setup available from the Web server. The second form pictured in 14.21 allows you to add any other project files needed to complete the installation.

FIGURE 14.20

Selecting the setup package items to deploy

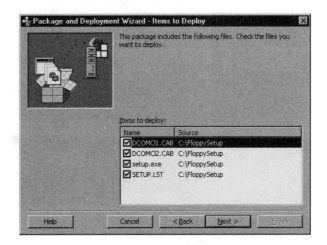

FIGURE 14.21

Selecting additional project files for Web deployment

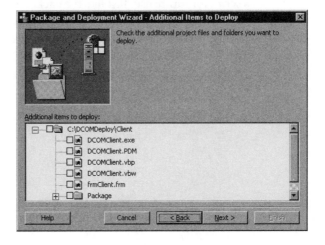

You must also indicate a resource on a Web server to which you will copy your setup package and supporting files. The next form in the Web deployment scenario allows you to specify the URL of the resource to which you want to copy the file. In addition, you can also select the mechanism, HTTP to FTP, that you want to use for the copying process. Select the appropriate copying method from the Web Publishing Protocol list box as pictured in Figure 14.22.

F I G U R E   14.22

Configuring the Web
deployment
properties

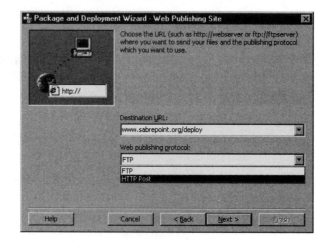

Completing the Deployment

The final form of the wizard allows you to save the deployment settings in a script for future use. Just like the packaging portion of the wizard, to repeat the deployment again in the future, you do not have to repeat all of the deployment settings. Simply select the saved deployment script from the list. This final form, pictured in Figure 14.23, looks very much like the final form for the packaging functionality and is the same for every deployment method previously discussed.

FIGURE 14.23

Saving the deploy-
ment script

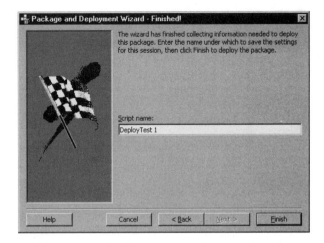

Deploying and Configuring MTS Components and Clients

Microsoft ✓ *Exam Objective*	**Create a package by using the MTS Explorer.** ▪ Use the Package and Deployment Wizard to create a package.

Microsoft ✓ *Exam Objective*	**Configure a client computer to use an MTS component.** ▪ Create packages that install or update MTS components on a client computer.

The word *package* is definitely an overloaded term. Do not get confused by its different uses. An MTS package is a collection of components that work within a single proxy process. The Package and Deployment Wizard creates setup packages that are used for installation and deployment. The MTS Explorer cannot create setup packages and the wizard cannot create MTS packages, but the two utilities can work together to complete the deployment process as described as follows.

One of the challenges of deploying distributed components is configuring all of the client applications to reference the components deployed in a central location. If you choose to deploy your components within the MTS environment, take advantage of the synergy between the Package and Deployment Wizard and the MTS Explorer to simplify the process.

We have already discussed the use of the wizard in creating packages for both the client applications as well as the components. To effectively distribute the components to the MTS server, create a package containing the desired components and deploy that package to the desired MTS server. Running the setup program on the Server installs and registers the components.

Once a component is registered, you can add it easily to an MTS package by importing the component into the MTS package. You can accomplish this by using the MTS menus or drag-and-drop. Once the components have been installed successfully on the server, configure the client computers to access these components.

For additional information and a description of importing components into an MTS package, refer to Chapter 5 of this book.

The MTS Explorer supports a client configuration feature that makes the process of configuring a client workstation to use an MTS component as simple as running an executable. By exporting an MTS package through the MTS Explorer, a client executable is created that configures the client workstation to use the MTS package.

This client application installs proxy stub DLLs that provide type library and interface information about the target package. Modifications that identify the components as remote components managed by MTS on the server computer are made to the registry on the client computer. Running this executable on the client should be sufficient to configure the client workstation to use the MTS components through DCOM.

It is very important that you do not run the client executable created by the MTS package export process on the server machine where the component is installed. Since the executable rewrites the system Registry, running the executable will render the MTS package unusable. If this happens inadvertently, you can fix the problem by deleting and recreating the MTS package.

To export the package and create the executable, right-click the desired package in the MTS Explorer and select Export from the resulting pop-up menu. This will bring up a dialog like the one pictured in Figure 14.24. In this dialog, specify the location of the exported package. The exported package will end with a .pak extension.

FIGURE 14.24

Configuring an MTS package export

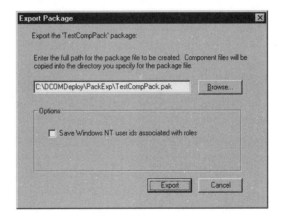

The export process will also create a Clients folder under the export directory. The client executable will have the same name as the package exported, but will end with an .exe extension rather than a .pak extension. Even if you do not intend to import this package to any other locations, you must run the export to create this client executable.

Using the DCOM Configuration Utility

Microsoft ✓ ***Exam*** ***Objective***	**Register a component that implements DCOM.**

Microsoft ✓ ***Exam*** ***Objective***	**Configure DCOM on a client computer and on a server computer.**

Microsoft ✓ ***Exam*** ***Objective***	**Implement load balancing.**

Another way to configure DCOM to access Component objects is to use the DCOM Configuration utility (DCOMCNFG.exe). This utility allows you to configure DCOM on both the client and server computers, including providing all necessary Registry entries for a component that implements DCOM.

The DCOM Configuration utility can be run on both the client and the server involved in the DCOM communication. From the client, you can point the client application to reference an installed component to a location where the component is not locally installed. This will make modifications to the Windows Registry to support these new locators.

On the server side, the DCOM Configuration utility gives you the ability to configure security and component identity. If you want to limit the creation of the remote component to only specific NT accounts, you can do this with the utility. You can also set an identity for the component, allowing the component to assume the security identity of the interactive user or a specific user account that you can configure.

Figure 14.25 illustrates the initial form of the DCOM Configuration utility. To access this utility, select Start ➤ Run from the Windows Desktop menu. In the text box labeled Open, enter the command **DCOMCNFG** and click the OK button. This dialog presents you with a list of Out-of-process COM servers (EXEs) and any COM DLLs that have been imported into MTS packages.

F I G U R E 14.25

The Components list in the DCOM Configuration utility

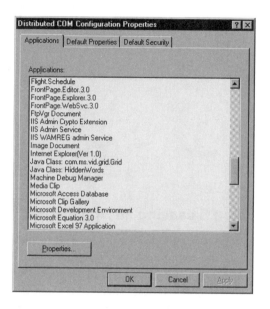

To view or modify the DCOM properties of any of the listed components, simply select the desired component from the list and click the Properties button on the dialog. The resulting dialog begins with a General tab that reports information about the component. Notice in particular the Local Path attribute at the bottom of the dialog. For the component pictured in Figure 14.26, the local handler is listed as `mtx.exe`. This is not a trivial matter because the `mtx.exe` executable is the MTS Executive, the service that manages all proxy processes for MTS packages. When a remote client makes a call to the components deployed under MTS, they are actually calling the MTS Executive, which handles the actual calls to the component in-process.

FIGURE 14.26

DCOM Component
properties

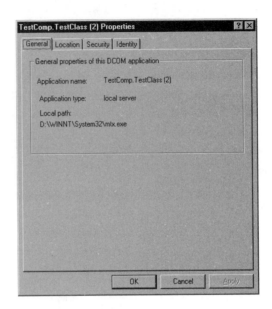

Load Balancing an Application

Clicking the Location tab, you will see the properties that pertain to where the component code is actually run. This tab can be used to aid in the load balancing of a distributed application. Just because you deploy your clients remotely doesn't mean that there won't be bottlenecks. DCOM can help.

MTS does not support any type of load-balancing functionality directly. To provide load balancing in your application, you must provide it through the application code or configuration. The most common approaches to load balancing in distributed Windows applications are:

- Clustering NT Enterprise servers

- Static load balancing through configurations and deployment

- Dynamic load balancing through code

Clustering   Using Windows NT Enterprise, two servers can be clustered together sharing a common set of drives. This clustering provides two main advantages. First, it provides increased scalability and load balancing by utilizing a pool of two servers to respond to client requests for components or database resources. NT clusters appear to the application as a single server and the traffic is balanced between them, significantly improving the scalability of the application.

The other advantage of the clustering solution is fail-over support. When an NT cluster is created, a signal (or "heartbeat") is passed between the two servers, enabling each server to detect if the other ever stops operating. In this case, all activity is transferred to the remaining server. While this will have a negative impact on scalability, the fail-over support allows the application to continue rather than crashing when a server on the network fails. SQL Server Enterprise Edition is cluster aware and gives you the ability to create a data tier with fail-over redundancy.

Static Load Balancing   Static load balancing is a commonly used practice in Windows-based distributed applications today. The concept is a simple one: the more servers actively working in an application, the better performance will be. One way to approach static load balancing is through the configuration of COM components. In the Location tab of the component properties window of the DCOM Configuration utility (pictured in Figure 14.27), you are presented with many options as to where the component will actually run. Although all of the client workstations may point to a single server to execute all components, configuring the component to execute at another location frees up some of the resources on the DCOM server machine.

FIGURE 14.27

Configuring execution locations in DCOM

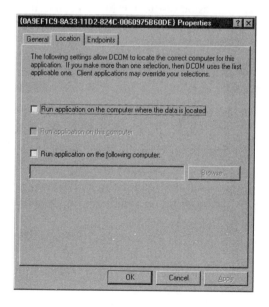

Another approach is to simply deploy components in multiple locations. This can have some advantages because it reduces the overhead associated with responding to user requests by allowing the users to contact the target server directly. This approach is quite simple to implement. You can have multiple component servers on the network, each responding to requests directed to them. Clients would be configured to access different components on different servers, rather than expecting a single server to handle all of the object requests.

No matter which method you choose, these solutions are merely static solutions. There is not a dynamic process sending creation requests to other servers only when reaching a specific threshold. This means that in order to employ static-load balancing techniques, you must be intimately familiar with the processing of your application. You must know the frequency of calls to specific components and the intensity of the server activity generated by those calls. Only then can you begin to compute the optimal allocation of resources throughout your network.

Dynamic Load Balancing   Since there are no automated approaches to dynamic load balancing, you must create these yourself. This means writing code in your client applications to distribute calls to components located in multiple locations or writing resource handlers in your components to allow dynamically allocated component instantiations as needed. Any serious discussion of the development of dynamic load balancing is beyond the scope of both this book and the exam.

Summary

Deploying the distributed application is one of the most critical phases of the application development cycle. A successful deployment requires extensive planning and a thorough understanding of the environment in which the application will be deployed. The process will vary somewhat depending on whether a floppy-, network-, or Web-based deployment option is selected.

Part of the deployment process should always include planning for application growth and upgrades. You should also consider performance implications in your deployment as well. Unlike desktop applications, the deployment of a distributed application has a direct impact on the performance. To maximize the performance of a distributed application, you should distribute the application elements across as many servers as needed and possible. The more servers actively involved in processing your application, the better the performance: This is called load balancing.

Visual Basic also supplies the Package and Deployment Wizard to assist in the deployment process. Using this wizard, the developer can create setup packages that contain client applications, COM servers, and even DCOM support files needed to allow the application to function.

Review Questions

1. Which of the following command line compilation switches allows you to provide Conditional Compilation arguments?

    A. /m

    B. /d

    C. /c

    D. /l

2. The DCOM configuration utility allows you to configure all of the following on a business objects server except:

    A. Out-of-Process components

    B. Executable applications

    C. MTS Components DLLs

    D. Non-MTS DLLs

3. Which of the following features of Windows NT Enterprise supports load balancing?

    A. 4GB Tuning

    B. Clustering

    C. Integrated Security

    D. MTS transaction support

4. Which of the following utilities would you use to create an executable that configures DCOM on the client workstation?

A. DCOMCNFG

B. Package and Deployment Wizard

C. MTS Explorer

D. Windows Explorer

5. Which of the following load-balancing techniques supports fail-over?

A. Static load balancing through deployment

B. Static load balancing through configuration

C. Windows NT Clustering

D. MTS Packages

6. Which utility would you use to create .cab files from your application?

A. MTS Explorer

B. DCOMCNFG

C. Package and Deployment Wizard

D. Windows Explorer

7. You are deploying a client application to 50 desktops, all located on the same LAN. The application package is approximately 20MB in size. Which application deployment strategy should you use?

A. Floppy

B. CD-ROM

C. Web

D. Network

8. You are deploying a client application to 500 desktops located throughout the region. These desktops are not connected directly to the same network. The setup package is about 3MB in size and is not a critical application. Which application deployment strategy should you use?

   A. Floppy

   B. CD-ROM

   C. Web

   D. Network

9. Which of the following is not a compiled file format supported by Visual Basic?

   A. DLL

   B. EXE

   C. OCX

   D. FRM

10. To be deployed within the MTS environment, a component must be compiled as a(n)

   A. DLL

   B. EXE

   C. OCX

   D. FRM

APPENDIX

A

Answers to Review Questions

Chapter 1 Answers

1. The Microsoft JET database engine is structured to be a very robust multi-user engine scaling to thousands of users.

   A. True

   B. False

   Answer: B

2. In a typical client/server implementation, the database engine will reside on a:

   A. Windows NT primary domain controller

   B. Central database application server

   C. Client workstation

   D. Business component object

   Answer: B

3. When dealing with data extraction, the database server application's primary role is:

   A. Data reduction

   B. Data formatting

   C. Reporting

   D. Sorting

   Answer: A

4. Which service defines data modification and data extraction?

   A. User

   B. Business

   C. Data

   D. Application

   Answer: C

5. Which service defines formatting and reporting activities?

  A. User

  B. Business

  C. Data

  D. Application

  Answer: A

6. Which service defines validation and data access logic?

  A. User

  B. Business

  C. Data

  D. Application

  Answer: B

7. You have decided to implement a two-tier client/server architecture, but you are concerned with the maintainability of business logic. Which architecture should you implement?

  A. Smart client

  B. Smart server

  C. Smart component

  D. Mixed

  Answer: B

8. You have decided that you will implement a two-tier client/server architecture, but you are concerned about the strain that may be placed on the server. The client workstations have excess processing capacity. Which architecture should you implement?

  A. Smart client

  B. Smart server

C. Smart component

D. Mixed

Answer: A

9. Business objects will most often be created as which type of object?

A. True DLL

B. Java applet

C. Active Server Page

D. COM object

Answer: D

10. Which of the following Microsoft tools provides for data availability by preventing a transaction from failing if the data source is unavailable?

A. Microsoft SQL Server

B. Microsoft Message Queue

C. Microsoft Transaction Server

D. Microsoft Windows NT Server Enterprise

Answer: B

11. Which of the following is not part of the ACID test by which transactions are measured?

A. Anonymity

B. Consistency

C. Isolation

D. Durability

Answer: A

12. The ability to provide support for user bases ranging from very small to very large without suffering performance degradation is called:

   A. Responsiveness

   B. Threading

   C. User pooling

   D. Scalability

   Answer: D

13. Which of the following is not a benefit of using Microsoft Visual SourceSafe?

   A. Each object can have different levels of permissions for every user created through the Visual SourceSafe Administrative Utility.

   B. SourceSafe provides for a historical repository of source code modifications.

   C. SourceSafe guarantees that a read/write copy of the source code will be available whenever it is requested by a user.

   D. SourceSafe protects source code from simultaneous revisions by multiple users.

   Answer: C

14. Which of the following database application classifications would be considered appropriate for a database designed to accept numerous real-time data modifications?

   A. Data warehouse

   B. Online Transaction Processing System (OLTP)

   C. Online Analytical Processing System (OLAP)

   D. Decision Support System (DSS)

   Answer: B

15. Which of the following is NOT considered a true relational database management system? (select two)

    A. Microsoft SQL Server

    B. Oracle

    C. Microsoft Access

    D. Microsoft FoxPro

    Answer: C, D

Chapter 2 Answers

1. If Table A, containing 25 records, and Table B, containing 50 records, are joined together with a cross join, how many records will be in the result set?

    A. 25

    B. 50

    C. 75

    D. 1250

    Answer: D

2. If Table A, containing 25 records, and Table B, containing 50 records, are joined together with a right outer join, how many records will be in the result set? (Assume a one-to-one relationship exists.)

    A. 25

    B. 50

    C. 75

    D. 1250

    Answer: B

3. If Table A, containing 25 records, and Table B, containing 50 records, are joined together with a left outer join, how many records will be in the result set? (Assume a one-to-one relationship exists.)

A. 25

B. 50

C. 75

D. 1250

Answer: A

4. A customer table contains a field identifying the employee number of an employee that is dedicated exclusively to servicing that customer's account. Which of the following statements is true concerning this scenario?

A. Violation of first normal form

B. Violation of second normal form

C. Violation of third normal form

D. No violation exists

Answer: D

5. In the same table as discussed in question 4, assume that a field has been added to the customer table that specifies the grade of the employee assigned to that customer. Which of the following statements is true concerning this scenario?

A. Violation of first normal form

B. Violation of second normal form

C. Violation of third normal form

D. No violation exists

Answer: C

6. A customer table has a field called *contact name* where the full name of the contact individual for that company is placed. Which of the following statements is true concerning this scenario?

 A. Violation of first normal form

 B. Violation of second normal form

 C. Violation of third normal form

 D. No violation exists

Answer: A

7. An order details table has a composite key of order number and product number. This table also contains a field that holds the customer number. Which of the following statements is true concerning this scenario?

 A. Violation of first normal form

 B. Violation of second normal form

 C. Violation of third normal form

 D. No violation exists

Answer: B

8. The field that identifies every record in the table as unique is called the

 A. Common Key

 B. Foreign Key

 C. Unique Key

 D. Primary Key

Answer: D

9. Which of the following is NOT a requirement of the Primary Key?

 A. It must be numeric.

 B. It must not allow nulls.

    C. It must be unique.

    D. It must be indexed.

Answer: A

10. Attributes of an entity are implemented as the:

    A. Rows of a table

    B. Tables of a database

    C. Columns of a table

    D. Key values in a table

Answer: C

11. Which of the following are advantages of using stored procedures in a database application? (Choose all that apply.)

    A. Abstraction of data access logic from the client and business tiers

    B. Interoperability among all popular relational database management systems

    C. Increased performance over submitting ad hoc queries to a database server

    D. Full support for advanced programming logic

Answer: A, C

12. Which of the following SQL WHERE clauses extracts rows from a table where the *lastname* column can be any number of characters but starts with the letter B?

    A. `WHERE lastname = 'B*'`

    B. `WHERE lastname = 'B_'`

    C. `WHERE lastname = 'B%'`

    D. `WHERE lastname = 'B?'`

Answer: C

13. Which of the following statements will drop the authors table entirely from the database?

A. `TRUNCATE TABLE authors`

B. `DROP TABLE authors`

C. `DELETE authors`

D. `DELETE TABLE authors`

Answer: B

14. The meaning of null is:

A. Nothing

B. Undefined

C. Zero

D. Empty

Answer: B

15. Which of the following is not a valid approach to enforcing database transactions?

A. Creating transactions at the data tier

B. Using Microsoft Transaction Server

C. Using the transaction support of a data access model

D. Storing data using a transacted file system

Answer: D

Chapter 3 Answers

1. Which of the following is not an element of the ADO model?

A. Database

B. Error

C. Connection

D. Parameter

Answer: A

2. Which of the following ADO recordset types provides the greatest degree of concurrency?

A. Static

B. Forward-only

C. Dynamic

D. Keyset

Answer: C

3. Which of the following cannot be included in the Open method of the recordset?

A. CursorType

B. User Name

C. CursorLocation

D. LockType

Answer: C

4. Which of the following code examples will not read data from the *au_fname* column of a recordset represented by the object variable *rs*?

A. `rs!au_lname`

B. `rs(au_lname)`

C. `rs.Fields("au_lname")`

D. `rs.Fields("au_lname").Value`

Answer: B

5. Which of the following locking types will lock a recordset only during an Update process and not immediately when the data modifications are requested?

A. Pessimistic

B. Update

C. Optimistic

D. Batch optimistic

Answer: C

6. A prepared statement is:

A. Query text cached on the client

B. Query text cached on the server

C. Compiled query cached on the client

D. Compiled query cached on the server

Answer: D

7. Which symbol in an ADO query should you use to identify a parameter?

A. !

B. ^

C. ?

D. *

Answer: C

8. Which of the following will provide the best aggregate execution performance for a query that is not executed repeatedly?

A. Direct execution

B. Stored procedures

C. Prepared statements

D. ADO Data Control

Answer: B

9. Which method of the Recordset objects should you use to navigate multiple recordsets returned by a stored procedure?

A. NewRecordset

B. NavigateRecordset

C. OpenFull

D. NextRecordset

Answer: D

10. Which of the following scenarios will perform a direct execution of a Command object?

A. The Execute method

B. The Prepare method

C. The ExecDirect method

D. The Open method

Answer: A

11. Which of the following statements is capable of abandoning a series of modifications made to a recordset locked with a BatchOptimistic lock?

A. CancelUpdate

B. AbandonBatch

C. CancelBatchUpdate

D. CancelBatch

Answer: D

12. Which of the following approaches to data modifications is the least efficient?

    A. Updating through a cursor using a recordset

    B. A stored procedure

    C. An update statement prepared and executed

    D. An update statement executed directly

Answer: A

13. Which of the following is not an advantage of using stored procedures?

    A. Developer focus on core competence

    B. Increased execution performance over direct execution

    C. Portability among various database server products

    D. Well-defined methods for calling from ADO

Answer: C

14. An ADO dynamic property is:

    A. A property that changes value at runtime

    B. A value defined by the user

    C. A property that dynamically resizes as needed to accommodate database parameters

    D. A property implemented by the OLE DB service provider

Answer: D

15. Which of the following will not create a read-only recordset?

    A. A lock type of read-only

    B. A client-side cursor location

C. A forward-only cursor type

D. A static cursor type

Answer: B

Chapter 4 Answers

1. Which principle of object design states that the implementation detail of the way an object works should be hidden from the developer?

   A. Abstraction

   B. Encapsulation

   C. Inheritance

   D. Polymorphism

   Answer: C

2. Which principle of object design states that the object model should represent as closely as possible the object or process described in the real world?

   A. Abstraction

   B. Encapsulation

   C. Inheritance

   D. Polymorphism

   Answer: A

3. Which principle of object design states that if multiple objects define the same interfaces, they can be implemented in the same way, regardless of their implementation methodology?

   A. Abstraction

   B. Encapsulation

   C. Inheritance

   D. Polymorphism

   Answer: D

4. Which principle of object design states that a class has the ability to pass its attributes on to other classes by creating a subclass?

A. Abstraction

B. Encapsulation

C. Inheritance

D. Polymorphism

Answer: C

5. An interface that can be seen only in the class in which it is defined is scoped as:

A. Public

B. Private

C. Friend

D. Reserved

Answer: B

6. An interface that can be seen everywhere the component is referenced, including a client application, is scoped as:

A. Public

B. Private

C. Friend

D. Reserved

Answer: A

7. An interface that can be seen only within the object model or component in which it is defined is scoped as:

A. Public

B. Private

C. Friend

D. Reserved

Answer: C

8. Collections usually have fixed membership.

    A. True

    B. False

Answer: B

9. Which of the following properties or methods is not commonly supported by collections?

    A. Count

    B. Expand

    C. Add

    D. Delete

Answer: B

10. How many types of class objects can a single collection hold?

    A. 0

    B. 1

    C. 2

    D. 3

Answer: B

11. Which of the following procedure types will execute when you assign a value to a property of an object?

    A. Property Get

    B. Property Let

    C. Property Set

    D. Public Sub

Answer: B

12. Which of the following statements should you write in a procedure to cause the component to fire an event?

A. RaiseEvent

B. DeclareEvent

C. FireEvent

D. DoEvents

Answer: A

13. Which of the following constants should you add to a custom component error to identify the error to the client as coming from a component object?

A. objError

B. vbClassError

C. vbComponentError

D. vbObjectError

Answer: D

14. The threading model that defines a set of isolated but identical processing spaces for thread execution is called:

A. Multithreading

B. Single threading

C. Apartment threading

D. Component threading

Answer: C

15. Which of the following compiled elements does not run in-process?

A. ActiveX EXE

B. ActiveX DLL

   C. ActiveX Control

   D. Standard DLL

Answer: A

Chapter 5 Answers

1. The Visual Basic project file that stores the design of a UserControl ends with which extension?

   A. `.ctx`

   B. `.ocx`

   C. `.ctl`

   D. `.uct`

Answer: C

2. Which event should you use to store property values into the PropertyBag?

   A. Terminate

   B. ReadProperties

   C. WriteProperties

   D. SaveProperties

Answer: C

3. Which of the following ActiveX control events does not occur as the application hosting the control is terminated?

   A. Terminate

   B. ReadProperties

   C. WriteProperties

   D. Resize

Answer: C

4. Which of the following situations would not cause the Initialize event of an ActiveX control to occur?

 A. When a control is placed on a form at design-time

 B. When a form designer containing a control is closed

 C. When a compiled application containing a control executes

 D. When an application terminates and re-enters design-time for the host application

Answer: B

5. Which of the following methods is used to inform an ActiveX control's container that one of its properties has been modified?

 A. CanPropertyChange

 B. PropertyModify

 C. Property_Change

 D. PropertyChanged

Answer: D

6. Which collection of an ActiveX control enumerates all of the properties that can be bound to a data source?

 A. DataFields

 B. DataMembers

 C. DataBindings

 D. DataProperties

Answer: C

7. Which event of an ActiveX control data provider runs every time a bound control extracts data through the provider?

 A. GetDataMember

 B. GetDataField

C. GetDataProperty

D. GetDataRow

Answer: A

8. Which event from the list below occurs only once in the entire life cycle of an ActiveX control?

A. Initialize

B. Resize

C. Terminate

D. InitProperties

Answer: D

9. Which parameter of the WriteProperty method can be omitted but should be included to increase the efficiency of the control?

A. Name

B. Value

C. PropBag

D. DefaultValue

Answer: D

10. Which method of an ActiveX control is used to interrogate a data provider for data update support?

A. CanPropertyUpdate

B. CanPropertyChange

C. PropertyModify

D. Updateable

Answer: B

11. Which event should be used to resize an ActiveX control as the user modifies the size of the control implementation on a form?

   A. Resize

   B. Paint

   C. Initialize

   D. SizeChanged

   Answer: A

12. Which Visual Basic dialog box is used to expose the data binding in a data consumer control?

   A. DataBindings

   B. Data members

   C. Procedure bindings

   D. Procedure attributes

   Answer: D

Chapter 6 Answers

1. What behavior occurs when a command button's default property is set to True?

   A. When clicked, that button acts to accept any changes that have been made to data contained in the form.

   B. That button's click event will be fired if the Enter key is pressed, regardless of focus.

   C. That button will respond to the Cancel key being pressed.

   D. Any properties of that button not explicitly defined are set to True.

   Answer: B

2. Presentation Tier applications are built using which Visual Basic template?

   A. Standard EXE

   B. ActiveX DLL

    C. ActiveX EXE

    D. ActiveX Control

Answer: A

3. Which property does every Visual Basic control contain?

    A. Text

    B. Caption

    C. Security

    D. Name

Answer: D

4. What are the two ways you can place a control on your form?

    A. Double-click the control's icon on the toolbox.

    B. Select the control from the Components dialog.

    C. Click the control's icon on the toolbox and drag the icon to your form.

    D. Click the control's icon on the toolbox, then click and drag across the form.

Answer: A, D

5. How do you add an ActiveX control to the toolbox?

    A. Drag the control's icon from the ActiveX button on the toolbar to the toolbox.

    B. Select Project ➢ Insert ActiveX Control from the menus.

    C. Register the control.

    D. Select the control from the Components dialog.

Answer: D

6. Which of the following is the correct syntax for registering an ActiveX control?

    A. `Regserver32.exe c:\Windows\System\neat.ocx`

    B. `Regsvr32.exe c:\Windows\System\neat.ocx`

    C. `Regsvr32.exe neat.ocx`

    D. `Regsvr32.exe /u c:\Windows\System\neat.ocx`

Answer: B

7. What happens when you register a component?

    A. The component is copied to the Controls directory.

    B. The component is installed onto your local hard disk, and the registry is updated to reflect its presence.

    C. The registry is updated to reflect the presence of the control.

    D. The licensing directory in the registry is checked for permission to use a component.

Answer: C

8. What does the ImageList control do?

    A. It displays items in the ListItems collection in one of four views.

    B. It displays the selected node(s) of the TreeView control.

    C. It holds images in memory for use by the TreeView control.

    D. It holds images in memory for other controls to use.

Answer: D

9. Which of the following uses the correct syntax for the Add method of the Nodes collection of the TreeView control?

    A. tvwNetwork.Nodes.Add RootNode, tvwChild, NewChild, "The New Child"

    B. tvwNetwork.Add "RootNode", tvwChild, "NewChild", "The New Child"

   C. tvwNetwork.Nodes.Add (tvwChild, "RootNode", "NewChild", "The New Child")

   D. None of the above

Answer: B

10. How do you program the ListView control to respond to clicks on the TreeView control?

   A. Script the TreeView_Changed event of the ListView control.

   B. Script the TreeView_Changed event of the ListItems collection.

   C. Place code in the TreeView_Clicked event of the ListView control.

   D. Place code in the NodeClicked event of the TreeView control.

Answer: D

11. How do arrays differ from collections? Select all that apply.

   A. Arrays require that all elements be of the same type.

   B. Collections allow the user to identify an object by its Index value.

   C. Menu items and other controls can be placed in arrays or collections.

   D. The For Each...Next statement is available for use in arrays.

Answer: A, C

12. Which of the following statements is false?

   A. Collections allow you to systematically manipulate objects.

   B. A control array has only one set of methods, but each control has its own properties.

   C. Controls in a control array must all have the same name, but a unique Index value.

   D. The Controls collection is created by dimensioning a variable of the type Collection.

Answer: D

13. How do you procedurally configure a pop-up menu?

    A. Call the Pop-upMenu method in the MouseUp event procedure, and pass a menu name.

    B. Create a root-level menu and set its visible property to False.

    C. Check the Pop-Up Menu Property check box in the Menu Editor.

    D. Place script in the RightMouseDown event that calls the Pop-up method of the desired menu.

Answer: A

Chapter 7 Answers

1. Which of the following cannot function as a data source?

    A. ADO Data Control

    B. MaskedEdit control

    C. Data-aware class

    D. DataEnvironment object

Answer: B

2. For which type of control would you not want to set the CausesValidation property to True?

    A. A command button labeled Help

    B. A command button labeled Validate

    C. The first text box on a form

    D. The last text box on a form

Answer: A

3. Which is not a property associated with data binding?

    A. DataSource

    B. DataMember

    C. DataFormat

    D. RecordSource

Answer: C

4. Which of the following events can tell whether a function key (e.g., F4) has been pressed?

A. Change

B. KeyUp

C. KeyDown

D. KeyPress

Answer: D

5. Which of the following is not a tool for validating data at entry?

A. The MaskEdit format property

B. The TextBox CausesValidation property

C. LostFocus Event

D. The TextBox MaxLength property

Answer: A

6. What does a data command do?

A. Enforces data integrity

B. Maintains data validity

C. Defines the database interaction

D. Defines the database query

Answer: D

7. You extract the value of the ClipText property of a MaskEdit control. What do you see?

A. The first five characters of information originally passed to the control

B. The last five characters originally passed to the control

C. The text that was originally typed into the service

D. The MaskEdit.text property with literals included

Answer: C

8. The Visual Basic 6.0 Data Form Wizard ignores which technology?

   A. ADO

   B. ODBC

   C. Data bound Grids

   D. OLE DB

   Answer: D

9. To automatically create data bindings, you can drag icons from the
_____ to _____ .

   A. Data View window – Form

   B. ToolBox – Data View window

   C. Data Environment window – Form

   D. Toolbox – Form

   Answer: C

Chapter 8 Answers

1. Which of the following COM interfaces supports automation?

   A. Invoke

   B. IUnknown

   C. IDispatch

   D. IDeclare

   Answer: C

2. Which method of the IDispatch interface is avoided through DispID
binding?

   A. Invoke

   B. GetTypeInfo

C. GetTypeInfoCount

D. GetIdsOfNames

Answer: D

3. Which of the following methods of the IDispatch interface is used when performing vTable binding?

A. GetIDsOfNames

B. Invoke

C. Both A and B

D. Neither A nor B

Answer: D

4. Which keyword is used when declaring a reference to an abstract class to support all of its public interfaces?

A. WithEvents

B. Public

C. Implements

D. ByVal

Answer: C

5. You are writing a component that performs some processing and then notifies a client application when the processing is complete. There is no need for the component to differentiate between client applications, nor will it continue processing after the client application's response to the notification, but you need the client to continue processing while waiting for a notification. Which technique should you use?

A. Asynchronous processing with callbacks

B. Asynchronous processing with events

C. Synchronous processing with API calls

D. Asynchronous processing using API

Answer: B

6. Which approach to binding will result in the best performance?

A. Late binding

B. DispID binding

C. vTable binding

D. All have identical performance

Answer: C

7. Which of the following is not an advantage of a type library?

A. Usually smaller than the full component.

B. Fully documents the component for early binding.

C. Can be viewed by the Visual Basic object browser.

D. When loaded, automation calls can execute without requiring the component to load.

Answer: D

8. Which of the following is the most efficient way to instantiate an object class when repeated instantiations will be made from the same class template?

A. Auto-instantiation with the New keyword

B. Using the New keyword with the Set statement

C. Using the CreateObject function with the Set statement

D. All of these methods offer generally the same performance

Answer: B

9. Which of the following declaration statements would result in late binding?

A. Dim xl as Excel.Application

B. Dim cmd as CommandButton

C. Dim obj as Project1.Class1

D. Dim frm as Form

Answer: D

10. Which of the following code statements terminates the instance of the object referenced in the object variable obj?

A. Set obj = Nothing

B. obj.Close

C. Set obj = TerminateObject()

D. obj.Terminate

Answer: A

Chapter 9 Answers

1. Which of the following component threading models does Microsoft Transaction Server support? Choose two.

A. Apartment threading

B. Free threading

C. Control threading

D. Single threading

Answer: A, D

2. Which package authentication level should you use if you want to ensure the highest level of encryption available as the packets cross the network?

A. Connect

B. Packet Privacy

C. Packet Integrity

D. Call

Answer: B

3. Which of the following code examples would allow a user to access a component functionality only if the user was a member of a Windows NT group called Managers that is associated with the Admins role of a component?

A. If IsCallerInGroup("Admins") Then

B. If IsCallerInRole("Admins") Then

C. If IsCallerInGroup("Managers") Then

D. If IsCallerInRole("Managers") Then

Answer: B

4. Which of the following is a firm requirement of MTS components?

A. They must be COM compliant.

B. They must be apartment-threaded.

C. They must be stateless.

D. They must interact with a data source.

Answer: A

5. Which of the following methods is used to inform the Context object that a transaction must be canceled?

A. CancelTran

B. SetCancel

C. SetAbort

D. RollBack

Answer: C

6. You should avoid using properties in an MTS component because:

A. MTS does not understand how properties are exposed.

B. All properties are private interfaces.

C. Properties execute differently than methods and can bypass MTS security.

D. Properties usually maintain state on the server.

Answer: D

7. Which transaction setting is most appropriate for the root component that enlists other components into a transaction if the component is always and only used as a root component?

A. Supports transactions

B. Requires a transaction

C. Requires a new transaction

D. Does not support transactions

Answer: C

8. Which transaction setting is most appropriate for the root component that enlists other components into a transaction if the component is only occasionally used as a root component?

A. Supports transactions

B. Requires a transaction

C. Requires a new transaction

D. Does not support transactions

Answer: B

9. MTS objects must be packaged as

A. In-process COM objects (DLLs)

B. Standard DLLs

C. Out-of-process DLLs (EXEs)

D. PAK files

Answer: A

10. Which of the following statements is not true about the MTS security model?

   A. It is an optional service provided for the Administrator.

   B. It is integrated with the Windows NT security system.

   C. It uses the Context object to allow the component to query security status.

   D. It is never enabled when the object does not support transactions.

   Answer: D

Chatper 10 Answers

1. Which of the following ASP objects should you use when constructing a message to send to a browser from a WebClass?

   A. Request

   B. Response

   C. Server

   D. Session

   Answer: B

2. Which of the following technologies does not require Microsoft Internet Explorer in order to function?

   A. Visual Basic WebClass

   B. VBScript in an HTML page

   C. Active document

   D. Visual Basic DHTML application

   Answer: A

3. Which event of an IIS application WebItem will fire when a request is made to load that WebItem from within the IIS application?

   A. Start

   B. Request

   C. Respond

   D. Navigate

Answer: C

4. Which of the following collections of the ASP Request object should the developer use to read the content of the body of an HTTP request message?

   A. Cookies

   B. Form

   C. QueryString

   D. ClientCertificate

Answer: B

5. Which method of the Response object is used in a WebClass to create the HTML response that is sent to the browser?

   A. Create

   B. Respond

   C. Navigate

   D. Write

Answer: D

6. Which of the following statements correctly identifies the class of an active document container as an Internet Explorer browser?

   A. TypeOf(UserDocument.Parent) = "ie4_browser"

   B. TypeName(UserDocument.Parent) = "ie4_browser"

   C. TypeOf(UserDocument.Parent) = "IWebBrowserApp"

   D. TypeName(UserDocument.Parent) = "IWebBrowserApp"

Answer: D

7. Which of the following is not a method of the hyperlink in an active document?

A. GoTo

B. GoBack

C. GoForward

D. NavigateTo

Answer: A

8. Which attribute of an HTML form defines whether form contents will be sent to the Web server in the head or the body of an HTTP request message?

A. Put

B. Action

C. Method

D. Value

Answer: C

9. Which of the following code element is not supported by VBScript?

A. Variant data type

B. Fixed arrays

C. GoTo statements

D. Event Recognition

Answer: C

10. When does a new session begin in an Active Server Pages application?

A. When a browser first accesses an HTML page in the Web

B. When a browser first accesses an ASP page in the Web

C. When the IIS Service starts on the Windows NT computer

D. Never; sessions are only supported by WebClasses.

Answer: B

11. If you do not specify which scripting language you wish to use in an HTML page, Microsoft Internet Explorer will default to:

A. VBScript

B. JavaScript

C. PerlScript

D. None, the <SCRIPT> tag will be ignored.

Answer: B

12. Which Active Server Pages object is used in the manipulating of cookies, either to read or to write?

A. Request

B. Response

C. Both

D. Neither, cookies are not supported in ASP

Answer: C

13. Which of the following events is not recognized by the WebClass?

A. Initialize

B. Terminate

C. Start

D. Respond

Answer: D

14. Which object in the Active Server Pages model is responsible for managing Session Start and End events?

A. The Global.asa file

B. The Session object

C. Each ASP file manages its own Session events

D. You must create a custom COM object to manage these events

Answer: A

15. When inserting an ActiveX control into a Web page using the <OBJECT> tag, which parameter of that tag identifies the control to the script on that page so that the control can be manipulated?

   A. ClassID

   B. Name

   C. ID

   D. CodeBase

Answer: C

Chapter 11 Answers

1. What is the greatest advantage developers gain by using HTML Help instead of WinHelp?

   A. HTML Help is much easier to configure and use than WinHelp.

   B. The HTML Help engine is already installed on most PCs.

   C. Existing content is easily reused in help files.

   D. There is no advantage; WinHelp is a better technology.

Answer: C

2. HTML topic files can be created with which of the following tools? (Mark all that apply.)

   A. A text-based HTML editor

   B. A graphical HTML editor such as Microsoft Front Page

   C. Internet Explorer 4

   D. HTML Help Workshop

Answer: A, B, D

3. Where in an application can the HelpFile be specified?

   A. At design-time, in the App object

   B. At design-time, in a control's property window

C. At runtime in the App.Helpfile property

D. At runtime in the Project Properties dialog

Answer: C

4. Which of the following is not a file type found in an HTML Help File?

   A. .hlp

   B. .hhk

   C. .hhc

   D. .chm

   Answer: A

5. When converting a WinHelp project to HTML Help using HTML Help Workshop WinHelp Converter Wizard, which of the following files is not created automatically?

   A. Project file

   B. Index file

   C. Contents file

   D. HTML topic files

   Answer: B

6. What data type is the HelpContextID?

   A. String

   B. Integer

   C. Single

   D. Long

   Answer: D

7. How are WhatsThisHelpIDs mapped to individual topics?

   A. What's This Help topics and their IDs are stored in a text file.

   B. IDs are mapped to topic files in a C header file that is included in the Project File.

   C. What's This Help uses the HTML Help topic mappings, and setting the WhatsThisHelp property to true overrides the regular context-sensitive help system.

   D. The help topics are stored locally, saved with each form or control.

   Answer: A

8. Which of the following is a true statement?

   A. Pathname is a valid method of the MSMQMessage object.

   B. Receive is a valid method of the MSMQQueue object.

   C. The Close method of the MSMQQueue object should always be executed immediately following receipt of a message.

   D. Messages from the message queue are synchronous, meaning they will only be delivered after other pending events have completed.

   Answer: B

9. Which of the following best describes the App object?

   A. It can be created as needed. It is used to bind a client application to a data source.

   B. It can be created as needed. It is used to set and retrieve properties of the current application.

   C. It is created automatically when an application is launched. It is used to set and retrieve properties of the current application.

   D. The App object provides an object handle for referencing component objects over a network.

   Answer: C

Chapter 12 Answers

1. Which property of the Err object returns the numeric value associated with the most recent runtime error?

A. Description

B. Number

C. NativeError

D. Source

Answer: B

2. You are creating a client application that calls ActiveX DLLs. Which of the following properties of the Err object provides the name of a component that sends an error back to the client application?

A. Number

B. Description

C. NativeError

D. Source

Answer: D

3. How many error conditions can the Err object report at any single point in time?

A. 0

B. 1

C. 65535

D. Unlimited

Answer: B

4. Which of the following statements forces inline error handling?

A. On Error GoTo *linelabel*

B. On Error GoTo Inline

C. On Error Resume Next

D. On Error GoTo 0

Answer: C

5. Which of the following statements discontinues error trapping for a procedure?

 A. On Error GoTo *linelabel*

 B. On Error Resume Next

 C. Err.Stop

 D. On Error GoTo 0

 Answer: D

6. You are creating an ActiveX component that raises user-defined errors. What is the valid range of error numbers that you can use for user-defined errors?

 A. 0 – 255

 B. 0 – 65535

 C. 0 – 1000

 D. 513 – 65535

 Answer: D

7. You are creating an ActiveX component that raises user-defined errors. Which of the following statements correctly raises an error to the client with error number 20000?

 A. Err.Raise vbObjectError + 20000

 B. Err.Raise vbObjectError, 20000

 C. Err.Number = 20000

 D. Err.NativeError = vbObjectError + 20000

 Answer: A

8. Which of the following is not a valid Resume statement in an Error handler?

   A. Resume

   B. Resume Next

   C. Resume Previous

   D. Resume line

   Answer: C

9. Which property is associated with every collection defined by Visual Basic?

   A. Clear

   B. Count

   C. Source

   D. Number

   Answer: B

10. Which ADO object acts as parent to the Errors collection in the ADO hierarchy?

   A. Command

   B. Recordset

   C. Parameter

   D. Connection

   Answer: D

Chapter 13 Answers

1. Which of the following debug tools would you use to locate the specific point that a variable is set to an unexpected value?

   A. Breakpoint

   B. Watch expression

    C. Locals window

    D. Callstack

    Answer: B

2. Which of the following could not be used to execute a conditional breakpoint?

    A. A STOP statement executed in a conditional IF block

    B. The Assert method of the Debug object

    C. A watch expression that breaks when an expression evaluates to true

    D. Setting a break in the Locals window

    Answer: D

3. You need to monitor the value of a variable called *intReturn* that is private to a general procedure called *ReturnProc* in Form1. Which of the following would be the most efficient context for a watch expression?

    A. Form1, ReturnProc

    B. Form1, All procedures

    C. All modules, ReturnProc

    D. All modules, All procedures

    Answer: A

4. You need to monitor the value of a variable called *intReturn* that is publicly declared in a module called *Module1*. The value of this variable is set and manipulated only in a procedure called *ReturnProc* in Form1 and read in other procedures in the application. Which of the following would be the most efficient context for a watch expression?

    A. Form1, ReturnProc

    B. Form1, All procedures

C. Module1, ReturnProc

D. Module1, All procedures

Answer: A

5. You need to monitor the value of a variable called *intReturn* that is publicly declared in a module called *Module1*. The value of this variable is set and manipulated in numerous procedures in the application. Which of the following would be the most efficient context for a watch expression?

A. Form1, All procedures

B. All Modules, All procedures

C. Module1, ReturnProc

D. Module1, All procedures

Answer: B

6. Which of the following debug tools would you use to locate your current position in a series of embedded procedure calls?

A. Locals window

B. Immediate window

C. Callstack

D. Debug object

Answer: C

7. Which of the following is not a valid watch expression setting?

A. Watch expression

B. Break When Value Is True

C. Break When Expression Changes

D. Break When Value Changes

Answer: C

8. Which of the following is not a valid stepping option?

A. Step Around

B. Step Into

C. Step Over

D. Step Out

Answer: A

9. Which of the following tools can be used to change the value of a variable or property during break mode of an application?

A. Watch window

B. Callstack

C. Locals window

D. Debug object

Answer: C

10. Which of the following project types cannot be included in a project group?

A. Standard EXE

B. ActiveX DLL

C. ActiveX Control

D. All of the above project types can be included in a project group

Answer: D

Chapter 14 Answers

1. Which of the following command line compilation switches allows you to provide Conditional Compilation arguments?

A. /m

B. /d

C. /c

D. /l

Answer: B

2. The DCOM configuration utility allows you to configure all of the following on a business objects server except:

 A. Out-of-Process components

 B. Executable applications

 C. MTS Components DLLs

 D. Non-MTS DLLs

 Answer: D

3. Which of the following features of Windows NT Enterprise supports load balancing?

 A. 4GB Tuning

 B. Clustering

 C. Integrated Security

 D. MTS transaction support

 Answer: B

4. Which of the following utilities would you use to create an executable that configures DCOM on the client workstation?

 A. DCOMCNFG

 B. Package and Deployment Wizard

 C. MTS Explorer

 D. Windows Explorer

 Answer: C

5. Which of the following load-balancing techniques supports fail-over?

A. Static load balancing through deployment

B. Static load balancing through configuration

C. Windows NT Clustering

D. MTS Packages

Answer: C

6. Which utility would you use to create .cab files from your application?

A. MTS Explorer

B. DCOMCNFG

C. Package and Deployment Wizard

D. Windows Explorer

Answer: C

7. You are deploying a client application to 50 desktops, all located on the same LAN. The application package is approximately 20MB in size. Which application deployment strategy should you use?

A. Floppy

B. CD-ROM

C. Web

D. Network

Answer: D

8. You are deploying a client application to 500 desktops located throughout the region. These desktops are not connected directly to the same network. The setup package is about 3MB in size and is not a critical application. Which application deployment strategy should you use?

A. Floppy

B. CD-ROM

C. Web

D. Network

Answer: C

9. Which of the following is not a compiled file format supported by Visual Basic?

A. DLL

B. EXE

C. OCX

D. FRM

Answer: D

10. To be deployed within the MTS environment, a component must be compiled as a(n)

A. DLL

B. EXE

C. OCX

D. FRM

Answer: A

APPENDIX

B

**Strategies for
Successful Test Taking**

This book is written for the express purpose of helping readers pass the 70-175 Visual Basic Distributed Application Development examination. This study guide focuses on the specific content material covered on the exam. Most of us have experienced at one time or another, however, that it is quite possible to do poorly on an exam, even after many long hours of study. To that end, we are including this appendix. Our aim here is to focus attention on the skills that can make your studying more effective and maximize your chances of passing the exam. We will cover two general classes of these skills in this appendix:

- Effective study techniques

- Test-taking skills

Remember, our point in this discussion is not to encourage you to take shortcuts in your preparations. We cannot overemphasize the necessity of a solid mastery of the exam content. The goal of this section is to make sure that you are studying effectively and that poor habits or other circumstances do not interfere with your chances of passing the exam.

Effective Study Techniques

Microsoft designs its certification exams to be difficult to pass. The reason for this is not to fail qualified individuals (though it may feel that way sometimes). All certification programs are by definition designed to certify competence. In the case of Microsoft, the driving goal is to certify that an MCP or MCSD is an experienced professional in the credentialed areas. The exams are written with this objective in mind. Exam objectives assess both a detailed knowledge of relevant technologies and a working knowledge of software usage patterns. Your study, then, should give you both a knowledge of important facts and specifications as well as the ability to relate to the tools like they are old friends.

There are several skills that can assist in your efforts to memorize important technical facts. We begin our discussion with coverage of these techniques.

Mnemonics

One of the most powerful (and least used) aids to memorization is the use of mnemonics, or individualized memory prompts. The key to mnemonics is to use word or visual associations that are unusual enough to remember easily. For memorizing lists, acronyms can be a useful prompting tool. A phrase or sentence that contains the key words can also be helpful. Perhaps the most famous instances of these techniques are from the music pedagogy camp. Practically every new piano student is taught that "Every Good Boy Does Fine" to represent the notes that fall on the lines of the treble clef, and F-A-C-E, the acronym that gives the notes that fall between the lines. Similarly, the list of Active Server Page Intrinsic Objects (Session, Application, Request, Response, and Server objects) can be remembered by finding a unique acronym like ASP-ARRSS. A phrase to aid recall of these objects might go something like this, "In a Web *application*, the browser *requests responses* from a *server*, simulating a *session*.

There are no right or wrong mnemonics; the key is that the cue have some sort of personal meaning that you can recall.

You may have been forced into using mnemonics by an over-vigilant system administrator. Many multi-user systems have such restrictive constraints on the selection of passwords that users must find a way to combine numbers, letters (in different cases), and punctuation in some way that they can remember.

The numbers 2 and 4 are particularly handy in making mnemonics. You can build sentences around their similarities to the words "to" and "for." For instance, a graduate of Florida State University might select went2FSU as a password string. This particular string will never show up in a dictionary of common passwords, yet the user is likely to remember it because it has a personal meaning.

Repetition

Why is it that you have no trouble remembering your social security number or the Pledge of Allegiance? How about your credit card, frequent flyer, or checking account numbers? These pieces of information may have little daily use or intrinsic personal meaning, but we retain them for years because of chronic exposure. In fact, you can tell a lot about a person and their life by the types of information they have committed to memory through repetition. If you have committed large portions of the Visual Basic language to memory from consistent use, you are probably on the path to passing the exam with ease. If this statement does not accurately describe you, your job is to make it so.

If you want to become familiar with Visual Basic and the elements of distributed application development and you don't work with Visual Basic regularly, find ways to expose yourself to these tools. Some of the means at your disposal for increasing your exposure to Visual Basic development include:

- working your way through the exercises in this book

- working through the exercises given in the Microsoft courses

- working through practice exams

This book is written to provide you with a review of the information likely to appear on your exam. We have also written the book to provide you with hands-on experience. Take advantage of the exercises. Work through each of them, and make sure you feel comfortable with the tasks and solutions. One of the ways this relatively brief exposure can aid in recall is by providing a visual experience for the student.

Visualization

Studies of learning styles have shown that different people learn best through different means. For some, optimal learning comes through the use of mnemonics. For others, hands-on experience is essential for any meaningful recall. Still others rely on simple repetition to embed information in their minds. Educational psychologists have found that learning is tied to our physical senses. If we listen to a certain piece of music while studying a topic, for instance, that information is recalled much more easily if we again listen to that piece of music. Multimedia presentations are especially effective in teaching, as multiple senses are used simultaneously.

Multimedia is not just a fancy use for technology. Based on sound, sight, and interaction, multimedia helps us learn faster and more thoroughly because we learn best when multiple senses are used.

One effective technique that you can use in the course of your study is to take advantage of visual aids wherever possible. Additionally, if your experience is that you learn well through visual experiences or hands-on practice, you should use that knowledge to your advantage while studying. As you read through example procedures, close your eyes and visualize the sequence of events as they transpire. If you then sit at your keyboard and actually work through the exercise, you are now reviewing what you have learned. It may also be helpful to stop at each step in the exercises and examine the various elements of the user interface. By following the changes in state of the user interface, visually cued learners can master complexities that are otherwise difficult to grasp.

Meaning-Making

Mnemonics, repetition, and visualization will aid you in storing and retrieving bits of data. However, the Microsoft certification exams are written to test your facility with the software, not just your ability to memorize static facts. In other words, the exam will also examine skills like problem solving, software development, and understanding which tools to apply to which jobs. If your brain is like a computer, you must do more than write a large amount of data to a text file on your hard disk. To pass the exam (and be an effective developer of distributed applications), you must also be able to take in information, process it, and store it in data structures that allow for future context-sensitive retrieval. These data structures can then, in turn, be used in the processing of future incoming information. In the realm of computer science, this is similar to neural networks or artificial intelligence.

The key to processing what you learn in this way is to consistently ask yourself the following questions while studying:

- How is this topic connected to the rest of the information in this chapter or book?

- How might I implement this feature or technology in a development project?

- How does this relate to my past experiences? Could I have used this in an earlier project? How did developers perform similar tasks before this particular technology was available?

Introducing this level of processing will definitely slow your acquisition of the information contained in this book. The lost efficiency, however, will be insignificant compared to the depth of understanding you will achieve. If you want to master the material and pass the exam, this type of rigorous effort will make the difference.

Why bother with this extra effort? Because when you incorporate information this way, you grasp the "big picture." When you know what the big picture looks like, you can make educated guesses about aspects of the picture you haven't explicitly studied. In an effort to assess your level of familiarity with their various developer tools and operating systems, Microsoft has created exam questions that probe the darker and more obscure areas of the image. In the first two chapters of this book we have attempted to lay out the major aspects of the big picture. We encourage you to read these chapters carefully. As you read the later chapters, push to see how each topic fits within the larger context.

If you want to be very thorough in your preparation, read this entire book twice. The first time through, you will only understand each chapter within the context of the previous chapters. During a second read-through, however, you can consider the entire book as you read—how all the features relate and what they do within those relationships.

Once you've reviewed the material contained in this book, you are ready to create a plan of attack for successfully passing the exam. The remainder of this appendix will deal specifically with ways to leverage what you have learned and maximize your exam score.

Test-Taking Skills

There are two important aspects of test preparation, the steps you take before beginning the exam and the little tricks that help you successfully recognize correct exam responses. While it may be tempting to skip to the section on selecting correct answers, we encourage you to review the "Before the Exam" items and use them as part of a comprehensive exam strategy.

Before the Exam

These pre-exam strategies may not directly *improve* your test score. We have included them here because of the potential *not* using these strategies has to *lower* your score. It is truly unfortunate when a person studies diligently for an exam and is then unable to perform to potential because of avoidable circumstances. Failing Microsoft certification exams is costly both financially and personally. Take full advantage of the effort you have spent in your studying by avoiding common obstacles.

Know Yourself

A little self-evaluation can go a long way toward preventing exam difficulties. The saddest sort of mistakes are the ones we make repeatedly. Think back over your past experience with test taking. If you have previously taken Microsoft certification exams, these experiences should be given special attention. What types of experiences have you had in prior exams? How successful have you been? Did you run out of time? Did you arrive late? Were you fully prepared? What can you learn from those past experiences that may help you prepare for a successful exam this time?

Your answers to the questions above will be individual. We encourage you to carefully plan ways to avoid any problems you may have previously had. Careful study and the techniques listed above may help with many problems. There are two relatively common test-taking challenges, however, that merit some specific mention.

Test anxiety has profoundly impaired millions of careers. Its symptoms are those associated with a "fight or flight" instinct; rapid heartbeat and breathing, sweating, general nervousness, and in more severe cases, an overwhelming sense of panic. If you suffer from mild to moderate anxiety when you take exams, try some of the following techniques to control your anxiety while testing.

- Remember that some anxiety is a normal reaction to the situation.

- Prepare well for the exam. The better prepared you are, the easier it will be to remain calm.

- Breathe slowly and deeply before and during the exam.

- Ensure you get adequate rest prior to the exam. If your body is fatigued, it will have a more difficult time responding well to the stress of the exam.

- Avoid consuming caffeine and nicotine. These chemicals are stimulants that act to increase the anxiety symptoms you feel.

- If you are so inclined and have a few weeks until you take the exam, a regular pattern of prayer or meditation is often helpful in learning to calm your body's reactions.

If your anxiety is more severe, you may want to seek assistance from a qualified psychotherapist. Alternatively, you may want to talk to your physician about medications that can help you cope with these brief and specific episodes of anxiety.

Another personal trait that sometimes keeps people from doing their best on exams is self-doubt. If you find that you tend to approach tests with an optimistic attitude but then midway through an exam you begin to doubt yourself and feel overwhelmed by the difficulty of the questions, there are some strategies that can help.

- Prepare well, including gaining a solid understanding of the topics to be covered and the level of detail you will need to know.

- Remind yourself before and during the exam that most tests beyond high school are written to assess students who vary significantly in their abilities. This includes students at the high end of the range of abilities. Some questions are quite difficult, but only seasoned professionals are expected to know the answers. Perfect scores on Microsoft exams are relatively uncommon. Remind yourself that not knowing all of the answers immediately is the way the test designers intended it to work. It does not automatically mean that you will fail the exam. Stay focused and use the knowledge you have acquired from study and the strategies given below to answer as many questions correctly as you can.

- Work smart. Since all questions are worth the same amount of points, don't linger on difficult questions. Select your best guess, then mark the question for review after you have completed the easier questions. This will have two positive effects: you won't use up time on hard questions that you could use more efficiently on easier questions, and you'll feel less frustrated as you move through the exam.

Finally, the last 24 hours before the exam can make a big difference in your performance. The next topic will cover some ways to take full advantage of those last hours.

Setting the Stage for Success: The Last 24 Hours

The essential element you should attend to in the final hours before the exam is concentration. Several factors can hamper your ability to concentrate, and you should do what you can to prevent any impairment. These concentration-reducing factors include fatigue, agitation, anxiety, and distractions. Below are some rules to help you avoid the most common of these:

- If you have not been to the testing site before, make a trip there prior to the testing day so you'll know where to park and how to get into the testing facility.

- Get a good night's sleep the night before the exam. If your style is to spend hours cramming just before the exam, schedule your exam for the afternoon. After a solid night of sleep, study for most of the morning and then go to the testing center. If this is difficult because of your work schedule, many larger cities have centers that are open on Saturdays. Don't underestimate the importance of good sleep. It may not explicitly improve your score, but without it your brain won't work as well, and on Microsoft exams that will hurt you.

- Arrive early. Go out of your way to arrive early at the testing center. A delay in travel can leave you arriving late and feeling flustered. Plan ahead. It's better to arrive early and spend a few moments relaxing or reviewing than to run in at the last moment and have to immediately begin concentrating. If you were unable to make a prior visit to the testing center, or if you are traveling to a different city to take the exam, this item is especially important. Before you begin the exam, prevent any distractions by visiting the restroom or getting a drink of water if needed. Don't let minor annoyances become big headaches.

- See "Things to Know about Microsoft Exams" for other details of the testing experience. Knowing what to expect will make the whole experience go more smoothly and allow you to focus all of your energies on the exam itself.

Things to Know About Taking Microsoft Exams

- You will need to present two forms of ID.

- You will be asked to agree not to tell others about the content of the exam.

- These are closed-book exams. Don't bring notes or other aids into the exam.

- You will be given scratch paper to use while taking the exam, but you'll have to give it back when you complete the exam.

- You may be monitored with audio or video equipment while taking the exam.

Selecting the Right Answer

Microsoft certification exams intend to measure the degree to which you have mastered the subject matter, and they do that quite well. However, the exams (like most exams) also indirectly test how well you have mastered the art of test taking. The remainder of this appendix will focus directly on techniques that can improve your general test-taking abilities.

The effect of test-taking skills is being able to test above your actual ability. The basic skill involved in effective multiple-choice testing is guessing well which answer is correct. We will present here some basic practices, or good habits, for test taking. You should learn to apply these practices every time you answer an exam question, whether it's from Microsoft or anyone else. Next, we present some more sophisticated strategies that may apply in certain circumstances.

Basic Practices

Six good habits for test taking are covered here. These basic practices generally should help you identify correct responses and avoid errors, while the advanced tools are primarily to help you guess effectively when you can't identify the correct answer directly. The basic practices covered below are:

- Read questions twice—watch for "not," "un," and double negatives.

- Guess the correct answer yourself before reading the given responses.

- Always read all of the responses before selecting one.
- Eliminate obviously wrong choices.
- Don't spend too much time on hard questions.
- Never change an answer unless you are sure it is wrong.

Jot this list on a small card, and review these items just before taking any practice exams. Also, review these just before taking your certification exam.

Read Questions Twice   Carefully read each question. Watch for words that may reverse the meaning of the question with prefixes like "un" or "im." Other ways meanings can be reversed are with words like "not" or the use of double negatives. Double negatives can be particularly difficult, as the second negative may arise in a response.

If a particular question is overly complex or initially confusing, you may want to diagram the question on your notepaper, noting the crucial elements of the question. You may question the extra time it will take to read the questions twice, but we recommend this method because with only one reading, the full meaning of the question is often not apparent. For example, consider the following question:

Which principle of object design states that the implementation detail of the way an object works should be hidden from the developer?

At first glance, readers may interpret this question, incorrectly, to be asking about hidden objects. The second time through, the reader re-reads the crucial phrase of the question, "Which principle of object design…" Reading the sentence twice enhances the accuracy of your understanding. Misinterpreting a question is more common in testing situations, because the reader is rushed and under pressure.

Some questions may have more than one correct response, and you will be asked to select a certain number of correct responses. Because there is no partial credit given, selecting only one response will be a wrong answer. Read directions carefully!

Guess the Answer Yourself Before Reading Response Options   If you are able to answer the question yourself, and your response is one of the listed options, the likelihood is very good that you have answered correctly. If you don't try to guess before seeing the given options, you may be misled by one of the incorrect responses. The main benefit to guessing early is this opportunity to bypass potential error.

Read All of the Responses Before Marking Your Choice   Your goal is to get as many questions correct as possible. Don't miss anything by answering a question without considering all of the possible responses. Some exam questions include two essentially correct responses, and you must select the one that is *most* correct. If you don't read them all, you may bypass the most correct response.

Eliminate Obviously Wrong Choices   If you cannot figure out the correct response, it is to your clear advantage to make an educated guess. This often means eliminating false options, and choosing among the remaining options. If you know the answers to half the questions on an exam, and guess randomly at the other half, you would on the basis of probability get a score of 62 percent (50 percent for the answers you knew, and 12 percent or so for the ones you got right by guessing randomly). If you are able to eliminate just one wrong response choice from each of the unknown questions, you will raise your score to 67 percent. If you reduce the pool by two on each question, your score increases to 75 percent. These figures are assuming that you select from the remaining responses randomly. Given a well-reasoned comparison of remaining responses using the tactics discussed below, you may be able to do even better.

Don't Spend Too Much Time on Hard Questions   As stated earlier, your score and your personal experience will be better if you are able to manage the inevitable difficult questions. Pick an answer, mark the question for review, and come back to it later, when you have completed the easier questions.

Never Change Your Answer Unless You Absolutely Know It Is Wrong   Several studies (and a huge collection of anecdotal evidence) have shown that when answers are changed, correct answers are changed to incorrect ones far more often than the other way around. About the only time you should feel comfortable in changing a response is if you find solid evidence in a subsequent question that your choice was wrong. There may be other times when you recognize problems and change answers, but you should always do so cautiously.

Advanced Strategies

So, now you've learned good habits for avoiding unnecessary errors. You will encounter some questions in your exam that you don't know the answers to. Good habits won't get you far on these questions. There are techniques, some of which we will present here, that can improve your chances of a correct response on these more difficult questions. To their credit, Microsoft puts great effort into their test-creation process, and these techniques will not always work.

The key to these techniques lies in an analysis of the response options given. In creating questions, the Microsoft staff has one basic goal, to create questions that will discriminate between testers with solid knowledge and experience and those without. There are several ways to create questions that may discriminate in this way.

- A question with a series of response options that are only finely distinguished from each other or that fall into clusters.

- A question with response options that are largely unique from each other.

- Some combination of the previous two.

These types of questions are handled differently. Your task then, is to determine which type of question it is. You can quickly determine which type of question you are facing and use the correct choice-selection strategies.

Clustered Responses   As noted above, some questions contain response sets with similar or clustered response options. The following question illustrates this type of question:

1. If an HTML form contains a text input field called Name, how would the value of that field be read in an Active Server Page (assuming that the method of the form is POST)?

   A. Request.QueryString("Name")

   B. Response.QueryString("Name")

   C. Request.Form("Name")

   D. Response.Form("Name")

The key to improving your success rate with this type of question is to look for the variation patterns in the response options. By giving a series of responses that differ systematically, the test developers are indirectly prompting you to remember certain issues relevant to the question. These questions are much easier to answer correctly than similar questions with random response options. This assumes, of course, that you have at least a basic knowledge of the subject matter.

In the example above, the four responses vary in two ways: half begin with a reference to the Request object, and half with the Response object. Additionally, two items reference a QueryString collection, and two reference a Form collection. In other words, by selecting these particular response options, the test creators are hinting that some combination of these two is the correct choice. The trick, then, is not so much figuring out the syntax as figuring out which structural elements are involved.

If the responses given for this question were more random, then you get fewer hints. In that case, you must be aware of many interacting issues, disproving three incorrect choices (including syntax or other meta information). When the only hope you have is to recall *anything* from a study guide, this reduction of noise is a great advantage.

Other examples of these "variations on a theme" questions are given below. Examine the available responses, and practice identifying the variance issues.

1. A CGI application is:

   A. Interpreted code running in a separate address space from the Web server.

   B. Interpreted code running in the same address space as the Web server.

   C. Compiled code running in a separate address space from the Web server.

   D. Compiled code running in the same address space as the Web server.

2. Which code statement would allow you to point the user's browser to a page called newpage.html?

   A. Request.Redirect newpage.html

   B. Request.Navigate newpage.html

    C. Response.Redirect newpage.htm

    D. Response.Navigate newpage.html

3. Which code sample would set a reference of the variable called EngObj to a running instance of the Truck.Engine object?

    A. `EngObj=CreateObject("Truck.Engine")`

    B. `Set EngObj=CreateObject("Truck.Engine")`

    C. `EngObj=Server.CreateObject("Truck.Engine")`

    D. `Set EngObj=Server.CreateObject("Truck.Engine")`

For Question 1 above, the crucial differences are the type of code being run (interpreted or compiled) and the location of the code processing (in process or out of process). Question 2 focuses on the essential differences between the Request and Response objects and the Navigate and Redirect methods. Question 3, in contrast, focuses attention on the syntax of the code rather than the objects or methods called.

Unique Responses When test responses do not have overlapping content, the strategies at your disposal are quite different. In this situation, there are more techniques available, but they are less reliable and not used on all unique-response questions.

The main advantage you have with this type of question is that the responses still have to be uniquely correct, so the alternatives can be more obviously unrelated. These answers are also frequently shorter and simpler than their overlapping cousins. The downside to these questions is that you get less information to aid you in extrapolating the correct answer.

The tools you have for these types of questions are as follows:

- These questions, especially if the responses are short and simple, are typically looking for recognition of a significant term. If one term looks like it might be related to the question and the others mean nothing to you, pick the one that rings a bell, even if it is a small bell.

- Unlike the overlapping-type responses, in the case of unique responses, a response that stands out from the group is likely to be the correct one.

- Watch for specific details. The more descriptors in use, the more likely this is the correct answer. Consider the following:

1. In a typical two-tier application, the database engine will reside on a:

   A. `NetWare server`

   B. `Central database application server`

   C. `Client workstation`

   D. `Windows NT computer`

In this case, the "B" answer is distinguishable over "D" because it carries extra defining adjectives.

- Watch for qualifiers. In other words, always and never are difficult standards to match, so correct responses will often contain words like "usually" or "typically."

- Some response sets will contain only a list of numbers. In general, test creators rarely choose one of the extremes for the correct answer. If you have no idea and are guessing, select one of the central responses. Consider the following example:

1. How many different types of class objects can a collection hold?

   A. 0

   B. 1

   C. 2

   D. 3

The answer to this question is 1, but if you don't know this at exam time, you can at least guess that A and D are probably not the correct responses. Using this technique, your chance of being correct improves from 25 percent to 50 percent.

A final comment on an old wives' tale: Many students have picked up the habit of always selecting "C" when the correct answer is not known. The rationale for this tactic is a fear that guessing at random may cause them to miss all correct responses and selecting "C" guarantees 25 percent probability on these guessed items (assuming four response options are given).

The "select C" logic has two flaws. First, it denies the laws of probability. If you select from four items randomly, you should consistently get approximately 25 percent correct. The more questions guessed randomly, the more narrow the range of variation around that 25 percent mark.

The second flaw in this logic is that by taking this conservative approach, potential opportunities are lost. As noted earlier, ruling out a few clearly false responses along the way raises your chances of guessing correct responses.

If you have previously used this method, we hope that reading this appendix has discouraged you from its use. You can do much better without necessarily knowing any more basic information.

The Microsoft certification exams are constructed by professionals trained in test creation procedures. Questions and response sets have been designed to reduce the effectiveness of these techniques. Using them is still likely to improve your scores, but these strategies will not compensate for inadequate study and preparation. The best approach to certification exams is a combination of thorough study, applied experience, and skilled test taking.

APPENDIX

C

Microsoft SQL Server 7 Primer

This appendix was written with Beta3 (build 517) of SQL Server 7. There may be some subtle differences between what you see in this chapter and the production release of SQL Server 7.

You cannot undertake any serious discussion of distributed application development without involving a Relational Database Management System (RDBMS). Microsoft SQL Server 7 is the most sophisticated RDBMS that Microsoft has developed to date. Along with standard RDBMS features such as a server-side engine and a relational data catalog, SQL Server boasts advanced features such as row-level locking, a security model tightly integrated with the Windows NT security system, and an extensive data transfer/transformation utility.

If you do not have a copy of SQL Server 7 for use in the exercises in this book, you can order a 120-day–evaluation copy from Microsoft for a nominal fee. Details can be found at `http://www.microsoft.com/sql`.

The intent of this appendix is to provide a basic degree of SQL Server 7 awareness to readers who have never used SQL Server before. In this appendix, we will discuss the installation of SQL Server and its client utilities as well as the basic navigation of the SQL Server clients. These clients include the SQL Enterprise Manager snap-in to the Microsoft Management Console and the Query Profiler utility. This appendix does not cover any detailed discussion of the SQL language. This information can be found in Chapter 2 of this study guide.

Installing SQL Server

Microsoft SQL Server 7 comes in two builds, one for the Intel X86 family of processors and one for the Compaq Alpha family of processors. For this discussion, we'll assume that you will be installing the Intel build of

SQL Server. In this section, we will discuss the different versions of SQL Server 7, their system requirements for installing SQL Server 7, and, finally, the installation process itself.

SQL Server 7 Versions

Microsoft SQL Server 7 comes in three different versions, the Desktop, Standard, and Enterprise editions. Each edition has its own strengths and pricing structures. Choosing the right version of SQL Server depends on your application needs and your network architecture.

SQL Server Desktop Edition

The Desktop edition is perfectly suited for mobile computing and small workgroup applications. Unlike the other versions of SQL Server, which require a Windows NT operating system, the Desktop edition can be installed on a Windows 95/98 computer. The Desktop edition runs as a background application rather than as a Windows NT service, which is the operating mode for the other versions of SQL Server. On a Windows NT operating system, the Desktop edition supports up to two processors. Windows 95/98 does not support multiprocessing. To install the Desktop edition of SQL Server 7 you will need:

- One of the following Microsoft Windows operating systems:
  - Windows 95
  - Windows 98
  - Windows NT Workstation 4 or later
  - Windows NT Server 4 or later
  - Windows NT Server Enterprise 4 or later
- Windows NT Service Pack 4 for all NT operating systems
- Microsoft Internet Explorer 4.1 Service Pack 1
- Installed Network Protocol
- Intel Pentium 166MHz or Alpha processor (up to two)
- 32MB RAM minimum
- 65-180MB hard disk space

SQL Server Standard Edition

The core SQL Server product is designed for most standard applications. It can be installed only on Windows NT operating systems. This edition of SQL Server supports additional processors (up to four), and runs as a Windows NT service. Since it runs as an NT service, it supports a greater degree of integration with Windows NT, including security integration and performance monitoring integration. To install the Standard edition of SQL Server you will need:

- One of the following Windows NT operating systems:
    - Windows NT Workstation 4 or later
    - Windows NT Server 4 or later
    - Windows NT Server 4 Enterprise Edition or later
- Windows NT Service Pack 4
- Microsoft Internet Explorer 4.1 Service Pack 1
- Installed Network Protocol
- Intel Pentium 166MHz or Alpha processor (up to four)
- 32MB RAM minimum
- 65-180MB hard disk space for SQL Server
- 35-50MB hard drive space for OLAP Server

SQL Server Enterprise Edition

The Enterprise edition of SQL Server 7 is designed to support the largest and most demanding applications. It can be installed only on Windows NT Server 4 Enterprise edition or later. This offers support for Enterprise features such as fail-safe support through clustering and increased application addressable memory. Using the Enterprise edition of SQL Server also increases the number of processors that SQL Server can use, to a maximum of 32. The installation requirements for the Enterprise edition are identical to the Standard edition of SQL Server except that the Enterprise edition must be installed on a Windows NT Enterprise server.

Installing SQL Server

SQL Server 7 supports an extremely intuitive installation process. The form-driven installation utility will gather all of the necessary information from you in a series of dialogs and then continue with the installation while you wait. Assuming that you have all of the necessary system requirements, you are ready to install SQL Server.

The Installation dialogs will change between the Beta3 and the retail version of SQL Server, so to avoid confusion we have refrained from displaying installation dialogs.

You should find the setup program in the root directory of the SQL Server CD. This setup program will detect your processor type and launch the appropriate setup utility for your Intel or Alpha processor. Launching this setup application will begin a series of dialogs that will prompt you to enter information about your desired installation. Below, you will find a short discussion of each of the more important elements of the installation.

Setup Type

SQL Server gives you three choices for setting up the server. You can select either a typical, custom, or minimum installation. The option that you select will affect the utilities that are installed as well as the server settings on installation.

The typical installation option should probably be renamed the default installation. If you choose this installation, it will continue without asking any more questions about the installation process, installing the server and all of the client utilities with all of the defaults. Use this option if you need to install a server quickly and can accept the installation defaults. We will identify these defaults later in this appendix. A typical setup can be used to perform all of the exercises in this book that require SQL Server.

The custom installation option offers you the most choice on how the installation should progress. It can install all or none of the client utilities and offers the installer complete options on how the installation should progress. This option is generally preferred for most installations.

The minimum installation option installs the server but only a basic set of the client utilities. This option may be chosen when no clients are needed or desired. Minimum installations are usually chosen when disk space is at a premium; however, the disk space required by these clients is comparatively insignificant, so this option is less desirable than a custom installation.

Destination Folder

The default installation location for the SQL Server files will be \MSSQL7. The data files created on installation will be located in the \MSSQL7\Data folder. If you do not change the options presented in this dialog, these settings will prevail.

Component Installation

In a custom installation, you will be presented with a dialog that allows you to select the components that will be installed. This list is divided into categories such as Server Components, Management Tools, Development Tools, etc. Select, from these categories, the components that you wish to install. The dialog that is presented before you make any alterations represents the default values that you will get with a typical installation.

Character Set, Sort Order, and Unicode Collation

These are very important options. If you change your mind about these options after installation, you will be required to rebuild the SQL Server master database to accommodate the changes. This will usually require you to rebuild your user databases as well, which is a very tedious task and is often prone to error. Make your selections here with care.

Character set is the ANSI code page that will be the source for all character data stored in the database. A code page is a mapping of code points to different character representations. You will want to select the code page that supports the characters you intend to store in your database. The default character set is the ISO or Latin1 character set, also known as code page 1252. Other popular character sets include multilingual (code page 850) and U.S. English (code page 437).

The sort order determines how character data sorts and compares with other character data. The most important distinction between sort orders is case-sensitivity. If you select a case-sensitive sort order, upper case characters will sort differently that lower case characters. This means that when doing a comparison operation such as writing a WHERE clause in a SQL query, the phrase *LIKE 'S%'* would yield different results that the phrase *LIKE 's%'*. The default sort order is dictionary order, case-insensitive.

Although they require additional care in implementation, case-sensitive sort orders are faster internally that insensitive sort orders. The fastest sort order available is binary.

SQL Server 7 supports special character data types for Unicode storage. While a standard code page stores a character as a single byte, the Unicode character set increases the storage to two bytes per character. While this may seem like a disadvantage because it requires additional storage space for data, it can actually provide a substantial benefit.

While a standard code page using one byte to store a character can only provide 256 code points, Unicode, with its 2-byte storage, increases the number of code points to 65,536. The intent of the Unicode character set is to provide a single character set that can store the majority of the world's most commonly used characters. The Unicode character set also stores mathematical and other special symbols in common use.

The Unicode collation order is the sort order for Unicode data. The default collation order is general, case-insensitive. You can also set the collation order to support certain locale preferences, if desired.

Network Libraries

SQL Server communicates with client applications across a network using network libraries. Although the names of some of the supported network libraries are the same as the network protocols with which they operate, installing the network libraries does not install the required network protocol. A network library is simply a layer of software that provides the SQL Server DBLib API with an abstraction of the network layer. In other words, the network library interfaces with the network so that SQL Server doesn't have to.

SQL Server supports numerous network libraries. Which libraries you install depends on which network protocols are in use in your network and how your client applications intend to communicate with SQL Server. You can install multiple network libraries if desired. Below is a list of the network libraries supported. Those that are installed by default are marked with an asterisk (*).

- Named Pipes*
- Multi-Protocol*

- TCP/IP Sockets*
- NWLink
- AppleTalk
- Banyan Vines

Some SQL Server functionality depends on a Named Pipes or Multi-Protocol connection. These network libraries can function with any Microsoft-supplied network protocol, but Multi-Protocol should be used if you run more that one network protocol on your network. Multi-Protocol also supports data encryption for the data as it moves across the wire.

You must have a network protocol installed before you can communicate with a SQL Server. Microsoft does not ship versions of the AppleTalk or Banyan Vines protocols. If you are using these protocols in your network, you must install them separately from the network library on the SQL Server machine.

Services Accounts

Each of the three services installed by SQL Server must have a Windows NT account in order to access Windows NT resources. If this server will not communicate with any other SQL Servers in the network to perform activities such as replication, remote stored procedures, or distributed transactions, then you can install the SQL Server using the Local System account. However, it is generally a good idea to provide a User account with administrative rights to it, and then use the same account for all SQL Server services.

Completing the Installation

After answering all of the installation questions, the SQL Server installer will begin the task of copying files to the hard drive and configuring the SQL Server according to your instructions. After the installation is complete, you will be returned to Windows NT. It is not required that you restart Windows NT, although it is generally a good idea.

Using SQL Server Client Utilities

SQL Server ships with a set of client utilities that allows the control and configuration of your SQL Server installation. They can be used to perform a full array of administrative functions. You can locate these utilities in the Windows Start menu by clicking Start ➤ Programs ➤ Microsoft SQL Server 7. Among the client utilities installed are:

- Service Manager
- Client Network Utility
- Server Network Utility
- Enterprise Manager
- Query Analyzer

This section will discuss these client utilities and their application in the SQL Server environment.

Service Manager

The SQL Service Manager utility is your primary interface for starting, stopping, and pausing the SQL Server installed services. Depending on your installation selections, up to four services can be installed.

MSSQLServer   The SQL Server engine. This service must be running to perform any SQL query or execute any Transact SQL statement.

SQLServerAgent   The SQL Server automation service. This service supports activities such as job scheduling, alert notifications, replication, etc.

Microsoft Search   The Full Text Search service. Allows the developer to create very sophisticated searches beyond basic SQL comparisons.

MSDTC   The Microsoft Distributed Transaction Coordinator. This service allows a SQL Server to enlist other servers within the context of a single transaction. This service is an integral part of the Microsoft Transaction Server product.

The Service Manager dialog, illustrated in Figure C.1, contains two drop-down lists. One list box allows you to select a server, while the other allows you to select a service. Once you have selected the desired server and service, click the Start/Continue, Pause, or Stop buttons to perform the desired action on the service.

F I G U R E   C.1

The Service Manager dialog

You can also start and stop services using the Control Panel Services applet or the Net Start and Net Stop command line utilities. The command lines can be especially helpful for batch operations.

Client Network Utility

Network libraries are essential to provide communication with a SQL Server, but it is not enough to simply install the network library on the server. You must also configure the client computer to talk with a SQL Server using a network library that is installed on the server. The Client Network Utility provides the flexibility of configuring a single client to communicate with different servers using different network libraries.

The Client Network Utility, pictured in Figure C.2, displays the network libraries that you will use to communicate with specific servers. If you wish to change the network library setting for communicating with a specific server, click the Edit button and make the change in the resulting dialog. To add a new server to your client list, click the Add button to present the dialog illustrated in Figure C.3. Type in the name of the server and select the appropriate network library. When you close the dialog, the settings are saved in the client computer's registry.

F I G U R E   C.2

The Client Network
Utility

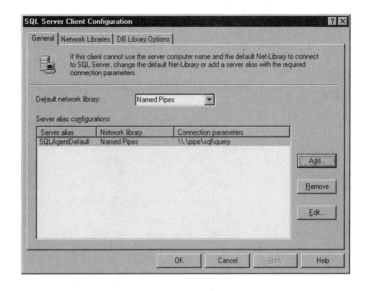

F I G U R E   C.3

Adding a new server to
the client

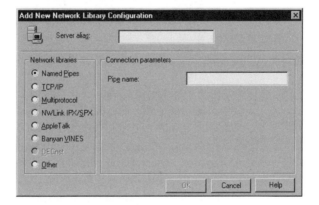

Server Network Utility

After installing a SQL Server, it is very easy to modify the SQL Server's network library support through the Server Network utility. This utility, pictured in Figure C.4, works in a similar fashion to the Client Network Utility.
You can modify an installed network library's settings by selecting the entry
in the list and clicking the Edit button. Clicking the Add button presents a

dialog that looks similar to the Client Add dialog in Figure C.3, except that you will not be able to change the name of the server. Select the desired network library for installation and click OK.

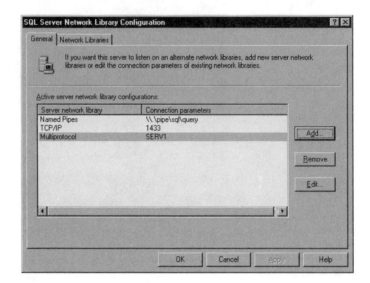

Enterprise Manager

The SQL Enterprise Manager is the primary graphical client utility for administering a SQL Server. The Enterprise Manager is implemented as a snap-in to the Microsoft Manager Console, an MDI application that provides a common shell for administering multiple services, such as Internet Information Server 4 and Microsoft Transaction Server 2.

The Enterprise Manager Snap-In, pictured in Figure C.5, provides a mechanism for viewing and administering multiple servers in the Enterprise from a single location. This utility is arranged in a standard Explorer interface, meaning that the tree view on the left side can be expanded to drill into any desired level of detail. Clicking the tree view will display the detail in the list view on the right side.

Some of the more important elements in the list view include:

Services   The first four nodes under the server display the current state of the SQL Server services. To change the state of the server, right-click the icon representing the service that you wish to affect and select Start, Stop, or Pause from the pop-up menu.

FIGURE C.5

The SQL Server
Enterprise Manager

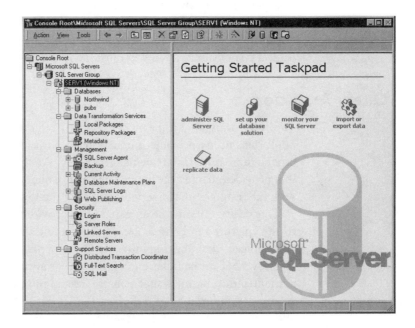

Logins This node contains all of the valid logins that this SQL Server will recognize. These might be either standard logins that are specific to SQL Server, or Windows NT accounts that have been added to the SQL Server login list.

Server Roles A list of security contexts under which a login can operate. Server Roles define a set of permissions to perform server level operations.

Databases Lists all databases managed by that server. You can drill into the databases folder to view the individual databases and drill further to view the objects within the databases. Database objects include tables, stored procedures, views, data types, database users, etc.

SQL Server Logs A set of error and status logs maintained by SQL Server. The most recent log is marked Current. Remaining logs are identified by archive number, lower numbers being the most recent.

Data Transformation Packages A list of saved Data Transformations created by the Data Transformation Services. This data transfer/transformation utility is a very sophisticated utility that allows the exchange of data between any OLE DB- or ODBC-compliant data formats.

If you are a database administrator (DBA) for SQL Server, you will be spending a great deal of time with the Enterprise Manager utility. If you are responsible for the development of a database and have no system administration responsibility, you will most likely use this utility less often.

Query Analyzer

This is the utility that is the most frequently referenced in the chapters in this book. This utility provides a basic interface for executing SQL queries and other Transact SQL statements. The Query Analyzer is a simple interface that provides an interface for entering a SQL query and executing that query, with the results of that query displayed in the lower pane of the window.

This utility can only be accessed after providing a valid login. The login form is pictured in Figure C.6. After selecting the target server, you have two choices when logging in to the Query Analyzer. You can use either Windows NT authentication or SQL Server authentication. Windows NT authentication requires that you are logged in to Windows NT under an account recognized by SQL Server. By default, all NT administrators are allowed access to the SQL Server through Windows NT authentication. This is sometimes referred to as trusted security, because SQL Server trusts that Windows NT has properly authenticated the user.

FIGURE C.6

Logging in to the
Query Analyzer

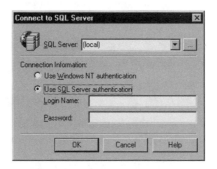

If you choose to use SQL Server authentication, you must provide a login from the list of SQL Server logins. This will not be a Windows NT login and password, but rather a login managed by SQL Server and authenticated by SQL Server exclusively. On installation, one user login account is created by default. That is the *sa* (system administrator) account. If you choose to use SQL Server authentication, use the login *sa* with no password.

Once you have been authenticated, you will see the Query Analyzer form as displayed in Figure C.7. When the form is first displayed you will see only one pane, not two as in the figure. Once you enter a query into the form and execute the query, the panes will split, displaying the query in the top pane and the query results in the bottom pane.

FIGURE C.7

The Query Analyzer utility

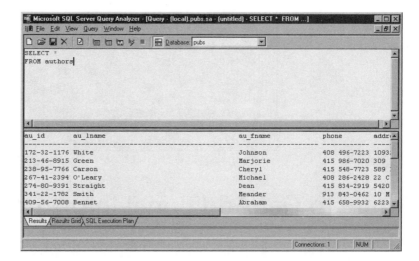

Every query assumes that it is using an individual database when executing. Some systems' administrative functionality assumes that you are using the master database, while queries that extract data from a user database assume that you are using that database. In Figure C.7, you will notice that the database drop-down list on the right side of the Query Analyzer toolbar shows that the query will be directed to the pubs database. To change the target database, open the drop-down list and select the desired database.

Once you have entered a query into the Query window, you can execute the query using numerous methods. By clicking the Query menu item, you will see options about query execution. The items labeled Results in Text and Results in Grid will toggle between these formats of displaying the query results. Results in Text puts the results in a fixed-width text format, while Results in Grid puts the results in a spreadsheet-like format. Selecting Execute from the Query menu will run the query. If you choose the Results in Grid option, you will see the results in a grid format as illustrated in Figure C.8.

FIGURE C.8

Executing into a grid

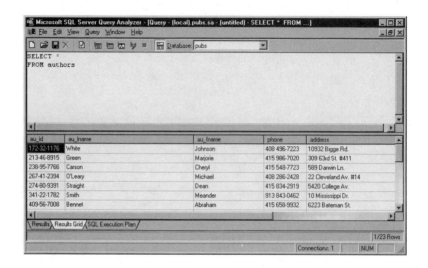

Where to Get Additional Information

This discussion of SQL Server has been brief, but there are many good resources available for you to continue your exploration of the SQL Server 7 product. These include Web sites, books, and other publications. Some of the better resources are listed below for your reference.

- Microsoft's SQL Server Web site, located at `http://www.microsoft.com/sql`

- *MCSE: SQL Server 7 System Administration Study Guide*, published by Sybex Network Press

- *Microsoft SQL Server 7 System Administration Training Kit*, published by Microsoft Press

- *Microsoft SQL Server 7 Database Implementation Training Kit*, published by Microsoft Press

Glossary

Abstraction The ability of an object to provide a virtual representation of a physical object or process. Using the concept of abstraction, you can reference an object without needing to describe in detail every individual attribute of the object.

Active Server Pages An ISAPI extension that allows HTML Script tags to execute on the server. HTML is placed in an Active Server Page. Script is marked for server-side execution and the executing script creates an HTML response to send back to the browser.

ActiveX An element of COM that defines the structure of client-side components and object models. Its use is particularly relevant for Internet development.

ActiveX Data Objects (ADO) A set of programmable objects designed to interface with OLE DB. The ADO object model showcases a more simplified hierarchy than its predecessors. The ADO object library is currently available from Microsoft free of charge in the OLE DB SDK.

Aesthetics The elements on an application interface that provide a visually pleasing environment. Fonts, complementary colors, and graphics can all provide aesthetic elements to an application interface.

Application Programming Interface (API) A set of functions or component interfaces that are available to other applications to provide programmability for a component or service. There are two major types of API interfaces. They are traditional call-level interfaces that are implemented as function calls in a DLL, or COM interfaces that are implemented as objects.

Atomic The attribute of a transaction that defines it as all-or-none. If a data modification is guaranteed to be atomic, then every element of the modification must succeed or the entire modification must be reversed.

Attribute A property or description of an entity used in database design. If the entity you are describing is a car, the attributes might be color, weight, etc. Attributes are represented in a database as the columns or fields in a table.

BackOffice A collection of Microsoft client/server applications bundled in a single package. BackOffice products includes SQL Server, Exchange Server, SMS, and SNA.

Bandwidth   The capacity of a network link to transmit data at a certain rate. Usually expressed in bits per second, 10 Mbps (mega-bits per second) is a common bandwidth for Ethernet networks. Bandwidth can either describe the total capacity of the network or the remaining capacity after all existing network traffic is taken into account.

Bidirectional Character Set   A character set that supports writing from both right to left and left to right. Middle Eastern languages in particular require bidirectional character sets. Although the native text is written from right to left, numbers and other European words which may be incorporated into the Middle Eastern language are written from left to right.

Business Services   Functionality in a database application that defines business logic. Data validation rules and other business rules make up the business services of an application.

Bytecode   The code resulting from the compilation of a Java class file. Rather than compiling into machine-specific code, Java code is compiled into bytecode, which must be executed by a Java Virtual Machine. This enables Java to execute on any hardware platform that has a Java Virtual Machine that is developed for it.

Class   The formal definition of an object. When an object is instantiated, the instantiation is based on the defining class. This class defines the interfaces, properties, and methods of an object.

Class ID   A unique 128-bit value that identifies a given COM interface as unique across all COM interfaces. This value is stored in the windows registry under CLSID subkeys. In an HTML object tag, the class ID identifies the object that is being inserted into the Web page.

Client/Server   A database application architecture that divides the processing tasks of the application between the server and a workstation. Other servers on the networks may also provide additional processing. There are two general forms of client/server architecture: two-tier and multiple-tier.

Codepage   A set of characters assigned to code points that is intended for a locale-specific implementation. ANSI code pages provide support for multiple characters by assigning each a number from 0 to 255. The computer stores the number internally and the character translation occurs through the code page.

Code Point   A single point in a code page or character set that identifies a single character. ANSI code pages define 256 code points. Each code point represents a single character that is rendered by a font written explicitly for that code page.

Collection   A group of one or more objects of the same type. A collection is an object that provides containership for other objects. All collections should support at least one property called *count,* which returns the total number of objects in that collection.

Common Gateway Interface (CGI)   An application that runs on a Web server designed to provide services and/or return HTML to a browser through the Web server. In IIS 3.0, CGI applications run in a separate process address space from the Web Server process itself.

Component   An object or group of objects compiled into a binary file (usually COM compliant) that can be accessed from applications.

Component Object Model (COM)   A specification that defines binary standards for object interfaces and specifies how objects relate and work with each other. Object Linking and Embedding (OLE) and ActiveX are both implementations of the Component Object Model.

Consistency   An attribute of a user interface to provide the same visual cues for the same actions without deviation. For example, if an opening file folder is used in one screen to symbolize a file open operation, the same metaphor should be consistently applied throughout the application. This includes all applications in a suite of which this application may be a member.

Console Interface   A legacy command window interface most commonly used for batch executions, emulations, and utility configurations.

Cookie   A small file hosted on the browser that allows the Web developer to store information concerning the preferences of the Web user making the connection. The cookie can also be used to maintain persistence of variables and other data across pages.

Cryptography API   The component of WOSA that provides support for cryptography services running under Microsoft Windows through a common API. Service providers that are Crypto API compliant will operate with any client application written to the Crypto API standard.

Data Access Objects (DAO)   The proprietary COM interface to Microsoft's JET database engine version 3.5 and earlier. The Data Access Objects provide support for JET databases, other ISAM databases through installable ISAM drivers, and ODBC databases.

Data Services   Functionality in a database application that interacts directly with the data storage. The data engine in a database application represents the data services interface.

Decision-Support System   A database that is used primarily as a reporting system. Decision-support databases are responsible for returning data to clients based on data selects, but rarely have any data modifications or insertions issued against them. Decision-support systems are often good candidates for denormalization.

Denormalization   The process of deliberately violating the rules of normalization in order to improve performance in a database.

Deployment   The process of installing applications on all the clients and servers that will run an application.

Device   In SQL Server, a preallocated unit of storage used to create databases.

Directness   The ability of an interface to give the user visual cues that indicate a direct response to an action taken by the user. For example, if a user double-clicks an icon, the mouse pointer will change to an hourglass. The hourglass is a direct result of the user's action.

ECMAScript   Defined by the European Computer Makers Association, ECMAScript defines a standard for JavaScript implementation in a Web page.

Encapsulation   The ability of an object to hide its implementation details from the object's consumers. The object becomes a "black box," where a set of interfaces is known, but how the interfaces are implemented is not known or needed by those calling the object.

Entity   An object or process that a database describes. In an inventory database system, an entity might be a customer or a product. Entities are represented in relational database structures as tables.

Event   A notification fired by an object altering the system of a condition that has occurred. In event-driven programming, events are the code catalysts. Nothing happens until an event fires. An event can be triggered by the user as in a click event of a command button, or it may be fired by the system, as in the load event of an HTML page.

Exchange Server   Microsoft BackOffice product that provides e-mail and groupware services. The e-mail services can be for the local network and also for Internet mail.

Feedback   The ability of an application to provide constant information to the user about application state and program flow. For example, when you press a toggle button, its shadowing changes, making the button appear to be pressed down. This informs the user that the feature symbolized by that button is engaged.

File-Server Database   A database architecture in which a data engine that resides on a client workstation accesses data stored in data files on a network file server. This approach is different from a client/server database in that the entire application and data engine resides on the client workstation. The server does nothing but store the file for shared access.

File Transfer Protocol (FTP)   A protocol used to transfer files (upload or download) over the Internet or intranets. The FTP interface is typically text-based, and WWW protocols are GUI-based.

Flat File   A data storage format in which all of the data is stored in few large tables rather than broken up into smaller tables and related together. Flat-file storage structures suffer from the disadvantage of storing a significant amount of redundant data.

Forgiveness   When a user takes an undesired action in an application, the application must provide a means of backing away from the action. For example, a prompt asking if a user really wants to close a window provides an element of forgiveness to the user who clicks the close button by mistake. He or she can reverse the process.

Globalization   The process of developing software with international distribution in mind. The globalization process becomes part of the initial planning phase. There is virtually no difference between a domestic distribution and an international distribution where the code is concerned.

Groupware   Software that allows groups to collaborate on projects. Tracks multiple accesses and changes to files so all the members of a group can see what other group members have done on the project.

HTML Form   An HTML structure that allows input to be received from a user and sent back to a process residing on a server. This server-side process might be a CGI application or an ISAPI application such as Active Server Pages.

HTML Tag   An identifier in a text file used to instruct Web browsers about how text should be formatted and displayed. Some tags are browser-specific as to their interpretation, while others will look the same displayed in almost any browser.

HTTP Response   The response to an HTTP request. The HTTP response usually contains the Web page requested by the browser, but it can also be a custom-created HTML page generated by an Active Server Page or some other server-side process.

HTTP Request   The message sent from the browser to the Web server when a page is requested or a form is submitted. The HTTP request message may contain values captured in an HTML form. These values can then be processed by a server-side process.

Hyperlink   Text marked by an anchor tag in an HTML page that, when clicked, points the browser to another location. Hyperlinks usually appear in another color, such as blue, when rendered on a Web page.

Hypertext Markup Language (HTML)   The language of the World Wide Web. HTML is not a programming language, it is a text markup environment like RTF in which tags that are used to mark the text are interpreted by the Web browser that loads the HTML file.

Inheritance   The ability of one class to define the interfaces, properties, and methods of another class. A class can be created based on another class. The new class will have the same properties and methods of the original base class, but the new class can add its own or take away from the base class behaviors.

Internationalization   A generic term that refers to the process of preparing software for international distribution. A developer can accomplish internationalization in one of two distinct ways. The developer can either localize the application or globalize the application.

Internet Server API (ISAPI)   An API set that allows the Web developer to create applications that run on the Internet Information Server in response to browser requests. ISAPI applications can provide services to a browser such as data connectivity or return HTML to the browser.

Intranet   The use of Internet protocols and programming within a local area network. An intranet works the same way as the Internet; however, only local users are allowed to access intranet content.

Internet Information Server (IIS)   Microsoft BackOffice product that provides Web publishing, FTP publishing, and on older versions Gopher publishing capabilities on an intranet or the Internet.

Java   A programming language developed by Sun Microsystems. Java is an object-oriented language very similar to C++ in structure. It can be used to create small applets that run in a Web browser and can be incorporated as part of a Website. It can also be used to create stand-alone applications that run independently from the Web. The interest in Java is primarily due to the fact that it can run on any hardware platform that supports a special interpreter called a Java Virtual Machine.

Java Applet   A small compiled Java class designed to run inside a Web browser. Applets are created with the Java language and are marked in an HTML file with an applet tag. The codebase attribute of the applet tag identifies the source of the applet's code. Applets are not permanently installed on the user's system and must be downloaded every time the Web page is accessed.

JavaScript   A programming language created by Netscape Communications that can be used inside of script tags on a Web page. JavaScript was formerly called LiveScript in its initial releases. It is usually added to a Web page to provide interaction with the user and other dynamic features in an internet application.

Java Virtual Machine   A Java interpreter used to execute Java bytecode on a host machine. A Java Virtual Machine can be created for any hardware platform, thereby enabling the bytecode to be cross-platform.

Joint Engine Technology (JET)   Microsoft's single-tier data engine. JET runs locally on each user workstation. Data can be stored locally or on a network server. JET ships as the native database engine in Microsoft Access, and it also ships with Microsoft Visual Basic.

JScript   In Internet Explorer, JScript is the Microsoft version of JavaScript. JScript is included with Microsoft Internet Explorer 3.0 and higher.

Keep Alive   The Keep Alive extension added to HTTP 1.1 allows a TCP connection to be maintained when the Web server would normally close it. This provides more responsiveness between the browser and the Web server, but it also increases the overhead on the Web server to maintain the open connection.

Key   Folders in the registry that hold values. Also referred to as subkeys.

License Service API (LSAPI)   The WOSA component that provides support for licensing services running under Microsoft Windows through a common API. Service providers that are LSAPI compliant will operate with any client application written to the LSAPI standard.

Locale   A specific language and sublanguage implementation. A locale is defined by its language, not by its geographical location.

Localization   The process of creating software for a specific locale. This means designing the application for implementation only in that locale and creating other distributions for alternate locales that the distributor wants to support.

Logo Compliance   Adherence to Microsoft's regulations allowing an ISV to include a Microsoft Logo on their products. Logo programs include Windows 95/NT compatible, Microsoft Office, and Microsoft BackOffice.

Many-to-Many Relationship   A method of relating two tables together such that one record in the first table relates the potentially many records in the second table and the reverse is also true. This approach requires a third table to act as an intermediary between the two related tables.

Messaging API (MAPI)   The WOSA component that provides support for e-mail and messaging systems through a common API. Service providers that are MAPI compliant will operate with any client application written to the MAPI standard.

Method   A behavior of an object that is defined in the class from which the object is instantiated. Methods cause things to happen in an object-based application.

Multiple Document Interface (MDI)   An application interface in which the main window is a container window that can hold multiple documents at the same time. Microsoft Word is an example of a multiple document interface application.

Multiple-Tier   A client/server database architecture that divides processing responsibility among many computers on the network. While the data engine resides on the application server and the client application resides on the client, there may be other servers that host business objects designed to process business rules.

Normalization   The process of removing data redundancy in data storage by following a set of rules known as the normal forms. A normalized database is the opposite of a flat-file database.

Object   An object is the implementation of a class. It is something that you can control through code. A object supports properties and methods that define how the objects appears and behaves.

OLE DB   A set of low-level COM interfaces designed to provide common support for database access. Similar in purpose to ODBC, OLE DB provides a COM interface and ODBC provides a traditional call-level interface.

One-to-Many Relationship   A method of relating two tables together such that one record in the first table relates to potentially many records in the second table. This type of relationship is the most common in relational database structure.

One-to-One Relationship   A method of relating two tables together such that one record in the first table can relate to a maximum of one record in the related table.

Online Transaction Processing System   A database that is used primarily to accept data modifications in the form of inserts, updates, and deletes. Online transaction processing systems are rarely used for heavy reporting. They are usually poor candidates for denormalization.

Open Database Connectivity (ODBC)   A component of the Windows Open Services Architecture that defines a generic standard for accessing databases. ODBC defines a call-level API set and a SQL grammar conformance requirement.

Package   Used by SMS to bundle software to be distributed and installed on SMS clients.

Package Description File (PDF)   A configuration file for SMS packages that specifies the installation options and other configuration information for the package.

Persistence   The ability of a variable or other piece of information to maintain its value across Web pages in a Web site. Using Active Server Pages, persistence can be achieved by using session-level and application-level variables.

Polymorphism   The ability to implement interfaces generically in your applications without regard to the code in the class that implements the interface. In other words, you can have multiple classes that define the same interfaces; however, the actual code behind these interfaces may perform different tasks depending on which class is used.

Property   An attribute or description of an object that is defined in the class from which the object was instantiated. One of the ways that developers implement an object is to modify its properties at run-time.

Proxy Server   Microsoft BackOffice product that provides a firewall to protect local resources from unauthorized Internet access and also controls access to Internet access from local users.

Pull Installation   A method of deploying applications over the network where the deployment process is initiated by the client by connecting to a server that contains the application. The application is pulled to the client.

Push Installation   A method of deploying applications over the network where the deployment process is initiated at a central server and is pushed down to the clients.

Record   An instance of an entity used in database design. Every record is a unique observation of an entity, complete with information regarding all attributes of that entity. Records are represented in a database as rows in a table.

REGEDIT   The registry editing tool provided with Windows 95. Also can be used in Windows NT 4.0 to edit that registry.

REGEDT32   The registry editing tool provided with Windows NT.

Registering Applications   The process of notifying the operating system about installed applications. This information must be written to specific locations in the registry.

Registry   A database used by Windows 95 and Windows NT operating systems to store system configuration information. Applications written for these platforms also store configuration information in the registry. Replaced .INI files under older Windows platforms.

Relationship   Commonality between two or more entities in a relational database. Relationships between entities allow data to be extracted from multiple sources and related together. There are three types of relationships: one-to-one, one-to-many, and many-to-many.

Remote Data Objects (RDO)   Developed by Microsoft, RDO is a thin, component layer that sits on top of the ODBC API. The RDO object model provides an alternative to the ODBC API for the database developer who must access ODBC data sources. RDO 2.0 is the last version of RDO available from Microsoft.

Scalability   The ability of a software component to handle very large amounts of traffic. For example, a component object that can handle a large number of requests coming from the Internet as easily as it handles a single request from one user is said to be scaleable.

Scope   The defined visibility of an object, variable, or procedure. For example, if a variable is declared to be visible to all procedures in an application, it is said to have public scope.

Shell Extension   An extension to the operating system interface that provides additional functionality that would be defined at the operating-system level rather than the application level. Modifying or customizing system elements is usually accomplished through shell extensions.

Simplicity   The ability of an interface to be accessible to users at all levels of sophistication. Interacting with a Windows application should be instinctive and simple.

Single Document Interface (SDI)   An application interface in which the main window is a document window. Only a single document can be loaded at any given time by the application. Notepad is an example of a single document interface application.

Single-Tier   A database architecture that places the entire responsibility for processing on a single computer. File-server databases are single-tier databases because the data engine resides on the workstation while the data used by the engine resides on a file server. Single-tier databases can also exist completely on a single computer as a stand-alone system.

SMS Installer   An add-on product to Microsoft's SMS that allows you to package applications together in a single self-extracting executable for easy installation.

SNA API   The component of WOSA that provides support for IBM System Network Architecture, allowing connectivity to IBM mainframe and AS/400 computers. The SNA API works with Microsoft SNA Server to provide gateway services to these systems without placing any of the implementation complexities in the client application.

System Network Architecture (SNA) Server   Microsoft BackOffice product that provides connectivity between a Windows NT network and IBM AS/400 or mainframe computers.

Speech API   The WOSA component that provides support for speech engines and text-to-speech services running under Microsoft Windows through a common API. Service providers that are Speech API compliant will operate with any client application written to the Speech API standard.

Structured Query Language (SQL) Server   The Microsoft BackOffice product that provides database capabilities. Many BackOffice products, such as SMS, use SQL Server to store their data. Programmers can also write custom databases by using Transact-SQL, the programming language of SQL Server.

Subkey   Folders in the registry that hold values. Also referred to as keys.

Subtree   The largest subdivision of the registry. The Windows NT registry has five subtrees; the Windows 95 registry has six subtrees.

Systems Management Server (SMS)   Microsoft BackOffice product that provides network management services. With SMS, the administrator can inventory network clients, remote control clients, and distribute software to clients.

Task Help   A help window that provides a user with step-by-step instructions to complete a task. The task help window is a pop-up, meaning that it remains on top of all other windows at all times so that it can be visible to provider instructions when needed.

Telephony API (TAPI)   The WOSA component that provides support for modems and other telephone equipment operating under Microsoft Windows through a common API. Service providers that are TPI compliant will operate with any client application written to the TPI standard.

Thunking   The process of converting a DLL call such that a 16-bit application can call a 32-bit DLL or the reverse. Windows 95 supports thunking in both directions, but Windows NT supports thunks only from 16-bit to 32-bit.

ToolTip   A small yellow window that appears when the mouse pointer is paused over an object, most commonly a tool on a toolbar. The window contains a one or two word description of the function of the tool.

Transaction Log   In SQL Server, the log portion of a SQL database. Modifications to SQL databases is usually first written to the transaction log and then written to the database.

Two-Tier   A client/server database architecture that divides processing responsibility between the client workstation and a networked application server. In this scenario, the data engine resides on the server, while the client application resides on a workstation. Business rules can be implemented on the server, workstation, or both.

Unicode   A character set that stores characters as two bytes rather than one. This allows up to 65,535 characters to be referenced from the character set rather than 256. The mission of Unicode is to provide a single character set under which all of the world's character's can be referenced.

User Control   The ability of a user to manage the interface and environment presented by an application. The user must have the ability to customize the interface and control the direction of all program flow.

User Services   Functionality in a database application that interacts directly with the user. User services include: receiving user input, formatting, reporting, etc.

Values   The configuration parameters in the registry. Values have three components, the name, type, and setting.

VBScript   A programming language created by Microsoft that can be used inside of script tags on a Web page. VBScript is based on the Microsoft Visual Basic programming language and is usually added to a Web page to provide interaction with the user and other dynamic features in an Internet application.

Windows Open Services Architecture (WOSA)   A set of APIs that provide a single system-level interface to enterprise computing environments, while hiding the complexities of heterogeneous environments from end users and developers.

World Wide Web (WWW)   A graphical method of publishing content over the Internet or intranets. Often referred to as the Web.

Index

Note to the Reader: Throughout this index **boldfaced** page numbers indicate primary discussions of a topic. *Italicized* page numbers indicate illustrations.

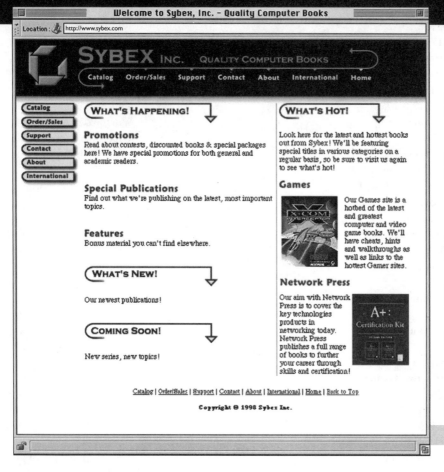

MCSD: Visual Basic 6 Distributed Applications Study Guide Companion CD-ROM

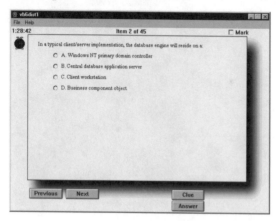

To start the CD-ROM included with this book, just pop it in your CD-ROM drive, use Explorer to locate the root directory for your CD-ROM, and double-click Clickme.exe. You'll see Sybex's easy-to-use interface.

The following productions are on the CD:

MCSD Test Engine. Created for Sybex by EdgeTest. All the questions and answers in this book are included on the test engine, an easy-to-use program for test preparation.

MCSD on the Web. Popular MCSD Web sites listed in order of importance to MCSD students.

MCSD Offline Update. The latest Microsoft information on the MCSD certification program. *NOTE:* Internet Explorer 4 or above is required to run this HTML-based document.

Internet Explorer 4.01. This powerful browser includes everything you need for accessing the Internet.

Microsoft SQL Server 7.0 Evaluation Edition. The leading Microsoft Windows database. *NOTE:* When run on Windows NT, SQL Server 7.0 Evaluation Edition requires the Windows NT Service Pack, which can be downloaded via the Web.

Using the Test Engine

The MCSD test engine is created for Sybex by EdgeTest. To prepare for the exam:

1. Close all active and minimized applications.

2. Access the test engine through the Sybex CD interface.

3. Follow the installation prompts to install and launch the engine.

4. If you choose not to run the program after it installs, you can start it later by clicking Start ➤ Programs ➤ The Edge Tests.

5. When the main screen appears, type your name and press Enter. Select an exam, select Start Practice Exam, and click Go.

To access other elements of the CD, use the Sybex interface.